Verbs Unleashed

A Writer's Guide to Impactful Prose

Abdullahi Hagar

afternoon
verbs

— approached, — began to, — brought, — came, — carried, — did, — drew, — drew down, — drew on, — drew to, — dropped toward, — followed, — lay, — made, — moved on, — passed, — passed away, — passed by, — passed in, — passed into, — put together, — sat at, — seemed like, — seemed to, — slid toward, — slipped away, — tried to, — turned into, — turned to, — walked through, — walked to, — went by, — went on, — wore on, — worked on, — worked through

air
verbs

asked —, blew out —, breathed —, breathed in —, broke into —, called to —, came through —, caught —, checked —, climbed into —, cut through —, drew in —, fell through —, felt —, filled —, flew into —, flew through —, followed from —, fought —, fought for —, gasped at —, gasped for —, gasped in —, got off —, got on —, grabbed —, hit —, jumped in —, jumped into —, jumped through —, kissed —, leaned into —, left by —, looked in —, looked into —, loved —, needed —, noticed —, pointed into —, reached into —, rolled in —, rose in —, rose into —, said over —, said to —, shot into —, shouted into —, smelled —, smiled into —, stared into —, stepped into —, stood in —, struck —, swallowed —, took in —, took to —, walked on —, wanted —, waved in —, went in —; — became, — began to, — blew, — blew across, — blew from, — blew in, — blew into, — blew off, — blew on, — blew out, — blew over, — blew past, — blew through, — blew up, — breathed out, — came, — came back, — came from, — came in, — came into, — came off, — came through, — carried, — caught, — caught at, — caught in, — changed, — cleared, — climbed from, — closed in, — continued, — continued to, — covered, — cut, — disappeared, — disappeared from, — entered, — fell, — fell down, — felt against, — felt like, — filled, — filled with, — forced, — forced into, — found, — gave, — got, — got before, — got in, — held, — helped, — helped to, — hit, — hit like, — hung, — lay, — lay on, — left, — left in, — lost, — made, — moved, — moved against, — moved at, — moved in, — moved past, — moved through, — needed for, — passed into, — passed through, — played on, — poured into, — pressed down, — pulled in, — ran, — ran out, — rang to, — rang with, — reached, — remained, — rolled out, — rolled over, — rose from, — rose up, — sat, — seemed, — seemed to, — settled in, — shifted, — shook, — shook with, — sighed, — sighed through, — slammed, — slammed against, — slammed from, — slammed into, — smelled, — smelled before, — smelled like, — smelled of, — sounded, — stayed, — stood behind, — stopped, — struck, — took, — took on, — touched, — turned, — turned from, — turned into, — turned to, — went, — went down, — went from, — went out, — whispered from, — wrapped around

aircraft
verbs

— appeared, — appeared above, — began to, — came, — came to, — carried, — climbed into, — finished off, — kept, — kept at, — landed, — landed on, — left, — lost, — made, — moved forward, — moved in, — opened, — picked up, — rose, — shook, — shook like, — took off, — tossed, — touched down, — waited to

aisle
verbs
came up —, continued down —, crossed —, cut down —, glanced across —, got up —, headed down —, leaned into —, left —, looked down —, looked into —, looked up —, moved down —, moved to —, moved up —, ran down —, ran up —, reached —, reached across —, slipped down —, started down —, started up —, stepped into —, stood in —, stopped in —, took —, turned into —, walked —, walked down —, walked to —, walked up —, went up —

alarm
verbs
asked in —, asked with —, called in —, felt —, gave —, glanced in —, heard —, hit —, jumped in —, laughed at —, looked in —, raised —, rose in —, said in —, said with —, saw —, set —, shouted in —, showed —, slept through —, sounded —, stood in —, swallowed in —, turned in —, turned off —, turned on —, waited for —, yelled in —; — appeared on, — began, — began to, — broke, — broke out, — brought on, — came, — came from, — came over, — continued, — continued to, — crossed, — cut off, — fell, — filled, — flew off, — grew, — gripped, — held, —

kicked up, — lay in, — lit up, — ordered, — passed across, — passed over, — raised, — raised in, — ran out, — ran through, — ran up, — rang, — rang in, — rang out, — rang through, — remained, — rose above, — rose from, — screamed, — set, — shot through, — shouted out, — shut off, — slammed into, — sounded, — sounded from, — sounded in, — sounded inside, — sounded on, — sounded through, — started to, — started up, — stayed in, — stopped, — turned to, — went, — went off, — went through, — went up

alley
verbs
approached from —, came in —, crossed —, crossed down —, cut down —, cut to —, disappeared into —, drove down —, drove up —, entered —, flew through —, glanced about —, glanced into —, headed down —, headed into —, headed out —, jumped across —, landed in —, left —, looked along —, looked down —, looked toward —, looked up —, moved down —, moved to —, nodded toward —, passed down —, ran across —, ran down —, ran into —, reached —, remained in —, remembered —, saw —, shifted down —, slipped into —, stared down —, stared into —, stared up —, started down —, started for —, stepped into —, stood before —, thought of —, turned down —, turned into —, walked —, walked down —, walked past —, walked to —, went down —, went to —; — appeared, — began to, — came out, — came together, — caught, — cried out, — crossed, — cut off, — fell, — filled, — held, — led, — led to, — looked for,

— looked like, — looked up, — opened onto, — opened out, — opened to, — ran along, — ran behind, — ran past, — remained, — seemed to, — smelled of, — stood, — stopped

altar
verbs
approached —, bowed at —, cleared —, climbed —, climbed onto —, continued to —, got to —, left —, looked at —, looked like —, moved around —, moved to —, moved toward —, passed —, reached —, stared at —, stepped around —, stepped to —, stepped toward —, stood at —, stood before —, stopped near —, walked around —, walked to —, went to —, worked on —

anger
verbs
added in —, asked in —, expected —, felt —, filled with —, forced down —, fought —, fought back —, fought down —, heard —, held in —, kept —, knew —, let —, liked —, noticed —, realized —, recognized —, replied in —, said in —, said with —, saw —, screamed —, screamed from —, screamed in —, set aside —, shook with —, shouted in —, shouted with —, showed —, smiled through —, spoke in —, spoke into —, spoke without —, swallowed —, swallowed around —, swallowed down —, threw —, understood —, wanted —; — became, — began to, — broke, — broke through, — came, — came at, — came into, — came off, — came out, — came through, — came together, — came upon, — came with, — carried, — cleared away, — crossed, — disappeared, — drove, — entered, — fell from, —

felt, — filled, — fought, — found, — gave, — got on, — grew, — grew in, — left to, — lit, — lit off, — lit up, — made, — opened, — passed, — put, — ran, — rang, — reached, — remained, — returned, — returned to, — rose, — rose in, — rose to, — rose up, — seemed to, — shook, — shot, — shot like, — shot through, — showed in, — showed on, — slammed into, — slid into, — slipped away, — took, — took up, — touched, — turned, — turned to, — went against, — went from, — went out, — woke, — worked, — worked over

animal
verbs
— began to, — broke into, — broke out, — brought to, — called, — called to, — came on, — came out, — caught, — caught in, — did, — died, — died out, — fell, — fell on, — fell to, — followed of, — fought over, — gave, — got, — got to, — held by, — knew, — lay on, — left of, — let, — let out, — lifted, — lived in, — looked, — looked around, — looked up, — lowered, — made, — made before, — made of, — moved, — moved in, — moved into, — paused, — pressed, — pressed against, — raised, — ran, — ran around, — ran in, — reached, — remained, — returned, — rolled away, — sank into, — sat back, — sat down, — sat in, — screamed, — screamed in, — seemed, — seemed to, — showed, — shut up, — sounded, — stared, — stared at, — stood, — stood with, — stopped, — stopped in, — struck, — took off, — took over, — turned, — understood, — waited inside,

— walked over, — went, — went down,
— went with

answer
verbs
asked in —, began —, believed in —,
breathed —, considered —, demanded
—, did —, expected —, found —,
frowned at —, gave —, got —, heard —,
hesitated over —, hesitated with —, hit
—, hoped —, knew —, laughed at —,
laughed in —, liked —, listened for —,
listened to —, looked up —, loved —,
made —, needed —, nodded —, nodded
in —, offered —, promised —, pushed
for —, repeated —, said in —, saw —,
shot back —, shrugged —, shrugged in
—, sighed in —, smiled in —, snapped
out —, thought about —, thought of —,
understood —, waited for —, wanted —
, watched for —, yelled in —; —
appeared, — appeared on, — became, —
came, — came at, — came back, — came
from, — came in, — came out, — came
to, — came with, — came without, —
drew, — dropped into, — forced, —
held, — helped, — kept, — lay, — lay
in, — made, — meant, — needed, —
rang in, — seemed, — seemed to, —
sent to, — shot, — shouted, — slipped
off, — sounded, — stayed, — stood in,
— struck, — threw into, — took, —
turned out, — went, — whispered in

apartment
verbs
approached —, arrived at —, called —,
came by —, came into —, came to —,
checked —, closed —, disappeared into
—, drove to —, entered —, found —,
glanced around —, got to —, headed to
—, kept —, left —, liked —, lived in —,

looked around —, lost —, loved —,
meant —, moved into —, moved
through —, nodded toward —, ran into
—, ran through —, ran to —, reached
—, remembered —, returned to —,
showed —, slipped inside —, slipped
into —, started to —, started toward —,
stayed at —, stayed in —, stepped inside
—, stepped into —, swung into —,
thought about —, tried —, walked
across —, walked around —, walked
inside —, walked into —, walked
through —, walked to —, walked
toward —, went by —, went into —,
went through —, went to —; — began,
— came, — came from, — closed with,
— fell, — felt, — filled with, — got, —
grew, — lay on, — lit up, — looked, —
looked like, — offered, — opened off,
— opened onto, — opened over, —
remained, — seemed, — seemed to, —
sent, — showed, — smelled, — smelled
like, — stood on, — stood open, —
swung open, — went, — went into, —
went up, — wore

area
verbs
appeared from —, came into —,
checked —, cleared —, did to —, drove
from —, entered —, found —, glanced
around —, glanced at —, headed for —,
headed into —, knew —, left —, lived in
—, looked around —, looked at —,
moved around —, moved into —, pulled
into —, pushed into —, rubbed —, saw
—, settled in —, stepped into —,
studied —, turned into —, walked
around —, walked into —, walked
toward —, went into —, went to —; —
appeared to, — became, — began to, —
called, — came down, — came into, —

caught, — closed, — closed off, — covered by, — covered with, — felt, — filled with, — followed, — grew, — held, — laid out, — lit up, — looked in, — looked like, — made, — moved, — offered, — remained, — seemed, — seemed to, — set aside, — set in, — smelled, — stared at, — stood out, — used for, — watched, — waved, — went, — worked at

arm
verbs
bent —, broke —, came —, caught —, caught at —, checked —, climbed into —, closed —, crossed —, cut at —, did in —, dropped —, fell from —, fell in —, fell into —, felt —, felt in —, followed —, gestured with —, glanced at —, grabbed —, grabbed for —, gripped —, held —, held in —, held onto —, held open —, held out —, held to —, held up —, hit —, hung from —, hung in —, hung on —, joined —, jumped from —, jumped in —, jumped off —, kept —, kicked —, kissed —, knew in —, knocked —, landed on —, lay in —, leaned on —, led with —, left —, lifted —, lifted up —, looked at —, lost —, lowered —, missed —, moved —, moved to —, needed —, nodded at —, noticed —, offered —, opened —, opened up —, picked up —, placed —, pointed —, pointed out —, pointed to —, pointed with —, pressed —, pulled —, pulled at —, pulled back —, pulled on —, pulled with —, pushed —, pushed against —, pushed off —, put down —, put out —, put up —, raised —, ran up —, reached for —, reached out —, recognized —, remained in —, remembered —, rolled on —, rose on —

, rubbed —, rubbed at —, sat on —, saw —, shifted —, shook —, shook out —, shot out —, slept in —, slid —, slid out —, slipped into —, smelled —, snapped out —, stared at —, started with —, stepped into —, stood in —, stopped —, struck —, swung —, swung out —, swung up —, threw —, threw open —, threw out —, threw up —, took —, touched —, turned in —, used —, walked into —, waved —, went for —, went into —, wrapped —; — appeared, — appeared in, — appeared to, — began to, — bent, — broke, — broke in, — broke out, — came, — came about, — came around, — came down, — came to, — came up, — caught, — caught between, — caught in, — closed about, — closed around, — closed over, — continued to, — covered, — covered in, — covered with, — crossed, — crossed across, — crossed against, — crossed beneath, — crossed in, — crossed on, — crossed over, — cut off, — did, — disappeared, — disappeared in, — disappeared inside, — drew, — dropped, — dropped away, — dropped down, — dropped like, — dropped off, — dropped to, — drove out, — ended in, — fell, — fell around, — fell at, — fell away, — fell back, — fell off, — fell out, — fell to, — felt, — felt like, — filled with, — flew, — flew across, — flew in, — flew out, — flew up, — followed after, — found, — gave, — gave out, — gave up, — gestured, — got through, — grew, — gripped, — held, — held down, — held in, — held out, — held over, — held up, — helped, — hit, — hung, — hung around, — hung at, — hung by, — hung from, — hung on, — hung outside, — hung over, — hung through,

— hung to, — kept, — landed across, — lay, — lay across, — lay along, — lay at, — lay between, — lay on, — lay over, — led, — left, — let, — lifted, — lifted onto, — lifted toward, — looked, — looked like, — lowered, — lowered to, — made, — made for, — made of, — meant to, — met with, — moved, — moved across, — moved in, — moved up, — moved with, — needed, — opened, — opened to, — opened up, — paused, — pointed, — pointed at, — pointed to, — pointed toward, — pointed up, — pressed against, — pulled, — pulled in, — pulled out, — pulled up, — raised, — raised above, — raised in, — raised over, — raised to, — raised up, — reached across, — reached from, — reached out, — reached through, — remained, — remained up, — rose, — rose from, — rose in, — rose to, — rose up, — said, — said without, — sank in, — screamed, — screamed at, — screamed in, — screamed with, — seemed, — seemed like, — seemed to, — sent, — sent out, — set down, — set in, — shook, — shook from, — shook in, — shook with, — shot, — shot forward, — shot out, — shot up, — shouted out, — showed, — slammed into, — slid about, — slid along, — slid around, — slid beneath, — slid down, — slid under, — slid underneath, — slipped, — slipped around, — slipped into, — slipped off, — slipped through, — slipped to, — spoke for, — started to, — stayed, — stayed open, — stood at, — stood on, — stood out, — stood up, — stopped, — struck, — swung, — swung about, — swung down, — swung forward, — swung in, — swung of, — swung on, — swung out, — swung with,

— told of, — took, — tossed across, — touched, — tried to, — turned, — turned to, — wanted, — wanted to, — waved, — waved above, — waved in, — went about, — went around, — went for, — went in, — went into, — went out, — went through, — went toward, — went under, — went up, — worked, — wrapped, — wrapped about, — wrapped across, — wrapped around, — wrapped over

armor
verbs
— appeared on, — became, — began to, — bent, — came up, — covered, — did to, — filled, — fought with, — gave, — grew, — held, — kept, — left, — left to, — made, — made of, — made up, — offered, — put, — ran down, — remained, — seemed to, — set, — shifted, — snapped into, — stepped up, — stood, — stood around, — stood like, — stood over, — stopped, — took, — turned, — went, — went back, — went into

arrow
verbs
added —, broke —, drew —, flew in —, followed —, found —, gestured at —, held —, killed by —, let —, let go —, let loose —, lowered —, picked up —, placed —, pointed —, pulled —, put —, reached for —, saw —, sent —, set —, set loose —, shot —, studied —, took — , took up —, tried —, wiped —; — appeared on, — arrived, — began to, — broke against, — broke beneath, — brought down, — came, — came forth, — came from, — caught, — caught in, — continued to, — covered, — crossed,

— cut, — cut by, — cut through, — dropped, — dropped away, — dropped to, — drove, — drove through, — ended, — fell, — fell like, — fell on, — flew, — flew at, — flew between, — flew from, — flew in, — flew into, — flew off, — flew over, — flew past, — flew through, — flew toward, — found, — glanced across, — glanced off, — hit, — hit to, — hung in, — kept, — knocked, — knocked to, — laid out, — landed in, — left, — left in, — made, — made for, — missed, — moved across, — moved on, — passed through, — pointed, — pointed at, — pointed down, — pointed to, — pointed toward, — poured down, — pulled back, — rang, — reached, — remained, — remained in, — sank into, — saw, — seemed to, — shot, — shot at, — shot by, — shot down, — shot forward, — shot into, — shot out, — shot past, — shouted at, — sighed, — slammed into, — snapped past, — started, — stood in, — stopped, — struck, — struck at, — struck into, — took, — took down, — took out, — turned into, — went, — went into, — went to, — worked

ash
verbs

— added to, — began to, — came into, — carried away, — dropped off, — dropped over, — fell, — fell away, — fell from, — fell into, — fell like, — fell on, — fell out, — filled, — hit, — hung in, — hung on, — left behind, — left off, — looked for, — remained, — rolled down, — rose, — rose from, — rose in

attack
verbs

began —, expected —, flew to —, heard about —, kept up —, let —, made —, met —, needed to —, pressed —, pressed with —, ran into —, recognized —, remembered —, repeated —, returned to —, stared at —, stayed —, swung to —, thought over —, tried —, used —, waited for —, went on —, wrote of —; — became, — began, — began at, — began to, — broke, — broke off, — came, — came after, — came along, — came at, — came from, — came on, — came up, — came without, — caught, — cleared, — continued, — continued to, — covered in, — did, — drew, — ended, — ended by, — fell from, — felt like, — followed, — forced, — gave, — happened, — happened at, — happened during, — happened in, — happened to, — hit, — kept, — left, — lived to, — looked for, — looked like, — made, — meant to, — missed, — moved down, — played on, — pulled, — seemed, — sent, — shook, — shut down, — slammed into, — started, — stopped, — struck, — threw, — took, — touched, — tried to, — turned, — used, — went, — wore off, — worked

attention
verbs

asked for —, came to —, caught —, demanded —, drew —, felt —, found —, got —, hated —, jumped to —, liked —, loved —, needed —, noticed —, remained at —, sat at —, saw —, shifted —, snapped to —, stayed at —, stood at —, stood to —, turned —, waited for —, wanted —; — caught, — caught by, — caught on, — fell from, — fell on, — flew to, — found, — jumped to, —

landed, — landed on, — remained on,
— returned to, — seemed, — shifted, —
shifted away, — shifted to, — shot, —
snapped back, — snapped to, — stayed
on, — swung, — touched, — turned, —
turned from, — turned to, — turned
toward, — went out, — went to, —
went with, — wore

audience
verbs
— began to, — believed, — called out,
— came to, — drew to, — entered, —
gave, — held, — hit, — laughed, —
laughed at, — leaned forward, — let out,
— remained, — rose to, — sat, —
screamed, — seemed to, — stared at, —
stood for, — thought of, — took to, —
turned with, — watched, — went

axe
verbs
called —, carried —, drew —, dropped
—, dropped under —, gestured with —,
got —, grabbed —, held —, hung up —,
lifted —, looked at —, lost —, lowered
—, nodded at —, picked up —, pointed
—, pointed with —, pulled —, pulled
out —, raised —, saw —, shrugged —,
swung —, threw —, took —, took down
—, took out —, took up —, used —; —
became, — came down, — caught, —
cut, — dropped, — dropped from, —
fell, — fell from, — felt, — filled, —
flew, — flew for, — flew from, — held,
— hung at, — hung from, — lay by, —
made, — passed, — paused, — pulled,
— pulled back, — raised, — raised
above, — raised to, — rang, — remained
in, — rose, — slammed into, — slid
over, — slipped from, — started to, —

stood, — swung, — swung in, — took,
— took off, — went down, — went up

back
verbs
agreed from —, approached from —,
asked from —, bent —, broke —,
brought —, brought up —, called —,
called from —, called to —, came
around —, came out —, carried —,
checked —, climbed in —, climbed into
—, climbed on —, climbed onto —,
closed —, continued to —, disappeared
into —, drew —, dropped onto —,
drove around —, entered through —,
explained from —, fell from —, fell on
—, fell onto —, fell to —, flew down —,
followed —, glanced toward —, got in
—, got into —, gripped —, headed
toward —, held —, hit —, jumped in —,
kissed —, knocked —, laid —, landed on
—, lay on —, left by —, looked at —,
looked in —, looked into —, looked on
—, looked out —, looked toward —,
moved to —, nodded to —, nodded
toward —, opened —, opened up —,
passed —, paused at —, pulled —,
pushed —, pushed to —, ran down —,
ran into —, ran to —, ran toward —,
rang —, reached —, reached around —,
reached behind —, reached for —,
reached in —, reached into —, remained
on —, returned to —, rode in —, rolled
—, rolled off —, rolled on —, rolled
onto —, rolled to —, rubbed —, rubbed
at —, said to —, sank onto —, sat across
—, sat at —, sat in —, saw —, settled on
—, shifted onto —, shifted to —,
shouted from —, shouted into —,
shoved —, slammed onto —, slept on —
, slid into —, slid on —, slid onto —,
slipped around —, slipped in —, slipped

into —, slipped onto —, spoke from —,
stared at —, stared out —, started at —,
started toward —, stayed in —, stayed
on —, stepped into —, stood in —,
stopped at —, studied —, swung around
—, took —, touched —, turned —,
turned on —, turned onto —, turned to
—, turned toward —, used —, walked
around —, walked out —, walked to —,
walked toward —, wanted —, watched
—, watched from —, watched out —,
waved —, went around —, went into —,
went out —, went to —, wrote —, yelled
from —; — appeared, — began to, —
bent, — broke, — called out, — came,
— came off, — disappeared down, —
disappeared into, — drove, — felt, —
felt like, — gave out, — grew, — hit, —
knew, — looked at, — looked like, —
pressed against, — pressed to, — ran
with, — rose above, — sank down, —
sank into, — screamed by, — seemed, —
settled against, — shook, — shook in, —
showed, — sighed with, — slammed
against, — slammed into, — snapped,
— started to, — stood, — stood up, —
threw out, — turned to, — went, —
went into, — went out

backpack
verbs
carried —, closed —, dropped —, got —
, got out —, grabbed —, lifted up —,
looked at —, lowered —, nodded
toward —, noticed —, opened —,
picked up —, pointed at —, pulled off
—, pulled on —, put down —, reached
for —, reached in —, reached inside —,
reached into —, returned —, set down
—, shifted —, shrugged off —, shrugged
on —, slid —, slipped off —, slipped on
—, stared at —, threw down —, took —

, took off —, tossed —, touched —,
wore —

backseat
verbs
answered from —, asked from —, called
from —, checked —, climbed in —,
climbed into —, cried from —,
demanded from —, dropped into —, fell
into —, gestured toward —, glanced in
—, glanced into —, glanced toward —,
got in —, got into —, jumped in —,
jumped into —, lay in —, leaned across
—, leaned from —, leaned into —,
leaned over —, looked in —, looked into
—, moved to —, muttered in —, opened
—, ordered from —, reached into —,
reached over —, reached to —, rolled
into —, said from —, sat in —, screamed
from —, slid across —, slid into —, slid
off —, slipped into —, smiled from —,
spoke from —, stood on —, took —,
turned to —, turned toward —

badge
verbs
carried —, checked —, drew —, drew
out —, found —, gave —, gave up —,
glanced at —, grabbed —, handed back
—, held out —, held up —, knew about
—, looked at —, needed —, offered —,
opened —, picked up —, pointed with
—, pulled —, pulled out —, put —, put
away —, put down —, reached for —,
read —, saw —, set —, showed —,
studied —, took —, took off —, took
out —, wanted —, wished for —, wore
—

bag
verbs

bent over —, bought —, brought —,
brought down —, carried —, caught —,
checked —, checked in —, climbed with
—, closed —, closed up —, crossed to —
, cut through —, drew out —, dropped
—, felt like —, filled —, finished with
—, found —, gestured to —, glanced at
—, got —, grabbed —, grabbed at —,
grabbed up —, grinned into —, gripped
—, handed —, handed back —, handed
over —, held —, held out —, held up —,
hit —, kept —, kept in —, laughed
behind —, leaned over —, left —, left in
—, lifted —, lit —, looked at —, looked
in —, looked inside —, looked into —,
looked through —, lost —, lowered —,
moved —, needed —, nodded at —,
nodded toward —, opened —, opened
up —, passed around —, passed over —,
picked up —, placed —, pointed at —,
pointed to —, pulled —, pulled down
—, pulled open —, pulled out —, put —
, put down —, reached for —, reached in
—, reached into —, reached to —, saw
—, set —, set down —, shifted —, shook
—, shook out —, shut —, stared at —,
started toward —, studied —, swung —,
threw —, took —, took down —, took
out —, tossed —, turned —, went into
—, went through —, went to —; —
arrived, — became, — began to, —
broke, — brought, — came, — came
from, — carried on, — closed, —
continued to, — covered, — cut across,
— cut into, — did, — dropped, —
dropped to, — fell, — fell away, — fell
from, — fell out, — fell over, — fell to,
— felt like, — filled by, — filled with,
— gave, — got off, — gripped in, —
held, — held out, — hit, — hung about,
— hung above, — hung at, — hung
down, — hung from, — hung off, —

hung on, — lay in, — lay inside, — lay
on, — lay open, — looked for, — looked
like, — made of, — made out, —
opened, — opened with, — passed, —
remained, — rolled down, — sat at, —
sat beneath, — sat between, — sat in, —
sat on, — sat open, — seemed to, — set,
— settled, — showed up, — shut, —
shut with, — slid down, — slid out, —
slipped from, — slipped off, — smelled,
— smelled like, — started to, — stood
by, — stood on, — swung, — swung on,
— took up, — used around, — used in,
— went, — went into, — went over, —
went to, — whispered open

balcony
verbs
called from —, called over —, crossed to
—, fell with —, found —, headed to —,
jumped off —, landed on —, left —,
moved off —, nodded at —, nodded
toward —, pointed to —, reached —,
remained on —, returned to —, sat by
—, sat in —, sat on —, stayed on —,
stepped onto —, stood on —, turned
from —, walked to —, went onto —,
went to —, yelled from —

ball
verbs
— appeared above, — appeared in, —
arrived, — asked, — began to, — came
away, — came in, — came near, — came
through, — crossed, — cut off, — did,
— disappeared, — disappeared into, —
drew up, — dropped between, —
dropped into, — ended, — fell in, —
felt, — filled with, — flew, — flew
across, — flew in, — followed, — hit, —
hit back, — hung from, — hung in, —
knocked, — landed on, — left, — left

in, — looked for, — meant, — passed, — passed through, — pointed at, — reached, — rolled, — rolled across, — rolled by, — rolled down, — rolled into, — rolled out, — rolled over, — rose above, — rose in, — said, — sank down, — sat at, — seemed to, — shot, — shot away, — sounded from, — stopped, — struck, — struck at, — swung, — swung in, — took, — took off, — took up, — used in, — wanted to, — went, — went in, — went on, — went onto, — went through, — went toward

band
verbs

— approached, — began, — began to, — called, — came onto, — came under, — came up, — caught, — climbed, — drew near, — fell against, — felt, — filled, — finished, — got, — held in, — hung from, — kicked up, — let out, — looked to, — made of, — made up, — met, — moved on, — moved onto, — moved through, — passed under, — played, — played at, — played on, — played under, — poured in, — pulled over, — put up, — sat around, — sat on, — saw, — set up, — shot between, — slept, — sounded, — sounded like, — started, — started to, — started up, — stood, — stopped, — struck up, — took, — turned up, — went over, — worked, — wrapped around

bank
verbs

appeared on —, approached —, arrived at —, called —, changed —, chose —, climbed —, climbed up —, crossed to —, demanded —, drove to —, entered —, fell onto —, got onto —, hit —, killed

—, lay on —, leaned against —, left —, looked along —, looked around —, looked to —, looked toward —, moved down —, passed —, passed through —, ran up —, reached —, sat against —, sat on —, shouted into —, stared toward —, stared up —, stayed with —, stood at —, stood on —, stood upon —, stopped by —, told —, turned toward —, walked past —, went into —, went to —, went up —, worked at —, worked in —; — appeared, — appeared to, — asked, — became, — began to, — brought, — called in, — came to, — caught, — continued, — covered with, — cried, — demanded, — drew, — drew in, — drew up, — dropped, — dropped to, — drove through, — filled, — filled with, — gave, — got, — got out, — got up, — grew down, — handed, — held, — lay, — lay like, — lay on, — leaned forward, — led to, — left, — lived in, — looked, — looked at, — looked for, — looked like, — lost, — moved up, — nodded, — nodded like, — opened, — pulled, — pulled out, — pulled up, — put, — put on, — replied, — rolled into, — said, — said from, — sat, — sat at, — shook, — shot, — shouted, — showed, — shrugged, — spoke with, — stood, — stopped for, — stopped with, — told, — tried to, — went into, — worked

bar
verbs

appeared in —, approached —, bought —, brought down —, called —, called from —, came around —, came into —, checked —, checked out —, continued behind —, continued to —, continued toward —, covered —, crossed to —, did like —, disappeared into —, drew up —, dropped —, entered —, fell over —, flew at —, found —, gestured to —, gestured toward —, glanced along —, glanced around —, glanced at —, glanced behind —, glanced into —, glanced toward —, got in —, got to —, grabbed —, gripped —, headed for —, hit —, jumped over —, kicked away —, leaned across —, leaned against —, leaned into —, leaned on —, leaned onto —, leaned over —, left —, left for —, lifted —, liked —, looked around —, looked at —, looked behind —, looked between —, looked through —, looked toward —, moved —, moved behind —, moved down —, moved to —, nodded toward —, opened —, ordered at —, passed —, picked up —, pointed beyond —, pointed to —, pointed toward —, pulled out —, pushed —, ran —, ran behind —, ran to —, reached —, reached across —, reached behind —, reached between —, reached over —, reached through —, reached under —, remained at —, returned to —, sat against —, sat at —, sat atop —, settled at —, shook —, shot —, shouted into —, shoved —, slid along —, slipped behind —, slipped into —, stared at —, started in —, started toward —, stayed along —, stepped around —, stepped down —, stepped from —, stepped into —, stepped to —, stood along —, stood at —, stood behind —, stopped at —, stopped by —, stopped in —, stopped outside —, struck —, suggested —, swung open —, swung through —, swung toward —, took —, took off —, turned from —, turned to —, turned toward —, waited at —, waited in —, walked from —, walked into —, walked past —, walked through —, walked to —, walked

toward —, waved from —, went behind —, went down —, went inside —, went into —, went through —, went to —, worked —, worked behind —, worked in —; — appeared, — appeared at, — appeared to, — began to, — blinked, — bowed, — called, — called out, — came, — came down, — cleared out, — closed, — covered, — did, — disappeared, — dropped, — dropped below, — dropped by, — dropped down, — fell, — fell under, — felt like, — filled up, — filled with, — flew open, — gasped at, — gave, — glanced up, — got, — grew, — held, — hung up, — jumped up, — knew, — laughed, — lay along, — lifted, — lifted from, — looked at, — looked like, — made, — made of, — met, — needed, — nodded, — noticed, — offered, — opened, — opened on, — played, — put on, — ran along, — ran down, — ran out, — rang with, — remained, — remained in, — rolled out, — rose up, — said, — sank, — screamed, — seemed, — seemed to, — set into, — set to, — set up, — shifted, — shut, — shut without, — slammed shut, — slid off, — smelled, — smelled like, — smelled of, — stood, — struck, — suggested, — swung open, — thought about, — told, — took, — took up, — turned to, — waited for, — went, — went up

barrel

verbs

— began, — came down, — came in, — came to, — cleared in, — closed, — covered with, — cut down, — filled with, — gestured, — held up, — made, — moved, — moved to, — placed in, — pointed, — pointed at, — pointed to, —

pointed toward, — pressed in, — returned to, — rolled around, — rolled up, — rose, — rose from, — rose toward, — set by, — shifted to, — started to, — stood, — stood in, — struck, — struck by, — swung, — swung to, — turned, — went to

bathroom
verbs
asked from —, called from —, came from —, came into —, changed in —, checked —, chose —, disappeared into —, entered —, finished in —, found —, gestured at —, gestured toward —, glanced into —, glanced toward —, got into —, got to —, headed for —, headed into —, headed to —, headed toward —, jumped into —, left —, looked around —, looked at —, looked for —, looked in —, looked into —, looked to —, looked toward —, loved —, moved across —, moved into —, moved through —, moved to —, nodded at —, nodded toward —, passed —, pointed at —, pointed out —, pointed to —, pushed into —, ran for —, ran into —, ran to —, reached —, returned from —, saw —, shouted from —, slipped into —, started for —, started in —, started toward —, stayed in —, stepped inside —, stepped into —, stepped to —, stepped toward —, stood in —, stood outside —, stopped in —, stopped outside —, thought about —, turned to —, used —, walked from —, walked into —, walked past —, walked through —, walked to —, walked toward —, went in —, went into —, went to —, yelled into —

battle

verbs
— added, — appeared in, — appeared to, — became, — began, — broke out, — came, — came back, — changed, — continued, — continued between, — continued by, — continued for, — continued to, — decided, — died down, — ended, — ended in, — entered, — fought, — fought at, — gave up, — got, — grew, — happened, — joined, — kept up, — lay in, — lost, — made, — moved, — needed, — needed to, — played out, — reached, — remained, — rolled up, — seemed, — seemed to, — started, — stayed, — stepped to, — stopped, — took, — turned, — turned in, — turned into, — turned on, — turned out, — went, — went on, — wore, — wore on

beach
verbs
approached —, came up —, drove to —, followed —, gestured toward —, glanced along —, glanced at —, glanced down —, headed down —, hit —, lay off —, lay on —, left —, looked around —, looked at —, looked down —, looked toward —, loved —, nodded at —, played on —, pointed at —, pointed down —, pointed toward —, ran down —, ran for —, ran on —, reached —, remained on —, remembered —, returned to —, stared at —, studied —, walked along —, walked on —, walked to —, wanted —, went to —

beam
verbs
— appeared in, — began to, — broke in, — came on, — came to, — came together, — caught, — crossed, — cut,

— cut across, — cut off, — cut through, — did, — disappeared, — dropped, — dropped from, — fell on, — fell over, — fell through, — gave up, — hit, — hung, — landed on, — left, — lifted, — lit up, — looked at, — lowered, — made, — meant to, — met, — missed, — moved across, — passed across, — passed over, — paused on, — reached, — remained of, — seemed to, — set on, — set up, — shifted, — shot out, — shot toward, — slammed into, — stopped, — struck, — swung into, — touched, — went, — went on, — went through

beard
verbs

— began to, — blew over, — came off, — came out, — came toward, — caught, — covered, — did, — ended, — felt, — gave, — grew out, — helped, — hung down, — lay on, — let, — let loose, — looked, — looked like, — made of, — played, — pulled back, — pulled to, — reached to, — replied, — said, — seemed like, — seemed to, — showed, — showed under, — spoke in, — stepped into, — stood out, — yelled

bed
verbs

approached —, asked from —, bent over —, bought —, called —, called from —, came around —, came off —, came to —, checked —, checked under —, climbed from —, climbed into —, climbed off —, climbed on —, climbed onto —, covered —, crossed to —, died in —, drank in —, drew before —, drew near —, dropped into —, dropped off —, dropped onto —, dropped to —, fell across —, fell against —, fell into —, fell on —, fell onto —, felt —, flew off —, flew to —, frowned at —, gestured at —, gestured to —, gestured toward —, glanced at —, glanced to —, glanced toward —, got in —, got into —, got off —, got on —, got to —, headed to —, hit —, hung over —, jumped from —, jumped into —, jumped off —, jumped on —, jumped onto —, kept to —, kicked —, kicked at —, landed on —, lay across —, lay in —, lay off —, lay on —, leaned across —, leaned against —, leaned off —, leaned on —, leaned over —, leaned toward —, left —, liked —, looked at —, looked beneath —, looked into —, looked to —, looked toward —, looked under —, loved —, made —, made up —, moved —, moved around —, moved from —, moved in —, moved near —, moved off —, moved on —, moved onto —, moved to —, moved toward —, moved up —, murmured from —, needed —, nodded at —, nodded toward —, passed —, paused beside —, paused by —, placed —, pointed at —, pointed to —, pushed off —, ran to —, reached —, reached across —, reached beneath —, reached under —, remained on —, returned to —, rolled across —, rolled from —, rolled in —, rolled off —, rolled under —, rose from —, rose off —, sank against —, sank on —, sank onto —, sank to —, sat beside —, sat by —, sat in —, sat on —, sat upon —, saw —, settled in —, settled into —, settled on —, shifted in —, shifted on —, shook —, shot off —, slept in —, slept on —, slid down —, slid from —, slid into —, slid off —, slid onto —, slipped from —, slipped into —, slipped off —, stared at —, started for —, started toward —, stayed in —, stayed on —, stayed under —, stepped to —, stepped toward —, stood above —, stood around —, stood beside —, stood by —, stood from —, stood in —, stood near —, stood over —, stopped beside —, studied on —, swung from —, swung off —, thought of —, thought on —, took to —, touched —, tried under —, turned down —, turned in —, turned on —, turned over —, turned to —, turned toward —, walked around —, walked past —, walked to —, walked toward —, wanted —, waved to —, went around —, went to —, went under —, worked in —; — began to, — bought with, — came into, — came up, — came with, — continued to, — covered in, — covered with, — did, — died, — fell onto, — felt, — filled with, — followed, — got to, — held, — hung, — hung from, — lay, — listened for, — lit up, — looked, — looked like, — looked out, — lost to, — made, — made of, — made up, — meant to, — moved, — moved for, — moved out, — opened, — opened to, — placed across, — pressed into, — pushed, — pushed against, — pushed together, — ran, — rang, — rose up, — said, — sat, — sat in, — screamed out, — seemed to, — set against, — set off, — set up, — shifted, — shook with, — sighed, — smelled, — smiled, — stared at, — stared into, — stood, — stood beneath, — took, — took up, — turned down, — turned over

bedroom
verbs

appeared from —, approached —, called from —, came from —, came into —, checked —, checked out —, cleared —,

continued into —, cried from —, crossed —, disappeared inside —, disappeared into —, entered —, entered from —, flew into —, found —, gestured at —, gestured toward —, glanced around —, glanced into —, glanced toward —, got to —, headed for —, headed into —, headed to —, headed toward —, laughed from —, left —, left for —, looked around —, looked at —, looked into —, looked toward —, moved across —, moved into —, moved through —, moved to —, nodded toward —, passed —, passed through —, pointed into —, pointed to —, ran for —, ran from —, ran in —, ran into —, ran to —, reached —, returned from —, returned to —, said in —, said to —, settled into —, shot toward —, shouted from —, slept in —, slipped into —, stared around —, started for —, started in —, started toward —, started with —, stayed in —, stepped into —, stepped toward —, stood in —, stood outside —, took —, tried —, turned into —, turned toward —, walked across —, walked from —, walked into —, walked through —, walked to —, walked toward —, went in —, went into —, went outside —, went through —, went to —, worked in —

beer
verbs

arrived before —, asked for —, bought —, broke off —, brought —, brought over —, chose —, decided on —, drank —, drank down —, drank from —, drew on —, dropped off —, finished —, finished off —, followed with —, frowned at —, frowned into —, gestured with —, got —, got out —, grabbed —, grinned into —, hated —, held —, held back —, held out —, held up —, kept —, killed —, lifted —, liked —, looked at —, looked into —, loved —, lowered —, meant —, needed —, nodded at —, offered —, opened —, ordered —, picked up —, pointed to —, poured —, pulled —, pulled out —, put —, put down —, raised —, reached for —, returned to —, returned with —, said to —, saw —, set down —, smelled —, smelled of —, smiled at —, smiled over —, stared at —, stared in —, stared into —, started —, studied —, swallowed —, took —, took out —, turned toward —, wanted —, worked on —

bell
verbs
— began, — began to, — continued to, — died away, — fell, — filled, — gave, — got, — hung, — hung above, — hung beside, — hung by, — hung on, — joined in, — looked at, — made, — rang, — rang above, — rang at, — rang behind, — rang for, — rang in, — rang on, — rang out, — rang over, — rang through, — rang to, — rang with, — reached, — said, — seemed, — shook, — sounded, — sounded for, — sounded in, — sounded like, — started, — stopped in, — struck, — swung up, — went off

belly
verbs
dropped onto —, dropped to —, fell on —, fell to —, felt —, glanced at —, grabbed —, grabbed at —, gripped —, held —, kissed —, landed on —, laughed from —, lay on —, leaned against —,

looked at —, opened —, pointed to —, pressed —, reached over —, rolled onto —, rolled to —, rubbed —, rubbed at —, touched —; — appeared in, — began to, — cut, — cut open, — drew near, — felt, — filled, — filled with, — gave, — grew, — grew with, — grinned down, — hit, — hit in, — led, — looked, — made, — made up, — pressed against, — remained, — rose, — shook, — threw, — touched, — turned, — woke up

belt
verbs
did —, dropped —, felt at —, found —, got —, grabbed —, gripped —, handed —, held —, looked at —, passed by —, picked up —, pointed to —, pulled on —, pulled up —, put on —, reached for —, reached onto —, reached to —, sent —, slipped off —, stopped —, threw on —, took —, took off —, touched —, wore —, wore at —, wore on —

bench
verbs
approached —, ate on —, came on —, came to —, chose —, cleared —, climbed on —, climbed over —, dropped onto —, found —, gestured to —, gestured toward —, got off —, lay on —, leaned across —, leaned against —, leaned on —, left —, looked at —, looked down —, looked underneath —, moved —, moved along —, moved on —, moved toward —, nodded to —, picked up —, pointed at —, pointed to —, pulled back —, pushed from —, reached —, reached under —, returned to —, rose from —, sank into —, sank to —, sat at —, sat below —, sat on —, saw

—, settled on —, shifted on —, slid
across —, slid along —, slid off —, slid
onto —, stayed on —, stepped onto —,
stepped over —, stepped to —, stood
before —, stood from —, stood on —,
took —, turned on —, walked to —,
walked toward —, waved at —

bike
verbs
climbed from —, climbed off —,
climbed on —, dropped —, drove —,
glanced at —, got —, got off —, got on
—, got onto —, held up —, jumped on
—, left —, lifted up —, looked at —,
loved —, missed —, nodded toward —,
passed —, picked up —, recognized —,
returned to —, rolled —, spent on —,
stared at —, stepped off —, stood from
—, stopped —, swung off —, swung on
—, swung onto —, walked —, went
toward —

bill
verbs
— appeared in, — began to, — came
into, — came to, — carried over, —
continued to, — did, — glanced at, —
got, — held, — jumped at, — kept, —
lay on, — left, — let, — looked at, —
made, — opened, — ordered, —
pressed, — pushed, — put, — raised, —
ran along, — sat in, — sat like, — sat on,
— seemed to, — sent to, — settled into,
— slammed, — slid, — slid behind, —
smiled over, — started to, — stepped in,
— stood at, — stood by, — threw, —
took, — turned, — turned on, — waited
on, — waved, — went into

bird
verbs

— appeared, — approached, — arrived,
— asked, — became, — began to, —
bowed, — broke from, — brought, —
brought to, — called, — called from, —
called in, — called out, — called to, —
came, — came at, — came from, —
came in, — came into, — came to, —
caught in, — considered, — cried from,
— cried out, — died, — died from, —
disappeared, — fell from, — fell in, —
fell into, — filled, — flew, — flew
across, — flew away, — flew by, — flew
from, — flew in, — flew into, — flew
off, — flew on, — flew over, — flew
past, — flew through, — flew to, — flew
up, — fought over, — gave, — got to, —
hung in, — hung over, — landed, — lay,
— lay on, — liked to, — looked, —
looked at, — made, — meant to, —
moved on, — opened, — picked, —
pulled up, — returned from, — rose, —
rose in, — rose into, — rose toward, —
said, — sat, — seemed, — seemed like,
— seemed to, — settled on, — shifted,
— shot out, — showed, — sighed, —
slammed into, — sounded, — spoke, —
stared at, — stopped, — struck up, —
swung to, — swung up, — threw back,
— took, — took off, — took to, —
touched down, — turned, — turned
into, — turned to, — used to, — waited,
— walked up, — wanted to, — went, —
went by, — went up

blade
verbs
asked for —, brought —, called up —,
came with —, carried —, caught —,
closed —, crossed —, drew —, drew
back —, drew forth —, drew out —,
dropped —, drove —, felt —, felt along
—, found —, glanced at —, grabbed —,

gripped —, held —, held up —, jumped —, knocked —, left —, lifted —, looked at —, lost —, lowered —, moved —, needed —, opened —, picked up —, placed —, pressed —, pulled on —, pulled out —, put down —, raised —, recognized —, said to —, sank —, saw —, slipped —, snapped open —, stared at —, stepped into —, studied —, swung —, took —, took out —, turned —, used —, watched —, wiped —, worked —; — appeared, — appeared in, — became, — began, — began to, — broke, — broke in, — broke off, — broke through, — brought to, — came, — came at, — came down, — came for, — came out, — came with, — came within, — caught, — caught in, — cleared, — closed, — continued, — continued to, — covered with, — crossed in, — cut, — cut down, — cut for, — cut in, — cut into, — cut out, — cut through, — did, — disappeared, — disappeared into, — disappeared with, — drank, — drew across, — drew back, — dropped from, — dropped to, — drove, — drove for, — drove into, — entered, — entered into, — fell, — fell from, — fell on, — fell to, — felt, — finished, — flew, — flew through, — found, — glanced across, — glanced off, — gripped in, — headed for, — held, — held out, — held to, — hit, — hung, — hung at, — hung from, — hung like, — kissed, — kissed by, — laid out, — lay, — lay across, — lay in, — lay on, — leaned against, — led, — left, — left in, — lifted, — looked, — lost, — made, — made for, — made of, — met, — met with, — missed, — moved, — moved toward, — opened, — opened up, — passed, — passed by, — passed through, — pointed at, — pointed toward, — pressed against, — pressed down, — pressed into, — raised to, — ran, — ran across, — ran like, — ran on, — ran through, — rang, — rang under, — reached, — rose, — rose above, — sank, — sank between, — sank in, — sank into, — seemed, — seemed to, — sent, — settled in, — shook, — shot forward, — shot out, — shot up, — showed, — slammed into, — slid, — slid from, — slid in, — slid into, — slid out, — slid through, — slipped, — slipped across, — slipped beneath, — slipped in, — slipped past, — slipped through, — snapped, — snapped off, — snapped up, — started to, — stayed, — stood from, — stopped, — stopped at, — struck, — struck against, — struck forward, — struck out, — swung across, — swung past, — swung to, — took, — touched, — turned, — waved around, — went, — went across, — went in, — went into, — went through, — went up

blanket

verbs

brought —, brought out —, carried —, drew —, dropped —, dropped like —, fell to —, felt —, fought off —, found —, got —, got out —, grabbed —, kicked off —, lay beneath —, lay on —, lay under —, left —, let —, lifted —, lifted off —, looked at —, lowered —, meant —, moved —, moved aside —, needed —, opened —, opened up —, picked up —, pulled —, pulled at —, pulled back —, pulled down —, pulled up —, pushed aside —, put —, reached under —, remained on —, returned to —, rolled into —, rolled up —, sat on —, settled into —, settled under —, shifted

under —, shook out —, shoved off —,
shrugged off —, shrugged under —, slid
under —, slipped under —, threw back
—, threw off —, took —, tossed —,
tossed aside —, tossed beneath —,
tossed off —, turned back —, went to —
, wrapped in —; — brought to, —
covered, — covered up, — dropped
from, — fell, — fell away, — fell over, —
fell to, — felt, — filled with, — flew
into, — lay behind, — lay on, — moved,
— pressed down, — pulled, — pulled
around, — pulled from, — pulled over,
— pulled up, — rolled, — rolled up, —
rose, — sat on, — seemed, — seemed to,
— shifted, — shifted with, — slid over,
— slipped down, — smelled, — smelled
like, — tossed, — went, — worked, —
wrapped, — wrapped about, — wrapped
around

block
verbs

appeared from —, came on —,
continued around —, continued down
—, continued up —, covered —, cut
through —, drove —, drove around —,
drove down —, found —, glanced up —,
got around —, headed down —, looked
beyond —, looked down —, looked up
—, made —, moved down —, picked up
—, ran —, stopped —, turned at —,
turned onto —, waited beside —,
walked —, walked around —, walked
down —, walked for —, went around —

blood
verbs

blinked away —, breathed in —,
brought —, checked for —, drank —,
drew —, felt —, felt in —, followed —,
found —, gave —, gestured at —,

glanced at —, got —, kissed —, knew —
, lay in —, left —, looked for —, lost —,
needed —, nodded at —, noticed —,
pointed to —, poured —, remembered
—, saw —, saw through —, slipped in —
, slipped on —, smelled —, smelled like
—, smiled through —, stared at —,
stepped in —, thought of —, told —,
took —, used for —, wanted —, went
for —, wiped —; — agreed, —
answered, — appeared, — appeared at,
— appeared on, — became, — began, —
began to, — broke out, — brought, —
brought out, — came, — came down, —
came from, — came out, — came
through, — came to, — came up, —
carried, — carried on, — caught in, —
cleared from, — continued to, —
covered, — cried down, — cried out, —
crossed, — cut off, — drew, — drove, —
entered, — fell, — fell from, — fell in,
— fell off, — fell on, — fell onto, — fell
out, — fell to, — felt, — felt like, —
filled, — flew, — flew from, — flew in,
— flew into, — flew through, — flew
up, — followed, — got, — got on, —
hit, — hung from, — hung in, — joined,
— joined with, — jumped, — knew, —
lay between, — led to, — left, — left in,
— left to, — lifted, — lifted from, — lit,
— lived, — looked, — looked like, —
made, — meant, — met, — moved, —
moved beneath, — moved through, —
offered, — passed down, — passed
through, — poured, — poured around,
— poured between, — poured down, —
poured forth, — poured from, —
poured in, — poured into, — poured
off, — poured onto, — poured out, —
poured over, — poured through, —
pushed past, — put on, — ran, — ran
across, — ran along, — ran between, —

ran down, — ran from, — ran in, — ran into, — ran like, — ran near, — ran off, — ran on, — ran out, — ran over, — ran through, — ran to, — ran together, — ran toward, — reached, — remained, — returned to, — rode on, — rolled from, — rolled over, — rolled toward, — rose, — rose from, — rose into, — rose on, — rose to, — rose up, — rubbed onto, — said, — sat on, — screamed in, — screamed into, — seemed to, — sent for, — settled, — settled over, — shot, — shot across, — shot forward, — shot from, — shot out, — shot up, — showed against, — showed in, — showed on, — slammed into, — slammed to, — slid across, — slid down, — slid toward, — slipped down, — slipped to, — smelled, — smelled like, — started from, — started to, — stepped up, — stopped, — struck, — suggested, — told, — took, — turned, — turned to, — went, — went back, — went from, — went in, — wiped from, — wore, — worked

blow
verbs

— became, — broke, — brought, — came, — came from, — carried, — caught, — cut, — cut down, — did, — drove, — fell, — fell by, — fell on, — felt like, — followed, — glanced, — glanced across, — glanced off, — got through, — hit, — knocked, — landed, — landed like, — landed on, — landed with, — lifted, — made, — meant to, — met, — missed, — opened, — rang, — rang in, — reached, — seemed to, — sent, — shook, — shot up, — slammed, — slammed into, — slipped down, — snapped, — stopped, — struck, —

struck by, — struck with, — took, — turned on, — went

board
verbs

brought —, came on —, checked —, climbed on —, dropped —, finished —, found —, gestured at —, gestured to —, glanced at —, got on —, got out —, gripped —, helped —, jumped on —, lifted —, looked at —, looked over —, looked toward —, made to —, moved —, moved along —, moved to —, needed —, nodded to —, opened —, paused by —, picked up —, pointed at —, pointed to —, pulled —, put down —, ran on —, remained on —, reminded —, sat at —, set up —, stared at —, stepped from —, stepped on —, stepped onto —, stood by —, stood on —, studied —, swung —, told —, took —, turned from —, turned to —, walked to —, went on —, went to —, worked on —; — became, — began to, — broke, — came out, — covered, — covered with, — did, — grew, — held, — held together, — hung from, — laid in, — laid on, — let, — made, — moved under, — placed over, — promised, — ran toward, — said, — seemed to, — set between, — showed, — slid across, — slid down, — smelled, — stood in, — stood on, — stopped, — struck, — touched, — turned, — turned toward, — went

boat
verbs

climbed aboard —, climbed from —, climbed in —, climbed into —, drew up —, dropped into —, fell off —, felt like —, found —, glanced at —, got —, got into —, got onto —, got to —, headed for —, landed beside —, left —, left for —, left with —, liked —, lived on —, looked at —, looked to —, needed —, passed —, pointed at —, ran to —, reached —, remained in —, returned —, returned to —, sat in —, saw —, shifted —, slept on —, started —, stayed in —, stayed with —, stepped from —, stepped into —, stopped —, took —, turned —, turned toward —, used —, walked off —, walked to —, wanted —, went to —; — appeared, — appeared in, — approached, — arrived, — began to, — broke, — called, — came back, — came into, — came off, — came to, — carried, — caught up, — cleared, — continued, — continued on, — continued to, — cut, — cut across, — cut through, — did, — disappeared, — disappeared around, — disappeared behind, — drew, — drew alongside, — drew up, — ended up, — entered, — felt, — filled with, — flew across, — flew away, — followed, — followed in, — fought, — found, — gave, — got, — grew, — held, — hit, — hung near, — hung on, — hung over, — jumped into, — lay, — lay at, — lay by, — left, — let fly, — lifted, — lifted on, — looked, — looked for, — lowered, — made, — made for, — made to, — moved, — moved across, — moved against, — moved away, — moved by, — moved forward, — moved on, — moved out, — moved through, — passed, — passed by, — passed out, — picked up, — played on, — pointed at, — pulled, — pulled away, — pulled to, — pulled up, — put out, — ran, — reached, — remained, — rolled on, — rose, — rose in, — rose into, — rose on, — sank, — sank by, — sank in, — sat, — sat back, — sat in, — saw, — screamed, — seemed, — sent out, — shifted, — shot forward, — shot out, — shoved against, — showed up, — slammed into, — slid, — slid along, — slid down, — slid forward, — slid in, — slid into, — slid over, — slid past, — slipped, — smelled, — stayed under, — stopped, — struck, — swung, — swung to, — threw up, — took, — touched, — tried to, — turned, — turned into, — turned toward, — waited at, — watched, — went, — went out, — went over, — wore, — wore out, — yelled

body

verbs

approached —, arrived at —, ate —, bent over —, bent to —, came into —, came upon —, carried —, caught —, checked —, checked out —, cleared —, climbed up —, covered —, covered up —, crossed to —, cut —, dropped —, entered —, entered with —, felt —, filled —, filled up —, found —, frowned at —, gestured at —, gestured to —, gestured toward —, glanced at —, got —, hated —, held —, hung from —, kicked aside —, kicked at —, kissed —, knew —, knew about —, leaned across —, leaned over —, left —, let —, lifted —, liked —, listened to —, looked around —, looked at —, looked down —, looked past —, looked toward —, loved —, lowered —, missed —, moved —, moved around —, needed —, nodded at —, nodded toward —, passed —, picked up —, pointed —, pointed at —, pointed to —, pulled on —, pushed —, put —, raised —, ran for —, ran over —, reached —, reached to —, remained with —, remembered —, rolled —,

rolled over —, rose from —, rubbed —, said to —, sat among —, sat beside —, saw —, settled —, shifted —, shifted behind —, shoved —, slept beside —, slid down —, slid into —, snapped into —, stared at —, stepped around —, stepped into —, stepped over —, stepped to —, stepped toward —, stood above —, stood over —, studied —, thought of —, took —, took in —, took on —, touched —, turned —, turned from —, turned to —, used —, walked around —, walked to —, wanted —, watched —, waved toward —, went for —, went over —, went to —, wore —, wrote about —; — added, — answered, — appeared, — appeared from, — appeared in, — appeared to, — became, — began, — began to, — bowed, — bowed in, — bowed out, — bowed with, — broke, — broke down, — broke out, — brought, — brought up, — came, — came between, — came down, — came into, — came to, — came together, — came up, — carried, — caught, — caught in, — changed, — changed into, — checked, — closed in, — continued, — continued to, — covered, — covered in, — covered with, — cried out, — cut through, — demanded, — demanded of, — did, — did at, — did to, — died, — died for, — disappeared, — drew together, — dropped, — dropped from, — dropped in, — dropped like, — dropped to, — drove, — drove into, — expected, — expected to, — fell, — fell away, — fell back, — fell in, — fell into, — fell on, — fell to, — felt, — felt like, — felt on, — felt together, — felt under, — filled, — filled with, — flew, — flew across, — flew past, — flew through, — flew to, — flew up, — flew with, —

followed, — followed in, — forced back, — fought, — fought on, — found, — found in, — gave, — gave out, — got, — got into, — got to, — grew, — headed into, — held in, — held with, — hit, — hung, — hung from, — hung in, — hung under, — hung up, — joined, — joined together, — jumped, — jumped with, — kicked, — kicked to, — knew, — knocked against, — laid, — laid out, — landed, — landed in, — landed on, — landed with, — lay, — lay against, — lay at, — lay beside, — lay by, — lay in, — lay inside, — lay like, — lay near, — lay on, — lay over, — led into, — left, — left behind, — left for, — left to, — let on, — lifted, — listened to, — lit by, — lit up, — looked, — looked like, — lost among, — lost to, — lowered to, — made, — made in, — made of, — met, — moved, — moved across, — moved around, — moved at, — moved back, — moved beyond, — moved down, — moved from, — moved in, — moved of, — moved through, — moved with, — needed, — needed in, — needed to, — nodded, — offered, — opened for, — passed under, — pressed, — pressed against, — pressed to, — pressed together, — pushed, — pushed into, — pushed to, — put, — raised above, — ran into, — ran with, — recognized, — remained, — remained in, — remained on, — remembered, — returned, — rolled, — rolled away, — rolled forward, — rose, — rose above, — rose in, — rose off, — rose toward, — said, — sank, — sank beneath, — sank to, — sat, — sat in, — screamed, — screamed at, — screamed for, — screamed from, — screamed in, — screamed with, — seemed, — seemed at, — seemed to, —

seemed with, — sent, — sent back, — settled, — settled in, — settled into, — settled on, — settled onto, — shifted, — shifted forward, — shifted in, — shifted on, — shook, — shook against, — shook from, — shook in, — shook like, — shook with, — shot, — showed, — sighed, — sighed in, — slammed, — slammed against, — slammed into, — slid, — slid down, — slid over, — slid under, — slipped, — slipped down, — slipped from, — slipped out, — snapped in, — snapped like, — spent, — spoke, — started, — started to, — stayed, — stayed in, — stood, — stood on, — stood up, — stopped, — struck, — suggested, — swung, — swung about, — swung in, — thought, — thought for, — threw, — threw off, — threw out, — threw up, — told, — took, — took off, — took on, — took over, — touched, — tried to, — turned, — turned away, — turned in, — turned into, — turned on, — turned to, — turned toward, — turned up, — turned with, — used, — used up, — waited for, — walked, — walked in, — walked out, — wanted, — wanted to, — went away, — went down, — went into, — went over, — went through, — went to, — went up, — woke, — wore, — worked, — worked at, — worked for, — worked like, — worked to, — wrapped around, — wrapped in

bolt
verbs

— appeared to, — began to, — broke, — closed, — continued to, — dropped to, — flew, — flew across, — followed, — gave, — glanced off, — held, — held on, — hit, — left, — moved, — passed

through, — pulled back, — put on, — sent, — shot, — shot from, — shot out, — shut, — slammed, — slammed into, — slid, — slid across, — slid into, — slipped down, — snapped back, — stood, — struck, — threw, — turned, — went between, — went off, — went through, — wore off

bone
verbs

— arrived, — began to, — broke, — broke with, — came from, — came together, — caught in, — changed, — continued to, — crossed, — crossed over, — dropped by, — ended, — fell with, — felt, — felt like, — filled with, — flew in, — followed in, — gave with, — grew, — held together, — hung around, — lay, — lay about, — lay at, — lay in, — lay under, — left behind, — left on, — looked, — lost, — met, — moved beneath, — moved under, — picked, — pressed out, — pressed together, — ran from, — rang, — rang like, — rose from, — rubbed, — rubbed together, — sat beside, — saw, — saw in, — saw on, — seemed to, — settled into, — shifted, — shifted in, — shifted throughout, — shook, — showed, — showed through, — showed up, — slammed into, — snapped, — snapped into, — snapped under, — snapped with, — stood, — stood out, — stopped, — turned, — turned away, — turned to, — waited in, — wanted to, — went, — whispered, — worked into

book
verbs

bent over —, bought —, brought —, carried —, checked —, checked out —,

chose —, closed —, closed up —,
continued through —, drew —,
dropped —, finished —, finished with
—, found —, frowned at —, gestured to
—, gestured toward —, glanced at —,
glanced through —, got —, grabbed —,
gripped —, handed over —, heard —,
held —, held out —, held up —, kept —
, kissed —, knew —, knew from —,
knocked over —, laid aside —, laid
down —, left —, lifted —, liked —, lived
for —, looked at —, lost —, loved —,
lowered —, moved —, moved through
—, needed —, nodded at —, nodded to
—, opened —, opened up —, picked up
—, pointed at —, pointed to —, pulled
down —, pulled out —, put —, put
aside —, put down —, raised —, rang up
—, reached for —, reached into —, read
—, recognized —, returned —, saw —,
sent —, set —, set aside —, set down —,
shifted —, shut —, slammed —, smiled
over —, spent on —, stared at —,
started —, started with —, studied —,
suggested —, thought of —, threw —,
took —, took down —, took out —,
took up —, tried —, used —, wanted —,
watched —, went through —, went to
—, worked at —, worked off —, worked
on —, wrapped —, wrote —, wrote in
—, wrote on —; — appeared, —
appeared in, — became, — began to, —
brought, — brought to, — called, —
came, — came out, — caught, —
cleared, — closed, — closed against, —
closed with, — covered, — crossed, —
did, — dropped onto, — fell around, —
fell into, — fell open, — fell to, — filled,
— filled with, — finished, — followed,
— got, — held, — held in, — helped to,
— hit, — hung beside, — hung from, —
knocked from, — laid open, — laid out,

— landed on, — lay, — lay on, — lay
open, — left at, — left out, — left to, —
looked at, — looked like, — lost, —
made, — made out, — offered to, —
opened across, — opened with, — put
together, — ran along, — read, — read
on, — remained, — returned to, —
rolled out, — said, — sat, — sat on, —
seemed, — seemed to, — sent out, —
settled on, — showed, — shut, —
slammed against, — slid across, — slid
from, — slid off, — smelled of, —
sounded, — spoke of, — stayed, —
stayed in, — stood, — took, — took up,
— touched, — tried to, — used in, —
waited underneath, — wanted to, —
went, — went on, — went onto

boot
verbs
bought —, carried —, checked —,
climbed into —, closed —, drove —,
finished with —, gave —, glanced inside
—, got —, grabbed —, gripped —, kept
—, kicked off —, knew —, lay in —,
lifted —, liked —, looked at —, loved —
, needed —, opened —, picked up —,
pointed to —, pulled off —, pulled on
—, put on —, raised —, rang up —,
reached for —, reached into —, reached
to —, said —, saw —, settled on —,
shifted —, shook off —, shut —,
slammed down —, slipped off —, stared
at —, stepped into —, stepped over —,
studied —, swung —, took —, took in
—, took off —, understood —, watched
—, went to —, wore —; — appeared
from, — appeared to, — approached, —
arrived, — asked for, — became, —
broke, — came, — came away, — came
down, — came from, — came in, —
came into, — came off, — came up, —

caught on, — cleared, — climbed into,
— continued to, — covered, — crossed
at, — cut, — disappeared in, — entered,
— felt, — felt like, — filled with, —
glanced off, — got, — grew, — gripped,
— headed from, — headed toward, —
hit, — hung over, — joined, — kicked,
— kicked at, — kicked up, — knocked
against, — knocked into, — landed
between, — landed in, — landed on, —
lay, — lay on, — left, — left in, — left
on, — lifted, — looked, — looked like,
— made, — made for, — made of, —
made on, — moved about, — moved
across, — nodded, — passed in, —
picked, — pulled off, — pushed, — ran
up, — rang against, — rang on, — rang
out, — remained open, — remained
outside, — rose into, — rubbed, — sank
in, — sank into, — sat on, — seemed to,
— shook with, — shut, — slammed, —
slammed into, — slid, — slid off, — slid
on, — slipped, — slipped in, — slipped
off, — slipped on, — sounded on, —
stared at, — stood up, — struck, —
struck up, — touched, — turned down,
— turned to

bottle
verbs
broke —, brought —, brought down —,
brought out —, carried —, caught —,
checked —, chose —, cleared —, closed
—, drank from —, drew on —, dropped
—, filled —, finished —, finished off —,
finished with —, found —, gestured
with —, glanced at —, glanced toward
—, got down —, got out —, grabbed —,
gripped —, handed over —, held —,
held out —, held up —, killed —, left —
, left for —, lifted —, lifted out —,
looked at —, lowered —, nodded to —,

nodded toward —, offered —, opened
—, passed back —, passed over —,
picked up —, placed —, pointed at —,
pointed to —, poured from —, pulled
out —, pushed —, put —, put away —,
put down —, raised —, raised up —,
reached for —, returned —, returned
with —, saw —, set —, set down —,
shifted —, shook —, slipped —, stared
at —, studied —, swung —, took —,
took out —, took up —, turned —,
turned up —, waved —, went into —,
went through —; — blinked, — broke
on, — brought, — brought to, — came
through, — considered, — dropped, —
fell, — fell from, — fell off, — fell out,
— fell over, — fell to, — fell with, —
filled with, — found at, — gave, —
glanced away, — glanced over, — held
in, — hit, — hung, — hung over, —
knocked down, — lay on, — leaned off,
— left, — lifted, — looked, — looked
like, — looked over, — looked up, —
made, — moved up, — nodded, —
nodded in, — pointed toward, —
pressed to, — ran along, — read, —
realized, — remained in, — rolled into,
— rolled onto, — rolled to, — rubbed
at, — sat on, — sat up, — shook, —
shrugged, — slipped in, — stared, —
stared at, — took off, — took up, —
turned up, — wanted to, — went onto,
— wrapped in

bow
verbs
broke —, called from —, carried —,
checked —, cut across —, drew —, drew
on —, dropped —, frowned at —, gave
—, gestured toward —, glanced at —,
grabbed —, grabbed for —, gripped —,
heard —, held —, landed on —, lay in

—, leaned on —, lifted —, lowered —, made —, moved to —, nodded toward —, offered —, passed —, picked up —, placed —, pointed over —, raised —, reached —, reached for —, replied with —, returned —, rose from —, said with —, sank into —, sat in —, stepped to —, stood near —, stood on —, stood upon —, took —, took out —, walked toward —, watched —; — began to, — called, — came about, — came up, — covered, — did, — fell from, — fell to, — grew, — held, — hung from, — lay across, — leaned against, — lifted, — lifted for, — looked, — made, — made of, — met, — opened for, — pointed, — pointed at, — pointed to, — pointed toward, — pressed, — remained, — rose, — rose up, — sat under, — saw from, — screamed, — shot, — slipped from, — slipped toward, — started to, — stood, — swung around, — took, — touched, — turned to

bowl
verbs
carried —, cleared —, filled —, finished —, found —, frowned at —, got —, got down —, grabbed —, held —, held out —, held up —, knocked over —, leaned over —, lifted —, looked at —, looked for —, loved —, nodded into —, opened —, passed —, picked up —, pointed at —, pointed to —, pushed away —, put —, put down —, raised —, reached for —, set down —, stared at —, stared into —, took —, worked over —

box
verbs
approached —, broke open —, came to —, carried —, caught —, checked —, checked behind —, checked inside —, climbed onto —, closed —, closed up —, covered —, crossed to —, crossed toward —, disappeared inside —, drew —, dropped —, filled —, finished —, found —, gestured to —, gestured toward —, glanced around —, glanced at —, glanced into —, got —, grabbed —, grew in —, held —, held out —, held up —, leaned into —, leaned over —, leaned with —, left —, lifted —, lifted down —, lifted open —, looked around —, looked at —, looked in —, looked into —, looked through —, managed —, moved —, moved into —, moved to —, nodded at —, nodded toward —, opened —, opened up —, picked up —, pointed at —, pointed inside —, pointed to —, poured from —, pulled down —, pulled open —, pulled out —, put —, put down —, reached —, reached behind —, reached for —, reached in —, reached inside —, reached into —, recognized —, returned to —, saw —, set —, set down —, shifted —, shook —, shut —, sighed over —, slept in —, stared at —, stared into —, stepped onto —, stood at —, stood before —, stood in —, thought outside —, threw down —, took —, took back —, took out —, turned from —, turned off —, turned toward —, walked around —, walked to —, walked toward —, watched —, went through —, went to —; — added to, — appeared, — appeared in, — began to, — came down, — came into, — came off, — came over, — came up, — checked out, — closed, — covered in, — disappeared, — fell away, — felt like, — filled with, — flew from, — followed, — found by, — gave, — held, — hung from, — hung in, —

hung on, — jumped, — laid out, — lay,
— lay in, — let out, — looked, — made,
— made for, — made of, — meant for,
— needed to, — opened, — put away,
— remained, — rolled, — said, — sat,
— sat in, — sat on, — saw to, — seemed
to, — settled, — shifted, — shook, —
showed, — shut, — slammed, — slid
into, — smelled, — stood, — stood out,
— stood up, — turned, — turned to, —
used, — waited for, — wrapped in

brain
verbs
— answered, — appeared, — began to,
— broke, — caught up, — cleared, —
cleared to, — continued to, — cried out,
— cut off, — did, — died, — felt, — felt
like, — filled up, — filled with, — flew
onto, — forced, — kept, — kicked in,
— kicked into, — knew, — left, — left
to, — listened to, — lit upon, — looked
like, — made, — muttered, — needed,
— played on, — put together, — ran
through, — recognized, — remained, —
rolled with, — said, — screamed, —
seemed to, — shifted, — shouted, —
started to, — took, — tried to, —
turned, — turned on, — turned to, —
wanted to, — went, — went back, —
went into, — woke up, — worked, —
worked to

branch
verbs
— became, — began to, — bent down,
— blew, — breathed out, — broke, —
broke in, — came down, — caught at,
— closed, — cut off, — did, — dropped,
— dropped into, — ended in, — fell, —
fell from, — fell on, — flew past, —
gave, — grabbed at, — held, — hit, —

hung, — hung down, — hung into, —
hung over, — joined, — knocked
against, — let, — lifted away, — lost, —
made, — moved in, — ran, — reached,
— reached down, — reached for, —
reached out, — reached toward, —
rubbed against, — seemed, — seemed
to, — shook, — slipped from, —
snapped, — snapped in, — snapped
inside, — snapped on, — snapped
under, — stood on, — stood out, —
struck, — suggested, — swung, —
touched, — turned, — waved in, —
wore, — wrote against

bread
verbs
ate —, broke —, broke up —, brought
—, brought out —, carried —,
considered —, finished —, finished up
—, found —, got —, got out —, hated
—, held up —, left —, left with —, lifted
—, loved —, made —, needed —,
offered —, picked up —, placed —,
pressed —, pulled —, pulled out —, put
—, put down —, reached for —, said —,
saw —, set —, smelled —, stared at —,
swallowed —, took —, tossed —, tried
—

breast
verbs
— arrived with, — began, — began to,
— came, — changed, — covered with,
— cut off, — felt, — filled, — grew, —
hit, — hung, — hung on, — lay, —
lifted, — looked, — looked like, — met,
— moved, — moved beneath, — moved
to, — needed, — pointed at, — pressed
against, — pressed into, — pressed to,
— pulled up, — pushed, — pushed
against, — pushed forward, — pushed

into, — pushed out, — rode, — rode above, — rose, — rose to, — seemed, — settled in, — shook with, — showed, — showed over, — slammed against, — slid up, — spoke with, — started, — started below, — stood around, — swung, — swung about

breath
verbs
added under —, agreed under —, answered under —, asked between —, asked under —, blew out —, caught —, demanded between —, drew —, drew in —, felt —, forced —, forced out —, fought for —, found —, gasped —, gasped between —, gasped for —, gasped in —, heard —, held —, laughed under —, let out —, lost —, missed —, murmured under —, muttered beneath —, muttered under —, needed —, paused for —, paused on —, promised under —, pulled —, pulled in —, pushed out —, repeated under —, said below —, said between —, said in —, said on —, said under —, said with —, shot —, sighed out —, smelled —, spoke under —, spoke with —, stared —, stood for —, stopped for —, swallowed —, took —, took in —, waited —, waited for —, watched —, whispered beneath —, whispered under —, wondered under —; — became, — began to, — blew, — blew across, — blew into, — blew like, — blew out, — blew over, — blew through, — brought, — came, — came back, — came from, — came in, — came into, — came like, — came out, — came through, — came to, — caught, — caught along, — caught at, — caught for, — caught in, — caught on, — caught to, — caught with, — continued, — cut, — died in, — drew in, — ended in, — ended on, — fell into, — fell out, — felt, — filled, — flew out, — found, — gave out, — got, — grew, — held, — held in, — hit, — hung, — hung about, — hung on, — joined in, — knocked from, — knocked out, — lay, — left, — left in, — left on, — left to, — made, — met, — moved, — moved in, — moved through, — murmured, — passed, — passed over, — ran through, — returned, — rolled between, — rolled out, — said, — sank, — sank back, — seemed, — seemed to, — set, — shook, — shook inside, — shot out, — showed, — slammed into, — slid down, — slipped, — slipped past, — smelled, — smelled like, — smelled of, — sounded, — sounded from, — sounded like, — started to, — stopped, — stopped for, — stopped in, — struck, — swallowed, — took, — took on, — tried to, — turned, — turned into, — turned to, — waited for, — went, — went by, — went in, — went on, — went out, — whispered across, — whispered against, — whispered in, — whispered past, — whispered up

breathing
verbs
— appeared, — became, — began to, — came, — came from, — came in, — caught, — caught for, — changed, — continued, — continued for, — continued to, — felt, — filled, — got, — grew, — looked, — made, — paused for, — picked up, — remained, — returned to, — seemed, — seemed to, — settled, — settled into, — shifted, — sounded, — sounded like, — stopped, — took over, — touched, — turned, — went

breeze

verbs

— became, — began, — began to, — blew, — blew across, — blew against, — blew around, — blew at, — blew from, — blew in, — blew off, — blew over, — blew through, — blew up, — blew with, — broke, — brought, — brought up, — came, — came down, — came from, — came in, — came off, — came over, — came through, — came up, — carried, — caught, — caught at, — did, — died, — died down, — died for, — disappeared, — dropped, — fell off, — felt, — felt on, — filled, — got at, — helped, — hit, — hung over, — kept, — kicked, — kicked in, — kicked up, — lifted, — made, — meant, — moved in, — moved with, — passed through, — picked up, — played along, — played among, — played over, — played through, — pushed, — pushed up, — rolled off, — rose, — rose off, — rose to, — seemed to, — sent, — settled in, — shifted, — shot down, — sighed through, — slipped over, — smelled of, — started to, — stopped, — took, — took over, — tossed, — touched, — worked

bridge

verbs

approached —, came to —, cleared —, climbed to —, continued onto —, crossed —, drove across —, drove onto —, drove over —, drove toward —, entered —, fell off —, followed along —, glanced across —, glanced to —, headed for —, hit —, jumped off —, killed on —, left —, looked about —, looked at —, looked toward —, made for —, moved across —, moved over —, passed across —, played —, pointed to —, pulled onto —, ran for —, reached —, returned to —, said on —, slept under —, slipped inside —, stared at —, stepped from —, stepped off —, stepped onto —, stood at —, stood by —, stood on —, stopped at —, stopped on —, studied —, turned across —, walked across —, walked off —, walked to —, walked toward —, walked under —, went to —; — appeared, — appeared to, — became, — began to, — broke beneath, — called, — came about, — came into, — caught, — continued, — crossed, — crossed over, — dropped into, — ended, — fell, — fell down, — fell like, — gave, — gave in, — grew, — held, — hung across, — hung in, — kept, — led into, — made of, — moved, — moved under, — passed, — poured, — ran beside, — ran to, — rose from, — sat, — seemed, — seemed to, — shook, — shook under, — shot out, — slid across, — slid under, — stood out, — went up

briefcase

verbs

brought —, carried —, closed —, closed up —, crossed to —, dropped —, finished —, found —, gestured toward —, glanced at —, glanced into —, glanced toward —, got —, grabbed —, handed over —, held —, held up —, kicked —, left behind —, lifted —, looked inside —, nodded at —, opened —, opened up —, picked up —, placed —, pointed at —, pointed to —, put —, put down —, raised —, reached for —, reached in —, reached into —, set down —, shifted —, shut —, snapped open —, stared at —, studied —, threw —, threw down —, took —, took out —, took up —, tossed —, went to —

brow
verbs
— began to, — came down, — came together, — caught, — cleared, — climbed in, — cut, — disappeared behind, — drew down, — drew in, — drew together, — drew up, — dropped, — dropped down, — dropped in, — dropped into, — flew up, — gave, — grew, — joined in, — joined together, — lifted, — lifted at, — lifted beneath, — lifted in, — lifted over, — lowered, — lowered in, — lowered into, — lowered over, — pressed against, — pulled down, — pulled in, — pulled into, — raised, — raised in, — remained, — rose, — rose at, — rose in, — rose to, — rose up, — rose with, — sank, — sank behind, — seemed to, — set off, — shot, — shot up, — stood, — stood out, — turned, — turned up, — went, — went down, — went up

building
verbs
approached —, arrived at —, bought —, called —, cleared —, continued —, continued around —, cut through —, did in —, disappeared into —, drove past —, drove to —, entered —, frowned at —, gestured at —, gestured toward —, glanced around —, glanced at —, glanced toward —, headed for —, headed toward —, left —, looked around —, looked at —, looked over —, looked to —, looked toward —, loved —, moved into —, nodded at —, nodded toward —, passed —, pointed at —, pointed to —, ran between —, ran for —, ran from —, ran into —, ran toward —, reached —, recognized —, returned to —, saw —, slipped inside —, slipped into —, stared at —, stared out —, started —, started around —, started toward —, stepped inside —, stepped into —, stopped beside —, studied —, swung into —, took in —, turned to —, turned toward —, walked around —, walked in —, walked inside —, walked into —, walked outside —, walked toward —, wanted —, watched —, went around —, went in —, went inside —, went into —; — appeared, — appeared in, — appeared to, — became, — began to, — called, — came, — came back, — came into, — came up, — came with, — carried, — carried out, — caught, — caught between, — continued to, — cut through, — did, — did in, — disappeared behind, — drew, — ended, — fell, — fell behind, — filled, — filled with, — fought for, — gave, — grew, — held, — knew, — laid out, — lay, — leaned, — leaned against, — left in, — left to, — lit by, — looked, — looked at, — looked down, — looked like, — looked to, — made, — made from, — made of, — met, — offered, — opened, — opened through, — promised, — raised, — rang with, — read, — remained, — rose, — rose about, — rose against, — rose in, — rose like, — rose on, — rose over, — rose to, — rose up, — said, — sat on, — seemed, — seemed to, — sent, — set, — set against, — set back, — settled in, — shook, — shook with, — slept, — slid, — slid past, — smelled of, — spoke to, — started to, — stepped out, — stood, — stood in, — stood out, — stopped, — swung open,

— took, — took on, — turned to, — used, — went down, — went up, — worked, — yelled

bullet
verbs

— began to, — blew in, — blew through, — broke, — came, — came at, — came into, — came through, — caught, — continued, — cut, — cut into, — cut off, — cut through, — did, — ended, — entered, — entered at, — filled, — flew, — flew at, — flew through, — found, — glanced against, — hit, — kicked, — kicked up, — kissed, — landed, — lay in, — left, — left to, — made, — made for, — made in, — meant for, — met, — missed, — passed through, — poured down, — put, — rang on, — rang out, — sank into, — shot off, — shot through, — showed, — slammed into, — snapped, — snapped off, — stood out, — stopped, — struck, — told, — went, — went around, — went by, — went into, — went over, — went through

bus
verbs

arrived in —, came by —, caught —, cleared —, climbed aboard —, climbed off —, climbed on —, cut off —, drove —, got off —, got on —, jumped from —, left on —, looked around —, looked at —, looked for —, missed —, nodded toward —, ran to —, remained aboard —, rode —, said on —, sat in —, saw —, slept in —, stepped across —, stepped onto —, thought of —, took —, turned off —, walked to —, went by —; — approached, — arrived, — arrived at, — became, — came, — came along, —

came to, — continued, — continued to, — disappeared into, — drew away, — drew up, — drove, — drove away, — drove by, — drove through, — felt like, — filled with, — flew by, — followed, — got, — headed for, — headed to, — headed toward, — hit, — left, — made, — moved, — moved into, — moved off, — moved through, — passed, — passed on, — picked up, — played, — pulled away, — pulled into, — pulled off, — pulled out, — pulled to, — pulled up, — put, — ran on, — ran through, — reached, — rolled, — rolled along, — rolled by, — rolled in, — rolled onto, — rolled over, — rolled past, — rolled up, — seemed to, — sighed, — slid down, — smelled of, — started to, — started up, — stopped, — stopped at, — swung out, — talked about, — took, — turned, — turned onto, — went, — went in, — went over, — went past, — went to

business
verbs

— appeared on, — began, — called, — came, — came on, — did, — finished, — followed, — kept, — led, — left, — looked, — made, — needed, — opened, — rode in, — sat, — seemed, — seemed in, — seemed like, — seemed to, — turned, — turned out, — walked in, — went by, — went into, — went on, — went through

cab
verbs

bought —, called —, called for —, caught —, checked —, climbed from —, climbed in —, climbed into —, found —, glanced in —, got —, got in —, got into —, grabbed —, jumped in —, jumped into —, left —, looked around —, looked into —, looked outside —, nodded toward —, ordered —, pulled around —, ran to —, ran toward —, reached —, reached across —, reached inside —, returned to —, sat in —, saw —, slid into —, slipped from —, started —, started toward —, stepped inside —, took —, waited in —, walked to —, watched —, waved for —; — appeared, — arrived, — began to, — came, — came on, — came to, — disappeared, — drew alongside, — drew up, — dropped, — dropped off, — drove, — drove away, — drove in, — drove to, — felt, — followed, — found, — left, — pulled away, — pulled into, — pulled onto, — pulled over, — pulled to, — pulled up, — rolled up, — sat, — seemed to, — settled into, — shot forward, — showed up, — smelled of, — stayed, — stopped, — stopped at, — stopped in, — took, — took off, — turned, — turned around, — turned into, — waited, — waited for

cabin
verbs
approached —, called across —, crossed —, entered —, fell into —, gestured at —, glanced around —, glanced at —, glanced toward —, headed for —, headed to —, headed toward —, jumped from —, left —, left for —, looked around —, looked at —, looked into —, looked toward —, meant —, moved about —, moved through —, pointed to —, pushed into —, ran from —, ran to —, reached —, returned to —, sat across —, saw —, slipped inside —, slipped into —, stared across —, stared around —, started for —, stayed in —, stepped into —, stepped outside —, stood

outside —, studied —, turned toward —, walked across —, walked into —, walked past —, went into —, went to —

cabinet
verbs
checked —, closed —, crossed to —, gestured at —, gestured toward —, grabbed —, hung —, kicked at —, leaned against —, looked into —, moved to —, moved toward —, nodded toward —, opened —, opened up —, pointed to —, reached inside —, reached into —, set —, shut —, slipped behind —, stepped from —, stepped to —, turned to —, walked to —, went into —, went through —, went to —

call
verbs
answered —, broke —, cleared —, closed —, cut —, cut off —, did —, ended —, ended up —, explained about —, felt —, finished —, finished up —, gave —, got —, got off —, heard —, hung up —, joined —, killed —, knew —, knew about —, listened to —, lost —, made —, met —, missed —, picked up —, placed —, pressed —, put —, put in —, put out —, ran to —, remembered —, repeated —, returned —, returned to —, sent —, sent out —, shook off —, shut off —, shut out —, thought of —, took —, took over —, turned at —, waved off —, wrapped up —; — appeared on, — asked for, — began to, — broke, — broke through, — brought, — brought back, — came, — came after, — came down, — came from, — came in, — came on, — came out, — came over, — came through, — came to, — came up, — continued, — crossed, —

cut off, — died, — dropped, — ended, — ended in, — ended with, — fell through, — fell to, — finished, — followed, — got, — happened, — happened with, — heard by, — jumped into, — leaned against, — leaned in, — left, — made, — made from, — meant for, — nodded toward, — rang, — rang out, — recognized, — repeated, — replied, — returned in, — rolled across, — said, — seemed, — sounded, — sounded from, — started, — stopped, — took, — turned, — turned out, — went, — went back, — went into, — went out, — went through, — went to, — went up, — woke up

camera
verbs

brought —, carried —, checked —, did like —, dropped —, found —, gestured at —, gestured toward —, gestured with —, glanced at —, glanced toward —, got —, got out —, grabbed —, grabbed at —, grinned at —, grinned for —, handed —, handed over —, held —, held out —, held up —, knew —, leaned into —, leaned toward —, lifted —, looked at —, looked into —, lowered —, moved —, nodded to —, nodded toward —, opened —, passed —, picked up —, pointed —, pointed to —, pulled out —, put down —, raised —, reached for —, reached to —, remembered —, returned to —, said into —, said to —, saw —, set —, set up —, showed to —, shut off —, smiled at —, smiled for —, smiled into —, spoke into —, spoke to —, stared at —, stared into —, started —, stepped behind —, stepped with —, stood behind —, studied —, thought of —, took —, took off —, took out —, turned

—, turned off —, turned on —, turned to —, turned toward —, used —, waved to —, went behind —, went for —, went on —; — arrived at, — began to, — brought out, — came, — caught, — caught of, — caught up, — closed in, — continued, — covered, — cut, — cut back, — cut to, — drew, — entered, — felt like, — flew into, — followed, — got, — got up, — held, — held up, — hung over, — joined, — kept, — landed, — left, — lit up, — looked like, — looked through, — lowered from, — lowered with, — made, — managed to, — moved, — moved across, — moved around, — moved away, — moved down, — moved in, — moved into, — moved to, — moved up, — passed, — paused at, — paused on, — picked up, — placed to, — pointed at, — pointed in, — pulled back, — pulled out, — pushed in, — remained, — rolled, — sat on, — seemed to, — sent, — set throughout, — set up, — shook, — shoved in, — shoved up, — showed, — showed up, — shut off, — snapped, — stared down, — started, — stayed, — stayed on, — stopped, — swung, — swung around, — swung to, — turned around, — turned from, — turned to, — waited outside, — watched at, — watched inside, — went, — went back

camp
verbs

broke —, came into —, checked —, climbed toward —, crossed —, entered —, found —, gestured to —, hated —, hit —, left —, looked around —, looked into —, made —, moved through —, nodded across —, pulled into —, ran across —, ran toward —, reached —, returned to —, saw —, set —, set up —, started toward —, struck —, turned to —, turned toward —, walked into —; — appeared, — arrived, — became, — began to, — broke up, — came for, — came into, — came up, — changed, — did, — filled with, — fought, — jumped from, — lay on, — left, — looked like, — meant, — rang to, — rose, — sat at, — seemed to, — sent, — set up, — settled for, — slept, — stood, — thought of

candle
verbs
added —, blew out —, called for —, carried —, demanded —, dropped —, held —, held up —, laid out —, left —, lifted —, lifted up —, liked —, lit —, loved —, lowered —, moved —, picked up —, pulled —, put out —, raised —, reached for —, remembered —, sat before —, saw —, set down —, set out —, stared at —, took —, took up —, turned —

cane
verbs
brought down —, dropped —, found —, gestured with —, got —, grabbed —, gripped —, held up —, leaned against —, leaned on —, leaned upon —, missed —, moved —, needed —, picked up —, pointed —, raised —, reached for —, remembered —, saw —, stood with —, swung —, took —, used —, walked with —

cap
verbs
— appeared, — blew over, — came into, — covered, — drew on, — fell off, —

filled with, — finished, — flew from, — glanced down, — glanced up, — held against, — held out, — lay in, — looked out, — looked up, — passed over, — placed on, — pulled, — pulled down, — pulled over, — rose to, — said, — sat on, — saw, — seemed to, — slipped from, — stopped, — turned around, — walked, — walked out, — walked over, — went into

car
verbs
approached —, arrived in —, asked for —, bought —, called —, called for —, called from —, called into —, came around —, came by —, came from —, came in —, came to —, caught —, changed —, checked —, climbed from —, climbed in —, climbed into —, closed —, considered —, continued toward —, crossed to —, did to —, disappeared into —, dropped —, dropped off —, drove —, entered —, fell into —, filled —, filled up —, found —, frowned at —, gestured at —, gestured to —, gestured toward —, glanced at —, glanced in —, glanced into —, glanced toward —, got —, got in —, got inside —, got into —, got to —, hated —, headed for —, headed to —, heard —, hesitated beside —, hit —, jumped for —, jumped from —, jumped in —, jumped inside —, jumped into —, jumped off —, kept —, kicked —, knew —, knew about —, leaned across —, leaned against —, leaned into —, leaned on —, left —, liked —, looked about —, looked around —, looked at —, looked behind —, looked in —, looked inside —, looked over —, looked under —, lost —, loved —, made for —, moved —,

moved around —, moved down —, moved to —, moved toward —, needed —, nodded at —, nodded toward —, noticed —, opened —, opened up —, passed —, passed between —, passed into —, passed on —, paused by —, picked up —, pointed to —, pointed toward —, pulled behind —, pushed off —, put —, ran around —, ran for —, ran past —, ran to —, ran toward —, ran up —, rang from —, reached —, reached across —, reached inside —, reached into —, reached under —, recognized —, remained near —, remembered —, returned to —, rode in —, rolled off —, said in —, said to —, sat in —, saw —, settled into —, shot into —, shut off —, slammed —, slept in —, slid —, slid from —, slid inside —, slid into —, slid off —, slipped inside —, slipped into —, stared at —, started —, started around —, started for —, started to —, started toward —, started up —, stayed by —, stayed in —, stayed with —, stepped from —, stepped inside —, stepped into —, stepped off —, stepped to —, stood alongside —, stood beside —, stood by —, stood outside —, stopped —, stopped at —, stopped behind —, stopped beside —, struck —, studied —, suggested —, swung —, swung toward —, thought about —, thought of —, threw —, took —, touched —, turned —, turned at —, turned from —, turned off —, turned on —, turned to —, turned toward —, waited by —, waited in —, walked around —, walked between —, walked to —, walked toward —, wanted —, watched —, watched from —, waved from —, waved toward —, went for —, went to —, worked on —; — appeared, — appeared at, — appeared from, — appeared in, — appeared on, — appeared over, — appeared to, — approached, — approached from, — approached on, — arrived, — arrived at, — arrived to, — ate, — ate up, — became, — began, — began to, — blew, — blew out, — blew up, — blinked, — bought in, — bought to, — broke, — broke down, — broke off, — brought, — brought around, — brought back, — brought out, — brought to, — called in, — came, — came along, — came around, — came back, — came by, — came down, — came from, — came in, — came into, — came on, — came out, — came over, — came through, — came to, — came up, — carried, — caught, — changed, — cleared, — climbed, — climbed out, — closed, — continued, — continued by, — continued down, — continued forward, — continued on, — continued to, — covered, — covered with, — cried out, — crossed, — cut, — demanded, — died, — disappeared, — disappeared around, — disappeared from, — drew, — drew alongside, — drew away, — drew out, — drew up, — dropped with, — drove, — drove across, — drove at, — drove away, — drove by, — drove down, — drove off, — drove on, — drove past, — drove through, — drove up, — entered, — fell, — fell into, — fell out, — felt, — felt like, — filled, — filled with, — flew away, — flew forward, — followed, — got, — grew, — headed, — headed in, — hit, — joined, — joined in, — jumped, — jumped forward, — jumped into, — kept on, — lay, — lay on, — leaned on, — left, — left at, — left behind, — lifted, — lifted with, — listened to, —

looked for, — looked like, — lost, — lowered, — made, — made in, — made of, — met, — missed, — moved, — moved about, — moved along, — moved by, — moved down, — moved forward, — moved in, — moved into, — moved off, — moved on, — moved onto, — moved past, — moved through, — moved toward, — moved up, — needed to, — opened, — opened on, — passed, — passed behind, — passed by, — passed down, — passed on, — passed over, — passed through, — paused, — paused at, — picked up, — pointed at, — pointed down, — pointed toward, — poured into, — pressed on, — pulled, — pulled away, — pulled down, — pulled in, — pulled into, — pulled out, — pulled over, — pulled to, — pulled up, — ran on, — reached, — remained, — remained behind, — remained in, — remained on, — rolled, — rolled by, — rolled down, — rolled forward, — rolled into, — rolled on, — rolled over, — rolled to, — rolled up, — rose, — said, — sank down, — sat, — sat at, — sat on, — saw, — screamed, — screamed around, — screamed at, — screamed in, — screamed into, — screamed to, — screamed up, — seemed, — seemed to, — sent, — set off, — settled into, — shifted into, — shifted to, — shook, — shot, — shot forward, — shot off, — shot out, — shot through, — shot to, — shot up, — showed up, — slammed into, — slammed to, — slid, — slid down, — slid into, — slid off, — slid to, — slipped, — slipped forward, — slipped into, — slipped on, — slipped onto, — smelled, — smelled like, — smelled of, — stared at, — started, — started down, — started to, — started

up, — stayed, — stayed at, — stayed in, — stayed on, — stood at, — stood between, — stood in, — stopped, — stopped at, — stopped by, — stopped in, — stopped on, — stopped out, — struck, — swung around, — swung into, — swung open, — swung out, — took, — took off, — took up, — tried to, — turned, — turned around, — turned at, — turned down, — turned in, — turned into, — turned off, — turned on, — turned onto, — turned out, — turned to, — used to, — waited, — waited along, — waited around, — waited at, — waited for, — waited in, — waited out, — went, — went around, — went by, — went down, — went into, — went off, — went on, — went out, — went past, — went through, — went up, — woke up, — worked on

card

verbs

checked —, closed —, drew —, dropped —, found —, gestured to —, gestured with —, glanced at —, glanced over —, got —, grabbed —, handed —, handed back —, handed over —, held —, held out —, held up —, kept —, knew —, laughed at —, left —, lifted —, looked at —, lowered —, nodded at —, offered —, picked up —, placed —, played —, pointed to —, pulled —, pulled at —, pulled out —, pushed —, put —, put away —, put down —, raised —, reached for —, reached to —, read —, returned —, saw —, sent —, showed —, shut —, slid —, slid in —, slid open —, stared at —, studied —, threw away —, threw down —, took —, took out —, touched —, turned over —, turned up —, waved —, wrote on —; — appeared, —

became, — came up, — covered, — disappeared into, — fell, — fell on, — fell onto, — fell out, — filled with, — got, — got for, — held together, — kept, — laid, — laid out, — lay on, — left, — left to, — lost, — read, — rolled out, — said, — set, — slid into, — slipped, — sounded, — stood in, — took, — turned into, — turned over, — wrapped in

carriage
verbs

approached —, arrived in —, called for —, called from —, called into —, came around —, checked —, climbed from —, climbed in —, climbed inside —, climbed into —, closed —, considered —, continued toward —, crossed to —, disappeared inside —, dropped off —, entered —, fell into —, found —, frowned at —, gestured at —, gestured to —, gestured toward —, glanced at —, glanced in —, glanced into —, glanced toward —, got —, got in —, got inside —, got into —, got to —, hated —, headed for —, headed to —, heard —, hesitated beside —, jumped for —, jumped from —, jumped in —, jumped inside —, jumped into —, jumped off —, kicked —, knew —, leaned across —, leaned against —, leaned into —, leaned on —, left —, looked around —, looked at —, looked behind —, looked in —, looked inside —, looked toward —, looked under —, loved —, made for —, moved —, moved around —, moved down —, moved into —, moved to —, moved toward —, needed —, nodded toward —, noticed —, opened —, opened up —, passed —, passed into —, passed on —, paused by —, pointed to —, pushed off —, ran around —, ran for —, ran past —, ran to —, ran toward —, ran up —, rang from —, reached —, reached across —, reached inside —, reached into —, reached under —, recognized —, remembered —, returned to —, rolled off —, said to —, sat in —, saw —, settled into —, slept in —, slid from —, slid inside —, slid into —, slid off —, slipped inside —, slipped into —, stared at —, started around —, started for —, started toward —, stayed by —, stayed in —, stayed with —, stepped from —, stepped inside —, stepped into —, stepped to —, stood alongside —, stood beside —, stood by —, stood near —, stood outside —, stopped —, stopped at —, stopped behind —, stopped beside —, studied —, swung —, swung toward —, thought about —, thought of —, took —, turned —, turned at —, turned from —, turned on —, turned toward —, waited by —, waited in —, walked alongside —, walked around —, walked to —, walked toward —, watched —, waved from —, waved toward —, went for —, went into —, went to —; — appeared, — approached, — approached along, — arrived, — asked, — began to, — came, — came down, — came for, — came in, — came into, — came out, — came to, — came up, — came with, — carried on, — changed in, — continued forward, — continued to, — crossed, — disappeared, — disappeared around, — disappeared from, — drew, — drew to, — drew up, — fell, — felt, — flew forward, — followed, — gave, — got, — grew, — hit, — jumped, — jumped forward, — kept on, — lay on, — left, — left at, — looked, — lost, — made,

— moved, — moved along, — moved away, — moved down, — moved forward, — moved from, — moved off, — moved on, — moved through, — moved up, — moved with, — opened, — passed, — passed behind, — passed by, — paused, — paused at, — picked up, — pressed on, — pulled away, — pulled into, — pulled out, — pulled to, — pulled up, — reached, — remained, — remained behind, — remained in, — rode, — rolled, — rolled by, — rolled down, — rolled forward, — rolled into, — rolled out, — rolled to, — sank down, — settled into, — shook, — shot, — shot forward, — shot through, — shot to, — slammed to, — slid to, — slipped onto, — started, — started down, — started to, — started up, — stayed, — stayed on, — stood in, — stopped, — stopped at, — stopped in, — swung around, — took off, — turned, — turned at, — turned in, — turned into, — turned on, — turned onto, — waited, — waited above, — waited for, — watched, — went, — went by, — went past, — woke up

cart
verbs

— arrived on, — bent to, — came back, — came in, — came to, — fell over, — filled, — filled with, — hit, — lay on, — left, — passed, — picked up, — pulled away, — rolled by, — rolled down, — rolled up, — said, — spoke in, — stood, — stood inside, — stopped at, — waited for, — waited on, — went from, — worked

case
verbs

approached —, closed —, closed up —, considered —, continued to —, found —, got —, held up —, knew about —, looked like —, lost —, made —, needed for —, opened —, passed —, picked up —, pressed —, promised in —, pulled on —, reached for —, recognized —, saw —, stared at —, studied —, thought about —, took —, tried —, wanted —, worked —; — arrived at, — ate, — began on, — began to, — began with, — brought about, — brought to, — came, — came from, — came in, — came to, — came up, — changed, — checked out, — closed, — decided, — decided by, — died down, — ended, — fell back, — fell between, — fell to, — fell under, — filled with, — got, — got down, — headed for, — heard on, — held, — hit, — hung over, — jumped from, — kept, — lay, — lay on, — lay open, — leaned against, — left, — lit by, — lowered, — made, — managed to, — moved in, — opened, — read, — replied, — sat on, — seemed, — seemed to, — sent across, — set, — settled, — shut, — slipped through, — stepped to, — stood around, — stood behind, — stood on, — told, — took, — waited in, — went around, — went down, — went on, — went to, — worked, — wrapped in, — wrapped up

castle
verbs

— appeared, — appeared at, — appeared on, — called, — came into, — came upon, — changed, — fell, — fell in, — fell into, — fell on, — lay, — left in, — looked, — looked like, — lost in, — made, — made of, — meant, — opened, — rang, — rang to, — rang

with, — remained, — rose, — rose
around, — rose beside, — rose to, — sat
above, — seemed, — seemed to, —
slept, — stood, — stood on, — went, —
went to, — woke to

cat
verbs
asked —, checked on —, drove —,
followed after —, fought like —,
grinned like —, hated —, kept —, knew
—, landed like —, liked —, looked at —,
looked like —, loved —, moved like —,
noticed —, picked up —, pointed to —,
put out —, reached for —, said —, said
to —, shifted into —, smelled of —,
smiled like —, stared at —, thought of
—, told —, watched —, went to —,
went with —, woke like —; — appeared,
— appeared from, — appeared in, —
approached, — became, — began, —
began to, — blinked, — brought, —
came, — came back, — came in, —
came through, — came to, — changed,
— climbed into, — continued to, —
cried, — cried under, — crossed, —
decided to, — did, — did at, — died on,
— dropped, — ended up, — fell to, —
flew forward, — followed, — forced, —
fought, — gave, — glanced over, — got,
— got in, — got up, — hesitated, —
hung to, — joined in, — jumped down,
— jumped into, — jumped onto, —
jumped up, — kept, — knocked, —
landed on, — lay, — let, — let out, —
lifted, — liked, — liked to, — lived, —
lived in, — looked down, — looked out,
— looked over, — lowered, — made, —
met, — moved forward, — moved in, —
nodded, — opened, — picked up, —
pushed, — put, — raised, — ran, — ran
up, — remained in, — returned to, —

rose from, — rubbed, — rubbed against,
— rubbed up, — said, — sat at, — sat
back, — sat down, — sat in, — sat on,
— sat with, — screamed, — seemed, —
seemed to, — sent back, — shook, —
showed, — shrugged, — slammed into,
— slept, — slept in, — slept like, —
slept on, — slipped behind, — slipped
between, — sounded, — stared at, —
started for, — started to, — stood, —
stood on, — stood up, — stopped, —
stopped in, — swung toward, — talked
to, — took, — tried to, — turned, —
turned around, — turned out, —
waited, — walked, — walked across, —
walked in, — wanted to, — watched, —
watched out, — went up, — woke on,
— worked out

cave
verbs
— became, — began to, — climbed, —
continued, — filled, — filled with, —
gave, — grew, — lit up, — looked like,
— opened up, — ran to, — rang with,
— rose, — set into, — shifted, —
shifted like, — smelled, — started to, —
stopped, — turned, — turned out, —
went, — went about, — went back, —
went on

ceiling
verbs
appeared on —, called to —, cried to —,
flew through —, gestured toward —,
glanced at —, glanced toward —, hit —,
jumped to —, looked at —, looked to —
, looked toward —, loved —, murmured
to —, nodded at —, nodded to —,
pointed at —, pointed to —, pointed
toward —, said to —, saw —, smiled at
—, spoke to —, stared at —, stared

toward —, studied —, told —, touched
—, watched —; — added to, —
appeared, — became, — bowed by, —
came down, — came into, — came on,
— came to, — came with, — covered
with, — did, — disappeared in, — fell
on, — forced, — gave, — held up, —
hung, — hung in, — hung with, —
lifted, — lit, — lit up, — lost in, —
made, — made of, — opened to, —
picked up, — ran down, — reached, —
rose to, — rose up, — seemed to, —
sent, — showed, — started, — struck,
— went, — went up

cell
verbs

answered —, approached —, called —,
checked —, closed —, continued to —,
drew out —, dropped —, entered —,
found —, gestured to —, glanced
around —, glanced inside —, glanced
into —, got near —, got on —, got out
—, got to —, grabbed —, gripped —,
held up —, hung up —, kept in —, left
—, looked around —, looked at —,
looked into —, lowered —, moved
toward —, opened —, passed —, picked
up —, pulled —, pulled out —, rang —,
reached —, reached for —, returned to
—, said into —, sat in —, screamed from
—, shouted into —, shut off —, slipped
from —, slipped into —, snapped open
—, spoke into —, stared around —,
stepped inside —, stepped into —, stood
outside —, stopped outside —, thought
of —, took out —, tried —, turned off
—, used —, walked along —, walked
into —, went into —, went to —,
worked in —; — appeared, — began to,
— blinked in, — called, — came, —
closed, — covered, — drew, — ended,

— fell to, — filled, — filled with, —
flew, — flew into, — flew open, — gave
off, — gave out, — grew, — held, —
hung, — jumped to, — made of, —
moved by, — opened, — opened onto,
— ran around, — rang, — remained in,
— replied, — sent, — shut, — shut up,
— slammed into, — snapped back, —
stared at, — started to, — stood on, —
swung, — swung open, — turned, —
waited for, — went off

chain
verbs

broke —, climbed —, dropped —,
glanced at —, grabbed —, grabbed onto
—, gripped —, held out —, hung from
—, lifted —, looked at —, needed —,
opened —, picked up —, pointed to —,
pulled —, pulled at —, put on —,
reached —, shook —, shrugged off —,
slid —, slipped —, spoke through —,
stepped over —, swung —, took —,
took off —, touched —; — appeared, —
broke, — broke off, — came, — came
back, — caught, — caught on, —
dropped, — dropped from, — dropped
into, — dropped to, — fell, — fell away,
— fell to, — felt, — forced, — gave, —
grew, — gripped in, — held, — hit, —
hung, — hung around, — hung from, —
hung off, — jumped, — lay, — lay
across, — lay against, — lay in, — left
on, — lifted, — looked, — looked to, —
made, — made of, — moved in, — put
on, — raised, — ran between, — ran
from, — ran to, — rang out, — read, —
sank into, — saw, — saw in, — saw to,
— seemed to, — shifted, — shifted in,
— shot out, — slid, — slid along, — slid
through, — slid to, — slipped off, —
snapped, — snapped like, — struck, —

struck off, — swung against, — swung in, — threw off, — waited on, — went, — worked against, — wrapped around

chair
verbs
asked of —, brought —, brought up —, came around —, came from —, came in —, came off —, came to —, climbed into —, climbed off —, climbed on —, climbed onto —, considered —, crossed to —, drew in —, drew out —, drew up —, dropped —, dropped in —, dropped into —, dropped on —, dropped onto —, dropped to —, fell against —, fell in —, fell into —, fell over —, felt for —, found —, gave up —, gestured at —, gestured to —, gestured toward —, glanced at —, got in —, got off —, got on —, grabbed —, grabbed for —, gripped —, headed for —, heard —, held —, held out —, jumped from —, jumped in —, jumped into —, jumped off —, jumped out —, kicked —, kicked at —, kicked out —, kicked over —, knocked over —, landed in —, lay behind —, leaned against —, leaned in —, leaned into —, leaned on —, leaned over —, left —, lifted —, lifted up —, looked at —, lowered —, lowered into —, lowered to —, missed —, moved —, moved in —, moved off —, moved on —, moved to —, moved toward —, nodded at —, nodded to —, nodded toward —, passed —, passed among —, picked —, picked up —, pointed at —, pointed to —, pulled —, pulled back —, pulled out —, pulled over —, pulled up —, pushed —, pushed away —, pushed back —, pushed from —, pushed in —, pushed off —, pushed out —, pushed over —, reached behind —, reached for

—, recognized —, remained in —, remained on —, returned to —, rolled —, rolled off —, rose from —, sank down —, sank in —, sank into —, sank onto —, sat in —, sat on —, saw —, settled against —, settled in —, settled into —, shifted —, shifted from —, shifted in —, shifted into —, shifted on —, shoved —, shrugged in —, slept in —, slid back —, slid from —, slid in —, slid into —, slid off —, slipped from —, slipped into —, slipped off —, slipped over —, snapped in —, stared at —, started in —, stayed in —, stepped onto —, stood at —, stood behind —, stood beside —, stood from —, stood near —, stood on —, stopped —, stopped by —, studied —, took —, tried —, turned —, turned around —, turned in —, turned on —, used —, walked around —, walked behind —, walked to —, walked toward —, wanted —, waved at —, waved to —, waved toward —, went to —; — added, — appeared to, — became, — broke, — came down, — came with, — carried on, — covered with, — died, — drank, — dropped forward, — fell, — fell away, — fell back, — fell into, — fell over, — fell to, — felt, — felt like, — flew, — flew across, — happened to, — held, — hit, — hung, — jumped back, — kicked, — kicked back, — lay on, — leaned against, — left of, — made, — made of, — made up, — moved, — moved behind, — needed, — offered, — placed against, — placed to, — pointed at, — pointed to, — pressed together, — pulled, — pulled up, — pushed back, — pushed in, — ran up, — rolled forward, — rolled over, — said, — sat, — sat at, — sat atop, — sat before, — sat in, — sat on, — sat under,

— seemed to, — set back, — set before, — set out, — set up, — settled amid, — shook, — shoved, — shoved together, — slammed against, — slid to, — snapped on, — stood, — stood behind, — stood on, — stopped, — took up, — turned, — turned to, — used by, — waited, — waited behind, — waited for, — worked in

chamber
verbs
arrived outside —, called —, checked —, continued across —, drove toward —, entered —, filled —, flew around —, glanced around —, grabbed —, left —, looked about —, looked around —, opened —, pointed across —, pushed into —, ran across —, reached —, returned to —, screamed at —, stared across —, stared around —, stepped into —, studied —, turned —, turned at —, walked around —, walked into —, went inside —, went into —, went toward —; — appeared, — became, — began to, — came, — came from, — fell, — filled with, — flew open, — grew, — lay, — lay beneath, — lay beyond, — lit up, — lit with, — made of, — meant to, — opened, — opened off, — rang with, — rose, — rose up, — sat, — seemed, — seemed to, — set aside, — shook, — slid into, — threw

charge
verbs
— blew, — blew out, — blew with, — came, — came from, — came off, — came to, — carried above, — dropped, — gave, — hit, — hung over, — left, — lit, — made, — placed against, — pressed, — pulled, — ran, — ran out, —

reached, — remained, — returned, — said, — sat in, — set, — slammed into, — slid, — slid down, — spent, — stepped up, — struck, — went off, — went to

cheek
verbs
— added, — appeared to, — began to, — came, — came to, — continued to, — covered with, — drew back, — fell into, — fell open, — felt, — felt like, — filled with, — gave, — got, — grew, — held, — hung in, — laid against, — lay, — lay against, — lay over, — left, — looked up, — made, — met, — pressed against, — pressed into, — pressed to, — pressed together, — pushed against, — pushed back, — pushed to, — put, — rose, — said, — seemed to, — shook, — showed, — slammed against, — started to, — stood, — stood out, — suggested, — touched, — turned, — went

chest
verbs
approached —, asked —, bent to —, checked —, closed —, continued to —, felt —, filled —, flew at —, frowned at —, gestured at —, gestured to —, gestured toward —, glanced at —, grabbed —, grabbed at —, gripped —, held —, held over —, hit —, kissed —, landed against —, landed on —, lay atop —, leaned into —, looked at —, looked inside —, moved to —, murmured into —, nodded against —, nodded into —, opened —, pointed at —, pointed to —, pointed toward —, pressed —, pressed on —, pushed —, pushed out —, reached for —, reached into —, reached

to —, rolled to —, rubbed —, rubbed at —, saw —, settled against —, shoved —, sighed against —, sighed into —, slammed into —, smiled against —, smiled into —, stared at —, took —, touched —, turned into —, walked to —, walked toward —, went to —; — appeared, — began to, — came, — caught, — closed, — covered in, — covered with, — did, — disappeared, — dropped down, — fell, — felt, — felt like, — filled, — filled with, — flew, — flew by, — followed, — fought to, — got, — grew, — grew with, — held, — hit, — lay, — lay on, — led, — lifted, — lifted underneath, — looked, — looked like, — made, — missed, — missed from, — moved, — moved against, — moved up, — nodded, — opened, — opened up, — pressed to, — pulled for, — remained, — reminded, — returned, — rolled over, — rose, — rose in, — rose up, — rose with, — sank in, — sat in, — screamed for, — screamed with, — seemed to, — settled into, — shifted, — shook, — shoved against, — showed, — shut, — sighed, — stared out, — started, — started to, — stood, — stood against, — stood on, — struck, — touched, — walked, — went, — went off, — went up, — worked like

chill
verbs

— began, — began to, — blew along, — came back, — came from, — came in, — came into, — came up, — caught, — climbed up, — covered, — entered, — felt like, — filled, — found, — gripped, — hit, — left by, — lifted, — made, — moved, — passed over, — passed through, — raised, — ran, — ran down,

— ran over, — ran through, — ran up, — reached, — remained, — returned to, — rolled off, — rose through, — rose up, — seemed to, — settled, — settled in, — settled into, — shot down, — shot through, — shot up, — slid across, — slid down, — slid over, — slid up, — slipped down, — started in, — took, — touched, — went, — went down, — went over, — went through, — went up, — whispered up, — worked

chin
verbs

caught —, dropped —, felt —, forced —, gestured with —, grabbed —, gripped —, held —, kissed —, led with —, lifted —, lifted up —, lowered —, nodded with —, pointed with —, pulled at —, put up —, raised —, rubbed —, rubbed at —, set —, threw up —, took —, tossed up —, touched —, wiped —, wiped at —; — began to, — came down, — came to, — came up, — climbed up, — covered in, — dropped, — dropped at, — dropped onto, — dropped to, — fell for, — fell onto, — fell to, — felt, — found, — got, — got in, — held, — hit, — hit with, — hung forward, — lifted, — lifted in, — lifted on, — lifted to, — lifted with, — lowered, — moved, — moved up, — nodded to, — pointed up, — pointed with, — pressed into, — pushed back, — raised, — raised to, — rolled on, — rose, — rose from, — rubbed along, — sank to, — settled, — settled atop, — shifted, — shot out, — shot up, — snapped up, — started to, — stood with, — turned, — went, — went up

chopper

verbs
— appeared, — approached, — began,
— began to, — came, — came back, —
came into, — cleared, — continued to,
— dropped into, — dropped onto, —
flew, — flew into, — followed, — grew
by, — happened to, — headed, —
hesitated, — kept, — landed, — landed
at, — landed with, — lay on, — lifted,
— lifted away, — lifted off, — lost, —
made, — moved, — moved forward, —
passed over, — reached, — returned, —
rose, — rose above, — rose from, — rose
through, — sank, — seemed to, — shot,
— stayed, — stayed on, — stood, —
took off, — took to, — touched down,
— turned

cigar
verbs
asked for —, bought —, drew on —,
drew out —, dropped —, finished —,
found —, grabbed at —, grinned around
—, held out —, held up —, lit —, lit up
—, looked at —, lowered —, nodded at
—, picked up —, pulled on —, pulled
out —, reached for —, slipped out —,
smelled of —, smiled around —, took —
, took out —, waved —, worked —

cigarette
verbs
blew on —, bought —, brought —,
checked —, drew on —, drew out —,
dropped —, finished —, finished with
—, found —, gestured with —, got out
—, grabbed —, grabbed for —, hated —,
held —, held out —, held up —, lit —,
lit up —, looked at —, lowered —,
needed —, offered —, passed —, picked
up —, played with —, pointed at —,
pointed to —, pointed with —, pressed

out —, pulled —, pulled at —, pulled on
—, pulled out —, put —, put down —,
put out —, raised —, reached for —,
returned —, returned to —, rolled —,
shook out —, smelled —, smelled of —,
spoke around —, stared at —, started
with —, stepped on —, struck —,
studied —, talked past —, thought
about —, threw —, threw away —,
threw down —, took —, took out —,
took up —, tossed —, tossed away —,
tossed down —, used —, wanted —,
watched —, waved —, wished for —; —
appeared between, — appeared to, —
became, — came back, — came on, —
dropped down, — dropped from, — fell
from, — fell on, — felt, — found, —
grew, — held, — held in, — hung, —
hung at, — hung from, — lit, — made
of, — paused in, — rolled, — rose over,
— rose to, — shook, — stopped, —
went out

circle
verbs
arrived in —, broke —, closed —,
entered —, fell into —, flew in —,
glanced around —, got to —, joined —,
left —, looked around —, made —,
moved around —, moved in —, nodded
toward —, ran in —, reached into —,
rubbed in —, sat outside —, shifted in
—, stepped into —, stepped through —,
stood from —, turned —, turned in —,
turned to —, walked around —, walked
in —, walked into —, walked toward —;
— appeared, — appeared on, —
appeared under, — began to, — broke,
— broke up, — closed, — covered with,
— disappeared, — fell, — found out, —
grew, — hung in, — lay, — looked, —
lowered, — met, — moved, — pressed

into, — raised, — rose, — rose beneath,
— seemed to, — set into, — turned to,
— went

city
verbs

approached —, came to —, drove
around —, drove into —, drove through
—, drove to —, drove toward —,
entered —, found —, gestured toward
—, glanced to —, got to —, hated —,
headed for —, headed to —, headed
toward —, held —, knew —, knew
about —, landed in —, left —, liked —,
lived in —, lived outside —, looked
toward —, loved —, missed —, passed
—, reached —, stared at —, stared
toward —, stayed in —, stopped outside
—, studied —, took —, took on —,
walked across —, went into —; —
appeared to, — arrived at, — became, —
began, — began to, — broke, —
brought into, — called, — came, —
came into, — came off, — came to, —
caught, — changed into, — chose, —
continued to, — covered, — cut off, —
did, — did by, — disappeared, — drew,
— dropped, — dropped away, — ended
with, — fell, — felt like, — filled with,
— followed, — found, — got, — grew,
— grew around, — kept up, — knew, —
lay, — lay about, — lay in, — lay under,
— left, — left for, — lifted off, —
listened, — lived on, — looked, —
looked for, — looked in, — looked like,
— lost, — made, — made for, — made
of, — made out, — made up, —
muttered in, — needed, — offered, —
opened, — remained under, — rolled
out, — rose, — rose above, — rose up,
— sat at, — screamed, — seemed, —
seemed to, — set on, — set upon, —

shut out, — slept, — slipped away, —
smelled, — smelled of, — spoke, —
stood, — swallowed by, — talked of, —
threw, — took, — took on, — took up,
— turned, — waited for, — went, —
went to, — wore, — worked

class
verbs

— began, — began to, — bowed, —
breathed, — broke into, — came to, —
carried, — drew in, — drew near, —
dropped to, — ended, — ended for, —
ended on, — filled, — flew by, —
followed, — got inside, — got into, —
laughed, — learned, — let out, —
listened, — met, — offered by, — put,
— ran against, — ran on, — sat, —
seemed, — seemed like, — settled, —
started, — turned into, — waited, —
waited for, — waited on, — wanted, —
wanted to, — went

claw
verbs

— answered, — appeared through, —
broke, — broke through, — came down,
— came near, — came up, — caught, —
caught at, — caught in, — did, —
disappeared, — disappeared from, —
disappeared into, — dropped down, —
ended, — fell away, — felt, — found, —
grabbed, — grew, — grew from, —
headed off, — helped in, — left, — left
on, — lifted, — looked like, — opened,
— passed, — played, — pressed against,
— pushed through, — raised, —
reached out, — reached through, —
sank into, — sent up, — settled on, —
slid, — slipped on, — slipped past

clip

verbs

— began to, — continued, — ended, — filled, — followed, — grinned, — held, — hung below, — jumped, — laughed, — ran out, — reached, — repeated, — rolled forward, — rose to, — sat back, — sat on, — shook, — showed, — smiled, — smiled in, — snapped into, — stood behind, — threw, — went inside

cloak

verbs

brought —, drew aside —, dropped —, felt beneath —, gestured at —, grabbed —, held —, hung —, lifted —, opened —, picked up —, pointed to —, pulled off —, pulled on —, put on —, raised —, reached for —, reached inside —, reached into —, reached under —, settled under —, shifted —, shook out —, shrugged into —, shrugged off —, shrugged on —, slipped off —, threw back —, threw off —, threw on —, threw open —, took —, took down —, took off —, took out —, touched —, wore —; — appeared, — became, — blew in, — caught, — caught in, — caught on, — cleared, — covered with, — did, — died in, — drew, — drove, — entered, — fell around, — fell away, — fell open, — fell over, — felt, — found, — held back, — hung, — hung from, — hung in, — hung on, — hung over, — hung to, — knocked, — laid over, — laughed, — lay, — lay on, — lay over, — looked, — made, — made of, — moved, — moved into, — moved through, — moved to, — opened, — pulled, — pulled about, — pulled down, — said, — sat, — seemed to, — shouted, — slipped, — slipped from, — snapped in, — stayed in, — stood, — took, —

tossed over, — waited at, — walked around, — waved, — went, — went down, — wore, — wrapped, — wrapped about, — wrapped around

clock

verbs

blinked at —, checked —, felt —, frowned at —, gestured toward —, glanced at —, glanced to —, glanced toward —, heard —, kicked aside —, lived by —, looked —, looked at —, looked to —, needed —, nodded at —, nodded to —, nodded toward —, picked up —, pointed to —, saw —, slept through —, stared at —, took —, watched —, worked around —; — appeared in, — appeared on, — began, — began to, — blinked away, — called out, — came, — changed, — fell, — felt like, — gave, — hung beside, — hung on, — lay on, — made, — made for, — moved, — moved in, — moved with, — ran at, — ran out, — read, — said, — sat at, — seemed like, — seemed to, — set at, — set on, — started to, — stopped, — struck, — tossed on, — turned to, — went off, — worked, — worked with, — wrapped around

closet

verbs

asked from —, came into —, checked —, closed —, crossed to —, disappeared into —, entered —, felt through —, finished in —, found —, gestured to —, headed for —, kept in —, left —, lived in —, looked in —, looked into —, looked through —, moved to —, nodded toward —, opened —, opened up —, passed —, pointed to —, pointed toward —, ran for —, ran into —, ran to

—, reached —, reached into —,
returned to —, saw —, shifted through
—, shut —, stared into —, started for —
, stepped into —, stood before —, stood
in —, tried —, turned to —, walked into
—, walked to —, went inside —, went
into —, went through —, went to —

cloth
verbs

— appeared, — became, — came away,
— came from, — caught, — covered, —
did, — fell away, — fell from, — fell out,
— held on, — held to, — held under, —
hung across, — hung from, — hung
over, — laid on, — lay in, — lifted into,
— looked, — made, — moved over, —
pressed against, — sat, — sat at, — sat
on, — seemed, — seemed to, — shot
through, — stayed behind, — worked
in, — wrapped around

clothes
verbs

brought —, changed —, checked —,
chose —, crossed to —, felt among —,
found —, gestured at —, gestured to —,
got —, grabbed —, hung up —, jumped
into —, kept —, kicked through —,
knew —, left —, looked at —, looked
for —, looked through —, loved —,
needed —, passed over —, picked out —
, picked up —, pulled off —, pulled on
—, pulled out —, put away —, put on
—, reached for —, reached into —,
recognized —, saw —, shook off —,
slept in —, studied —, threw off —,
threw on —, took —, took off —, tossed
—, touched —, wanted —, wore —; —
became, — began to, — bought with, —
bowed to, — came around, — came
down, — came off, — caught, —

changed, — covered, — covered in, —
drew, — dropped to, — entered, — fell
away, — fell out, — felt in, — flew, —
followed, — held, — held against, —
helped, — hit, — hung, — hung from,
— hung in, — hung off, — hung on, —
laid out, — lay in, — lay on, — left to,
— looked, — made, — made to, —
meant for, — passed down, — picked
up, — pulled from, — put together, —
remained in, — rolled under, — seemed,
— seemed to, — showed, — smelled, —
smelled of, — stared at, — took, — took
on, — turned to, — went into, — went
on, — went to, — went up

cloud
verbs

— appeared, — appeared in, —
appeared on, — appeared over, —
approached from, — arrived, — became,
— began to, — blew, — blew away, —
blew through, — broke, — broke into,
— broke open, — broke up, — came
from, — came over, — came up, —
caught, — cleared away, — climbed, —
closed about, — closed on, — continued
to, — covered, — crossed, —
disappeared, — drew back, — fell on, —
filled, — grew, — hung, — hung across,
— hung on, — hung over, — lay along,
— lay on, — left, — lifted, — lit, — lit
by, — looked like, — lowered, — meant
to, — moved, — moved across, —
moved in, — moved on, — moved
toward, — opened, — opened like, —
passed, — passed across, — passed
before, — passed in, — passed over, —
pushed up, — ran, — ran before, — ran
in, — rolled, — rolled across, — rolled
over, — rolled toward, — rolled up, —
rose, — rose above, — rose across, —

rose along, — rose from, — rose into, — rose over, — seemed, — seemed to, — settled, — shifted, — shifted to, — showed through, — slid across, — slipped across, — slipped over, — swallowed, — took away, — turned, — went away

club
verbs
arrived at —, ate at —, called —, came into —, entered —, glanced around —, glanced at —, grabbed —, grabbed for —, held up —, hit —, left —, let —, looked around —, looked at —, picked —, put away —, raised —, stared at —, swung —, took —, took outside —, turned for —, used —, went into —, went to —; — became, — began, — called, — caught, — cleared out, — continued to, — cut through, — did to, — fell to, — grew, — hit, — kept, — knocked, — lay at, — looked like, — made in, — made of, — met, — opened, — raised, — raised for, — rang, — rang on, — rose, — sat on, — seemed to, — slammed against, — smiled, — struck, — wrapped around, — yelled

coat
verbs
dropped —, found —, got —, grabbed —, held out —, held up —, hung —, hung up —, kept on —, left —, loved —, missed —, moved aside —, nodded at —, nodded into —, opened —, picked up —, pulled —, pulled off —, pulled on —, put —, put on —, reached beneath —, reached for —, reached inside —, reached into —, reached over —, reached under —, saw —, set —, shook off —, shook open —, shrugged into —,

shrugged off —, shrugged on —, slid into —, slipped behind —, slipped into —, slipped off —, slipped on —, swung on —, thought —, threw —, threw off —, threw on —, took —, took down —, took off —, tossed —, tossed off —, wanted —, wore —; — came away, — came in, — came into, — came out, — carried, — caught, — closed, — closed against, — covered, — covered in, — dropped to, — fell, — fell across, — fell from, — fell open, — fell to, — flew in, — grew, — held, — hung by, — hung from, — hung in, — hung on, — hung open, — hung over, — landed in, — lay open, — led, — lifted, — looked, — looked out, — made of, — moved toward, — paused for, — pulled over, — read, — remained, — remained on, — said, — said in, — sat, — sat to, — seemed to, — shut, — slid open, — stood behind, — stood over, — stopped, — swallowed, — turned, — turned up, — walked into, — walked over

cockpit
verbs
asked from —, called toward —, came from —, came into —, climbed into —, closed —, entered —, flew into —, glanced toward —, headed for —, jumped into —, lay in —, leaned into —, left —, looked about —, looked around —, looked into —, looked toward —, moved to —, opened —, ran into —, ran to —, reached —, reached across —, returned to —, sat in —, shouted from —, slipped from —, stared at —, started for —, stepped into —, swung toward —, took in —, watched from —

coffee

verbs
added to —, admitted over —, agreed to
—, arrived with —, asked for —, asked
over —, blew on —, bought —, broke
for —, brought —, brought in —, came
with —, chose —, continued with —,
demanded —, drank —, drank up —,
dropped —, finished —, finished off —,
found —, frowned into —, got —,
grabbed —, handed over —, hated —,
headed for —, held up —, leaned for —,
left —, lifted —, liked —, looked at —,
looked into —, loved —, made —,
managed over —, moved —, needed —,
offered —, opened —, ordered —,
passed around —, passed on —, passed
out —, picked up —, placed —, played
with —, pointed to —, poured —,
poured out —, pushed away —, put —,
put down —, put on —, rang for —,
reached for —, returned to —, said over
—, said to —, sat with —, saw —, set —,
set aside —, set down —, sighed in —,
smelled —, stared at —, stared into —,
started —, started with —, stayed with
—, stopped for —, studied —,
swallowed —, took —, took up —, tried
—, waited for —, waited until —,
wanted —, went for —, went with —;
— appeared, — appeared at, — arrived,
— arrived on, — brought, — came, —
came in, — closed, — ended at, — filled,
— grew, — helped, — kicked in, — left
in, — looked up, — remained, — sat, —
sat in, — sat on, — set up, — settled, —
smelled, — sounded, — started to, —
touched, — turned, — waited by, —
waited for, — went

coin
verbs

drew out —, dropped in —, found —,
frowned at —, gave —, glanced at —,
got —, handed back —, handed over —,
held out —, held up —, kept —, left —,
lifted —, looked at —, offered —, passed
across —, picked up —, pointed to —,
pulled out —, put away —, said —, slid
—, stared at —, threw in —, took —,
took out —, took up —, tossed —,
touched —, watched —; — appeared,
— came down, — came from, — came
to, — changed, — dropped by, —
dropped from, — dropped into, —
dropped to, — fell, — fell into, — gave,
— hit, — laid by, — landed in, — left
behind, — left in, — rose in, — sat in,
— sent, — set aside, — slid on, —
slipped off, — slipped through, — stood
in, — struck, — told, — took up, —
went back

color
verbs
— appeared, — appeared behind, —
appeared in, — appeared to, — became,
— began to, — broke through, —
brought, — came, — came back, —
came from, — came into, — came out,
— came to, — caught, — changed with,
— covered, — died, — filled, — flew
back, — flew from, — grew, — jumped
out, — left, — looked, — made, —
moved, — needed, — played across, —
remained, — remained on, — returned,
— returned to, — rode up, — rose, —
rose from, — rose in, — rose into, —
rose to, — rose with, — seemed, —
seemed to, — set, — settled, — shot, —
showed, — started to, — struck at, —
tried to, — turned out

column

verbs

— added up, — appeared, — appeared at, — approached, — arrived, — became, — began, — began to, — broke down, — carried, — caught up, — closed up, — continued on, — continued to, — crossed, — fell, — fell back, — followed, — followed behind, — grew, — headed, — kept, — led to, — left, — left behind, — looked like, — looked to, — lost, — met, — moved forward, — passed down, — passed over, — picked up, — ran into, — reached, — remained, — returned from, — rode out, — rose through, — rose up, — seemed, — set off, — set to, — snapped, — started down, — stopped, — turned, — turned around, — turned to

company
verbs

— agreed, — appeared to, — arrived, — ate, — began, — began to, — bought, — broke out, — broke up, — brought, — brought in, — called, — came, — came for, — came from, — came out, — came to, — closed, — crossed, — crossed through, — cut, — did, — drank in, — drew, — fell, — fell back, — figured out, — followed, — found, — glanced at, — got, — headed out, — held, — hung on, — lay in, — left, — looked at, — lost, — made, — managed, — moved, — moved onto, — passed over, — passed through, — paused to, — pushed, — pushed in, — pushed on, — ran, — ran into, — reached out, — remained, — rode, — rode away, — rose to, — said, — sank, — sank like, — sat, — sat on, — set out, — set up, — showed, — slept, — smelled, — stared out, — started down,

— started up, — stopped, — stopped for, — took, — took over, — tried to, — turned out, — turned to, — wanted to, — watched in, — went, — went forward, — went into, — went with, — worked, — worked on

computer
verbs

asked from —, caught —, checked —, checked with —, closed —, closed down —, closed up —, crossed to —, found —, found in —, gestured at —, gestured to —, gestured toward —, glanced at —, glanced toward —, got on —, grabbed —, headed to —, held up —, hit —, kept —, leaned over —, left —, looked at —, looked over —, moved to —, needed —, nodded at —, nodded to —, nodded toward —, opened —, picked up —, pointed at —, pointed to —, pulled out —, put down —, ran by —, ran to —, reached behind —, replied to —, returned to —, said —, said to —, sat at —, sat before —, sat by —, shifted to —, shut —, shut down —, shut off —, snapped on —, stared at —, started —, stayed at —, stood by —, studied —, swung to —, told —, took —, took in —, took out —, turned —, turned from —, turned off —, turned on —, turned to —, walked to —, waved to —, went into —, went on —, went to —, woke —, woke up —, worked —, worked at —, worked on —, yelled at —; — answered, — asked, — began to, — blinked off, — came, — came to, — came up, — closed, — did, — felt like, — finished, — hit on, — kicked back, — lay on, — left, — looked, — needed, — ran through, — replied, — returned, — said, — sat in, — sat on, — sat open, — sat to, —

seemed to, — set up, — showed, — shut, — shut down, — spoke, — stopped, — understood, — went

concern
verbs
answered —, asked in —, asked with —, frowned —, frowned in —, heard —, knew —, looked —, nodded with —, repeated with —, replied without —, said in —, said with —, said without —, saw —, showed —, shrugged off —, smiled through —, smiled without —, spoke from —, spoke with —, understood —, waved aside —, waved away —, waved off —, whispered with —, wondered with —; — appeared between, — began to, — brought, — came to, — crossed, — drew, — entered, — fell over, — felt, — flew back, — followed, — gave, — grew, — grew with, — left, — passed over, — passed through, — pushed, — ran, — ran like, — seemed, — seemed to, — sounded, — took, — tried to, — turned, — went

confusion
verbs
— began to, — broke, — broke out, — brought on, — came, — caught, — cleared, — cleared up, — closed, — covered, — crossed, — crossed over, — drew, — fell upon, — filled, — grew, — gripped, — held, — passed across, — passed over, — passed through, — poured out, — ran under, — remained, — seemed, — sent, — set in, — slid into, — took over, — turned into, — turned to

connection
verbs

— became, — broke, — broke off, — came through, — came to, — cut, — cut in, — cut off, — cut out, — died, — disappeared from, — dropped, — ended, — entered, — fell into, — grew, — grew after, — looked, — lost, — made, — reached, — seemed, — seemed to, — sent through, — snapped, — went, — went through

control
verbs
checked —, dropped —, felt —, felt in —, fought —, fought for —, found —, glanced at —, grabbed —, gripped —, kept —, kept under —, liked —, looked in —, lost —, moved to —, needed —, picked up —, played with —, remained in —, returned to —, stayed in —, took —, touched —, turned on —, turned to —, wanted —, worked —

conversation
verbs
ate without —, began —, broke off —, carried —, continued —, did beyond —, ended —, expected —, finished —, followed —, grabbed —, heard —, joined —, jumped into —, leaned into —, left —, liked —, listened to —, made —, missed —, moved into —, needed —, opened —, picked up —, remembered from —, repeated —, returned to —, started —, stepped into —, thought about —, turned from —, waited without —, walked without —, wanted —, wrapped up —; — appeared to, — became, — began, — began with, — broke, — broke down, — broke like, — broke off, — came back, — came from, — came to, — carried through, — changed, — changed to, — continued,

— continued along, — continued for, — continued in, — continued over, — continued throughout, — continued to, — continued with, — cut off, — died, — died away, — died out, — ended, — ended in, — fell, — fell away, — fell for, — fell off, — felt, — felt like, — filled, — followed, — gave, — got on, — grew, — happened, — happened in, — happened on, — held without, — joined, — kept up, — left off, — made, — made up, — managed to, — meant to, — moved on, — moved onto, — moved to, — paused, — ran out, — returned to, — rose, — seemed, — seemed to, — settled on, — shifted in, — sounded, — sounded like, — started, — started with, — stopped, — stopped at, — stopped in, — took, — took from, — turned, — turned away, — turned into, — turned to, — went, — went on, — went through, — went with

corner
verbs
appeared around —, asked from —, broke off —, came around —, came to —, checked from —, chose —, cleared —, continued around —, cut —, disappeared around —, drove around —, drove past —, drove to —, found —, gestured to —, glanced around —, glanced at —, glanced toward —, got to —, grabbed —, headed around —, hung —, kept to —, lay in —, leaned around —, leaned into —, left —, lifted —, looked around —, looked in —, looked to —, made —, moved into —, moved to —, moved toward —, nodded from —, nodded to —, nodded toward —, paused at —, pointed around —, pointed to —, pressed into —, pulled

down —, ran around —, ran to —, ran toward —, reached —, returned to —, rolled into —, said from —, sank into —, sat in —, shot to —, slid around —, slipped around —, slipped at —, slipped into —, snapped from —, spoke from —, stayed by —, stayed in —, stepped around —, stepped into —, stepped to —, stood at —, stood in —, stood on —, stopped at —, stopped on —, swung around —, took —, turned —, turned at —, turned to —, waited on —, walked around —, walked into —, walked to —, walked toward —, went around —, went to —; — appeared, — began, — began to, — came, — caught, — covered in, — dropped, — fell over, — felt, — glanced at, — held, — led to, — left to, — lifted, — looked, — picked, — played on, — pulled down, — remained, — sat, — screamed for, — showed, — started to, — stood, — touched, — turned, — turned down, — turned over, — used for

corpse
verbs
approached —, bent over —, carried —, covered —, crossed to —, dropped —, felt —, found —, frowned at —, gestured at —, glanced at —, grabbed up —, jumped over —, kicked —, lay like —, leaned over —, left —, lifted —, looked at —, looked like —, moved —, moved about —, nodded at —, passed under —, picked up —, pointed at —, pointed to —, pushed past —, reached —, returned to —, said to —, saw —, stared at —, stayed by —, stayed with —, stepped around —, stepped over —, stood by —, stood over —, studied —, told —, took —, walked around —,

walked to —, went past —, went to —;
— added to, — began to, — brought in,
— came to, — continued off, — did, —
fell forward, — fell to, — filled, — flew
into, — found in, — hit, — hung, —
hung above, — kept in, — laid out, —
landed, — landed with, — lay, — lay in,
— lay on, — left behind, — left to, —
let out, — looked, — made, — missed,
— moved in, — opened, — ordered, —
paused, — pulled, — raised, — ran, —
reached to, — remained to, — rose, —
rose from, — rose into, — said, —
seemed to, — settled on, — slid, —
smelled, — smelled like, — stepped in,
— stood at, — stood up, — took, —
turned, — turned into, — went, —
went down, — wore, — wrapped in

—, stepped down —, stepped into —,
stood in —, stopped in —, studied —,
turned —, turned along —, turned
down —, waited in —, walked —,
walked across —, walked along —,
walked down —, walked into —,
watched from —, went down —, went
into —, went up —, yelled into —; —
appeared, — became, — began, — began
to, — called, — came, — caught, —
disappeared into, — drew, — fell on, —
grew, — lay behind, — led, — led into,
— led to, — lit by, — looked like, —
offered, — opened, — opened into, —
passed, — ran, — ran off, — reached, —
remained, — sat, — seemed, — seemed
to, — set with, — showed, — stood, —
turned, — turned to, — went forward

corridor

verbs

appeared in —, asked from —, called
down —, came into —, came through
—, came to —, came up —, checked —,
continued along —, continued down —,
crossed —, disappeared into —, entered
—, filled —, flew down —, followed —,
glanced around —, glanced down —,
glanced into —, glanced up —, headed
down —, headed into —, landed down
—, lay in —, left —, listened at —,
looked around —, looked down —,
looked toward —, looked up —, moved
along —, moved down —, moved into
—, moved through —, nodded toward
—, passed down —, pointed along —,
pointed down —, pointed into —,
pointed toward —, ran along —, ran
down —, ran into —, ran through —,
ran to —, returned to —, sat in —, slid
into —, slipped into —, stared down —,
started down —, started up —, stayed in

couch

verbs

asked from —, came around —, chose
—, climbed onto —, crossed to —,
dropped on —, dropped onto —,
dropped to —, fell against —, fell off —,
fell on —, fell onto —, fell to —, flew to
—, gestured at —, gestured toward —,
glanced at —, got off —, got on —,
jumped from —, jumped off —, landed
onto —, lay on —, leaned against —,
leaned on —, leaned over —, leaned
toward —, left —, looked at —, moved
—, moved down —, moved to —,
moved toward —, opened —, paused by
—, pointed at —, pointed to —, pointed
toward —, pushed off —, ran around —
, reached behind —, remained on —,
returned to —, rolled off —, rose from
—, rose off —, said from —, said onto
—, said to —, sank against —, sank into
—, sank on —, sank onto —, sank to —,
sat on —, saw —, settled into —, settled

on —, settled onto —, shifted on —,
shoved —, shoved off —, slept on —,
slid across —, slid off —, stared at —,
stayed on —, stepped to —, stood
behind —, stood by —, stood from —,
took —, took in —, turned on —,
walked around —, walked to —, walked
toward —, went to —

counter
verbs

— appeared in, — brought out, — came
up, — dropped to, — filled with, —
gave, — glanced up, — held, — jumped,
— looked, — made, — moved, —
offered, — opened into, — ran, — said,
— sat, — screamed, — seemed, —
shook, — shot up, — showed, — smiled,
— smiled at, — stood, — watched, —
wiped

country
verbs

— appeared to, — ate, — ate before, —
became, — began to, — began with, —
called, — changed, — continued to, —
did with, — died from, — fell into, —
felt, — fought in, — got, — looked, —
looked for, — looked like, — lost, —
made, — made of, — missed, — passed
through, — put, — saw, — screamed
for, — seemed, — seemed to, —
sounded, — started to, — waited

course
verbs

— added, — answered, — brought to,
— called, — changed, — drove into, —
ended, — filled up, — followed, — got,
— laid out, — led to, — left, — made,
— offered, — raised, — realized, — said
into, — saw, — set forth, — smelled, —

stayed, — took, — turned aside, —
went, — wore

court
verbs

— agreed to, — began, — began to, —
broke into, — brought, — called for, —
came to, — fell, — fell into, — fell upon,
— felt toward, — found, — held up, —
laid, — laughed, — left, — looked, —
looked on, — moved to, — moved
toward, — murmured, — ordered, —
placed on, — rang with, — rose, —
seemed to, — spent, — took, — tried to,
— turned to, — waited

courtroom
verbs

— began to, — cleared, — cut out, —
expected, — fell, — filled in, — filled
up, — filled with, — flew open, —
gasped, — grew, — led into, — opened,
— remained, — sat back, — sat down,
— seemed to, — started to, — stayed, —
stood, — swung open, — took, —
wanted to, — watched, — went, —
yelled

cover
verbs

blew —, broke —, broke from —,
climbed underneath —, closed —, fell
on —, glanced at —, held up —, jumped
for —, jumped from —, left —, lifted
—, lifted off —, looked at —, looked inside
—, opened —, picked up —, pulled —,
pulled off —, pushed aside —, pushed at
—, raised —, ran for —, read from —,
recognized —, rose from —, rubbed —,
shut —, slept atop —, slid behind —,
stared at —, stepped into —, threw aside
—, threw off —, took —, took off —,

touched —, turned —; — answered, — appeared on, — asked, — began to, — came to, — caught, — closed, — dropped into, — fell over, — flew back, — flew off, — flew through, — gave, — got up, — held, — lifted, — looked, — made, — pulled back, — pulled off, — pulled over, — pulled to, — pulled up, — read, — remained, — rolled forward, — showed, — slid, — swallowed, — threw

crack
verbs

— appeared, — appeared along, — appeared in, — appeared on, — appeared with, — began to, — brought, — called, — came back, — caught up, — closed with, — cut, — demanded, — filled, — followed by, — followed in, — left by, — let in, — met, — opened among, — opened between, — opened in, — opened on, — ran, — ran across, — ran after, — ran down, — ran through, — ran under, — rang in, — rang out, — shook, — showed in, — sounded, — sounded in, — threw

creature
verbs

— brought to, — carried, — caught like, — continued, — covered with, — died by, — died on, — dropped to, — flew above, — gave, — got, — happened to, — held, — hesitated, — kept, — landed with, — lay in, — left in, — lifted, — lived in, — looked like, — made, — made for, — made of, — managed to, — moved across, — moved into, — moved through, — opened, — paused to, — pointed at, — raised, — ran around, — remained under, — rode on, — sat in,

— screamed in, — settled on, — shifted on, — shook, — stepped through, — stood, — stood in, — swung to, — thought in, — tried to, — turned, — waited for, — wore

crow
verbs

— added, — answered, — asked, — ate, — began to, — came in, — came to, — chose to, — fell over, — flew, — found, — gave, — got, — landed, — landed on, — liked to, — looked, — opened, — picked at, — picked up, — pushed off, — replied, — rode, — rode together, — rose from, — said, — screamed, — spoke, — started on, — took off, — took to, — turned, — waited, — waited on

crowd
verbs

appeared from —, approached —, called to —, disappeared into —, entered —, followed —, fought —, fought through —, glanced at —, heard —, joined —, knew —, looked around —, loved —, moved with —, pushed through —, reached through —, said from —, said to —, stared into —, stood amid —, told —, turned to —, wanted —, worked —; — became, — began, — began to, — broke, — broke into, — broke up, — brought back, — called out, — came, — came back, — came from, — came in, — came over, — came through, — came to, — caught, — changed, — closed, — closed in, — continued, — continued to, — cried, — crossed, — decided to, — demanded, — did, — drew, — drew back, — drew in, — dropped to, — fell, — fell away, — fell into, — filled, —

followed, — followed after, — found, — found out, — gasped, — gasped in, — gave, — gave forth, — gestured, — got out, — got to, — grew, — grew on, — grew to, — headed for, — held, — hesitated, — hung around, — joined in, — kicked into, — knew, — laughed, — laughed like, — leaned on, — leaned toward, — let, — let out, — listened to, — looked, — looked at, — looked for, — looked like, — looked on, — looked toward, — loved, — made, — moved, — moved away, — moved on, — moved to, — moved toward, — murmured, — murmured in, — nodded, — noticed, — opened, — opened out, — opened to, — opened up, — passed on, — poured, — poured into, — pressed together, — pushed, — pushed in, — rose, — rose in, — said, — sat, — screamed, — screamed in, — screamed like, — seemed, — seemed to, — sent up, — set off, — settled down, — settled in, — settled into, — settled to, — shifted, — shifted on, — shouted, — showed up, — sighed, — sighed like, — stared at, — started, — started to, — stood, — stopped, — stopped to, — took, — took up, — turned, — turned from, — turned on, — waited, — waited around, — waited for, — waited in, — waited outside, — waited to, — walked up, — walked with, — watched, — waved, — went, — went down, — went with, — yelled

cry
verbs
— became, — broke from, — broke out, — brought, — came, — came from, — came out, — came to, — carried over, — caught, — caught in, — changed, —

continued from, — continued to, — cut through, — died away, — died in, — died into, — disappeared, — ended, — ended in, — fell out, — felt like, — filled, — flew, — flew from, — gave, — grew, — joined with, — kept, — lost in, — picked up, — rang along, — rang in, — rang out, — rose, — rose behind, — rose from, — rose in, — rose over, — rose to, — rose up, — seemed to, — sent, — sent up, — shifted into, — shook, — slipped past, — sounded, — sounded behind, — started, — turned, — turned into, — went away, — went up, — woke, — woke up

cup
verbs
blew into —, brought —, carried in —, caught —, cleared away —, drank —, drank from —, dropped —, filled —, finished —, found —, frowned at —, gestured with —, glanced at —, glanced toward —, got —, grabbed —, gripped —, handed out —, handed over —, held —, held onto —, held out —, held up —, laid —, leaned over —, lifted —, lifted up —, looked at —, looked for —, looked into —, lowered —, nodded at —, nodded over —, offered —, passed around —, picked up —, placed —, pointed to —, poured —, poured out —, pulled out —, pushed —, pushed away —, put —, put aside —, put down —, put out —, raised —, reached for —, reached into —, read on —, remembered —, set —, set aside —, set down —, shoved —, slid —, slipped —, smiled into —, stared at —, stared into —, studied —, threw down —, took —, took up —, tried —, turned —, turned with —, went to —; — appeared, —

appeared on, — began to, — came off,
— came to, — covered, — dropped out,
— entered, — fell away, — fell from, —
fell to, — filled, — filled with, —
followed, — followed by, — held, —
left, — looked like, — paused, — rang,
— rang together, — sat, — sat on, — set
on, — shook, — slipped from, —
smelled, — stared out, — stood on, —
waited on, — watched

curtain
verbs
bought —, called from —, came through
—, closed —, disappeared behind —,
disappeared through —, drew —, drew
aside —, drew back —, dropped —,
gestured toward —, glanced at —,
glanced toward —, held back —, left —,
looked at —, looked through —, loved
—, moved —, moved to —, opened —,
ordered —, pulled —, pulled aside —,
pulled back —, pulled open —, pushed
—, pushed aside —, pushed back —,
pushed through —, reached for —,
reached under —, shut —, slipped
behind —, stepped through —, stepped
to —, threw back —, touched —,
walked behind —, walked to —, went
behind —; — began to, — blew in, —
closed, — closed against, — closed to, —
covered, — disappeared, — dropped to, —
— fell, — fell back, — fell on, — fell
over, — fell through, — hung, — hung
along, — hung in, — lifted, — lowered
to, — made, — met, — moved, —
opened, — passed out, — pulled, —
pulled back, — pulled over, — rose, —
rose to, — shut, — shut over, — slid
open, — turned, — turned into, —
waited, — went down, — went up

cut
verbs
— began above, — began to, — came,
— came out, — caught, — covered, —
disappeared in, — ended above, —
followed, — got on, — hit, — left, —
left by, — looked, — looked like, —
made, — meant to, — opened, —
opened on, — opened up, — poured
down, — ran, — ran along, — sent, —
stayed in, — stood out, — took off, —
went, — went through

dagger
verbs
asked for —, bent over —, carried —,
drew —, dropped —, felt for —, got —,
grabbed —, gripped —, held —, held up
—, laid down —, left —, lifted —, lost
—, lowered —, picked up —, pointed at
—, pressed on —, pulled —, pulled out
—, raised —, reached for —,
remembered —, returned to —, saw —,
stared at —, took —, took out —, used
—; — appeared, — appeared in, —
began to, — came, — came down, —
crossed, — crossed over, — cut through,
— did, — disappeared, — drove into, —
fell, — fell away, — fell from, — fell to,
— flew, — flew from, — flew toward,
— followed, — grew, — gripped, —
gripped in, — held, — held in, — hit, —
hung, — hung at, — hung on, — laid
under, — landed, — landed at, — lay,
— lay on, — left, — made, — made of,
— raised in, — settled, — slammed, —
slid, — slid in, — struck, — went into

dark
verbs
answered with —, arrived after —, asked
—, asked in —, came through —, drove

down —, entered —, fell into —, flew in —, frowned in —, gestured across —, gestured toward —, glanced at —, grew —, grinned in —, hated —, headed along —, held —, knew —, laughed in —, lay in —, leaned in —, left at —, let —, liked —, listened in —, looked at —, looked into —, looked up —, moved through —, nodded in —, pulled —, raised —, ran into —, ran through —, reached in —, recognized —, said to —, sank into —, sat in —, saw —, shot —, shouted from —, slipped into —, smiled in —, smiled into —, smiled through —, stared at —, stared into —, stepped into —, stood in —, stopped before —, talked about —, talked of —, thought about —, thought of —, took —, waited in —, waited until —, walked into —, went —, went into —, whispered from —, whispered in —, woke in —, worked until —

darkness

verbs

arrived in —, asked —, asked in —, believed in —, blinked in —, blinked into —, called into —, continued in —, disappeared into —, drank in —, drove into —, entered —, fell into —, fell through —, felt —, flew into —, frowned in —, gestured into —, grinned in —, grinned through —, jumped into —, kissed in —, lay in —, liked —, listened into —, listened through —, listened to —, looked into —, loved —, moved through —, murmured to —, muttered into —, nodded in —, pointed at —, pointed into —, ran through —, reached —, reached into —, reached through —, remained in —, remembered —, rode in —, rode into —

, rolled in —, rose in —, said from —, said into —, sank into —, sat in —, saw —, screamed in —, shot in —, shouted at —, shouted in —, shouted into —, shrugged in —, smiled in —, smiled into —, spoke after —, spoke from —, spoke into —, stared at —, stared into —, stared through —, stepped into —, stood in —, stopped in —, turned in —, waited in —, walked in —, wanted —, went into —, went through —, whispered in —, whispered into —, whispered through —, whispered to —, woke in —, woke into —, woke to —; — added, — appeared to, — approached, — became, — began to, — broke, — brought, — called for, — came, — came around, — came back, — came in, — came into, — came on, — came over, — came to, — came up, — came upon, — changed, — climbed through, — closed, — closed about, — closed around, — closed down, — closed in, — cried, — did, — disappeared within, — drew back, — drew in, — fell, — fell about, — fell across, — fell around, — fell in, — fell like, — fell on, — fell outside, — fell over, — fell upon, — felt, — felt like, — filled, — followed, — forced, — gave, — grew, — held, — hung over, — lay, — lay beyond, — lay on, — lay upon, — left, — lifted, — lit by, — lit up, — made, — met, — moved, — moved in, — pressed at, — pressed in, — pressed like, — pulled back, — put, — raised, — ran, — rang with, — remained, — returned, — returned to, — rolled inside, — rolled over, — rose, — said, — seemed, — seemed to, — settled, — settled in, — settled over, — shifted, — shot, — shot through, — slammed, —

slammed like, — stared at, — started to,
— swallowed, — took, — took on, —
turned to, — went by, — went on, —
went with, — whispered inside, —
wrapped about

dawn
verbs

— appeared, — appeared against, —
approached, — arrived, — arrived in, —
arrived with, — began, — began on, —
began to, — blew on, — broke, — broke
across, — broke beyond, — broke in, —
broke like, — broke on, — broke over,
— broke through, — brought, — came,
— came after, — came in, — came over,
— came to, — came with, — entered, —
filled, — gave, — got, — held, — lit, —
lived in, — looked, — made, — moved
into, — reached across, — returned, —
rose, — rose in, — rose on, — said, —
seemed to, — showed, — started to, —
struck, — took off, — touched, —
turned, — walked down, — went

day
verbs

arrived —, asked —, asked about —,
bought —, called —, came —, changed
—, did —, died on —, drove —, figured
out —, finished for —, fought until —,
got —, got in —, got through —, got up
—, kept —, lay —, learned —, left —,
left for —, lived —, lived until —, made
—, needed —, passed —, picked —,
played —, remembered —, returned —,
returned on —, rode —, said —, said on
—, sat —, saw —, slept —, slept during
—, snapped —, spent —, stayed —,
stayed in —, thought on —, thought to
—, told —, took —, tried —, used —,
waited —, walked —, walked for —,

wanted —, went —, went by —,
wondered on —, wore —, wore to —,
worked —, wrote —; — added to, —
added up, — appeared to, —
approached, — arrived, — asked after,
— asked for, — became, — began, —
began in, — began to, — began with, —
blew, — broke, — broke off, — broke
over, — brought, — brought forward,
— called, — came, — came at, — came
back, — came before, — came for, —
came from, — came in, — came on, —
came to, — came upon, — came with,
— carried, — caught up, — changed to,
— climbed, — closed with, —
continued to, — covered with, —
crossed, — decided to, — did, — died
off, — drew, — drew in, — drew near,
— drew on, — drew to, — ended, —
ended in, — fell in, — fell into, — felt,
— felt like, — filled with, — flew by, —
followed, — gave, — got, — got away,
— grew, — happened to, — held, — hit,
— kicked in, — killed, — lay, — lay
across, — lay in, — left, — left before,
— left in, — let out, — lifted, — lived
by, — looked over, — looked to, — lost,
— lost in, — made, — made in, —
missed before, — opened in, — passed,
— passed away, — passed by, — passed
for, — passed in, — passed into, —
passed through, — passed to, — passed
until, — passed with, — passed without,
— placed, — played on, — played out,
— played upon, — ran, — rang, —
reached, — read, — realized, —
remained, — rode about, — rode past,
— rolled by, — rolled on, — sat, — sat
by, — saw, — seemed, — seemed like,
— seemed to, — set aside, — set out, —
set up, — settled into, — shot to, —
showed in, — shut, — slid by, — slid

into, — slipped, — slipped away, — slipped by, — slipped into, — slipped past, — spent, — spent in, — spent on, — stared at, — started, — started out, — started to, — started with, — stayed with, — stood, — thought about, — took, — tried to, — turned, — turned about, — turned out, — turned to, — waited for, — walked, — watched, — watched toward, — went, — went around, — went by, — went into, — went on, — went over, — went to, — wore, — wore on, — wore to, — worked, — worked in, — worked on, — worked with, — wrapped up

death
verbs
— appeared to, — arrived, — began, — began to, — began with, — breathed down, — broke, — brought, — came, — came around, — came back, — came for, — came in, — came through, — came to, — came up, — continued to, — did in, — died of, — disappeared, — drew, — entered, — fell on, — filled, — followed, — followed in, — grew, — happened, — held in, — hung, — hung above, — hung in, — hung like, — hung over, — lay, — lay at, — left, — lived, — looked, — looked like, — made, — made to, — meant, — met at, — played on, — pointed to, — put, — reached for, — reached to, — remained, — rode, — rode into, — seemed, — seemed to, — sent, — sounded, — started to, — struck, — took, — took on, — waited at, — waited for, — waited in, — waited on, — walked in

deck
verbs

appeared on —, arrived on —, came across —, came down —, came on —, came to —, checked —, closed across —, crossed —, cut —, dropped to —, fell against —, fell to —, gestured toward —, hit —, jumped off —, landed on —, leaned across —, leaned against —, learned between —, lifted off —, looked along —, looked around —, looked over —, moved along —, nodded toward —, picked up —, pointed across —, pushed off —, put aside —, reached —, reached for —, remained on —, rolled across —, sat on —, shifted on —, slept on —, slid down —, stared at —, stared down —, started on —, stayed on —, stepped off —, stepped onto —, stood on —, studied —, took —, took out —, turned for —, walked across —, walked along —, walked on —, walked onto —, walked toward —, went below —, went on —; — became, — began to, — broke, — came, — came into, — came near, — came to, — cleared, — closed, — covered with, — fell upon, — jumped with, — kept, — lay, — lay around, — left, — looked out, — made, — made of, — met, — moved, — moved under, — paused at, — ran with, — returned, — rolled beneath, — rose up, — sat, — sat on, — saw, — seemed, — seemed to, — set up, — shifted beneath, — shook with, — shouted, — shouted down, — slammed into, — slid open, — sounded, — swung open, — swung under

desk
verbs
approached —, arrived at —, asked at —, blinked at —, bought —, called —, called from —, came around —, came to —, checked —, cleared —, climbed over

—, closed —, closed up —, continued to —, crossed —, crossed behind —, crossed to —, drew near —, dropped —, fell behind —, fell on —, fell onto —, found in —, gestured at —, gestured to —, gestured toward —, glanced across —, glanced at —, glanced toward —, got —, got off —, got to —, grabbed —, grinned across —, headed around —, headed for —, headed to —, hit —, jumped from —, kept at —, kept on —, kicked —, leaned across —, leaned against —, leaned at —, leaned behind —, leaned from —, leaned in —, leaned on —, leaned over —, left —, left for —, left on —, looked across —, looked around —, looked at —, looked behind —, looked past —, looked toward —, moved —, moved around —, moved behind —, moved to —, moved toward —, nodded at —, nodded to —, nodded toward —, opened —, passed —, passed by —, paused at —, picked up —, pointed at —, pointed to —, pulled out —, pushed from —, pushed off —, pushed on —, put away —, ran behind —, ran to —, reached —, reached across —, reached behind —, reached below —, reached into —, reached over —, reached to —, reached under —, remained at —, remained behind —, returned to —, rode —, rose behind —, rose from —, sat across —, sat at —, sat behind —, sat on —, saw —, settled behind —, shifted —, shifted on —, shoved from —, slid across —, slid behind —, slid into —, slid off —, slipped off —, stared at —, started around —, started at —, started for —, stayed at —, stayed behind —, stepped around —, stepped behind —, stepped to —, stepped toward —, stood at —,

stood before —, stood behind —, stood beside —, stood by —, stood from —, stood over —, stopped at —, stopped by —, studied —, swung around —, took over —, turned from —, turned off —, turned to —, waited at —, walked around —, walked behind —, walked by —, walked from —, walked past —, walked to —, walked toward —, waved at —, went around —, went behind —, went past —, went through —, went to —, worked at —, worked behind —, yelled across —; — appeared at, — approached, — ate up, — began to, — called to, — came, — came by, — cleared, — covered in, — covered with, — fell across, — filled with, — frowned, — gave, — got, — held, — knew, — lay, — left behind, — looked, — looked at, — looked out, — looked through, — looked to, — looked up, — made, — met, — murmured, — opened, — pulled in, — pushed, — pushed to, — pushed up, — rang, — rang without, — remained, — rose into, — rose to, — said, — said without, — sat, — sat across, — sat in, — saw, — set, — set on, — set up, — shook, — shoved onto, — stared at, — stood, — stood in, — stood to, — struck, — studied, — talked on, — took, — turned over, — waited for, — went over, — wore, — worked on

detail

verbs

— appeared on, — began to, — called out, — came, — came into, — came off, — came up, — caught, — did, — disappeared into, — filled, — filled in, — flew back, — got, — lay, — left out, — made, — meant, — opened, —

poured forth, — pulled together, —
remained with, — seemed, — worked,
— worked out

dinner
verbs
ate —, brought —, called —, called
during —, came to —, finished —, got
—, left for —, liked —, made —, made
for —, missed —, ordered —, picked at
—, remembered —, said at —, said of —
, said over —, sat at —, sat through —,
stayed for —, talked about —, thought
about —, thought of —, took —,
wanted —, wanted for —, went to —,
wore to —

direction
verbs
changed —, followed —, glanced in —,
headed in —, kicked in —, knew —,
looked in —, moved in —, needed —,
nodded —, nodded in —, picked —,
pointed —, pointed in —, pressed in —,
ran without —, shifted —, shouted in
—, smiled in —, stared in —, started in
—, stepped in —, turned in —, wanted
—, went —, went in —

dirt
verbs
drew in —, dropped to —, drove up —,
fell in —, fell onto —, felt —, got —,
hated —, hit —, kicked —, kicked at —,
knocked off —, landed in —, lay in —,
needed —, pointed at —, pushed at —,
rose from —, sat in —, saw —, slept on
—, smelled —, smelled of —, stared at
—, stayed in —, stood in —, touched —
; — began to, — blew up, — caught in,
— cleared, — drank, — fell, — fell to,
— filled, — filled in, — flew in, — flew

into, — flew up, — followed, — grew,
— hit, — kicked, — kicked up, — lay,
— lay around, — looked, — made, —
shifted, — snapped, — struck, — went

disbelief
verbs
answered in —, asked in —, blinked in
—, blinked with —, breathed in —,
cried in —, demanded in —, frowned in
—, gasped in —, laughed in —, listened
in —, murmured —, realized in —,
repeated in —, replied in —, said in —,
said with —, sat in —, saw —, settled on
—, shook off —, shouted in —, stared in
—, thought in —, turned in —, watched
in —, whispered in —, wondered in —

distance
verbs
called across —, checked —, chose —,
cleared —, closed —, covered —,
entered —, flew for —, followed at —,
followed from —, frowned into —,
hung at —, kept —, kept to —, listened
from —, looked into —, made —,
needed —, noticed in —, pointed into
—, remained at —, said —, slid for —,
stared into —, stayed at —, thought
about —, took in —, wanted —,
watched at —, watched from —; —
appeared to, — began to, — brought, —
came, — caught, — closed, — closed in,
— covered, — cried out, — cut through,
— ended, — felt, — grew, — grew
between, — helped, — kept, — left to,
— made, — opened out, — remained,
— rolled, — rolled like, — rose, —
seemed, — seemed to, — set against, —
stood

document

verbs

brought out —, checked over —, closed —, drew out —, drew up —, found —, glanced at —, glanced toward —, grabbed —, handed over —, held up —, laid aside —, looked at —, looked over —, looked through —, needed —, nodded to —, opened —, passed —, picked up —, pointed to —, pulled —, pulled out —, put down —, reached for —, read through —, rolled —, stared at —, studied —, took —, took over —, turned to —, wanted —

dog

verbs

approached —, asked —, ate —, bent over —, bent to —, brought up —, called —, called to —, checked —, dropped —, felt like —, finished with —, followed —, found —, gestured at —, gestured to —, gestured toward —, glanced at —, glanced to —, glanced toward —, got —, grabbed —, grabbed at —, hated —, held —, kicked —, killed —, kissed —, knew —, left —, left with —, lifted —, liked —, looked at —, loved —, managed —, meant —, met —, moved between —, murmured to —, muttered to —, needed —, noticed —, opened —, ordered —, passed —, passed out —, paused beside —, picked up —, played with —, reached around —, reached for —, reminded —, said to —, saw —, screamed at —, sent —, settled —, shouted at —, shouted for —, smelled like —, smiled at —, spoke to —, stared at —, stepped over —, stood beside —, stood like —, studied —, thought about —, thought of —, told —, took —, turned from —, turned into —, turned toward —, walked —, walked on —, walked toward —, wanted —, watched —, waved to —, went to —, went with —, worked like —, wrote about —; — answered with, — appeared, — appeared at, — appeared in, — arrived, — ate, — ate in, — ate up, — began, — began to, — blinked, — blinked in, — broke loose, — broke off, — called to, — came, — came along, — came back, — came for, — came forward, — came in, — came inside, — came out, — came over, — came to, — came toward, — came up, — caught, — changed, — climbed into, — closed, — closed in, — continued to, — covered in, — cried in, — crossed, — decided to, — did, — died, — dropped, — drove, — drove through, — fell, — fell in, — fell upon, — felt, — figured out, — filled, — finished, — followed, — followed at, — fought, — found, — gave, — glanced over, — got, — got away, — got back, — got into, — got out, — got to, — got up, — grew, — heard, — held, — helped, — hesitated, — hit, — hit by, — hung, — jumped, — jumped for, — jumped into, — jumped like, — jumped off, — jumped on, — jumped onto, — jumped out, — jumped up, — kept, — knew, — knocked, — landed in, — laughed to, — lay, — lay at, — lay in, — lay on, — lay under, — learned, — led, — left to, — let, — let out, — let up, — lifted, — lived, — looked, — looked after, — looked at, — looked up, — lost, — made, — made out, — meant, — moved, — moved between, — moved by, — moved down, — needed, — nodded, — noticed, — opened in, — paused, — picked at, — picked up, — pointed inside, — poured into, — pressed, — pulled, — pulled at,

— put, — raised, — raised in, — ran, —
ran across, — ran alongside, — ran away,
— ran between, — ran forward, — ran
from, — ran in, — ran into, — ran off,
— ran out, — ran to, — ran up, —
reached, — remained, — remained in,
— returned, — rolled, — rolled over, —
rose, — rose in, — rose to, — rubbed
against, — said, — sank to, — sat, — sat
at, — sat by, — sat down, — sat for, —
sat in, — sat on, — sat out, — sat to, —
sat up, — saw, — seemed, — seemed to,
— sent up, — set, — set off, — settled,
— shifted, — shook, — shot, — shot
away, — shot forward, — shot out, —
shoved down, — showed up, — shut up,
— sighed, — slammed into, — slept by,
— slept in, — slept on, — slipped
through, — snapped, — snapped at, —
sounded, — stared, — stared at, —
stared down, — started, — started to, —
started up, — stayed, — stayed near, —
stood, — stood in, — stood on, — stood
up, — stopped, — stopped in, — struck,
— thought of, — threw, — took, —
took off, — tried to, — turned, —
turned into, — turned to, — waited by,
— walked, — walked across, — walked
in, — watched, — watched for, —
watched from, — went, — went after,
— went back, — went for, — went into,
— went to, — whispered, — woke

door
verbs
answered —, appeared at —, appeared
in —, appeared outside —, appeared
through —, approached —, arrived at —
, asked about —, asked through —, blew
through —, broke for —, broke through
—, called from —, called through —,
called toward —, came in —, came out

—, came through —, came to —, caught
—, checked —, checked behind —,
chose —, climbed out —, climbed
through —, closed —, continued past —
, continued to —, continued toward —,
covered —, cried at —, crossed —,
crossed through —, crossed to —,
crossed toward —, demanded at —,
disappeared behind —, disappeared
from —, disappeared inside —,
disappeared out —, disappeared through
—, dropped —, entered —, entered
through —, fell against —, felt —, filled
—, flew out —, followed through —,
forced —, found —, frowned at —, gave
—, gestured at —, gestured for —,
gestured out —, gestured outside —,
gestured through —, gestured to —,
gestured toward —, glanced at —,
glanced out —, glanced to —, glanced
toward —, got —, got in —, got to —,
grabbed —, headed for —, headed out
—, headed through —, headed to —,
headed toward —, heard —, held —,
held open —, hesitated at —, hesitated
by —, hesitated inside —, hesitated
outside —, hit —, hung —, hung at —,
hung in —, hung out —, hung over —,
jumped out —, jumped through —,
kept —, kept near —, kept to —, kicked
—, kicked at —, kicked for —, kicked in
—, kicked open —, kicked through —,
kicked toward —, knew —, knocked at
—, knocked on —, lay before —, lay by
—, leaned against —, leaned in —,
leaned inside —, leaned on —, leaned
out —, leaned through —, leaned to —,
leaned toward —, left —, left by —, left
on —, left through —, lifted —, listened
at —, listened near —, listened outside
—, listened through —, lived with —,
looked at —, looked for —, looked in —

, looked out —, looked through —, looked to —, looked toward —, lowered —, made —, made for —, moved for —, moved off —, moved out —, moved to —, moved toward —, needed —, nodded at —, nodded to —, nodded toward —, noticed —, opened —, opened up —, passed —, passed by —, passed through —, paused at —, paused by —, paused inside —, paused near —, paused outside —, paused to —, picked up —, pointed above —, pointed at —, pointed behind —, pointed out —, pointed through —, pointed to —, pointed toward —, pressed against —, pressed open —, pulled —, pulled at —, pulled open —, pulled up —, pushed —, pushed against —, pushed at —, pushed off —, pushed on —, pushed open —, pushed out —, pushed over —, pushed through —, ran at —, ran for —, ran out —, ran through —, ran to —, ran toward —, reached —, reached around —, reached behind —, reached for —, reached inside —, reached through —, reached to —, reached toward —, remained at —, remained by —, remained in —, remained near —, returned from —, returned to —, rolled back —, said —, said at —, said by —, said from —, said through —, said to —, sank against —, sat against —, saw —, screamed at —, screamed through —, shifted against —, shook —, shot —, shouted from —, shouted through —, shoved —, shoved against —, shoved aside —, shoved at —, shoved open —, shoved through —, shut —, slammed —, slammed into —, slammed through —, slid —, slid back —, slid inside —, slid open —, slid toward —, slipped in —, slipped open —, slipped out —, slipped through —, slipped to —, slipped toward —, smiled at —, smiled from —, spoke at —, stared at —, stared between —, stared out —, stared toward —, started for —, started out —, started to —, started toward —, stayed at —, stayed by —, stayed near —, stepped against —, stepped behind —, stepped from —, stepped in —, stepped inside —, stepped into —, stepped out —, stepped past —, stepped through —, stepped to —, stepped toward —, stood across —, stood against —, stood at —, stood before —, stood behind —, stood beside —, stood by —, stood from —, stood in —, stood inside —, stood near —, stood outside —, stopped —, stopped at —, stopped before —, stopped by —, stopped in —, stopped inside —, stopped near —, stopped outside —, struck —, studied —, swung —, swung open —, swung through —, swung to —, swung toward —, threw open —, told —, took —, touched —, tried —, turned at —, turned for —, turned from —, turned out —, turned outside —, turned to —, turned toward —, waited at —, waited behind —, waited by —, waited outside —, walked —, walked from —, walked in —, walked out —, walked through —, walked to —, walked toward —, watched —, watched from —, waved at —, waved from —, waved to —, waved toward —, went for —, went in —, went out —, went through —, went to —, went toward —, yelled at —, yelled through —; — added to, — appeared, — appeared to, — asked, — asked for, — became, — began, — began to, — blew off, — blew open, — blew out, — blew to, — blinked, — broke, — broke down, — broke open, — brought, — brought back, — came, — came away, — came down, — came into, — came off, — came open, — came to, — came up, — carried, — caught, — chose, — closed, — closed against, — closed around, — closed at, — closed behind, — closed between, — closed for, — closed of, — closed on, — closed to, — closed with, — continued to, — covered in, — crossed, — cut into, — cut off, — did, — disappeared, — drew, — drew shut, — dropped against, — dropped open, — fell down, — fell forward, — fell in, — fell open, — fell to, — felt, — felt like, — filled, — finished, — flew, — flew back, — flew off, — flew open, — forced, — gave, — gave for, — gave off, — gave on, — gave onto, — gave up, — gave with, — got, — got away, — grew, — happened to, — held, — held up, — helped, — hit, — hit with, — hung, — hung open, — joined, — kicked back, — kicked in, — landed on, — laughed, — lay, — lay in, — lay open, — leaned on, — led, — led from, — led into, — led off, — led onto, — led to, — led under, — left open, — left to, — let in, — let off, — lifted, — lit off, — lit up, — looked, — looked at, — looked down, — looked into, — looked like, — looked up, — lowered, — made, — made of, — meant for, — met with, — moved, — moved on, — moved to, — needed to, — offered, — opened, — opened across, — opened against, — opened at, — opened behind, — opened between, — opened by, — opened down, — opened for, — opened from, — opened in, — opened into, — opened of, — opened off, — opened on, — opened onto, — opened out, —

opened to, — opened under, — opened up, — opened with, — opened without, — played on, — pulled back, — pulled off, — pulled out, — pulled up, — pushed open, — pushed out, — put, — raised, — raised on, — ran in, — ran off, — rang, — rang like, — reached by, — read, — remained open, — replied, — rolled, — rolled down, — rolled open, — rolled up, — rose into, — rose to, — said, — sat, — screamed, — seemed, — seemed to, — sent, — set in, — set into, — shook, — shook against, — shook from, — shook on, — shoved open, — showed, — shut, — shut at, — shut behind, — shut in, — shut on, — shut to, — shut with, — shut without, — slammed, — slammed at, — slammed behind, — slammed in, — slammed into, — slammed on, — slammed open, — slammed shut, — slammed to, — slept, — slid, — slid forward, — slid open, — slid shut, — slid to, — slid toward, — slid up, — slipped open, — smelled of, — snapped back, — snapped open, — sounded, — stared at, — started in, — started to, — stayed, — stayed open, — stepped, — stood, — stood behind, — stood between, — stood for, — stood on, — stood open, — stopped, — suggested, — swung, — swung back, — swung down, — swung in, — swung into, — swung on, — swung open, — swung out, — swung shut, — swung with, — tried to, — waited across, — went up, — whispered open, — wore, — worked, — wrapped in

doorway
verbs

added from —, appeared at —, appeared in —, appeared near —, approached —, arrived at —, asked from —, bowed from —, called from —, came from —, came through —, came to —, cleared —, crossed to —, demanded from —, disappeared through —, entered through —, fell in —, fell through —, filled —, gestured to —, glanced at —, glanced into —, glanced through —, glanced to —, glanced toward —, got to —, gripped —, headed for —, hesitated at —, hesitated in —, hit —, hung in —, hung near —, jumped through —, lay in —, leaned against —, leaned in —, leaned into —, left —, listened at —, looked at —, looked like —, looked through —, managed from —, moved into —, moved past —, moved through —, moved to —, moved toward —, muttered from —, nodded at —, nodded to —, passed —, passed by —, passed into —, passed through —, paused at —, paused by —, paused in —, paused inside —, pointed from —, pointed to —, pointed toward —, pulled —, pushed through —, ran through —, ran to —, reached —, remained in —, returned to —, said from —, said in —, sank in —, sat in —, saw —, screamed from —, shifted at —, shifted near —, shouted at —, shouted from —, shoved through —, slipped into —, smiled from —, spoke from —, stared at —, stared through —, stared toward —, started for —, started toward —, stayed in —, stayed near —, stepped from —, stepped into —, stepped past —, stepped through —, stepped to —, stood at —, stood before —, stood by —, stood from —, stood in —, stood near —, stood outside —, stopped at —, stopped in —, stopped inside —, stopped outside —, stopped past —, swung from —, turned at —, turned from —, turned in —, turned into —, turned to —, turned toward —, waited at —, waited by —, waited in —, walked in —, walked into —, walked through —, walked to —, walked toward —, watched —, watched from —, waved from —, went through —, went to —, whispered from —, yelled from —

doubt

verbs

— began to, — broke, — called, — called upon, — came into, — came to, — continued to, — covered, — crossed, — disappeared, — dropped away, — entered, — expected, — fell away, — fell upon, — felt, — filled, — found, — grew, — grew like, — gripped, — headed, — headed for, — heard, — helped, — helped by, — killed, — lay, — lay in, — led to, — liked, — listened in, — listened to, — looked for, — made, — meant to, — passed across, — passed over, — ran, — ran down, — ran like, — rang in, — recognized, — remained, — returned, — rose off, — said, — saw, — seemed to, — set in, — settled in, — settled on, — showed in, — slid under, — spent, — stared at, — struck, — thought, — tried to, — turned to, — waited on, — went for, — whispered

dragon

verbs

— approached from, — arrived to, — began to, — bent, — blew, — blinked, — broke off, — came back, — chose to, — cleared, — continued to, — fell, —

filled, — glanced at, — glanced over, — grew, — hung in, — leaned forward, — let out, — lowered, — made, — moved, — opened, — paused, — rode through, — rose, — sank toward, — seemed to, — sent, — settled down, — shifted on, — shot past, — smiled, — spoke, — took, — tried to, — turned, — turned to, — watched, — wished to

drawer
verbs
checked —, closed —, found in —, glanced at —, gripped —, headed for —, heard —, kept in —, kicked at —, looked at —, looked into —, looked through —, moved to —, nodded at —, opened —, pointed to —, pulled —, pulled open —, pulled out —, reached for —, reached in —, reached into —, rolled open —, shut —, slammed —, slid open —, slipped open —, stared into —, took out —, tried —, walked to —, walked toward —, went through —, went to —

dread
verbs
— appeared to, — became, — began to, — came into, — came on, — closed around, — closed in, — dropped, — entered, — fell on, — filled, — grew, — gripped, — landed in, — made, — ran up, — returned to, — rose in, — rose up, — sank into, — sat in, — screamed up, — set upon, — settled, — settled in, — slammed into, — went down, — went into, — went through

dream
verbs

answered in —, believed —, believed in —, came in —, did —, entered —, explained —, filled —, fought —, hated —, held onto —, kissed like —, knew —, moved in —, nodded into —, remembered —, repeated —, replied in —, rose with —, said in —, saw —, seemed —, shook off —, slept without —, slipped into —, spoke of —, thought about —, thought of —, understood —, walked in —, walked through —, went into —, woke from —; — approached, — became, — began, — began in, — began to, — broke up, — brought, — came, — came back, — came from, — came into, — came to, — came with, — changed, — continued, — crossed over, — did, — died, — disappeared, — ended, — filled with, — gave, — grew, — happened, — helped, — left, — made, — meant, — put on, — seemed, — seemed like, — seemed to, — set in, — slipped away, — started on, — started to, — stood, — stopped, — turned to, — went, — went away, — went on, — wished for, — wore on

dress
verbs
approached —, bought —, bought for —, changed into —, gave —, gestured at —, grabbed —, held up —, hung up —, lifted —, liked —, loved —, made —, moved inside —, opened —, picked up —, pointed to —, pulled on —, pulled out —, pulled up —, put on —, raised —, ran with —, reached for —, recognized —, slipped into —, slipped off —, slipped on —, stared at —, stepped into —, stepped on —, thought of —, threw off —, threw on —, took off —, tried on —, watched —, wore —;

— blew up, — bought for, — bowed
forward, — came off, — came through,
— came to, — caught, — caught in, —
cut, — did, — dropped past, — dropped
to, — ended, — fell forward, — fell to,
— gave away, — hung from, — hung in,
— hung on, — jumped around, — left,
— lifted in, — looked, — made, —
made of, — made out, — offered, —
pulled across, — pulled along, — pulled
off, — remained, — replied, — rode up,
— said, — sat in, — seemed, — showed,
— showed off, — slid, — slid between,
— slid down, — slid open, — slid to, —
slipped, — slipped over, — stayed on, —
stood, — stood to, — turned, — went
over, — worked

drink
verbs
arrived with —, asked for —, bought —,
brought —, did —, drank like —, drew
—, dropped off —, felt like —, finished
—, finished off —, finished up —,
gestured for —, gestured to —, got —,
grabbed —, handed over —, held —,
held up —, helped —, killed —,
knocked back —, laid —, lifted —, liked
—, looked at —, lowered —, made —,
needed —, nodded to —, offered —,
opened —, ordered —, passed out —,
picked up —, pointed to —, poured —,
poured out —, put down —, raised —,
reached for —, remembered —,
returned to —, returned with —, saw —
, set —, set down —, set out —, shot
back —, smiled at —, smiled into —,
stared at —, stared into —, stood with
—, stopped for —, studied —, threw
back —, took —, took up —, tossed
back —, tried —, wanted —, went for
—, went into —

drive
verbs
approached on —, continued up —,
disappeared down —, drove down —,
frowned at —, gestured at —, headed up
—, held out —, held up —, hit —, left
—, left for —, made —, pulled into —,
ran down —, shifted into —, started up
—, stood on —, swung into —, took —,
took out —, turned into —, understood
—, walked down —, walked up —, went
for —, went up —

driveway
verbs
blew off —, called from —, checked —,
continued up —, crossed —, drove
down —, drove into —, drove up —,
followed —, found —, glanced around
—, headed toward —, headed up —, hit
—, looked at —, looked down —,
looked toward —, nodded toward —,
paused in —, paused on —, pulled into
—, pulled onto —, pulled up —, ran
down —, ran up —, rolled down —,
rolled into —, rolled up —, shot up —,
started up —, stepped down —, stood in
—, turned down —, turned into —,
turned onto —, turned up —, walked
down —, walked up —, waved at —,
went up —

drone
verbs
— began to, — came into, — changed,
— continued, — continued to, — cut
out, — entered, — fell into, — filled, —
flew in, — flew on, — followed, —
found, — got, — hit, — kept, — landed,
— looked like, — made, — reached, —
remained on, — rose, — rose to, —

settled on, — showed, — stopped, — turned, — turned to, — used, — went out

drop
verbs

— appeared at, — began to, — came, — came out, — fell, — fell against, — fell from, — fell in, — fell into, — fell off, — fell on, — fell upon, — flew like, — grew, — grew under, — hit, — landed on, — landed with, — left, — made, — ran, — ran down, — remained, — remained in, — rolled down, — slid down, — slipped off, — went into

drug
verbs

— became, — began to, — called, — came, — changed, — did to, — entered, — found, — hit, — kicked in, — left, — looked, — made, — pressed against, — seemed to, — shot into, — stepped into, — stopped, — took, — took over, — used to, — went, — went into, — wore off, — worked

dusk
verbs

— approached, — arrived, — began to, — brought, — came, — came down, — came on, — came to, — climbed over, — drew, — drew down, — drew near, — fell, — fell on, — fell over, — fell upon, — gave, — headed for, — lay across, — lay over, — rolled in, — settled down, — settled in, — settled into, — settled over

dust
verbs

— appeared, — appeared with, — became, — began to, — blew, — blew across, — blew away, — blew in, — blew like, — blew over, — blew up, — came from, — came off, — caught in, — cleared, — climbed, — covered, — fell behind, — fell from, — fell in, — felt like, — filled, — flew, — flew at, — flew from, — flew in, — flew into, — flew through, — flew toward, — flew up, — followed in, — forced into, — got in, — headed, — hung in, — kicked up, — lay, — lay over, — lay upon, — lifted, — made, — moved in, — remained, — remained of, — rolled over, — rose, — rose above, — rose from, — rose in, — rose into, — rose under, — rose with, — seemed to, — settled, — settled around, — settled for, — settled in, — settled to, — shot out, — started to, — stopped, — turned to, — went up

ear
verbs

asked by —, bent —, breathed into —, carried in —, caught —, changed —, checked —, cleared —, closed —, covered —, cried in —, filled —, gasped in —, gestured to —, got into —, grabbed —, held —, hit —, kissed —, laughed in —, leaned into —, leaned to —, leaned toward —, murmured against —, murmured below —, murmured in —, murmured into —, muttered in —, muttered into —, noticed —, pointed to —, pressed —, pulled at —, pulled on —, raised —, reached for —, reached to —, rubbed —, said against —, said beside —, said in —, said into —, saw —, screamed into —, shouted in —, shouted into —, shut —, spoke against —, spoke by —, spoke in —, spoke into

—, talked in —, touched —, went for —
, whispered against —, whispered in —,
whispered into —, worked —, yelled in
—; — appeared to, — began to, —
came, — came to, — carried, — caught,
— continued to, — covered with, — cut
off, — did, — felt, — felt like, — filled
with, — grew, — heard, — laid, —
lifted, — listened of, — listened to, —
made, — picked out, — picked up, —
pointed at, — pressed against, —
pressed to, — raised, — rang, — rang at,
— rang for, — rang from, — rang with,
— rose to, — said, — seemed, — shifted
in, — shut down, — shut in, — smelled
of, — stared at, — started to, — stood
up, — took, — took on, — turned, —
turned to, — waited for, — went, —
went through, — went up

earth

verbs

— answered, — became, — began to, —
broke open, — brought, — came, —
came down, — closed up, — continued
to, — did, — died, — disappeared
within, — dropped, — dropped away,
— drove back, — fell into, — felt, —
felt like, — filled, — flew, — gave, —
grew, — happened to, — held, — made,
— moved, — moved against, — moved
beneath, — opened up, — passed
through, — pressed, — pulled back, —
pushed back, — ran, — remembered, —
rolled down, — rose, — rose behind, —
rose from, — rose to, — rose up, —
seemed, — seemed to, — shook, —
shook beneath, — shook to, — shook
under, — shook with, — shot up, —
shouted out, — showed, — showed
through, — slipped beneath, — smelled,

— swung beneath, — took in, —
turned, — turned to, — wanted

edge

verbs

asked with —, called from —, came to
—, crossed to —, drove to —, felt on —,
flew over —, found —, glanced over —,
got to —, grabbed —, hit —, jumped
over —, leaned against —, leaned over
—, lived on —, looked on —, looked
over —, lost —, moved to —, needed —,
nodded toward —, paused at —, ran to
—, reached —, rolled over —, said with
—, sat on —, seemed on —, slid onto —
, slipped over —, stared at —, stepped
off —, stepped over —, stepped to —,
stepped toward —, stood at —, stopped
at —, turned on —, used —, walked to
—, went over —, went to —; —
appeared, — appeared in, — began to,
— came, — came into, — caught, —
closed in, — continued to, — covered
in, — cut, — cut into, — cut to, —
grew, — hit, — left, — let, — looked, —
made, — met, — met on, — pulled, —
returned to, — rose, — rubbed, — sat
forward, — seemed, — seemed to, —
shifted, — slammed, — stood, — turned
up, — walked

effort

verbs

— became, — began to, — brought, —
came, — came from, — came to, —
continued to, — drew, — got to, — left,
— made, — made to, — managed to, —
met with, — needed to, — opened, —
pulled, — put in, — recognized, —
remained in, — seemed, — seemed to,
— slid, — thought about, — took from,

— tried to, — turned out, — went beyond, — worked

elbow
verbs
appeared at —, bent —, caught —, checked —, drew —, grabbed —, gripped —, held —, held out —, kicked —, lay on —, leaned on —, leaned onto —, led with —, lifted —, lifted to —, lifted up —, muttered at —, offered —, put —, raised —, remained on —, returned —, rolled onto —, rose on —, rose to —, rubbed —, said at —, shifted —, shot out —, stayed at —, stood at —, struck with —, swung —, threw —, took —, touched —, used —

elevator
verbs
added —, called —, came to —, climbed into —, continued toward —, crossed to —, disappeared into —, entered —, found —, gestured to —, gestured toward —, glanced at —, glanced toward —, got in —, got into —, got off —, got on —, got to —, headed for —, headed to —, headed toward —, heard —, hit —, left —, looked around —, looked at —, made for —, moved toward —, passed —, passed by —, pointed to —, pointed toward —, pressed for —, pushed onto —, ran to —, rang for —, reached —, returned to —, rode —, rode in —, screamed inside —, shouted into —, slipped into —, stared at —, started for —, started toward —, stepped across —, stepped inside —, stepped into —, stepped off —, stepped on —, stepped onto —, stood inside —, stopped at —, stopped outside —, took —, turned toward —, waited for —, walked into —, walked past —, walked to —, went down —, went to —, whispered across —; — arrived, — arrived at, — arrived on, — arrived with, — began, — began to, — came, — came at, — came to, — came up, — carried, — chose, — climbed, — closed, — continued to, — dropped, — dropped like, — felt, — gave, — hesitated, — kicked, — landed, — led to, — made, — moved, — moved up, — opened, — opened behind, — opened in, — opened into, — opened on, — opened onto, — opened up, — opened with, — passed, — ran, — ran up, — rang, — reached, — remained, — returned, — rose, — rose at, — rose to, — rose with, — said, — sank, — sank away, — sank to, — sank toward, — seemed, — settled, — settled with, — shook, — shot, — showed, — shut down, — slid open, — smelled, — smelled like, — sounded, — started down, — started to, — started up, — stopped, — stopped at, — stopped on, — stopped with, — worked

emotion
verbs
— added to, — appeared to, — began to, — broke, — broke through, — came, — came back, — came out, — caught in, — crossed, — did, — entered, — felt, — filled, — got, — got in, — held, — lay, — lay like, — left, — made, — passed over, — played across, — played out, — poured into, — ran, — ran through, — rolled out, — rose, — rose into, — rose to, — rose up, — rose within, — sat in, — seemed, — seemed to, — settled, — shook, — shut down, — slipped into, — slipped through, — struck, — touched, — worked

end
verbs

added at —, approached —, came at —, came on —, came to —, considered —, fought to —, headed to —, held —, hit —, leaned on —, lifted —, lived on —, played —, pressed —, reached —, said on —, sat at —, started at —, stood at —, waited at —, walked to —, wanted —, wanted for —, went off —; — answered, — appeared at, — asked, — bent into, — came, — came at, — came from, — came of, — came to, — came up, — caught on, — cleared, — closed, — decided to, — dropped, — dropped on, — fell, — fell away, — felt like, — got, — held, — held in, — hung, — hung from, — hung off, — hung over, — knew, — lay, — led down, — let out, — looked like, — made, — meant, — met, — passed through, — picked up, — pointed at, — pointed in, — replied, — said, — sank into, — sat, — seemed to, — slammed into, — slid beneath, — slipped into, — snapped down, — sounded, — spoke for, — stared at, — stepped over, — stood, — stopped, — struck, — waved above

energy
verbs

— appeared, — appeared across, — appeared around, — appeared between, — appeared from, — appeared in, — appeared on, — appeared to, — ate, — began to, — blew through, — came, — came from, — came off, — came out, — came through, — came to, — continued to, — cut down, — drew to, — felt, — flew above, — hit, — joined in, — kept up, — left, — left to, — looked to, —

made, — moved through, — needed to, — passed through, — played over, — poured forth, — poured into, — poured out, — pushed through, — ran through, — returned to, — sank into, — seemed, — seemed to, — shot down, — shot forward, — shot out, — shot up, — slammed into, — slammed through, — spent, — stopped, — struck, — took over, — touched, — went into, — went out

engine
verbs

bent over —, checked —, cut —, cut off —, got —, heard —, kicked —, kicked up —, killed —, let off —, opened up —, pushed —, reached below —, rolled to —, shouted over —, shut —, shut down —, shut off —, snapped off —, started —, started up —, stopped —, turned off —, turned on —, turned over —, waited until —, worked —; — became, — began to, — blew, — breathed, — broke through, — brought, — came, — came to, — caught, — caught at, — caught on, — changed, — continued to, — cut, — cut off, — cut out, — died, — dropped, — fell, — filled, — gasped, — gave, — grew, — hit, — jumped to, — kicked, — kicked in, — killed with, — knocked, — lay, — looked, — made, — missed, — muttered through, — pulled up, — ran, — ran at, — ran for, — ran in, — rose to, — screamed, — screamed by, — screamed in, — screamed with, — seemed to, — settled, — shook, — shut down, — shut off, — slid, — sounded, — sounded like, — started, — started on, — started to, — started up, — started with, — stayed, — stayed together, — stopped, — took, — took

on, — turned off, — turned over, —
wanted to, — went

entrance
verbs

appeared at —, approached —, arrived
at —, asked from —, called —, cleared
—, climbed to —, covered —,
demanded —, drove to —, found —, got
to —, got under —, headed for —,
headed toward —, hesitated at —,
hesitated near —, left through —,
looked at —, looked to —, looked
toward —, made —, made for —,
moved to —, nodded to —, nodded
toward —, passed —, paused at —,
paused by —, paused near —, pointed to
—, pointed toward —, pulled into —,
ran for —, ran through —, ran to —, ran
toward —, reached —, remained at —,
returned to —, saw —, shot through —,
slipped through —, stared at —, started
toward —, stepped through —, stepped
to —, stepped toward —, stood at —,
stood outside —, stood within —,
stopped at —, turned into —, turned
toward —, waited at —, waited near —,
walked out —, walked to —, walked
toward —, watched —, waved at —,
went in —, went to —

envelope
verbs

brought out —, checked —, closed —,
closed up —, cut open —, drew —, drew
out —, dropped —, found —, frowned
at —, gestured at —, glanced at —,
glanced into —, got —, grabbed —,
handed —, handed over —, held out —,
held up —, laid —, left —, lifted —,
looked at —, looked in —, looked inside
—, looked into —, nodded to —,

nodded toward —, opened —, opened
up —, picked up —, placed —, pointed
to —, pulled down —, pulled out —,
put —, put down —, reached for —,
reached into —, remembered —, saw —,
shook —, shoved —, slid open —,
smelled —, stared at —, studied —, took
—, took out —, touched —, tried —

evening
verbs

— approached, — became, — began, —
began to, — came, — came back, —
came behind, — came on, — chose
between, — climbed up, — closed in, —
did, — drew, — drew on, — drew to, —
ended, — fell, — fell into, — fell like, —
felt, — felt from, — flew by, — made,
— opened, — passed, — passed into, —
passed out, — remained, — rolled
around, — rolled on, — sat near, —
seemed, — seemed to, — set down, —
slipped away, — started out, — took, —
took on, — turned, — turned into, —
turned out, — went, — went before, —
wore on, — wore to, — worked out

excitement
verbs

— began to, — came from, — came
through, — closed on, — crossed, —
disappeared, — drew, — entered, — fell
away, — filled, — found, — gave, —
grew, — grew at, — grew in, — grew to,
— left, — lit, — played across, — played
through, — raised, — ran through, —
ran up, — rang in, — rode, — rose in,
— rose to, — seemed to, — sent, — shot
out, — slid down, — took, — touched,
— turned to, — went through

exit

verbs
began —, chose —, continued toward
—, felt —, found —, gestured to —,
gestured toward —, glanced at —,
glanced to —, glanced toward —,
headed for —, headed toward —, knew
—, looked for —, made —, missed —,
moved for —, moved to —, moved
toward —, pointed to —, pointed
toward —, ran out —, ran toward —,
reached —, shot for —, shoved through
—, slid off —, stared toward —, started
for —, started toward —, stayed by —,
stepped out —, stood near —, stood
outside —, stopped by —, swung toward
—, took —, turned for —, turned
toward —, walked to —, walked toward
—, watched —, went out —, went to —

explosion
verbs
— began, — began to, — blew, — blew
out, — came, — came from, — came
over, — did, — died away, — ended in,
— filled, — finished, — followed, —
happened, — hit, — kicked, —
knocked, — left, — lit, — lit up, —
meant to, — passed over, — pushed up,
— rang out, — rose in, — seemed to, —
sent, — set off, — shook, — sounded,
— sounded like, — started in, —
stopped, — struck, — took, — took out,
— turned, — turned to, — went, —
went down, — went off

expression
verbs
answered with —, caught —, checked —
, felt —, frowned at —, got —, kept —,
knew —, laughed at —, listened without
—, looked at —, lost —, nodded with —
, noticed —, paused with —, put on —,
read —, recognized —, replied with —,
said with —, said without —, saw —,
saw in —, smiled at —, studied —, took
in —, took on —, watched —, wore —;
— answered, — appeared on, —
became, — broke, — came across, —
came into, — came over, — caught, —
caught between, — changed, — changed
from, — changed to, — cleared, —
continued, — crossed, — crossed over,
— disappeared like, — drew into, —
fell, — fell away, — fell back, — fell
into, — felt, — filled, — filled with, —
gave, — got, — grew, — held, — hit, —
kept, — left, — lit up, — looked, —
looked like, — lost, — made, — meant,
— moved from, — passed like, — passed
over, — pulled at, — ran over, —
remained, — returned to, — said, —
seemed, — seemed to, — set in, —
settled, — settled into, — settled on, —
shifted, — shifted across, — shot, —
showed, — shut down, — slipped back,
— slipped from, — slipped toward, —
spoke, — stayed, — stopped, —
suggested, — told, — took, — took on,
— took over, — turned, — turned from,
— turned into, — turned to, — went
from, — went to, — went with, —
wiped

eye
verbs
answered with —, blinked —, blinked
open —, called —, caught —, checked
—, closed —, covered —, crossed —, did
open —, drew —, dropped —, felt —,
felt for —, filled —, followed —, forced
open —, found —, found in —, glanced
into —, got —, held —, kept —, kissed
—, knew —, let —, lifted —, liked —, lit
—, looked at —, looked in —, looked

into —, looked like —, looked to —, looked with —, lost —, loved —, lowered —, met —, missed —, moved —, needed —, nodded with —, noticed —, opened —, opened up —, pointed at —, pointed to —, raised —, reached to —, read —, recognized —, remembered —, returned to —, rolled —, rubbed —, rubbed at —, said —, said with —, saw —, saw in —, shifted —, shoved away —, shut —, slipped open —, smiled with —, snapped open —, stared at —, stared into —, started with —, stayed under —, studied —, swung —, thought —, thought about —, thought of —, took —, touched —, tried —, turned —, turned to —, used —, wanted —, watched —, watched through —, watched with —, wiped —, wiped at —; — answered, — appeared, — appeared along, — appeared at, — appeared in, — appeared to, — asked, — ate, — ate up, — became, — began, — began to, — bent down, — blinked, — blinked against, — blinked at, — blinked away, — blinked behind, — blinked in, — blinked into, — blinked like, — blinked open, — blinked up, — blinked with, — broke, — broke away, — broke from, — called, — came, — came away, — came back, — came down, — came from, — came into, — came open, — came through, — came to, — came up, — caught, — caught by, — caught on, — changed, — changed from, — checked, — checked out, — cleared, — climbed, — closed, — closed against, — closed at, — closed down, — closed for, — closed in, — closed like, — closed on, — closed to, — closed with, — considered, — continued, — continued down, — continued to, — covered, — covered with, — crossed, — crossed with, — cut, — cut in, — cut into, — cut out, — cut through, — cut to, — demanded, — did, — did open, — died away, — disappeared, — disappeared into, — drank, — drank in, — drew, — drew up, — dropped, — dropped away, — dropped for, — dropped from, — dropped in, — dropped to, — dropped with, — fell, — fell away, — fell back, — fell below, — fell from, — fell into, — fell like, — fell off, — fell on, — fell onto, — fell out, — fell to, — fell upon, — fell with, — felt, — felt like, — filled, — filled up, — filled with, — flew, — flew into, — flew open, — flew to, — flew up, — followed, — followed by, — followed to, — fought, — fought open, — fought to, — found, — gave, — gave away, — glanced, — glanced at, — glanced down, — glanced over, — glanced to, — glanced toward, — glanced up, — got, — got to, — grabbed, — grew, — grew in, — grinned, — happened on, — heard, — held, — held on, — helped to, — hesitated, — hit, — jumped, — jumped around, — jumped between, — jumped in, — kept, — landed on, — laughed, — laughed at, — lay, — lay on, — leaned over, — left, — let, — lifted, — lifted to, — lifted up, — lit, — lit for, — lit like, — lit on, — lit up, — lit with, — lived, — looked, — looked after, — looked around, — looked at, — looked away, — looked down, — looked in, — looked into, — looked like, — looked out, — looked over, — looked past, — looked through, — looked to, — looked toward, — looked up, — lost, — lost in, — loved, — lowered, — lowered for, — lowered in, — lowered to, — made, —

made of, — met, — met for, — met in, — met over, — missed, — moved, — moved about, — moved across, — moved along, — moved around, — moved away, — moved back, — moved between, — moved down, — moved from, — moved in, — moved like, — moved on, — moved over, — moved past, — moved to, — moved up, — moved with, — nodded, — opened, — opened in, — opened onto, — opened to, — opened with, — passed, — passed over, — paused on, — picked out, — picked up, — played, — played over, — played up, — pointed, — pointed at, — pressed to, — promised, — pulled, — pulled at, — put out, — raised, — raised at, — ran, — ran along, — ran down, — ran on, — ran over, — ran up, — ran with, — reached, — reached out, — remained, — remained on, — remained open, — remained to, — returned, — returned to, — rolled, — rolled away, — rolled behind, — rolled beneath, — rolled from, — rolled in, — rolled into, — rolled to, — rolled toward, — rolled up, — rolled with, — rose, — rose to, — rose up, — rubbed, — said, — sank, — sank into, — sat, — sat at, — sat on, — saw, — saw along, — saw for, — saw into, — saw past, — saw through, — screamed, — seemed, — seemed to, — sent, — set, — set about, — set on, — set with, — settled, — settled on, — settled onto, — settled upon, — shifted, — shifted across, — shifted away, — shifted from, — shifted in, — shifted outside, — shifted over, — shifted through, — shifted to, — shifted up, — shook, — shot, — shot across, — shot around, — shot in, — shot open, — shot over, — shot to, — shot toward, —

shot up, — shot with, — shouted, — showed, — showed above, — showed behind, — showed in, — showed over, — shut, — shut against, — shut beneath, — shut for, — shut in, — shut like, — shut to, — shut with, — slammed shut, — slid, — slid across, — slid along, — slid away, — slid down, — slid from, — slid open, — slid over, — slid shut, — slid to, — slid toward, — slid up, — slipped, — slipped away, — slipped down, — slipped open, — slipped through, — slipped to, — smiled, — smiled at, — snapped, — snapped back, — snapped down, — snapped open, — snapped to, — snapped up, — snapped with, — spoke, — stared, — stared across, — stared at, — stared down, — stared from, — stared in, — stared into, — stared off, — stared on, — stared out, — stared through, — stared toward, — stared with, — started, — started from, — started on, — started to, — started with, — stayed, — stayed away, — stayed in, — stayed on, — stayed open, — stepped to, — stood, — stood beside, — stood in, — stood up, — stopped, — stopped at, — studied, — suggested, — swung, — swung to, — threw, — threw off, — told, — took, — took in, — took on, — touched, — touched with, — tried to, — turned, — turned away, — turned down, — turned from, — turned in, — turned into, — turned to, — turned toward, — turned up, — turned without, — walked from, — wanted to, — watched, — watched from, — went, — went across, — went around, — went back, — went beyond, — went from, — went in, — went on, — went out, —

went over, — went to, — worked, — worked to

eyebrow
verbs
— appeared to, — came together, — climbed, — climbed in, — climbed into, — climbed to, — climbed toward, — did, — disappeared beneath, — disappeared under, — drew, — drew down, — drew into, — drew together, — drew up, — dropped, — explained, — fell on, — flew, — flew up, — got, — jumped, — lifted, — lifted at, — lifted in, — lifted over, — looked, — looked like, — lowered, — made, — met in, — moved up, — opened against, — pulled, — pulled down, — pulled together, — pushed, — pushed together, — raised, — raised in, — rode, — rolled up, — rose, — rose in, — rose toward, — rose with, — seemed, — shot, — shot toward, — shot up, — stepped forward, — told, — tried to, — went, — went up

eyelid
verbs
— began to, — blinked open, — closed, — closed in, — closed on, — did, — dropped, — fell back, — fell shut, — fell to, — felt, — felt like, — flew, — flew open, — grew, — hung, — lifted, — looked, — lowered, — lowered with, — opened, — sank, — seemed to, — snapped open, — snapped up, — started to, — turned

face
verbs
blew in —, bowed —, breathed in —, called —, changed —, checked —, covered —, cut —, did to —, drew —,

dropped —, fell on —, felt —, filled out —, finished —, finished with —, found —, glanced at —, got —, got in —, grabbed —, gripped —, hated —, held —, hit —, kept —, kicked —, kissed —, knew —, landed on —, laughed in —, leaned into —, lifted —, lifted up —, liked —, listened with —, looked at —, looked into —, looked upon —, loved —, lowered —, made —, managed —, noticed —, offered —, placed —, pointed at —, pointed to —, pointed with —, pressed —, pulled —, put —, put on —, raised —, ran into —, read —, recognized —, remembered —, rubbed —, rubbed at —, saw —, screamed into —, set —, shook —, shouted in —, shouted into —, showed —, shrugged —, stared at —, stared into —, started with —, stepped into —, struck —, studied —, threw in —, touched —, turned —, watched —, went for —, wiped —, wiped at —, wiped off —, wore —; — added, — answered, — appeared, — appeared above, — appeared against, — appeared at, — appeared behind, — appeared beneath, — appeared beside, — appeared between, — appeared from, — appeared in, — appeared on, — appeared over, — appeared through, — appeared to, — became, — became like, — began to, — bent down, — blew off, — blinked out, — bowed, — bowed down, — broke, — broke into, — broke out, — broke through, — broke with, — brought, — brought back, — brought up, — came, — came around, — came back, — came from, — came into, — came on, — came to, — came together, — came toward, — came up, — carried, — caught, — caught in, — caught on, — changed, — cleared, —

cleared for, — cleared of, — cleared with, — closed, — closed down, — closed in, — closed off, — closed up, — continued to, — covered, — covered above, — covered in, — covered with, — crossed, — cut, — cut away, — cut from, — cut in, — cut open, — demanded, — did, — died, — disappeared, — disappeared for, — disappeared in, — disappeared into, — drew, — drew back, — drew in, — drew into, — drew with, — dropped, — dropped from, — dropped with, — drove, — explained, — fell, — fell at, — fell away, — fell in, — fell into, — fell like, — fell with, — felt, — felt like, — filled, — filled with, — forced, — fought to, — found, — frowned, — gave, — gave away, — glanced at, — glanced in, — got, — got to, — grew, — happened in, — held, — held in, — hit, — hung in, — hung upon, — jumped off, — kept, — kissed, — landed in, — landed on, — laughed, — lay against, — lay in, — left, — let, — lifted, — lifted into, — lifted to, — lifted up, — lit, — lit by, — lit in, — lit on, — lit up, — lit with, — looked, — looked at, — looked away, — looked down, — looked like, — looked off, — looked out, — looked up, — lost, — lost behind, — lost in, — lost of, — lost to, — lowered, — lowered against, — lowered into, — lowered to, — lowered within, — made, — made for, — made of, — meant, — met, — moved back, — moved behind, — nodded, — offered, — opened, — paused on, — played, — pointed, — pointed down, — pointed into, — pointed to, — pressed, — pressed against, — pressed into, — pressed out, — pressed to, — pressed together, —

pulled, — pulled against, — pulled at, — pulled down, — pulled into, — pulled out, — pushed, — pushed into, — pushed through, — pushed up, — put, — put away, — raised to, — ran, — ran with, — rang with, — remained, — remained without, — reminded, — returned, — returned to, — rolled over, — rose above, — rose from, — rose in, — rose inside, — rose up, — said, — sank, — sank behind, — sank in, — sank into, — sat in, — saw, — screamed, — seemed, — seemed at, — seemed in, — seemed to, — sent, — set, — set in, — set into, — set with, — settled into, — shifted, — shifted toward, — shook with, — showed, — shut down, — slammed against, — slammed into, — slammed to, — slammed up, — slid behind, — slid forward, — slipped, — slipped back, — smiled, — smiled from, — smiled out, — snapped, — snapped into, — snapped up, — sounded, — spoke, — spoke of, — spoke to, — stared, — stared at, — stared into, — stared out, — stared through, — stared up, — started to, — stayed, — stood, — stood among, — stood in, — stood out, — stood up, — stopped, — struck, — studied, — suggested, — swung around, — swung to, — talked to, — told, — took, — took on, — tried to, — turned, — turned away, — turned from, — turned into, — turned out, — turned to, — turned toward, — turned up, — walked down, — walked over, — walked to, — watched from, — watched without, — went, — went down, — went from, — went out, — went through, — went to, — went up, — wore, — worked, — worked with, — wrote

fact

verbs

— admitted to, — arrived, — broke, — brought, — caught, — did, — fell into, — felt like, — filled with, — found, — got into, — helped to, — led to, — lived with, — made for, — offered, — opened, — put down, — rang, — remained, — saw, — seemed, — seemed to, — sent, — set forth, — spent, — spoke for, — stood, — threw up, — took, — tried to, — worked

fan

verbs

— arrived after, — blew at, — blew on, — broke down, — came in, — came on, — continued, — covered, — did, — dropped from, — followed along, — headed to, — headed toward, — jumped up, — lay against, — left, — lit, — made of, — moved, — opened, — raised, — sat on, — seemed, — showed up, — shut, — shut with, — started to, — stayed on, — stood, — stopped, — took, — turned on, — used to, — waited on, — went, — went off, — went out, — went up, — worked

fang

verbs

— began to, — broke, — brought on, — brought out, — came at, — came down, — drove for, — felt, — filled, — found, — grew, — left, — left in, — pressed against, — pressed into, — promised, — put, — ran out, — sank, — sank in, — sank into, — seemed, — seemed to, — sent, — shot out, — showed, — showed in, — slid out, — went, — went through

fear

verbs

brought —, climbed without —, cried in —, cried with —, crossed without —, felt —, filled with —, followed —, fought —, fought back —, fought down —, fought off —, gasped in —, hated —, heard —, held —, jumped in —, knew —, lay in —, lived in —, lived on —, muttered in —, pushed aside —, read —, recognized —, remembered —, said in —, saw —, shook from —, shook off —, shouted with —, showed —, smelled —, smelled like —, smelled of —, swallowed —, swallowed away —, thought of —, understood —, whispered in —, yelled in —; — became, — began, — began to, — believed, — blew through, — breathed on, — broke through, — came, — came back, — came into, — came on, — came to, — came upon, — came with, — caught in, — changed, — cleared, — climbed on, — closed about, — closed around, — closed in, — closed up, — continued to, — crossed, — died on, — disappeared, — ended up, — fell, — fell across, — fell away, — fell on, — fell upon, — filled, — followed, — gave, — grabbed, — grew, — grew in, — gripped, — handed down, — held, — hit, — hung in, — jumped into, — kept, — kicked in, — lay, — left, — left behind, — let loose, — lifted, — lifted from, — lit, — made, — met, — moved through, — moved up, — opened in, — passed, — passed over, — passed through, — played across, — played over, — poured in, — poured through, — pressed against, — pushed into, — put, — ran, — ran down, — ran like, — ran through, — ran up, — realized, — remained, — returned, — returned like,

— returned to, — rolled down, — rolled over, — rolled through, — rose, — rose from, — rose in, — rose through, — rose to, — rose up, — said, — seemed, — seemed to, — set in, — settled in, — settled into, — settled on, — shot down, — shot through, — shot up, — showed, — showed in, — showed on, — slammed into, — slid down, — slid into, — slid up, — slipped into, — started, — stayed, — stood on, — stood with, — stopped, — struck, — talked through, — took, — took over, — touched, — turned, — turned to, — walked, — went, — went away, — went down, — went through, — went up, — went with, — whispered up, — wore off, — worked against

feature
verbs
— appeared, — became, — began to, — broke into, — called, — came into, — came out, — came to, — changed, — changed by, — continued to, — covered, — drew down, — ended, — fell, — fell into, — grew, — held, — lifted into, — lit with, — lowered into, — made, — played in, — remained, — seemed, — seemed to, — set, — set in, — set like, — settled into, — shoved forward, — showed, — stood out, — took on, — turned, — went, — went from

feeling
verbs
arrived with —, asked with —, explained with —, felt —, fought —, fought against —, fought off —, got —, hated —, heard —, knew —, laughed at —, liked —, lost —, loved —, nodded with —, recognized —, remembered —, replied with —, returned —, said with —, settled into —, shook off —, shut down —, smiled at —, spoke with —, swallowed past —, understood —, wanted —, wondered at —; — began to, — came, — came from, — came into, — continued to, — crossed, — disappeared, — disappeared from, — fell away, — felt, — felt like, — got, — grew, — grew in, — left, — left in, — left to, — loved, — made, — moved beyond, — opened up, — passed, — passed into, — passed through, — ran, — remained, — returned, — returned to, — rose in, — rose up, — sank, — seemed, — seemed to, — settled in, — settled into, — showed in, — shut down, — started to, — stopped, — turned to, — understood, — went, — went away, — went through, — wrapped about

fence
verbs
arrived at —, came at —, came past —, came to —, cleared —, climbed —, climbed onto —, climbed over —, climbed through —, crossed —, crossed to —, dropped from —, fell off —, gestured toward —, glanced at —, grabbed —, gripped —, hit —, jumped —, jumped over —, leaned against —, leaned on —, leaned over —, looked over —, moved along —, moved to —, moved toward —, paused beside —, pointed to —, pushed off —, ran at —, ran for —, ran to —, ran under —, reached —, recognized —, remained by —, saw —, slid off —, slipped through —, slipped under —, stared at —, stayed by —, stood against —, stood at —,

stopped at —, stopped by —, turned to —, turned toward —, walked along —, walked around —, walked to —, went inside —, went over —

field
verbs
approached —, cried in —, disappeared into —, filled out —, gestured to —, glanced about —, glanced across —, glanced at —, headed across —, knew —, left —, looked across —, looked around —, looked at —, looked over —, looked past —, needed —, nodded toward —, passed —, played —, pointed across —, pointed beyond —, pointed to —, ran across —, ran onto —, ran through —, ran toward —, saw —, shut off —, stared across —, started across —, started in —, started into —, stepped into —, stood on —, turned from —, turned toward —, walked on —, watched —, waved at —, went into —, worked —; — appeared, — appeared beneath, — became, — began to, — came back, — came to, — caught, — covered in, — cut, — ended, — fell, — felt, — felt like, — filled, — filled with, — gave, — lay, — looked, — made, — opened, — opened out, — opened up, — placed, — ran, — ran in, — remained, — returned to, — sat, — seemed, — set into, — shook, — showed, — touched, — watched, — went down, — wore

fight
verbs
— began, — began to, — broke out, — continued, — continued below, — ended, — ended with, — forced, — happened, — left, — left to, — looked,

— looked like, — rang out, — remained in, — seemed like, — seemed to, — set, — shifted to, — started, — started at, — started in, — took, — turned, — turned into, — went, — went on, — went out

file
verbs
asked for —, brought —, brought out —, brought up —, checked —, checked through —, closed —, continued through —, dropped —, finished —, finished with —, found —, gestured to —, glanced at —, glanced over —, grabbed —, handed over —, held up —, laid aside —, laid down —, left with —, lifted —, lifted off —, lifted out —, looked at —, looked in —, looked over —, looked through —, meant —, moved —, nodded at —, nodded to —, nodded toward —, offered —, opened —, opened up —, passed over —, picked up —, pointed to —, pointed toward —, pulled —, pulled out —, pulled over —, pushed —, put —, put down —, ran through —, reached for —, reached in —, reached into —, read —, read through —, recognized —, returned to —, returned with —, shut —, stared at —, studied —, took —, took out —, touched —, turned —, wanted —, went into —, went through —, went to —; — appeared, — appeared on, — became, — came through, — came up, — closed, — closed in, — did in, — ended at, — filled with, — finished up, — gave, — grew, — laid out, — lay on, — moved, — opened, — opened up, — put, — put together, — remained in, — remained on, — said, — sat in, — slid onto, — started to, — stayed in, — turned up, —

waited on, — went, — went back, — wrapped in

finger
verbs
added —, approached —, asked through —, ate —, ate with —, blew on —, broke —, caught —, closed —, crossed —, cut —, did —, dropped —, felt —, felt with —, followed —, gestured with —, got —, grabbed —, gripped —, held —, held out —, held up —, kissed —, laid —, laughed behind —, let —, lifted —, lifted up —, looked at —, looked through —, lost —, lowered —, made —, met —, moved —, noticed —, opened —, picked up —, played with —, pointed —, pointed with —, pressed —, pulled on —, pulled out —, pushed —, put —, put out —, put up —, raised —, reached —, reached for —, reached out —, reached with —, remembered —, rolled —, rubbed —, said through —, saw —, shifted —, shook —, shook out —, shot up —, slid —, slipped —, slipped through —, smelled —, snapped —, spoke through —, stared at —, struck —, studied —, thought of —, took —, touched —, tried —, turned to —, used —, watched —, waved —, wiped —, wiped off —, wore on —; — appeared to, — became, — began, — began to, — broke, — came, — came across, — came away, — came down, — came in, — came into, — came to, — came up, — came upon, — caught, — caught in, — closed, — closed about, — closed around, — closed into, — closed on, — closed over, — closed with, — continued to, — covered, — crossed, — cut into, — cut off, — did, — disappeared, — disappeared under, —

drew, — drew down, — dropped, — dropped down, — dropped to, — drove, — drove through, — ended in, — entered, — fell away, — fell on, — felt, — felt against, — felt along, — felt around, — felt for, — felt like, — flew, — flew across, — flew down, — flew forward, — flew into, — flew on, — flew out, — flew over, — flew to, — flew with, — followed, — forced, — found, — gestured, — glanced over, — got, — grabbed, — grew, — grew on, — gripped, — happened on, — held, — held on, — held to, — hesitated, — hit, — jumped, — kept up, — knew, — knocked off, — landed, — landed on, — lay on, — left, — left on, — lifted, — lifted from, — lifted into, — lit on, — looked, — looked like, — looked off, — looked under, — lost, — lowered, — made, — made for, — met, — missed from, — missed on, — moved, — moved across, — moved against, — moved along, — moved around, — moved down, — moved in, — moved into, — moved on, — moved onto, — moved over, — moved through, — moved to, — moved under, — moved up, — moved with, — opened, — passed over, — passed through, — paused, — paused in, — paused on, — picked, — picked up, — played in, — played over, — played with, — pointed, — pointed at, — pointed down, — pointed in, — pointed out, — pointed to, — pointed toward, — pressed, — pressed against, — pressed into, — pressed on, — pressed to, — pressed together, — pulled, — pulled at, — pulled out, — pushed, — pushed at, — pushed into, — raised, — raised on, — raised to, — ran, — ran across, — ran

along, — ran down, — ran out, — ran
over, — ran through, — ran up, —
reached, — reached behind, — reached
for, — reached out, — reached within,
— remained, — remained at, —
remained beneath, — repeated, —
returned, — returned to, — rolled, —
rose, — rubbed, — rubbed against, —
rubbed at, — rubbed over, — sank in, —
sank into, — sat at, — screamed, —
screamed with, — seemed, — seemed to,
— sent, — settled on, — settled over, —
shifted, — shook, — shook against, —
shook around, — shook with, — shot
toward, — shot up, — shoved over, —
slid, — slid across, — slid along, — slid
beneath, — slid between, — slid down,
— slid from, — slid inside, — slid into,
— slid off, — slid over, — slid through,
— slid under, — slid underneath, — slid
up, — slipped, — slipped beneath, —
slipped between, — slipped from, —
slipped inside, — slipped off, — slipped
on, — slipped open, — slipped over, —
slipped through, — slipped under, —
slipped up, — snapped, — snapped into,
— snapped like, — snapped up, —
started to, — started toward, — started
up, — stayed on, — stopped, — stopped
for, — stopped in, — struck, — studied,
— threw, — took, — touched, —
turned, — walked down, — walked
over, — walked through, — waved, —
went back, — went down, — went in,
— went inside, — went on, — went out,
— went past, — went to, — went up, —
wiped, — wore, — worked, — worked
at, — worked on, — worked over, —
worked through, — worked to, —
worked with, — wrapped, — wrapped
around, — wrapped between, —
wrapped in

fire

verbs

added —, approached —, asked —,
broke up —, brought —, called —, came
to —, came under —, caught —, caught
on —, caught over —, died by —, died
in —, drew out —, felt —, felt on —,
frowned into —, gave up —, gestured at
—, glanced across —, glanced at —,
glanced to —, glanced toward —, heard
—, heard about —, held —, jumped to
—, knew —, laid —, lay before —,
leaned over —, left —, liked —, lit —,
looked at —, looked into —, made —,
managed —, moved to —, needed —,
opened —, paused before —, pointed at
—, pointed to —, pointed toward —,
ran toward —, reached —, remembered
—, returned —, returned to —, rose
from —, rose in —, sat before —, sat
beside —, sat by —, saw —, sent —, set
—, smelled —, smiled at —, stared
around —, stared at —, stared into —,
started —, started like —, stepped
around —, stood by —, stood near —,
studied —, thought of —, threw —,
threw up —, turned from —, turned off
—, turned to —, used —, walked
around —, walked to —, wanted —,
watched —, went into —, went to —,
wished for —, wrote with —; —
appeared on, — appeared to, — ate at,
— ate away, — ate into, — ate up, —
became, — began, — began in, — began
to, — blew from, — broke, — broke
out, — broke up, — brought, —
brought under, — came, — came from,
— came in, — carried across, — caught,
— caught in, — climbed, — climbed
over, — climbed through, — climbed
toward, — closed between, — closed in,

— continued, — continued to, — did,
— died, — died at, — died away, —
died down, — died in, — died out, —
died to, — disappeared, — disappeared
from, — drew, — drove, — drove back,
— entered, — fell on, — felt, — filled,
— flew, — flew from, — followed, —
fought against, — gave, — got away, —
got out, — grew, — grew in, — grew
with, — gripped, — held on, — hit, —
hung, — hung around, — joined, —
kicked up, — laid down, — lay, — lay
on, — led, — left, — left behind, — let
out, — let up, — lit, — lit by, — lit up,
— looked, — looked up, — lost, —
made, — made of, — meant for, — met,
— moved through, — needed, — played
in, — poured forth, — poured from, —
poured out, — put, — ran along, — ran
down, — ran out, — ran through, —
ran to, — ran up, — rang out, —
reached, — reached out, — remained
behind, — remained in, — rolled over,
— rose about, — rose above, — rose in,
— rose into, — rose up, — sank, — sank
down, — sank into, — sat against, — sat
on, — seemed, — seemed to, — sent, —
sent forth, — set in, — shifted, — shot,
— shot from, — shot in, — shot into,
— shot out, — shot through, —
slammed into, — slid off, — snapped,
— snapped in, — sounded, — sounded
like, — started, — started in, — started
inside, — started to, — started under,
— stopped for, — struck, — suggested,
— took, — took on, — touched, —
turned, — turned to, — waited for, —
wanted to, — went, — went in, — went
off, — went out, — went over, — went
up, — whispered, — whispered within,
— wore, — worked, — worked at

firm
verbs
— agreed to, — became, — began to, —
called, — caught, — changed, — chose,
— cut, — decided to, — did, — filled
with, — fought, — found, — grew, —
grew by, — happened to, — looked, —
looked into, — met, — reached, —
rolled in, — sat on, — set to, — spent,
— spent over, — swallowed, — took, —
turned, — wanted, — went on

fish
verbs
— added to, — ate, — began to, —
came, — came back, — came from, —
came to, — caught in, — caught on, —
caught up, — cleared, — did, —
disappeared, — dropped on, — filled, —
followed by, — helped by, — hit, —
jumped, — jumped at, — lived in, —
looked like, — lost, — lost at, — moved
past, — pulled from, — put down, —
ran, — rode on, — rolled over, — sat, —
seemed to, — swallowed, — walked out,
— went by

fist
verbs
brought up —, closed —, drew back —,
dropped —, filled —, glanced at —,
grabbed —, gripped —, held out —,
held up —, leaned on —, led with —,
lifted —, looked at —, lowered —, made
—, noticed —, opened —, put up —,
raised —, rubbed —, shook —, swung
—, touched —, used —; — became, —
began to, — broke, — called, — came at,
— came down, — came up, — caught,
— caught through, — closed, — closed
around, — closed on, — closed over, —
covered, — covered with, — drew back,

— dropped on, — drove up, — filled with, — flew, — found, — glanced at, — glanced off, — got, — gripped, — held, — held up, — hit, — landed in, — looked, — looked down, — lowered, — made by, — moved to, — nodded, — opened, — ordered, — pressed against, — pushed against, — raised, — rose, — rose in, — said, — settled against, — shook with, — shot across, — shot out, — shoved, — shoved in, — slammed against, — slammed down, — slammed into, — slipped through, — snapped, — snapped out, — stared, — started to, — stood to, — struck, — struck against, — struck at, — swung, — took, — touched, — turned, — turned to, — walked away, — wiped, — wrapped around

flame

verbs

blew out —, blinked into —, breathed —, caught —, cleared —, disappeared into —, flew onto —, found —, heard —, leaned into —, liked —, loved —, nodded at —, pointed at —, pointed beyond —, pointed to —, remembered —, rose through —, said to —, saw —, shook out —, stared at —, stared into —, stepped toward —, stood before —, struck —, studied —, turned down —, turned to —, walked through —, watched —, went for —, went into —; — added to, — appeared, — appeared at, — appeared in, — became, — began, — began to, — blew out, — breathed into, — broke, — broke through, — came in, — came out, — carried away, — caught, — caught despite, — caught in, — caught on, — climbed, — continued to, — did, — died, — died

away, — died down, — died on, — disappeared, — drove, — drove away, — fell, — fell back, — felt, — filled, — flew at, — forced, — grew, — headed up, — hit, — joined, — jumped, — jumped from, — kept, — kissed, — left, — lit, — lit for, — lit up, — looked, — looked like, — made, — played across, — played on, — played with, — poured into, — poured out, — pulled, — pulled back, — ran up, — reached, — reached to, — remained, — rolled off, — rolled over, — rose, — rose from, — rose into, — rose to, — rose up, — seemed to, — set to, — shot, — shot forward, — shot from, — shot out, — shot over, — shot through, — shot to, — shot up, — snapped, — started to, — started up, — stood out, — threw, — took, — turned to, — went, — went out, — went up, — woke

flash

verbs

— appeared around, — appeared on, — blinked, — broke out, — came, — came behind, — caught, — cut off, — died into, — disappeared from, — drove, — ended, — followed by, — grew, — hit, — lit, — lit up, — looked like, — made, — ran over, — rang out, — returned to, — sank in, — seemed to, — struck out, — went off

flashlight

verbs

bought —, brought —, brought up —, came with —, carried —, dropped —, followed with —, found —, gave up —, gestured with —, got —, grabbed —, handed back —, held —, held out —, killed —, led with —, lifted —, lit up —,

lowered —, moved —, passed over —,
picked up —, pointed —, pulled —,
pulled out —, put —, put down —,
raised —, reached for —, remembered
—, set down —, shifted —, shut off —,
snapped on —, stood with —, swung —,
threw down —, took —, took out —,
turned off —, turned on —, turned out
—, used —, walked with —, waved —;
— appeared behind, — arrived, —
blinked, — called, — came on, —
caught, — cut across, — cut through, —
disappeared, — dropped, — fell, — felt,
— flew from, — found, — hit, — lay on,
— led, — left behind, — lit, — looked
into, — moved, — moved across, —
moved down, — passed over, — played
across, — pointed at, — pointed to, —
ran out, — seemed, — shot around, —
slipped from, — swung to, — swung
toward, — went, — went on, — went
out, — went up, — worked

flesh
verbs
— became, — began to, — broke, —
brought, — came, — came from, —
came off, — came out, — came upon, —
closed, — closed over, — continued to,
— cut from, — demanded, — dropped
to, — fell away, — fell from, — fell off,
— felt, — filled, — filled out, — flew
across, — flew in, — gave, — gave off,
— hung, — hung from, — hung off, —
lay open, — left, — looked, — made, —
met, — opened, — remained, — rose,
— rose in, — rose up, — seemed, —
seemed to, — slid, — slid against, — slid
from, — slipped around, — went, —
wrapped

floor

verbs
asked from —, blinked at —, came off
—, came to —, cleared —, climbed to —
, continued across —, covered —, cried
from —, crossed —, disappeared off —,
disappeared onto —, drew on —,
dropped onto —, dropped to —, drove
to —, fell against —, fell on —, fell onto
—, fell to —, felt —, flew across —,
found —, gestured toward —, glanced
around —, glanced at —, got on —, got
to —, headed for —, hit —, jumped off
—, jumped onto —, jumped to —,
kicked at —, kissed —, knew about —,
laid —, landed on —, lay on —, leaned
to —, left —, left on —, lived on —,
looked around —, looked at —, looked
on —, looked to —, lowered to —, met
—, nodded at —, nodded to —, passed
—, pointed at —, pointed to —, pushed
off —, reached —, reached to —,
remained on —, returned to —, rolled
across —, rolled off —, rolled on —,
rolled onto —, rolled to —, rose from —
, rose off —, said to —, sank through —,
sank to —, sat on —, saw —, settled on
—, shook —, shouted from —, sighed at
—, slept on —, slid across —, slid to —,
slipped on —, slipped to —, smiled at —
, spoke to —, stared at —, stared toward
—, started across —, started on —,
stayed on —, stepped onto —, struck —,
studied —, took —, turned onto —,
turned to —, walked across —, walked
onto —, watched —, went to —, woke
on —, worked on —; — appeared to, —
asked, — began to, — broke away, —
came, — came from, — came over, —
came to, — came up, — caught, —
cleared in, — closed to, — covered by,
— covered with, — dropped, —
dropped out, — ended, — ended at, —

fell away, — felt, — felt like, — filled, —
filled with, — gave, — got, — helped, —
hung from, — laid out, — laughed, —
lay, — led to, — lit up, — looked, —
looked to, — looked up, — made, —
made up, — met, — moved, — moved
like, — moved under, — opened, —
picked up, — pushed, — ran, —
remained, — sat at, — saw, — seemed,
— seemed like, — seemed open, —
seemed to, — shifted, — shook, —
shook beneath, — shook under, —
shook with, — showed, — shut off, —
slid open, — started to, — stood, —
stopped, — took up, — turned to, —
walked along, — went, — went out, —
went up, — worked for, — wrapped in

flower
verbs

ate —, bought —, brought —, called —,
gestured at —, gestured to —, glanced at
—, got —, grabbed —, held out —, laid
down —, lay —, left —, left with —,
liked —, looked at —, loved —, nodded
at —, nodded to —, noticed —, offered
—, picked up —, put —, reached over
—, saw —, sent —, set down —, showed
—, smelled —, smelled like —, smelled
of —, studied —, thought about —,
took —, touched —, turned to —,
walked past —; — arrived, — arrived at,
— asked, — began to, — blew from, —
breathed into, — brought in, — came
from, — came out, — cleared, —
covered, — disappeared, — fell to, —
filled, — grew from, — grew in, — grew
on, — grew outside, — hit, — kissed, —
lay, — made, — nodded to, — opened
to, — played upon, — poured in, —
raised, — rang with, — said, — sat, —

sat on, — seemed to, — stood on, —
struck, — swung upon, — went

fog
verbs

— appeared, — appeared to, — became,
— began to, — blew through, — came,
— came up, — carried, — cleared, —
cleared from, — closed in, — continued
to, — covered, — ended, — fell on, —
grew, — hung, — hung across, — lay, —
lifted, — lifted from, — lowered over,
— made, — pressed, — reached for, —
remained, — returned, — rolled, —
rose, — rose from, — said, — seemed to,
— settled over, — slipped over, —
started to, — stayed, — turned, — went
on

folder
verbs

brought out —, brought over —, closed
—, dropped —, glanced at —, grabbed
—, handed over —, held out —, held up
—, left with —, lifted —, looked at —,
looked through —, nodded at —,
opened —, opened up —, picked up —,
placed —, pulled out —, reached for —,
reached into —, returned with —,
shook —, shut —, stared at —, studied
—, took —, took out —, waved —

food
verbs

added —, asked about —, asked for —,
ate —, bought —, brought —, carried —
, caught for —, cleared away —, did like
—, did without —, dropped —,
explained about —, finished —, fought
—, found —, frowned at —, gave —,
gestured to —, glanced at —, got —,
handed over —, kept —, left —, liked —

, looked at —, loved —, needed —,
nodded at —, offered —, ordered —,
passed —, passed on —, paused for —,
picked at —, picked up —, played with
—, pointed to —, poured out —,
pushed away —, put down —, returned
to —, returned with —, sent in —,
smelled —, stared at —, stopped at —,
swallowed —, thought about —, threw
—, took —, took up —, turned to —,
wanted —, waved at —, went for —; —
appeared beside, — appeared on, —
arrived, — arrived in, — brought, —
came, — came from, — came into, —
came on, — caught in, — cut into, —
did, — drew, — felt, — filled, — flew
from, — followed, — held, — helped,
— hit, — jumped, — laid out, — left, —
left for, — left in, — looked, — made,
— offered, — picked, — placed in, —
ran out, — rose above, — said, — sat, —
sat in, — seemed, — seemed to, — set
on, — settled, — smelled, — sounded,
— went, — wrapped in

foot
verbs
approached on —, arrived on —,
brought down —, came on —, came to
—, caught —, climbed to —, crossed —,
drew —, drew off —, drew up —,
dropped —, dropped to —, felt in —,
felt with —, flew —, flew off —, flew to
—, followed on —, forced —, fought to
—, found —, frowned at —, glanced at
—, got —, got on —, got to —, grabbed
—, grabbed at —, grabbed for —,
gripped —, held —, held down —, held
out —, helped with —, jumped —,
jumped about —, jumped to —, kept —,
kept on —, kept to —, kicked —, kicked
out —, kicked with —, landed on —,

landed upon —, lay at —, lay near —,
left —, left on —, lifted —, lifted to —,
looked around —, looked at —, looked
to —, lost —, lowered —, moved —,
nodded at —, noticed —, picked up —,
placed —, pointed at —, pointed to —,
pressed with —, pulled to —, pushed off
—, pushed to —, put —, raised —, ran
—, reached —, reached toward —,
realized —, remained on —,
remembered —, rolled onto —, rolled to
—, rose to —, rubbed —, said to —, saw
—, set —, settled at —, shifted —,
shifted on —, shifted to —, shook —,
shot to —, shoved to —, shoved with —,
slammed to —, slid —, snapped to —,
stared at —, stared below —, started at
—, started to —, stayed on —, stepped
back —, stood —, stood in —, stood on
—, stopped by —, studied —, swung —,
swung to —, thought on —, took —,
took down —, touched —, tried —,
turned —, used —, walked —, watched
—, went —, wiped —; — added, —
appeared, — appeared in, — ate, —
became, — began to, — broke, — broke
through, — came, — came back, —
came down, — came from, — came
into, — came off, — came on, — came
out, — came through, — came to, —
came up, — carried, — caught, —
caught in, — caught on, — checked, —
continued, — covered with, — crossed,
— crossed at, — cut by, — cut off, —
did, — disappeared through, — drank,
— drew, — drew back, — drew up, —
dropped over, — ended in, — fell, —
fell to, — felt, — felt like, — flew across,
— flew forward, — flew off, — flew
over, — flew up, — followed, — found,
— frowned, — gave, — got, — grew, —
gripped, — held, — held in, — hit, —

hung off, — hung over, — kept, — kicked, — kicked above, — kicked in, — kicked out, — kicked up, — kissed, — knew, — knocked against, — landed in, — landed on, — lay, — leaned, — leaned back, — left, — lifted, — lifted from, — lifted in, — lifted off, — looked, — looked like, — looked up, — lost, — lost in, — made, — made of, — made with, — met, — missed, — moved, — moved from, — moved in, — moved into, — moved on, — moved toward, — nodded, — passed, — passed beyond, — passed over, — paused, — paused beneath, — placed, — pointed, — pointed down, — pointed forward, — pointed up, — pressed against, — pressed to, — pressed together, — pushed against, — pushed up, — put on, — raised, — ran down, — remained, — remained on, — rolled, — rose, — rose above, — rose from, — rubbed, — said, — sank, — sank into, — sat, — screamed in, — seemed, — seemed to, — set, — set down, — set on, — shifted, — shook, — shot out, — shot through, — shot up, — showed, — shrugged, — slammed down, — slammed into, — slammed onto, — slid, — slid across, — slid down, — slid from, — slid off, — slid on, — slid out, — slid under, — slid up, — slipped, — slipped from, — slipped in, — slipped into, — slipped off, — slipped on, — slipped onto, — slipped through, — smelled up, — snapped out, — started to, — started up, — stayed, — stood, — stood out, — stopped, — stopped in, — struck, — swung, — swung from, — swung in, — swung up, — took, — took over, — touched, — touched down, — touched with, — tried to, — turned, — used, —

walked to, — went, — went around, — went back, — went by, — went down, — went from, — went on, — went out, — went over, — went past, — went through, — went up, — whispered up, — wrapped in

footstep
verbs
— approached, — approached along, — approached at, — approached from, — became, — began, — broke, — broke into, — came, — came back, — came behind, — came down, — came from, — came through, — came to, — came toward, — came up, — closed to, — continued, — continued on, — crossed, — did, — died away, — disappeared into, — dropped to, — drove, — entered, — fell behind, — filled, — gave, — got, — grew, — headed, — hesitated by, — left, — made, — moved, — moved across, — moved around, — moved away, — moved back, — moved down, — moved on, — moved toward, — moved up, — ran, — ran across, — ran through, — rang off, — rang on, — rang out, — reached, — returned, — sent, — shook, — sounded, — sounded above, — sounded across, — sounded along, — sounded behind, — sounded from, — sounded in, — sounded off, — sounded on, — sounded out, — started up, — stopped, — stopped outside, — walked, — walked to, — walked toward, — went

force
verbs
— approached, — became, — began to, — broke through, — came from, — came on, — came over, — closed in, —

closed to, — continued, — continued on, — continued to, — decided to, — did, — died with, — drove, — filled, — flew, — found, — gave, — got, — got to, — grew, — held, — held off, — left to, — looked for, — looked on, — made, — made up, — met, — moved in, — moved on, — needed to, — played, — pressed, — pressed out, — pulled, — pulled at, — pulled on, — pushed, — reached, — remained, — remained in, — returned through, — rose up, — said, — sent to, — set out, — shook, — shot, — shot out, — shot up, — slammed, — slammed into, — stepped forward, — stepped up, — stood in, — struck, — took, — tried to, — turned, — used, — went back

forehead
verbs
— began to, — broke out, — came into, — came toward, — covered in, — covered with, — dropped onto, — dropped to, — felt, — got, — grew, — hit, — hung over, — leaned against, — leaned into, — looked, — lowered, — meant, — met, — picked out, — poured, — pressed, — pressed against, — pressed to, — ran into, — remained, — set down, — showed, — started to, — struck, — touched, — touched in

forest
verbs
broke from —, chose —, cleared —, continued through —, disappeared into —, entered —, frowned at —, gestured to —, glanced into —, hated —, kept to —, lived in —, looked at —, looked into —, looked to —, pointed into —, ran into —, ran through —, returned to —,

saw —, slipped into —, smelled —, smelled of —, stared across —, stared around —, stared at —, stared into —, stepped into —, stood in —, stopped in —, turned toward —, walked into —, walked through —, watched —, waved to —, went into —, whispered to —; — appeared to, — became, — began, — began to, — breathed in, — called, — came, — came to, — carried, — climbed, — closed in, — continued to, — cut down, — disappeared, — dropped into, — ended, — ended at, — filled with, — followed, — gave, — grew, — held, — lay on, — looked, — looked for, — made, — met, — opened into, — opened out, — opened through, — opened up, — remained, — rose along, — seemed, — seemed to, — shifted, — shook, — shook with, — smelled of, — started to, — stayed, — stood, — stood in, — swallowed up, — took on, — turned to, — used, — waited for, — went on

fork
verbs
brought back —, dropped —, found —, gestured with —, got —, grabbed —, held up —, laid aside —, laid down —, left at —, lifted —, looked at —, lowered —, picked —, picked up —, placed —, played with —, pointed —, pointed with —, put down —, raised —, reached —, reached for —, set —, set aside —, set down —, threw down —, took —, took up —, turned at —, used —, waved —

form
verbs

— appeared, — appeared at, —
appeared from, — appeared in, —
appeared on, — appeared to, —
appeared within, — became, — began
to, — blinked on, — breathed, — called,
— came, — came across, — came from,
— came to, — came up, — climbed
into, — closed about, — continued, —
covered with, — disappeared, — drew,
— fell from, — fell over, — filled, —
grew, — jumped on, — laughed, — lay
in, — lay on, — leaned in, — looked, —
looked like, — made, — missed, —
moved, — moved from, — moved in, —
moved through, — opened, — passed,
— picked out, — pressed against, — ran
with, — remained, — rolled with, —
rose, — rose from, — rose up, —
seemed, — seemed to, — shifted, —
slammed into, — slid past, — slipped by,
— stood, — stood in, — took, —
turned away

foyer
verbs

appeared in —, arrived at —, called from
—, came into —, crossed —, crossed to
—, crossed toward —, entered —,
gestured toward —, glanced around —,
glanced into —, hit —, landed in —,
looked toward —, moved into —,
moved through —, passed through —,
paused in —, pointed toward —, ran to
—, reached —, returned to —, started
toward —, stayed in —, stepped into —,
stood in —, stopped in —, waited in —,
walked into —, walked to —

frame
verbs

— began to, — broke, — came into, —
caught on, — filled, — filled out, —

flew open, — held, — laid on, — led to,
— looked, — looked like, — made out,
— moved, — pressed, — put on, —
remained, — seemed to, — set on, —
shifted, — shifted in, — shook, —
showed, — stood, — suggested, —
turned, — wrapped in

fright
verbs

— blew through, — brought, — came
from, — came to, — caught in, —
closed around, — closed up, — crossed,
— fell across, — filled, — grew in, —
gripped, — lifted from, — lit, — made,
— played across, — played over, —
poured through, — pressed against, —
ran down, — ran through, — ran up, —
rolled down, — rolled through, — rose
in, — settled in, — shot down, — shot
up, — showed in, — showed on, —
slammed into, — slid down, — turned

front
verbs

appeared at —, asked from —, came
around —, came out —, checked —,
climbed into —, hit —, kept —, moved
—, moved to —, pushed to —, put on
—, put up —, ran in —, reached —,
rode up —, sat at —, sat up —, saw out
—, slammed —, stood —, stood at —,
stood near —, stood up —, took —,
walked in —, walked out —, walked up
—; — appeared to, — began to, — came
to, — carried, — continued to, —
covered with, — dropped, — fell back,
— held, — held up, — left, — let in, —
made, — pulled out, — raised, —
reached, — rolled over, — seemed to, —
spoke in, — stood, — turned, — turned

to, — turned up, — waited, — walked over, — went in

frown
verbs
— appeared on, — brought on, — came to, — cleared, — covered, — crossed, — cut, — disappeared, — filled, — gave, — grew, — left, — made, — passed over, — pulled at, — pulled down, — remained, — returned, — seemed to, — settled between, — shifted, — slipped, — started to, — stayed in, — took up, — touched, — turned, — turned into, — went

frustration
verbs
admitted in —, asked in —, caught —, cried in —, demanded in —, felt —, frowned in —, gasped in —, laughed in —, muttered in —, nodded in —, replied in —, said in —, screamed —, screamed in —, screamed with —, shook in —, shook with —, shouted in —, sighed —, sighed in —, sighed with —, smiled in —, snapped in —, swallowed —, thought in —, turned —, understood —, wondered in —, yelled in —

fury
verbs
— became, — began to, — blew into, — brought, — called for, — came, — came out, — came over, — caught, — continued to, — cut, — entered, — filled, — gave, — grew, — left, — made over, — poured out, — put, — ran, — ran like, — rang against, — rang out, — returned, — returned at, — rolled off, — rolled through, — rolled up, — rose,

— rose from, — rose in, — rose to, — settled into, — shut away, — slammed into, — spent, — turned to, — went out, — went through, — went up

game
verbs
— approached, — became, — began, — began to, — broke, — broke up, — brought, — brought to, — called, — came for, — came from, — came on, — came to, — caught, — changed, — continued in, — ended, — entered, — finished, — flew by, — got under, — happened, — hung from, — lay open, — left for, — made by, — opened up, — picked up, — played at, — played on, — played with, — ran on, — seemed, — seemed to, — started, — started out, — started up, — stopped, — took, — took on, — took over, — turned on, — went, — went on, — went to, — worked, — worked for

garage
verbs
appeared from —, approached —, checked —, closed up —, crossed —, died in —, drove into —, drove toward —, entered —, entered through —, fell into —, gestured toward —, glanced around —, glanced at —, glanced into —, glanced toward —, got to —, headed to —, knew —, knocked down —, leaned against —, left —, left through —, looked around —, looked in —, looked into —, moved through —, nodded toward —, opened —, pointed to —, pointed toward —, pulled into —, ran inside —, ran into —, ran to —, reached —, sat in —, started in —, stayed in —, stepped inside —, stepped into —,

thought about —, turned into —,
walked around —, walked into —,
walked through —, walked to —,
walked toward —, waved from —, went
in —, went into —, went through —,
went to —

garden
verbs
approached —, arrived at —, checked —
, considered —, crossed —, entered —,
gestured at —, hated —, landed in —,
left —, looked across —, looked at —,
looked over —, looked toward —, loved
—, moved toward —, nodded down —,
nodded to —, passed —, pointed across
—, pointed to —, ran across —, ran into
—, reached —, remembered —,
returned to —, saw —, slipped into —,
stared across —, stared down —, stayed
in —, stepped into —, stopped in —,
studied —, thought about —, took in —
, walked through —, went through —,
went to —; — added, — began to, —
came, — changed, — continued to, —
covered in, — did, — disappeared from,
— ended, — filled with, — fought, —
grew, — grew in, — looked, — looked
like, — looked up, — made, — meant,
— met, — seemed, — seemed to, — set
out, — slid, — slid open, — slid past, —
stood, — stood beside, — stood open,
— worked in

gate
verbs
appeared at —, approached —,
approached to —, arrived at —, blew
through —, came through —, came to
—, checked —, climbed —, climbed
over —, closed —, continued to —,
dropped through —, drove out —,

drove through —, entered —, entered
through —, flew through —, found —,
gestured toward —, glanced across —,
got to —, headed for —, headed through
—, headed toward —, heard —, hit —,
jumped into —, jumped over —, kicked
—, kicked open —, leaned on —, left
through —, lifted —, looked at —,
looked through —, looked toward —,
made —, made for —, moved through
—, nodded at —, nodded toward —,
opened —, passed —, passed through —
, paused at —, paused outside —,
pointed to —, pressed open —, pulled at
—, pulled open —, pulled through —,
pushed against —, pushed at —, pushed
on —, pushed open —, pushed through
—, raised —, ran for —, ran out —, ran
to —, reached —, reached for —, rode
out —, rode to —, said at —, sat at —,
sat by —, saw —, shook —, shoved at —
, shoved open —, shut —, slid back —,
slipped through —, stared at —, started
toward —, stayed at —, stayed near —,
stepped into —, stepped through —,
stepped toward —, stood at —, stood by
—, stood outside —, stopped at —,
stopped before —, stopped by —,
studied —, swung open —, took back —
, tried —, turned for —, turned to —,
waited at —, waited by —, walked out
—, walked through —, walked to —,
walked toward —, walked under —,
watched —, went inside —, went
through —, went to —; — appeared, —
began to, — came, — came down, —
came into, — carried, — closed, —
closed across, — closed behind, —
closed by, — closed with, — covered, —
covered with, — disappeared from, —
fell, — fell away, — fell behind, — felt,
— flew open, — gave, — hung on, —

hung open, — lay in, — led into, — led to, — left, — lifted, — lowered, — made of, — moved under, — needed, — opened, — opened for, — opened in, — opened on, — opened to, — put up, — rang out, — remained open, — rose, — said, — said in, — set in, — shook, — shouted, — shut, — shut behind, — slammed against, — slammed behind, — slid across, — slid open, — stood, — stood between, — stood open, — swung, — swung open, — told, — took, — waited for, — went, — went up

gaze
verbs
broke —, caught —, did —, drew —, dropped —, felt —, followed —, forced —, found —, grabbed —, held —, kept —, let —, lifted —, looked into —, lowered —, met —, moved —, noticed —, raised —, recognized —, returned —, sat under —, saw in —, shifted —, slid —, slipped —, stared into —, turned —, watched —; — answered, — became, — began to, — broke to, — came back, — came down, — came to, — came up, — carried over, — caught, — caught on, — considered, — continued, — continued to, — did, — drank, — drank in, — drew, — dropped, — dropped away, — dropped down, — dropped for, — dropped from, — dropped to, — fell, — fell away, — fell down, — fell for, — fell from, — fell on, — fell over, — fell to, — fell upon, — felt, — felt like, — filled with, — flew about, — flew back, — flew to, — flew up, — followed, — found, — glanced, — glanced over, — grew, — held, — held for, — jumped, — jumped to, — landed on, — left, — lifted, — lifted to, — lifted up, — lit, — lit on, — lit up, — looked, — lowered, — lowered to, — lowered with, — made, — met, — met over, — met through, — met with, — moved, — moved back, — moved down, — moved from, — moved over, — moved past, — moved to, — passed over, — passed through, — pointed out, — ran over, — ran up, — reached, — remained, — remained on, — returned, — returned to, — rose, — rose from, — rose to, — said, — sat, — seemed to, — settled, — settled on, — settled over, — shifted, — shifted away, — shifted to, — shot, — shot to, — shot up, — slid, — slid across, — slid around, — slid away, — slid behind, — slid down, — slid from, — slid off, — slid over, — slid past, — slid to, — slid toward, — slipped, — slipped down, — slipped over, — slipped past, — snapped back, — snapped to, — snapped up, — stared out, — stayed, — stayed on, — stopped, — swung, — swung between, — swung to, — told, — took, — took in, — took on, — touched, — touched for, — turned away, — turned down, — turned on, — turned to, — turned toward, — went, — went back, — went beyond, — went from, — went past, — went through, — went to, — went toward, — went up

gear
verbs
— appeared in, — began to, — came up, — climbed out, — fell away, — laid out, — left, — lost in, — made, — passed by, — pointed, — poured into, — poured out, — sat, — sat at, — set, — set up, — started to, — stood, — stood down, —

took, — took up, — turned in, — went, — worked behind, — wrapped up

glance
verbs
— became, — began to, — came, — came over, — fell on, — fell to, — felt like, — filled with, — followed, — left, — met, — moved away, — moved over, — passed around, — rose up, — said, — seemed to, — shifted, — shifted from, — shifted to, — slid, — slid away, — slid from, — took in, — took to, — turned on, — went, — went from, — went to, — went toward, — went with

glass
verbs
appeared through —, approached —, breathed onto —, broke —, cleared out —, considered —, demanded —, drank —, drank from —, dropped —, felt —, filled —, filled up —, finished —, finished off —, found —, frowned at —, frowned into —, frowned through —, gestured with —, glanced at —, glanced through —, glanced toward —, got —, grabbed —, grabbed up —, gripped —, handed over —, held —, held out —, held up —, hit —, kicked in —, knew about —, knocked on —, laughed into —, leaned against —, leaned toward —, lifted —, looked at —, looked into —, looked like —, looked over —, looked through —, looked to —, looked toward —, lowered —, moved —, nodded at —, offered —, picked up —, played with —, pointed at —, pointed to —, poured —, pressed against —, pulled back —, put —, put down —, raised —, reached for —, rubbed —, sat at —, sat behind —, saw —, set down —, settled —, shook

—, shouted through —, slid down —, smiled over —, spoke into —, stared at —, stared into —, stared through —, stepped over —, stepped to —, stepped toward —, stood at —, stood behind —, stood with —, studied —, threw —, took —, took away —, took in —, took out —, took up —, touched —, turned from —, turned to —, waved —, went for —, worked in —; — began to, — broke, — broke away, — came, — came back, — came down, — came from, — came to, — came up, — covered, — cut, — cut into, — did, — dropped, — dropped inside, — dropped to, — fell, — fell from, — fell like, — fell off, — fell out, — fell to, — felt, — filled to, — filled with, — flew across, — followed, — held, — held by, — held in, — hit, — joined by, — knocked out, — laid out, — looked like, — lost, — lowered to, — made, — raised to, — reached toward, — read, — remained, — rose up, — sat on, — seemed, — set at, — set in, — set into, — set on, — shook, — shook to, — showed, — slid, — slid across, — slid down, — slid open, — slipped, — slipped from, — snapped in, — sounded from, — started to, — stood on, — stopped, — struck, — took on, — turned, — turned out

glasses
verbs
blinked through —, breathed on —, brought out —, carried —, cleared —, dropped —, filled —, found —, frowned at —, got —, hated —, held up —, lifted —, looked for —, looked over —, looked through —, lowered —, needed —, passed —, passed out —, picked up —, pulled off —, pulled on —, pushed

up —, put down —, put on —, reached for —, set down —, shoved up —, slid on —, slipped off —, slipped on —, swung —, took —, took off —, took out —, touched —, wiped —, wore —; — appeared at, — came, — caught, — covered, — did, — fell from, — fell off, — fell to, — filled with, — gave, — held in, — held on, — hung against, — hung around, — hung down, — hung on, — jumped out, — knocked, — lay on, — left behind, — lifted, — looked, — looked like, — looked up, — made, — offered, — pushed down, — pushed up, — raised, — raised in, — returned, — said, — sat in, — sat on, — seemed, — set on, — slid down, — slid forward, — slipped down, — stared at, — stood at, — stood up, — told, — turned to, — worked, — worked behind

gloom
verbs

— came, — came into, — closed in, — crossed, — entered, — fell on, — felt, — filled, — filled with, — gave, — grew in, — headed toward, — hung across, — lay in, — lifted, — passed over, — pressed in, — pulled back, — rose off, — screamed in, — seemed, — settled, — settled down, — settled on, — showed in

glove
verbs

blew into —, drew off —, drew on —, felt —, got —, kept on —, lifted —, looked at —, looked for —, picked off —, picked up —, placed —, pulled off —, pulled on —, pulled up —, put aside —, put on —, set —, set aside —, shook off —, shrugged on —, slipped off —,

slipped on —, snapped off —, snapped on —, took —, took off —, wore —

glow
verbs

— appeared, — appeared on, — became, — began, — began to, — came from, — came under, — covered, — died beneath, — disappeared behind, — drew, — fell in, — fell upon, — filled, — found, — grew, — joined, — left, — lit, — lit in, — lit up, — made, — paused for, — poured out, — pushed back, — returned, — rose, — seemed, — seemed to, — shot out, — started to, — stopped, — turned, — went back

gold
verbs

bought —, brought —, found —, glanced at —, hit —, kept —, knew —, knew about —, lifted —, lifted up —, liked —, looked at —, looked past —, meant —, nodded at —, offered —, put —, put on —, reached for —, recognized —, spoke of —, struck —, turned —, used —, wanted —, went for —, wore —

grace
verbs

— appeared to, — asked for, — blinked, — came upon, — crossed, — did, — disappeared, — drew out, — entered, — gave in, — got, — joined, — lay on, — led, — loved to, — opened, — pointed out, — pulled from, — said, — said with, — set, — took, — tried to, — walked down, — wanted to

grass
verbs

added —, approached —, came over —,
crossed —, cut —, dropped to —, fell
into —, fell to —, felt —, glanced at —,
hit —, kicked —, kicked at —, kicked
into —, landed in —, landed on —, lay
in —, lay on —, lay upon —, passed
through —, picked at —, pointed into
—, pointed out —, ran through —, ran
up —, reached —, rose from —, sat in
—, sat on —, settled to —, shifted on —
, shot across —, slipped on —, smelled
—, smelled like —, smelled of —, stared
at —, started across —, stepped into —,
stepped onto —, stepped through —,
stood among —, stood on —, stopped in
—, walked across —, walked through —
; — approached, — began to, — bent,
— came, — caught, — caught on, —
covered with, — felt, — filled, — gave,
— grew, — grew in, — grew on, — grew
through, — grew under, — grew up, —
lay of, — looked, — looked like, — lost,
— made, — made by, — met, —
nodded in, — rolled up, — rose in, —
rose to, — rubbed up, — seemed, —
seemed to, — set, — slipped across, —
smelled, — took over, — waited on, —
waved, — waved in, — whispered in, —
wrapped around

grin

verbs

added with —, admitted with —, agreed
with —, answered —, answered with —,
asked with —, broke into —, caught —,
continued with —, covered —, dropped
—, explained with —, finished with —,
forced —, fought back —, fought down
—, gave —, got —, grinned —, held
back —, held in —, hung onto —,
leaned with —, liked —, lost —,
managed —, missed —, murmured with

—, nodded with —, offered with —,
replied with —, returned —, said
through —, said with —, saw —, settled
for —, shot —, shrugged with —, stayed
with —, suggested with —, swallowed
—, thought with —, tried —, turned
with —, wore —; — appeared, —
appeared on, — became, — began on, —
began to, — broke, — broke across, —
broke out, — broke over, — broke
through, — came, — came back, —
came onto, — came over, — came to, —
carried through, — changed, — covered,
— crossed, — did, — died, —
disappeared, — dropped from, — fell,
— fell away, — felt, — filled, — filled
up, — followed, — found, — got, —
grew, — grew on, — grew under, —
held, — landed upon, — left, — lifted,
— lit, — lit up, — looked, — made, —
opened, — played in, — pulled at, —
remained, — returned, — returned
with, — said, — seemed to, — set, —
showed, — slid from, — slipped, —
slipped away, — slipped out, — stayed,
— stopped, — suggested, — touched, —
turned, — turned into, — turned to, —
went

ground

verbs

bent to —, bowed to —, considered —,
cut across —, died on —, dropped to —,
fell on —, fell onto —, fell to —, felt —,
felt for —, found on —, frowned at —,
gave —, glanced toward —, grabbed —,
grinned at —, held —, hit —, jumped to
—, kept —, kicked —, kicked at —,
kicked off —, kissed —, knew —, landed
on —, lay on —, left —, lifted off —,
lived above —, looked around —,
looked at —, looked from —, looked to

—, looked toward —, lost —, met —, nodded at —, pointed at —, pointed to —, pointed toward —, pushed off —, ran across —, ran to —, reached —, remained in —, rolled on —, rose from —, said to —, sank to —, sat on —, settled onto —, shouted from —, slammed to —, slid to —, slipped to —, spoke to —, stared at —, stepped to —, stood —, stood on —, struck —, studied —, swung to —, touched —, watched —, went to —; — appeared, — appeared to, — became, — began, — began to, — blew up, — came up, — cleared, — closed, — continued to, — did, — did with, — disappeared beneath, — dropped away, — ended, — fell away, — felt, — felt like, — forced, — gave, — got up, — grew, — heard, — held, — held up, — jumped, — lay, — lifted into, — lit up, — looked, — looked at, — made, — made for, — moved under, — opened up, — ran, — ran along, — ran in, — rolled, — rolled by, — rose, — rose beneath, — rose from, — rose in, — rose toward, — said, — sank beneath, — seemed, — seemed to, — set up, — shifted beneath, — shook, — shook beneath, — shook from, — shook under, — shook with, — slid, — smelled of, — started to, — stood, — turned to, — used, — worked, — worked in

growl
verbs

— answered, — began, — began to, — came back, — came from, — came out, — cut, — did, — disappeared into, — drew, — filled, — followed, — got into, — grew, — made, — repeated, — rolled over, — rolled up, — rose above, — rose from, — rose in, — rose to, — seemed,

— seemed to, — sent, — sounded, — sounded from, — sounded in, — sounded like, — turned into, — went up

guilt
verbs

— ate at, — came back, — closed in, — crossed over, — drove, — entered, — filled, — followed, — held, — hit, — hung, — made, — poured off, — pressed against, — ran into, — remained, — rose into, — sank, — sat in, — seemed to, — settled in, — slammed against, — slid down, — stepped up, — turned to, — wore off

gun
verbs

asked about —, blinked at —, bought —, broke —, brought out —, brought up —, called for —, came off —, carried —, caught —, checked —, covered —, drew —, drew back —, drew out —, dropped —, felt —, found —, gave up —, gestured with —, glanced at —, got —, got out —, grabbed —, grabbed for —, gripped —, handed over —, hated —, heard —, held —, held onto —, held out —, held up —, hung up —, jumped —, kept —, kicked at —, kicked away —, knew —, knew about —, lay beside —, leaned with —, led with —, left —, lifted —, liked —, looked at —, looked for —, looked like —, looked over —, looked past —, lost —, loved —, lowered —, moved —, needed —, nodded at —, nodded to —, nodded toward —, noticed —, opened —, passed —, picked up —, placed —, pointed —, pointed at —, pointed to —, pulled —, pulled at —, pulled out —, put —, put away —, put back —, put down —, raised —, ran —, ran past —, reached for —, reached out —, reached to —, recognized —, remembered —, returned —, returned with —, rolled off —, said of —, saw —, saw of —, sent —, set down —, shifted —, slipped —, slipped on —, slipped out —, stared at —, stayed with —, stepped over —, swung —, thought of —, threw away —, took —, took out —, took up —, tossed —, tossed down —, touched —, turned —, understood —, wanted —, watched —, waved —, went for —, wiped off —, wore —; — added to, — appeared, — appeared in, — began, — began to, — broke in, — brought up, — came, — came around, — came away, — came back, — came down, — came into, — came on, — came out, — came to, — came up, — caught, — closed, — continued, — continued to, — disappeared, — dropped, — dropped away, — dropped from, — dropped into, — dropped onto, — dropped to, — dropped with, — entered, — fell, — fell from, — fell on, — fell out, — fell to, — felt, — felt like, — flew, — flew from, — flew open, — followed, — gave, — gripped in, — held, — held by, — held down, — held in, — held to, — hung from, — joined in, — kicked, — kicked against, — landed with, — lay, — lay by, — lay inside, — lay on, — lit, — lit up, — looked, — looked like, — lost, — lowered, — made, — managed to, — meant to, — moved, — moved into, — opened, — opened up, — paused, — pointed, — pointed at, — pointed down, — pointed out, — pointed to, — poured, — pressed against, — pressed into, — pressed to, — raised, — raised in, — raised to, —

ran to, — remained, — rolled, — rolled away, — rose, — rose to, — said, — sat, — sat by, — screamed, — seemed, — sent, — set across, — shook in, — shut with, — slid across, — slipped, — slipped from, — smelled, — snapped in, — snapped open, — spoke, — spoke in, — spoke with, — stayed, — stayed at, — stayed in, — stayed up, — stood, — stood at, — stood in, — stopped, — struck, — swung around, — swung to, — took, — touched, — turned, — turned out, — turned over, — used, — used in, — watched, — waved, — went, — went back, — went down, — went into, — went off, — went over, — went through, — went to, — went up, — worked

gunfire
verbs

— began, — broke out, — came, — came from, — continued, — continued above, — continued on, — died, — died away, — died out, — ended, — filled, — heard in, — lit up, — made, — meant, — paused, — rang in, — rang outside, — returned on, — shook, — sounded, — sounded behind, — sounded from, — sounded in, — stopped, — went, — went off

hair
verbs

blew —, breathed into —, caught —, changed —, checked —, covered —, cut —, did —, dropped —, felt —, felt for —, felt of —, finished with —, found —, gestured at —, got —, grabbed —, grabbed at —, gripped —, hated —, hoped —, kept —, kissed —, lifted —, liked —, lost —, loved —, moved —, murmured against —, murmured into —, picked at —, played with —, pointed at —, pulled —, pulled at —, pulled on —, pushed at —, reached for —, rubbed —, rubbed at —, saw —, set —, settled into —, shook —, shook out —, shoved at —, smelled —, spoke against —, stared at —, stopped above —, studied —, swung —, thought of —, tossed —, touched —, wanted —, watched —, whispered against —, wiped at —, wore —, worked in —, worked on —; — answered, — appeared, — appeared over, — appeared to, — became, — began, — began to, — blew, — blew about, — blew across, — blew around, — blew in, — blew like, — blew up, — bowed, — brought up, — came, — came away, — came down, — came from, — came into, — came off, — came out, — came through, — came to, — came up, — came with, — caught, — caught in, — caught on, — caught up, — chose, — climbed out, — covered, — covered by, — covered in, — cut, — cut above, — cut in, — cut into, — cut off, — did, — disappeared, — drew, — fell, — fell about, — fell across, — fell against, — fell around, — fell away, — fell back, — fell between, — fell down, — fell forward, — fell from, — fell in, — fell into, — fell like, — fell off, — fell on, — fell onto, — fell over, — fell past, — fell to, — felt, — felt like, — felt on, — filled, — flew, — flew against, — flew around, — flew in, — flew on, — flew out, — found at, — found in, — found under, — gave, — got, — got off, — got out, — got up, — grew, — grew between, — grew from, — grew into, — grew on, — gripped in, — happened to, — held, — held back, — held down, —

held up, — hung, — hung about, — hung across, — hung against, — hung around, — hung down, — hung from, — hung in, — hung loose, — hung on, — hung over, — hung past, — hung to, — jumped, — jumped up, — kissed, — landed, — landed on, — laughed, — lay, — lay across, — lay against, — lay like, — lay on, — lay over, — led, — left, — left on, — left to, — lifted, — lifted up, — looked, — looked like, — looked up, — made, — met, — missed from, — moved, — moved in, — moved like, — moved over, — moved with, — needed, — opened, — passed on, — played over, — played with, — pointed, — pointed in, — pointed of, — poured out, — pulled back, — pulled behind, — pulled down, — pulled forward, — pulled from, — pulled into, — pulled out, — pulled up, — put, — put up, — raised, — ran down, — ran in, — ran into, — rang, — reached, — read, — remained, — remained by, — remained on, — replied, — rolled into, — rose along, — rose at, — rose on, — said, — sat, — sat at, — sat behind, — sat with, — seemed, — seemed to, — set in, — set off, — settled down, — shifted, — shifted at, — shifted like, — shook, — shook with, — shot up, — shouted for, — showed, — showed up, — slammed into, — slid across, — slid down, — slid off, — slid over, — slid to, — slipped from, — slipped off, — slipped over, — smelled, — smelled like, — snapped against, — snapped with, — started away, — stepped forward, — stepped from, — stepped out, — stood at, — stood behind, — stood beneath, — stood in, — stood on, — stood out, — stood up, — stopped at, — suggested, — swung,

— swung above, — swung against, — swung around, — swung forward, — swung from, — swung like, — talked on, — told, — tossed around, — tossed in, — touched, — tried to, — turned, — turned in, — turned into, — turned to, — waved, — waved around, — went, — whispered over, — wrapped in

hall
verbs
added from —, appeared from —, appeared in —, arrived at —, arrived outside —, asked from —, called across —, called down —, called from —, came down —, came into —, checked —, continued down —, crossed —, disappeared down —, disappeared into —, entered —, flew down —, gave —, gestured around —, gestured down —, gestured toward —, glanced around —, glanced down —, glanced toward —, glanced up —, got to —, headed down —, headed for —, headed into —, headed toward —, headed up —, hesitated in —, hung in —, left —, looked across —, looked around —, looked at —, looked down —, looked up —, moved down —, moved into —, moved toward —, nodded to —, passed through —, paused in —, pointed across —, pointed down —, pointed to —, pointed toward —, pushed into —, ran across —, ran down —, ran for —, ran into —, ran to —, reached —, returned to —, rolled down —, set —, shot down —, shouted across —, shouted down —, slid into —, slipped across —, slipped down —, slipped from —, slipped into —, stared down —, started down —, started toward —, started up —, stayed in —, stepped down —, stepped into —,

stood in —, stopped in —, swung toward —, turned down —, turned toward —, waited in —, walked —, walked across —, walked down —, walked from —, walked into —, walked through —, walked to —, went across —, went down —, went in —, went into —, went through —, went to —, yelled down —, yelled from —, yelled into —; — appeared to, — became, — began to, — called, — came back, — cleared, — continued, — disappeared into, — drew, — ended in, — fell, — fell on, — felt, — filled with, — grew, — joined, — lay, — led, — led away, — led to, — let, — lit by, — lit with, — looked, — looked out, — made, — meant, — opened, — opened into, — ran off, — rang to, — rang with, — remained, — remained in, — returned to, — seemed, — seemed to, — showed through, — started to, — stood on, — stopped, — thought about, — turned, — turned to, — wanted to, — watched, — went, — went back, — went on, — went past, — wore

hallway
verbs
added from —, appeared from —, appeared in —, asked from —, broke for —, called down —, called from —, called into —, came down —, came into —, checked —, continued down —, continued up —, crossed —, disappeared down —, disappeared into —, entered —, gestured down —, gestured toward —, glanced around —, glanced down —, glanced into —, glanced toward —, got to —, happened into —, headed down —, headed toward —, hit —, leaned into —, left through

—, looked around —, looked down —, looked into —, looked up —, loved —, moved down —, moved into —, moved through —, nodded down —, nodded toward —, nodded up —, opened onto —, passed into —, paused at —, paused in —, pointed down —, pointed to —, pointed toward —, ran down —, ran into —, ran toward —, reached —, remained in —, returned to —, said in —, screamed into —, slid down —, slipped into —, stared down —, stared into —, started down —, started toward —, stepped in —, stepped into —, stood in —, stopped in —, thought of —, turned down —, turned in —, turned toward —, waited in —, walked —, walked along —, walked down —, walked into —, walked through —, walked to —, walked toward —, went along —, went down —, went into —, went to —, whispered from —; — appeared, — appeared to, — became, — bent, — came, — continued on, — covered with, — cut across, — drew, — ended at, — ended in, — fell, — filled with, — got, — headed for, — headed toward, — held, — laid in, — lay, — led into, — led to, — lit up, — looked, — looked for, — made, — made of, — offered, — opened, — opened into, — opened out, — opened up, — ran, — ran in, — remained in, — seemed, — showed, — smelled like, — smelled of, — stared at, — stayed, — told, — took, — took on, — waited for, — wore, — wrapped in

hammer
verbs

brought down —, chose —, dropped —, followed behind —, found —, got —,

grabbed —, gripped —, heard —, held up —, leaned on —, lifted —, loved —, lowered —, picked up —, pointed at —, pointed to —, pulled back —, put down —, raised —, saw —, set —, stared at —, stopped —, studied —, swung —, thought about —, took —, took out —, tossed —, used —; — came down, — covered with, — did, — dropped, — dropped on, — fell, — fell like, — fell on, — glanced off, — held, — held in, — hit, — kept, — looked like, — pulled back, — rang, — rang along, — rang in, — rang on, — rang out, — returned, — rose, — snapped forward, — snapped on, — started to, — struck, — took, — tried to, — wrapped in

hand
verbs

added —, asked for —, ate with —, began in —, bent —, bent over —, blew into —, blew on —, brought down —, brought up —, came to —, carried in —, caught —, caught up —, changed —, checked —, climbed into —, closed —, considered —, covered —, crossed —, cut —, died at —, died by —, drew away —, drew out —, dropped —, dropped to —, drove with —, fell into —, fell on —, fell onto —, fell to —, felt —, felt of —, felt with —, followed on —, forced —, forced up —, found —, gestured at —, gestured with —, glanced at —, glanced to —, glanced toward —, got —, got on —, got to —, grabbed —, grabbed onto —, grabbed with —, grinned behind —, gripped —, gripped in —, held —, held in —, held open —, held out —, held to —, held up —, hit —, hit with —, hung by —, joined —, kept —, kept on —, kissed —, knew about —, laid —, laid down —, landed on —, laughed behind —, leaned on —, let —, lifted —, lifted away —, lifted up —, liked —, looked at —, looked down —, looked in —, looked into —, looked to —, looked toward —, lost —, lowered —, moved —, needed —, needed into —, needed on —, nodded at —, nodded behind —, nodded in —, nodded into —, nodded toward —, noticed —, offered —, offered up —, opened —, opened out —, picked at —, picked up —, placed —, played with —, pointed at —, pointed to —, pointed with —, pressed —, pressed into —, pulled —, pulled away —, pulled out —, pulled with —, pushed forward —, pushed to —, pushed with —, put —, put down —, put out —, put up —, raised —, raised up —, ran —, reached —, reached for —, reached out —, reached up —, reached with —, remained on —, remembered —, rode with —, rolled —, rolled onto —, rolled to —, rose on —, rose to —, rubbed —, rubbed at —, sat on —, saw —, set —, settled —, shifted —, shook —, shook off —, shook out —, shot —, shot out —, shot up —, shoved —, shoved out —, showed —, shrugged off —, slammed —, slid —, slipped —, smelled —, smiled at —, snapped out —, stared at —, stayed —, stayed on —, stepped on —, stopped —, studied —, swung —, swung with —, talked behind —, talked with —, thought about —, thought of —, threw —, threw off —, threw out —, threw up —, told —, took —, took away —, took out —, tossed —, tossed up —, touched —, tried —, turned —, turned on —, turned over —, used —, waited on —, wanted —, watched —, waved —, waved with —,

went to —, whispered behind —, wiped —, wiped off —, wore on —, worked —, worked with —, wrapped —, wrote by —; — appeared, — appeared at, — appeared beside, — appeared between, — appeared from, — appeared in, — appeared over, — appeared to, — asked, — became, — began, — began to, — bent, — broke, — broke out, — broke through, — broke with, — brought, — called, — came, — came about, — came across, — came against, — came around, — came away, — came back, — came behind, — came beneath, — came between, — came down, — came forward, — came in, — came into, — came off, — came on, — came out, — came over, — came to, — came together, — came toward, — came up, — came upon, — carried, — caught, — caught at, — caught in, — changed into, — climbed, — climbed up, — closed, — closed about, — closed around, — closed in, — closed into, — closed of, — closed on, — closed over, — closed up, — closed upon, — continued, — continued to, — covered, — covered in, — covered with, — crossed, — crossed at, — crossed behind, — crossed on, — crossed over, — cut, — cut off, — demanded, — did, — disappeared, — disappeared into, — disappeared under, — drew, — drew away, — drew back, — drew near, — dropped, — dropped away, — dropped down, — dropped for, — dropped from, — dropped into, — dropped like, — dropped on, — dropped onto, — dropped through, — dropped to, — ended, — ended in, — entered, — entered in, — fell, — fell away, — fell back, — fell down, — fell from, — fell in, — fell into, — fell off,

— fell on, — fell onto, — fell open, — fell to, — felt, — felt against, — felt along, — felt around, — felt like, — filled with, — flew, — flew at, — flew like, — flew out, — flew over, — flew to, — flew toward, — flew up, — flew with, — followed, — forced, — fought to, — found, — gave, — gestured, — gestured against, — gestured in, — gestured to, — gestured toward, — glanced off, — got, — got through, — got to, — grabbed, — grabbed at, — grabbed for, — grabbed onto, — grew, — gripped, — gripped in, — gripped into, — gripped on, — gripped under, — happened in, — happened to, — headed, — held, — held above, — held at, — held forth, — held in, — held on, — held open, — held out, — held over, — held to, — held up, — hesitated, — hesitated above, — hesitated for, — hesitated on, — hit, — hung, — hung at, — hung beside, — hung by, — hung in, — hung over, — joined, — jumped, — kept on, — kept up, — knocked against, — knocked on, — laid on, — landed on, — lay, — lay in, — lay like, — lay on, — lay upon, — leaned on, — left, — left behind, — let, — lifted, — lifted from, — lifted in, — lifted to, — lifted up, — lifted with, — lit, — lit along, — looked, — looked at, — looked like, — looked over, — looked to, — lost, — lowered, — lowered from, — lowered in, — lowered like, — made, — made of, — managed, — meant, — met, — missed, — moved, — moved around, — moved at, — moved beneath, — moved between, — moved by, — moved down, — moved from, — moved in, — moved inside, — moved like, — moved of, — moved on, — moved onto,

— moved over, — moved through, — moved to, — moved toward, — moved under, — moved until, — moved up, — moved with, — offered in, — opened, — opened on, — passed across, — passed down, — passed over, — passed through, — paused, — paused at, — paused before, — paused for, — paused in, — paused on, — paused over, — picked, — picked up, — placed against, — played along, — played with, — pointed, — pointed at, — pointed to, — pressed, — pressed against, — pressed at, — pressed between, — pressed down, — pressed into, — pressed on, — pressed over, — pressed to, — pressed together, — pulled, — pulled at, — pulled away, — pulled down, — pulled into, — pushed, — pushed against, — pushed beneath, — pushed between, — pushed into, — pushed through, — pushed up, — put, — raised, — raised above, — raised in, — raised to, — raised toward, — raised with, — ran, — ran down, — ran over, — ran through, — ran up, — rang, — reached, — reached across, — reached down, — reached for, — reached forward, — reached in, — reached into, — reached out, — reached past, — reached through, — reached to, — reached toward, — reached under, — remained, — remained across, — remained behind, — remained in, — remained on, — remained over, — returned, — returned to, — rose, — rose before, — rose from, — rose into, — rose of, — rose off, — rose to, — rose up, — rose with, — rubbed, — rubbed against, — rubbed at, — rubbed up, — said, — sank, — sank into, — saw, — screamed with, — seemed, — seemed on, —

seemed to, — sent, — settled against, — settled around, — settled at, — settled down, — settled in, — settled on, — settled onto, — settled upon, — shifted to, — shifted toward, — shook, — shook against, — shook around, — shook at, — shook in, — shook inside, — shook like, — shook on, — shook over, — shook with, — shot, — shot across, — shot around, — shot down, — shot forward, — shot into, — shot out, — shot through, — shot to, — shot up, — shouted in, — shouted to, — shoved, — shoved at, — shoved between, — shoved down, — shoved in, — shoved into, — shoved up, — showed, — showed to, — shut, — shut off, — slammed, — slammed on, — slammed onto, — slid, — slid across, — slid along, — slid around, — slid away, — slid beneath, — slid between, — slid down, — slid from, — slid inside, — slid into, — slid off, — slid over, — slid through, — slid to, — slid toward, — slid under, — slid up, — slipped, — slipped around, — slipped away, — slipped behind, — slipped down, — slipped from, — slipped in, — slipped inside, — slipped off, — slipped on, — slipped onto, — slipped over, — slipped through, — slipped to, — slipped under, — slipped up, — smelled, — smelled of, — snapped, — snapped around, — snapped back, — snapped in, — snapped into, — snapped on, — snapped out, — snapped up, — stared into, — started, — started to, — started up, — stayed, — stayed down, — stayed in, — stayed on, — stayed over, — stood, — stood out, — stood over, — stopped, — stopped at, — stopped in, — struck, — struck down, — swung at, — swung beside, — swung out, — took, — took in, — took off, — took on, — took over, — touched, — touched down, — tried to, — turned, — turned into, — turned off, — turned to, — used up, — waited, — waited for, — wanted to, — waved, — waved at, — waved from, — waved in, — waved through, — went about, — went around, — went at, — went back, — went behind, — went between, — went down, — went for, — went forward, — went from, — went in, — went inside, — went into, — went off, — went out, — went over, — went through, — went to, — went under, — went up, — whispered like, — wiped across, — wore, — worked, — worked at, — worked between, — worked to, — worked together, — worked up, — worked with, — wrapped, — wrapped about, — wrapped along, — wrapped around, — wrapped in, — wrote

handle

verbs

bent to —, dropped —, felt —, flew off —, found —, grabbed —, grabbed for —, gripped —, held —, hit —, lifted —, lifted up —, looked at —, pointed to —, pressed —, pressed down —, pulled —, pulled against —, pulled on —, reached —, reached for —, reached to —, shook —, shoved —, touched —, tried —, turned —, used —

hat

verbs

added —, bought —, checked —, considered —, dropped —, felt —, got —, grabbed —, handed —, held up —, hung —, hung up —, kept —, knocked

off —, lifted —, lifted up —, looked at
—, lost —, moved —, passed —, picked
up —, pointed at —, pointed to —,
pointed with —, pulled down —, pulled
off —, put —, put on —, raised —,
reached for —, reached under —,
returned —, slid on —, thought about
—, threw —, threw off —, threw on —,
took —, took off —, took out —,
touched —, used —, waved —, wore —;
— answered, — appeared on, —
approached, — became, — blew off, —
bought at, — covered, — fell off, — fell
to, — flew from, — flew off, — got, —
hung off, — looked, — looked into, —
made of, — moved, — moved through,
— pulled, — pulled down, — pulled
over, — pushed to, — rode, — rolled
into, — sat in, — sat on, — shouted, —
shoved into, — slid, — slid from, —
started to, — stepped around, —
stepped out, — stood in, — stood up, —
struck, — turned to, — waited for, —
went

head
verbs
asked over —, bent —, bowed —, broke
—, carried in —, cleared —, covered —,
cut off —, did —, dropped —, felt —,
felt behind —, finished in —, flew above
—, flew over —, followed —, found —,
gestured above —, gestured with —,
glanced above —, got —, grabbed —,
gripped —, heard in —, held —, held up
—, hit —, hung —, kept —, kicked —,
kissed —, laid —, landed on —, leaned
—, let —, lifted —, lifted up —, listened
to —, looked like —, looked over —,
lost —, lowered —, made —, moved —,
moved to —, nodded —, picked up —,
pointed —, pointed above —, pointed at

—, pointed to —, pulled around —,
pulled away —, pushed —, put down —,
raised —, raised up —, reached above —
, reached behind —, reached for —,
reached over —, reached to —,
remembered —, rolled —, rubbed —,
sat —, sat at —, saw —, screamed inside
—, shifted —, shifted to —, shook —,
shrugged —, slipped —, snapped —,
spoke in —, spoke over —, stared at —,
stared over —, stood —, struck —,
studied —, swung —, threw back —,
threw up —, took —, tossed —, tossed
up —, touched —, touched inside —,
turned —, turned away —, turned up —
, used —, wanted —, went for —, went
inside —, went into —, wiped —, wore
over —, worked on —, wrapped —; —
agreed, — answered, — appeared, —
appeared above, — appeared around, —
appeared at, — appeared in, — appeared
on, — appeared over, — appeared to, —
asked, — became, — began to, — bent,
— bent down, — bent in, — bent
together, — blew off, — bowed, —
bowed against, — bowed beneath, —
bowed for, — bowed in, — bowed into,
— bowed like, — bowed over, — bowed
to, — bowed toward, — bowed upon,
— broke, — broke out, — broke
through, — brought, — brought on, —
called out, — came, — came above, —
came around, — came away, — came
back, — came down, — came forward,
— came from, — came into, — came
off, — came out, — came through, —
came to, — came together, — came up,
— came with, — came within, —
carried, — caught, — caught on, —
changed to, — checked, — cleared, —
cleared with, — continued, —
continued to, — covered, — covered by,

— covered with, — cried, — cut off, — did, — disappeared, — disappeared below, — disappeared beneath, — disappeared from, — disappeared in, — disappeared into, — disappeared under, — drew back, — dropped, — dropped between, — dropped down, — dropped forward, — dropped in, — dropped into, — dropped on, — dropped onto, — dropped to, — dropped under, — ended, — fell, — fell across, — fell against, — fell back, — fell between, — fell forward, — fell from, — fell in, — fell into, — fell off, — fell on, — fell onto, — fell to, — felt, — felt like, — felt on, — filled, — filled up, — filled with, — flew, — flew back, — flew off, — flew past, — flew through, — flew up, — followed, — gave, — gestured toward, — glanced off, — got, — grew, — gripped between, — held, — held down, — held up, — hit, — hit with, — hung, — hung at, — hung between, — hung down, — hung forward, — hung from, — hung in, — hung off, — hung over, — hung to, — kept, — kept on, — kicked back, — killed, — knocked, — knocked into, — landed in, — landed on, — landed with, — lay, — lay beside, — lay in, — lay on, — leaned, — leaned against, — leaned back, — leaned out, — leaned over, — leaned through, — leaned to, — leaned together, — left, — left to, — lifted, — lifted in, — lifted on, — lifted up, — lifted with, — liked to, — looked, — looked like, — looked out, — looked to, — looked up, — lost in, — lowered, — lowered against, — lowered between, — lowered in, — lowered inside, — lowered into, — lowered on, — lowered to, — lowered toward, — made, — met, — met beneath, —

moved, — moved across, — moved around, — moved back, — moved beyond, — moved by, — moved in, — moved through, — moved to, — moved up, — needed, — nodded, — nodded around, — nodded in, — nodded with, — ordered, — placed on, — pointed, — pointed down, — pointed in, — pointed toward, — poured, — pressed, — pressed into, — pulled back, — pushed, — pushed forward, — pushed into, — pushed up, — raised, — raised to, — raised upon, — ran with, — rang, — rang in, — rang with, — reached above, — remained, — remained above, — remained down, — replied, — returned, — rode, — rolled, — rolled against, — rolled away, — rolled down, — rolled from, — rolled on, — rolled to, — rose, — rose above, — rose from, — rose off, — rose to, — rose up, — rose with, — rubbed against, — said, — sank, — sank below, — sank beneath, — sank down, — sank in, — sank into, — sat at, — sat behind, — sat on, — screamed, — screamed out, — seemed, — seemed to, — sent, — set off, — set with, — settled, — shifted, — shook, — shook from, — shook in, — shook like, — shook on, — shook up, — shot, — shot off, — shot out, — shot through, — shot to, — shot up, — showed, — showed above, — slammed, — slammed against, — slammed into, — slammed on, — slammed onto, — slammed open, — slid across, — slid into, — slid through, — slipped from, — slipped over, — slipped under, — smelled, — snapped around, — snapped back, — snapped down, — snapped forward, — snapped in, — snapped off, — snapped on, — snapped to, — snapped toward,

— snapped up, — sounded, — spoke, — spoke of, — stared at, — started to, — stayed, — stayed in, — stepped out, — stood, — stood at, — struck, — struck like, — suggested, — swung about, — swung around, — swung away, — swung in, — swung into, — swung to, — swung toward, — swung up, — told, — took, — took in, — tossed from, — tossed in, — touched, — tried to, — turned, — turned around, — turned aside, — turned at, — turned away, — turned by, — turned from, — turned in, — turned into, — turned on, — turned over, — turned to, — turned toward, — turned up, — turned with, — waited, — walked through, — watched over, — waved, — went, — went back, — went below, — went down, — went on, — went out, — went through, — went to, — went under, — went up, — whispered, — wore, — wrapped in, — wrapped up, — yelled

headlight
verbs
— appeared, — appeared at, — appeared in, — appeared on, — appeared over, — approached in, — approached up, — blew, — blinked off, — came from, — came on, — came through, — came to, — came up, — caught, — cut, — cut through, — did, — died, — drew, — grew, — hit, — lit up, — made, — moved away, — passed, — picked out, — rolled, — rose over, — shot across, — shut off, — slid past, — stood in, — stopped at, — swung across, — swung around, — swung into, — threw, — turned, — turned down, — turned off, — went, — went off, — went on, — went out

heart
verbs
answered from —, ate —, broke —, cried in —, crossed —, died with —, felt —, felt in —, filled —, followed —, gave with —, heard —, knew —, knew by —, laid —, laid to —, laughed in —, laughed without —, lifted out —, listened to —, looked at —, looked into —, lost —, missed —, opened —, picked up —, poured out —, put —, said in —, said to —, showed —, smiled with —, spoke against —, spoke from —, started —, stopped —, studied —, took —, took to —, touched —, wanted —, went with —, whispered in —; — added to, — appeared beside, — became, — began to, — blew, — blew open, — broke, — broke at, — broke for, — broke in, — broke into, — brought, — came near, — caught, — caught at, — caught in, — climbed into, — climbed up, — closed, — continued to, — cried, — cried in, — cried out, — cut out, — did, — died, — dropped, — dropped into, — dropped like, — dropped to, — fell, — fell into, — fell to, — felt, — felt like, — filled, — filled up, — filled with, — flew in, — flew up, — fought on, — found, — gave, — gave out, — got away, — grew, — gripped with, — held, — helped to, — hit, — jumped, — jumped at, — jumped from, — jumped into, — jumped through, — jumped to, — jumped with, — kicked, — kicked in, — kicked into, — kicked up, — knew, — knocked, — knocked in, — knocked like, — lay, — lay down, — lay in, — lifted, — lifted at, — lifted for, — lifted up, — lifted with, — lived in, — looked, — looked for, — lost, — made, — missed, — needed, —

opened, — paused, — picked up, —
pulled into, — pulled to, — pushed
against, — reached out, — remained, —
remembered, — remembered to, —
returned, — returned to, — returned
with, — rose, — rose at, — rose in, —
rose into, — said, — sank, — sank at, —
sank down, — sank in, — sank inside,
— sank into, — sank like, — sank on, —
sank to, — sank with, — sat, — sat like,
— seemed, — seemed to, — set on, —
set up, — set upon, — settled, — settled
to, — shook, — shot, — sighed, —
sighed with, — slammed, — slammed
against, — slammed in, — slammed
into, — sounded, — spoke, — started,
— started to, — stepped, — stepped in,
— stood, — stopped, — stopped for, —
stopped in, — stopped with, — threw,
— took, — took in, — took over, —
touched, — tried to, — turned, —
turned over, — turned to, — wanted to,
— went, — went into, — went out, —
went up, — whispered of, — wished to

heat
verbs
— appeared in, — ate through, —
became, — began to, — blew on, —
broke, — broke in, — broke out, —
brought, — came, — came in, — came
off, — came on, — came out, — came
through, — came up, — climbed up, —
continued to, — did, — died away, —
died down, — disappeared, —
disappeared from, — drove, — fell on,
— felt, — filled, — followed, — got, —
grew, — gripped, — held, — held on, —
hung, — hung on, — lay over, — left, —
left through, — lifted into, — lit, —
lost, — made, — met, — moved in, —
moved through, — passed through, —

poured down, — poured out, — poured
over, — poured through, — pressed
down, — pushed, — ran down, — ran
over, — reached, — reached out, —
returned, — returned to, — rolled off,
— rolled out, — rose, — rose from, —
rose in, — rose off, — rose on, — rose
over, — rose to, — rose up, — sank, —
screamed from, — seemed, — seemed
to, — shot down, — shot out, —
shrugged off, — started in, — turned on,
— went, — went on, — went through,
— went up

hedge
verbs
— blinked, — continued, — cut down,
— drew off, — fell against, — felt, —
found, — gestured, — glanced, —
glanced away, — glanced over, — knew,
— laughed, — looked, — looked
around, — moved, — moved up, —
nodded, — opened, — pointed, —
raised, — ran along, — ran down, —
reached, — rubbed at, — said, — sat, —
saw, — seemed to, — settled, — shook,
— shouted, — shrugged, — smiled, —
spoke, — stared, — stared down, —
stared for, — stood, — stood over, —
studied, — threw, — took, — walked,
— watched, — wiped

heel
verbs
felt like —, followed at —, followed on
—, got on —, gripped —, held —, kept
to —, kicked at —, kicked off —, kicked
with —, liked —, placed —, pointed at
—, sank on —, sank to —, sat on —,
settled onto —, slammed —, slid off —,
slipped into —, slipped off —, snapped
—, stayed on —, struck with —, swung

on —, took off —, took to —, turned —
, turned on —, wore —; — came, —
came along, — came off, — came out, —
caught, — caught in, — caught on, —
drove into, — found, — headed for, —
hit, — hung over, — kicked up, —
looked, — moved up, — pointed, —
pressed against, — pressed into, —
promised to, — pushed against, — rang
against, — rang on, — sank into, —
slammed down, — slid across, — slipped
on, — sounded, — started, — struck, —
took, — touched, — turned, — walked
in

helicopter
verbs
— appeared, — appeared above, —
appeared on, — approached, — became,
— began, — began to, — blew up, —
came, — came around, — came down,
— came in, — came into, — came to, —
changed, — climbed, — climbed above,
— continued to, — crossed, —
disappeared from, — drew, — dropped,
— dropped down, — dropped from, —
dropped into, — entered, — fell from,
— filled, — flew, — flew in, — flew
over, — flew past, — flew up, —
followed, — got in, — grew, — hit, —
hung, — hung in, — hung on, —
landed, — landed in, — landed on, —
lay on, — left, — let loose, — lifted, —
lifted away, — lifted into, — lifted off,
— lifted up, — lost, — made, — passed,
— reached, — returned, — rose, — rose
from, — sat on, — seemed to, — set
down, — settled onto, — shook, —
snapped through, — sounded, —
sounded like, — started to, — stopped,
— swung, — swung around, — swung
toward, — took, — took off, — took

on, — took to, — touched down, —
tried to, — turned, — waited, — went
down, — went up

hesitation
verbs
added without —, admitted without —,
agreed without —, answered without —
, came without —, caught —, continued
without —, dropped —, explained —,
felt —, heard —, left without —, missed
—, moved without —, nodded without
—, noticed —, offered without —, read
—, replied with —, replied without —,
returned without —, said after —, said
with —, said without —, saw —,
showed —, spoke without —, stepped
without —, understood —, walked
without —, wondered about —

highway
verbs
came to —, crossed —, drove across —,
drove along —, drove down —, drove
onto —, found —, glanced toward —,
got off —, got to —, hit —, left —,
looked down —, looked up —, pulled
off —, pulled on —, pulled onto —, ran
along —, reached —, settled onto —,
smelled like —, stared at —, started
toward —, stayed off —, stayed on —,
stopped at —, turned off —, turned
onto —, walked toward —

hill
verbs
came over —, climbed —, climbed
through —, climbed up —, continued
down —, continued up —, drove down
—, drove past —, drove up —, entered
—, found —, glanced down —, glanced
toward —, headed toward —, headed up

—, lived over —, looked around —, looked at —, looked down —, looked toward —, looked up —, moved up —, nodded down —, nodded toward —, pointed along —, pointed down —, pointed to —, pointed up —, ran down —, ran up —, saw —, slid down —, stared at —, started down —, started for —, started up —, stood on —, stopped up —, used —, walked down —, walked up —, went down —, went up —; — appeared to, — brought, — came, — changed, — climbed to, — drew near, — dropped away, — ended in, — felt, — grew, — led from, — led to, — looked like, — made, — made of, — met, — offered, — ran, — rang, — rose, — rose in, — rose into, — rose toward, — rose up, — seemed to, — shook from, — slid, — slid in, — stood, — stood upon, — took, — turned, — went down, — went on, — went up

hip
verbs
broke —, caught —, grabbed —, gripped —, held —, kissed —, landed on —, leaned on —, lifted —, moved —, nodded at —, raised —, reached for —, reached to —, rolled —, rolled to —, rubbed —, settled —, shifted —, shoved at —, swung —, swung from —, touched —, turned —, wore at —, wrapped up —; — became, — began, — began to, — bent, — came back, — caught, — drew back, — drove into, — fell, — fell between, — felt, — felt against, — fought, — gave, — got, — hit, — left, — lifted, — met, — moved, — moved against, — moved in, — moved into, — opened, — pressed into, — pulled back, — pushed, — pushed

forward, — pushed together, — pushed up, — rang, — rolled in, — rolled into, — rose, — rubbed along, — seemed to, — sent, — shifted, — shook in, — snapped, — started to, — stepped forward, — stood out, — swung in, — took on, — took over, — touched, — worked

hole
verbs
blew into —, climbed from —, climbed into —, climbed through —, did —, disappeared into —, dropped through —, entered —, fell down —, fell into —, filled —, filled in —, found —, gestured at —, jumped into —, looked around —, looked at —, looked into —, looked through —, nodded at —, nodded into —, pointed out —, pointed to —, poured into —, reached —, reached into —, reached through —, reached to —, saw —, shouted into —, spoke into —, stared at —, started for —, stepped into —, stepped through —, stepped to —, studied —, watched —, waved to —, went through —, went to —, yelled into —; — appeared, — appeared about, — appeared between, — appeared in, — appeared to, — began to, — called, — came, — closed, — cut for, — cut in, — cut into, — cut out, — disappeared, — fell away, — filled by, — filled in, — filled with, — grew, — held, — led to, — left by, — left to, — looked, — looked down, — looked like, — made, — opened, — opened at, — opened in, — opened up, — played, — put in, — ran down, — rose, — said, — seemed, — seemed to, — took, — waited

home

verbs

arrived —, arrived at —, broke into —, brought —, called —, called from —, came —, came from —, came to —, carried —, considered —, continued —, continued on —, did at —, did like —, died at —, drove —, drove toward —, entered —, felt at —, flew —, followed —, found —, glanced around —, got —, got to —, headed —, headed for —, headed into —, knew from —, left —, left at —, left for —, liked —, lived at —, looked at —, loved —, made —, missed —, moved between —, needed —, opened —, passed —, pointed toward —, pushed —, ran —, ran from —, ran toward —, reached —, returned —, returned to —, sat at —, saw —, saw at —, sent —, set off —, settled into —, slid —, started —, started for —, stayed —, stayed at —, stepped into —, thought about —, thought of —, took —, tried —, turned for —, turned toward —, walked —, walked from —, walked into —, wanted —, watched —, went —, went on —, went to —, whispered of —, worked at —, worked from —; — appeared to, — began to, — called, — came to, — changed, — cried, — did, — felt, — felt like, — filled with, — grew, — knew, — left, — looked, — looked like, — looked out, — made, — meant, — put to, — rang, — read, — remained, — rose in, — sat, — sat astride, — sat on, — seemed, — seemed to, — set on, — settled, — settled in, — showed, — stared at, — stood, — stood open, — turned into, — watched, — went about, — went by, — went over

hope
verbs

— answered, — began to, — blew out, — came down, — came into, — came to, — climbed up, — died, — died in, — dropped, — entered, — fell, — filled, — gave, — grew, — lay in, — lay with, — left, — left for, — left to, — lit, — made, — rang in, — remained, — returned with, — rose, — rose in, — sank, — sank down, — sank in, — seemed, — seemed to, — showed on, — slid through, — started, — took, — turned to, — went out, — went up, — woke up

horn
verbs

— began to, — blew, — blew for, — blew in, — blew on, — blew out, — broke off, — broke with, — called through, — came, — came down, — continued, — continued to, — died, — died away, — drove, — fell, — filled, — flew from, — grew above, — hit, — laid, — lay at, — made, — rang out, — returned, — screamed, — seemed, — seemed to, — set upon, — sounded, — sounded across, — sounded behind, — sounded from, — sounded in, — sounded like, — sounded on, — sounded to, — stared at, — stayed, — stopped, — struck, — took, — took up, — turned

horror
verbs

asked in —, felt —, gasped in —, gasped with —, paused in —, realized in —, realized with —, remembered —, repeated with —, said in —, said with —, screamed in —, screamed with —, shook with —, shouted in —, stared at —, stared in —, started in —, started

with —, stood in —, swallowed in —,
thought in —, watched —, watched in
—, watched with —, whispered in —;
— appeared on, — became, — began to,
— broke through, — came back, —
came into, — came on, — came out, —
came over, — came upon, — crossed, —
felt, — filled, — hit like, — landed on,
— lay at, — lay in, — passed over, —
passed through, — returned, — rolled
through, — rose, — saw, — seemed, —
seemed to, — shook, — showed on, —
sounded on, — struck, — went out, —
went up

horse

verbs

appeared astride —, approached —,
asked —, ate like —, brought —, called
for —, caught —, checked —, checked
on —, climbed from —, climbed on —,
demanded from —, dropped from —,
fell from —, fell off —, felt —, followed
with —, found —, glanced at —, got —,
got off —, got on —, heard —, helped
with —, jumped off —, jumped on —,
kept —, kicked —, kicked at —, killed
—, knew —, leaned from —, led —, left
—, liked —, looked at —, looked toward
—, lost —, loved —, made for —,
missed —, moved —, ordered —, pulled
—, pushed —, ran to —, reached —,
recognized —, returned to —, rode —,
said to —, sat —, sat atop —, sat on —,
saw —, slid from —, slid off —, slipped
off —, smelled —, stared at —, stepped
from —, stood between —, stopped —,
struck at —, studied —, swung from —,
swung off —, told —, took —, turned
—, turned to —, used —, walked —,
walked past —, walked to —, walked
toward —, watched —, went to —,

whispered to —, yelled at —; —
appeared like, — approached, —
became, — began to, — blinked, —
broke, — broke from, — broke into, —
brought back, — brought to, — called
out, — came, — came by, — came
down, — came on, — came onto, —
came up, — carried, — caught, —
cleared, — climbed, — closed, —
continued on, — continued to, —
covered, — crossed, — cut, — did, —
died, — dropped, — dropped in, —
dropped on, — fell, — fell into, — fell
like, — fell on, — filled, — flew out, —
flew past, — followed in, — fought, —
found, — gave, — gave out, — heard, —
held in, — hung, — jumped, — jumped
forward, — kept on, — kicked, —
kicked at, — kicked in, — kicked up, —
knew, — landed, — lay, — lay at, — lay
on, — left, — let out, — lifted, —
looked, — looked up, — lowered, —
made, — made of, — meant, — missed,
— missed from, — moved, — moved
forward, — moved in, — moved up, —
passed, — pulled, — pulled through, —
put, — put down, — put on, — raised,
— ran down, — ran in, — ran on, —
ran up, — reached, — remained, — rode
out, — rode over, — rolled, — rose, —
rose from, — saw, — screamed, —
screamed in, — seemed, — seemed to,
— set down, — set off, — settled down,
— shifted, — shot out, — slammed
into, — slipped, — slipped under, —
snapped, — stared at, — stepped past,
— stood, — stood on, — stood up, —
stopped, — stopped in, — swung, —
threw, — took, — took off, — tossed,
— tried to, — turned, — waited, —
waited behind, — walked, — walked in,
— walked off, — walked under, —

wanted to, — went, — went by, — went down, — went in, — went into, — wore

hospital
verbs
arrived at —, called —, called from —, came at —, checked into —, drove to —, entered —, found —, got from —, got to —, knew —, left —, left for —, lived at —, needed —, nodded toward —, passed in —, pointed toward —, reached —, remained in —, rolled into —, stayed at —, turned at —, walked past —, walked toward —, went to —, worked at —, worked in —

host
verbs
— added, — appeared above, — approached, — approached through, — arrived at, — asked, — broke, — came, — came against, — came at, — came behind, — came forth, — drew up, — entered, — gave, — laid aside, — lay, — leaned forward, — made, — nodded, — ordered, — passed, — pointed to, — pressed, — pushed through, — read, — replied, — returned, — rode on, — said, — seemed, — shook, — sighed, — smiled into, — talked to, — took, — turned, — went

hotel
verbs
called —, checked into —, continued past —, drove past —, drove to —, entered —, found —, gave —, got —, got to —, knew —, left —, looked at —, moved into —, nodded toward —, pointed toward —, ran inside —, reached —, returned to —, stayed in —,

walked into —, went into —, went to —, worked at —, wrote —

hour
verbs
arrived —, arrived within —, asked —, began —, called —, came within —, climbed through —, cried for —, did after —, died in —, drew for —, drove —, drove for —, felt —, filled —, got —, hated —, kept —, knew —, left —, left after —, liked —, looked for —, played for —, put —, ran for —, remembered for —, returned —, sat for —, slept —, slept for —, spent —, spoke for —, stared for —, stayed —, stayed about —, stayed for —, stood for —, stopped —, talked for —, thought about —, thought by —, thought of —, tried —, waited —, waited for —, walked for —, watched —, watched for —, woke —, worked —, worked for —, worked through —, wrote for —; — approached, — arrived from, — became, — began, — began to, — brought, — came, — came up, — covered, — dropped, — ended, — fell into, — felt, — filled in, — flew by, — gripped, — hung around, — lay in, — leaned over, — left, — left of, — lived, — lived in, — looked over, — looked through, — lost in, — made, — meant, — moved through, — moved toward, — passed, — passed in, — passed with, — pushed, — rang, — remained before, — rolled around, — rolled away, — rolled by, — sat by, — sat in, — seemed, — seemed like, — seemed to, — showed, — slid by, — slipped away, — slipped by, — spent, — spent on, — stared at, — started, — stopped, — stopped to, — tossed in, — turned into, — turned to, — walked, — went, —

went by, — went on, — went over, —
wore on, — worked, — worked on, —
worked out

house
verbs
approached —, arrived at —, began at
—, began with —, blew into —, bought
—, broke into —, called —, called about
—, called around —, called into —,
came among —, came into —, came
near —, came to —, came with —,
checked through —, chose —,
considered —, continued into —,
continued past —, did —, died in —,
disappeared behind —, disappeared
inside —, disappeared into —, drove by
—, drove past —, drove to —, entered
—, fell against —, flew from —, flew
through —, found —, found beneath —
, gestured at —, gestured to —, gestured
toward —, glanced around —, glanced
at —, glanced into —, glanced toward
—, got —, got in —, got to —, gripped
—, hated —, headed for —, headed into
—, headed through —, headed toward
—, held up —, helped around —, helped
in —, hit —, kept —, kept up —, knew
—, knew about —, leaned against —,
leaned into —, left —, liked —, listened
to —, lived at —, lived in —, looked
about —, looked around —, looked at
—, looked between —, looked over —,
looked through —, looked toward —,
lost —, loved —, meant —, missed —,
moved —, moved around —, moved
into —, moved through —, moved up
—, nodded at —, nodded to —, nodded
toward —, passed —, passed between —
, passed by —, passed through —,
paused inside —, paused outside —,
played before —, pointed at —, pointed
in —, pointed inside —, pointed out —,
pointed to —, pointed toward —, put
—, ran —, ran at —, ran behind —, ran
for —, ran from —, ran into —, ran
through —, ran to —, ran toward —,
reached —, recognized —, remained in
—, remained outside —, remembered
—, returned to —, sat around —, sat in
—, saw —, shouted into —, slept in —,
slipped between —, slipped in —,
slipped inside —, slipped into —, spent
at —, stared at —, stared toward —,
started for —, started to —, started
toward —, stayed at —, stayed in —,
stepped inside —, stepped into —, stood
against —, stood outside —, stopped at
—, stopped before —, stopped outside
—, studied —, thought about —,
thought of —, told —, told about —,
took —, took in —, tried —, turned into
—, turned to —, turned toward —,
waited at —, walked —, walked around
—, walked between —, walked from —,
walked in —, walked inside —, walked
into —, walked through —, walked to
—, walked toward —, wanted —,
watched —, went around —, went by —
, went in —, went inside —, went into
—, went past —, went through —, went
to —, wondered about —, wore around
—, worked around —, worked on —,
yelled into —; — appeared, — appeared
in, — appeared on, — appeared to, —
became, — began to, — blew down, —
blew out, — called, — came, — came
down, — came from, — came into, —
came on, — came over, — came up, —
came with, — carried, — caught, —
caught on, — closed, — continued, —
continued on, — continued to, — did,
— disappeared, — disappeared from, —
disappeared on, — dropped by, —

ended in, — entered, — fell, — fell
down, — fell into, — fell on, — felt, —
felt like, — filled up, — filled with, —
flew, — flew open, — fought for, —
gave, — gave away, — gave back, — got,
— grew, — held, — laid in, — landed
on, — lay, — lay across, — lay in, — lay
on, — led on, — looked, — looked
about, — looked at, — looked for, —
looked in, — looked like, — looked
through, — made, — made of, — met,
— moved, — moved around, — moved
past, — needed, — offered, — opened,
— opened onto, — opened to, —
opened with, — pulled, — put, — put
into, — ran in, — rang, — remained, —
returned, — returned to, — rose, —
rose into, — said, — sat, — sat at, — sat
by, — sat in, — sat on, — sat upon, —
seemed, — seemed like, — seemed to, —
sent, — set, — set back, — set on, —
settled at, — settled into, — shook, —
shook from, — shook on, — showed, —
slept, — slid, — slid past, — smelled, —
smelled like, — smelled of, — sounded,
— sounded like, — started to, — stayed,
— stayed on, — stood, — stood for, —
stood in, — stood on, — stood open, —
stood out, — struck, — talked about, —
took, — touched, — tried to, — turned,
— turned out, — waited, — waited for,
— watched, — went back, — went into,
— went on, — went out, — went up, —
whispered, — wore, — worked, —
worked into, — worked like

hunger

verbs

— added to, — became, — began to, —
came, — came upon, — cut through, —
did, — drew, — felt in, — forced, —
grew, — grew between, — hit, —

kicked, — kicked in, — knew, — left, —
left in, — made, — passed, — poured
down, — reached for, — returned, —
returned with, — rose in, — sank, —
seemed to, — shot through, — stopped,
— took over, — woke, — woke like, —
worked through

ice

verbs

— became, — began to, — broke loose,
— broke with, — brought back, —
closed about, — closed in, — closed
over, — covered, — cut through, —
disappeared, — fell, — fell like, — fell
to, — filled, — flew in, — gave, — got,
— held, — hung from, — hung off, —
kicked in, — knocked against, — lay, —
left, — poured down, — poured in, —
ran down, — ran through, — rang, —
rang like, — remained, — rose, — rose
beyond, — rose from, — rose on, —
seemed to, — settled in, — shifted, —
shot through, — slammed into, — slid
into, — slid through, — struck, — took
on, — waited to, — wrapped around

idea

verbs

— began to, — broke through, — broke
up, — brought, — came, — came along,
— came from, — came into, — came to,
— came with, — caught, — crossed, —
dropped into, — ended in, — entered,
— fell, — filled in, — flew in, — gave,
— grew, — happened to, — held, — hit,
— led to, — left, — made, — ran
through, — sat, — seemed, — seemed
like, — seemed to, — sent, — sounded,
— struck, — took, — worked

image

verbs

appeared in —, blinked at —, blinked away —, called up —, came to —, caught —, cleared —, closed down —, glanced at —, grabbed at —, held —, held up —, learned of —, liked —, looked at —, looked over —, nodded to —, paused —, pointed at —, pointed to —, pulled —, pulled up —, recognized —, saw —, sent —, set up —, shook away —, shook off —, showed —, smiled at —, stared at —, studied —, took —, turned to —, worked at —; — appeared, — appeared against, — appeared in, — appeared on, — became, — began, — began to, — blinked, — blinked out, — broke, — brought, — came, — came back, — came from, — came in, — came into, — came of, — came through, — came to, — came up, — came with, — caught in, — changed, — changed to, — closed, — continued to, — cut to, — did, — disappeared, — fell away, — filled, — filled with, — flew at, — followed, — grew, — hit, — joined to, — jumped, — jumped onto, — looked to, — made, — moved, — moved beneath, — moved in, — moved past, — opened, — played, — played across, — played in, — played of, — played through, — poured through, — pulled from, — pushed, — remained, — remained in, — reminded, — returned to, — rose behind, — rose in, — rose to, — rose up, — said, — seemed, — seemed to, — sent, — set to, — shifted, — shifted to, — shook, — shot around, — showed, — slammed into, — snapped into, — spoke to, — started to, — stood up, — took, — turned into, — went, — went away, — went by, — worked

impact
verbs

— blew, — came, — came on, — caught, — felt in, — felt like, — finished, — forced, — knocked, — knocked over, — lifted, — looked like, — lost in, — made, — missed, — pushed, — ran up, — sent, — shook, — shot, — shot up, — slammed into, — snapped, — sounded in, — took, — took off, — turned

information
verbs

— answered, — appeared, — became, — brought, — came, — came after, — came at, — came back, — came from, — came in, — came out, — came through, — came up, — came with, — changed, — flew across, — found, — helped, — made, — needed to, — passed through, — poured through, — remained, — rolled up, — seemed to, — turned out, — went to

instinct
verbs

— answered, — brought, — called on, — came, — kept, — kicked, — kicked back, — kicked in, — kicked into, — knew, — knocked around, — lit up, — made, — picked up, — reached out, — rolled, — said, — screamed at, — screamed for, — seemed to, — sent, — told, — took, — took over, — tried to, — turned, — went, — went into, — went on, — went through, — whispered into

intercom
verbs

asked over —, asked through —, called over —, came on —, demanded through —, got on —, hit —, leaned over —, leaned toward —, looked at —, picked up —, pointed to —, pressed —, pushed —, rang —, said into —, said over —, said through —, shut off —, spoke into —, spoke through —, told —, took over —, turned off —, turned on —, went to —

jacket
verbs
bent for —, checked —, checked inside —, closed —, dropped —, found —, got —, got on —, grabbed —, grabbed onto —, grabbed up —, gripped —, heard —, held up —, hung —, hung up —, left —, left with —, let —, lifted up —, liked —, loved —, moved —, needed —, opened —, picked through —, picked up —, pulled at —, pulled off —, pulled on —, pulled open —, pulled out —, put —, put on —, ran for —, reached beneath —, reached for —, reached in —, reached inside —, reached into —, reached under —, recognized —, saw —, shook off —, shrugged into —, shrugged off —, slid —, slid back —, slid off —, slipped between —, slipped into —, slipped off —, slipped on —, threw —, threw off —, threw on —, took —, took off —, tossed —, tossed off —, tossed on —, touched —, went into —, wished for —, wore —; — appeared in, — approached, — blew on, — came from, — came off, — closed, — covered, — covered with, — cut off, — entered, — fell open, — filled, — flew onto, — flew past, — hung, — hung around, — hung off, — hung on, — hung open, — hung over, — lay on, — looked, — made, —

made of, — opened, — raised, — read, — said, — sent up, — slid open, — slipped from, — smelled, — stepped forward, — stepped out, — stood in, — talked to, — tossed over, — turned up, — waited, — worked

jaw
verbs
— became, — began to, — came, — came up, — closed around, — closed in, — closed on, — closed over, — closed to, — closed with, — drew, — dropped, — dropped around, — dropped at, — dropped in, — dropped open, — dropped to, — fell off, — fell open, — felt, — filled with, — gave, — held, — held open, — hung, — hung down, — hung for, — hung loose, — hung open, — jumped, — lifted, — lifted in, — looked, — met, — moved, — moved at, — opened, — pulled, — pulled back, — remained, — seemed to, — set, — set against, — set in, — set into, — set like, — set with, — shifted, — shook, — shut, — shut on, — shut with, — snapped, — snapped at, — snapped down, — snapped over, — snapped through, — stood out, — took on, — turned into, — turned to, — went back, — went for, — went on, — went to, — worked, — worked in, — worked through, — worked with

jeans
verbs
appeared in —, arrived in —, changed into —, chose —, dropped —, fought off —, glanced at —, got into —, grabbed —, helped with —, kicked off —, liked —, picked up —, pulled —, pulled off —, pulled on —, pulled up —,

put on —, reached for —, reached into —, sat in —, shoved —, slipped on —, snapped —, stepped into —, studied —, threw —, threw on —, took off —, touched —, wore —; — came into, — covered, — dropped to, — felt, — filled with, — followed, — got out, — held up, — hit, — hung, — hung off, — left, — looked, — looked at, — made, — moved, — moved along, — picked out, — ran down, — rode, — rolled up, — seemed to, — shoved in, — slid open, — stepped forward, — stood, — stood on, — walked by

key
verbs
asked for —, bent toward —, brought —, brought out —, caught —, drew —, drew out —, dropped —, felt for —, forced —, found —, frowned at —, gave back —, got —, got out —, grabbed —, grabbed for —, handed —, handed over —, heard —, held —, held onto —, held out —, held up —, hit —, jumped for —, kept —, knew —, knew about —, lifted —, looked at —, lost —, managed —, needed —, offered —, picked up —, placed —, pointed to —, pressed —, pulled —, pulled out —, pushed —, put —, raised —, reached for —, remembered —, returned with —, set down —, slid in —, slipped in —, stared at —, threw —, threw away —, told —, took —, took off —, took out —, tossed —, touched —, tried —, turned —, turned back —, used —, waited for —, worked —; — answered, — became, — began to, — came, — decided, — did in, — dropped to, — entered, — fell from, — fell into, — fell out, — felt, — filled, — found, — gave, — glanced from, —

held, — hung, — hung from, — hung near, — hung on, — landed on, — lay in, — lay on, — left, — let out, — lowered, — made, — made of, — made under, — meant, — missed, — opened, — pressed into, — pressed to, — sat in, — slid, — slid in, — slid into, — slipped in, — slipped into, — sounded, — struck, — turned, — turned in, — turned over, — turned to, — went, — went into, — went under, — worked

keyboard
verbs
bent over —, dropped —, frowned at —, hit —, leaned into —, leaned over —, left —, looked at —, looked over —, moved —, pointed at —, pressed —, pulled out —, pulled over —, reached for —, returned to —, sat at —, slid —, slid between —, stared at —, swung to —, touched —, turned on —, turned to —, went at —, went to —, worked —, worked on —

kiss
verbs
blew —, broke —, broke from —, broke off —, came for —, changed —, did during —, drew from —, ended —, felt —, felt about —, held —, leaned into —, liked —, meant —, met —, moved into —, paused in —, remembered —, returned —, said with —, sank into —, saw —, sighed into —, took —, turned into —, wanted —; — became, — broke, — caught, — continued, — did, — ended, — ended with, — felt, — filled with, — got, — grew, — grew in, — landed in, — left, — made, — meant, — moved, — moved like, — moved to, — pulled, — put, — said, — sent, —

sent through, — set off, — spoke for, — started, — stopped, — took, — took away, — took on, — turned from, — turned into, — went on, — went through

kitchen
verbs

appeared from —, approached —, arrived at —, arrived in —, asked from —, called from —, came across —, came from —, came inside —, came into —, came through —, came to —, came toward —, checked —, checked on —, cried to —, crossed —, crossed to —, did —, disappeared into —, disappeared to —, entered —, entered through —, fell into —, finished —, flew into —, found —, gestured around —, gestured toward —, glanced around —, glanced at —, glanced in —, glanced into —, glanced toward —, got to —, headed for —, headed into —, headed through —, headed to —, headed toward —, heard from —, helped in —, hit —, kept in —, laughed from —, left —, left for —, liked about —, lit up —, lived in —, looked around —, looked at —, looked into —, looked through —, looked toward —, lost —, loved —, moved around —, moved from —, moved into —, moved through —, moved to —, moved toward —, nodded across —, nodded toward —, passed —, passed through —, paused in —, pointed to —, pointed toward —, pushed through —, ran around —, ran into —, ran over —, ran to —, ran toward —, reached —, remained in —, replied from —, returned from —, returned to —, rolled between —, said from —, sat in —, settled in —, shouted from —, shouted into —, slammed into —, slipped into —, slipped through —, smiled around —, stared across —, stared around —, stared into —, started for —, started in —, started into —, started to —, started toward —, stayed in —, stepped across —, stepped from —, stepped inside —, stepped into —, stepped toward —, stood in —, stood near —, stopped at —, stopped in —, studied —, took —, took over —, turned into —, turned to —, turned toward —, waited in —, walked across —, walked from —, walked into —, walked past —, walked through —, walked to —, walked toward —, watched from —, waved at —, went across —, went in —, went inside —, went into —, went through —, went to —, went toward —, whispered in —, worked in —, yelled from —; — began to, — came, — came into, — carried, — closed, — dropped, — explained, — fell, — felt, — filled with, — finished, — flew open, — gave off, — gripped at, — happened to, — held, — laughed, — lay, — left open, — looked, — looked in, — looked like, — looked out, — made, — opened, — opened into, — opened to, — put, — sat, — seemed, — seemed to, — sent, — sent up, — set to, — showed, — shut up, — smelled, — smelled of, — tried, — waited for, — watched, — went

knee
verbs

bent —, bent at —, brought to —, brought up —, came on —, came to —, climbed to —, drew up —, dropped on —, dropped onto —, dropped to —, drove —, fell on —, fell onto —, fell to —, gestured to —, got —, got off —, got

on —, got onto —, got to —, grabbed —
, gripped —, held —, hung over —,
kissed —, landed on —, leaned on —,
leaned onto —, leaned over —, lifted —,
looked at —, lowered —, lowered to —,
offered —, pressed —, pulled up —,
pushed onto —, pushed to —, raised —,
raised to —, reached toward —,
remained on —, returned to —, rolled
on —, rolled onto —, rolled to —, rose
from —, rose on —, rose to —, rubbed
—, sank onto —, sank to —, sat on —,
settled to —, shifted on —, shot to —,
shoved to —, slid on —, slid onto —,
slid to —, slipped to —, stayed on —,
stepped between —, struck —, thought
about —, took —, touched —, used —,
went for —, went on —, went to —,
yelled into —; — answered, —
appeared, — appeared to, — asked, —
began to, — bent, — bent for, — bent
in, — bent under, — broke open, —
came down, — came up, — closed into,
— crossed, — drew up, — fell out, —
felt, — felt like, — filled with, — found,
— gave, — gave out, — got, — held, —
hit, — hung in, — knocked beneath, —
lifted to, — lifted under, — looked like,
— lost, — made, — moved, — pointed
at, — pressed against, — pressed down,
— pressed into, — pressed to, — pressed
together, — pulled to, — pulled toward,
— pulled up, — pushed between, —
raised, — rubbed against, — sank into,
— screamed in, — shifted, — shook, —
shook from, — shook under, —
slammed against, — slammed into, —
slipped, — snapped, — snapped
together, — started to, — stayed, —
stayed for, — stood out, — stopped, —
struck, — took, — touched, — tried to,

— turned to, — went, — went into, —
went out, — went to

knife

verbs

brought —, brought out —, carried —,
caught —, closed —, crossed —, drew —
, drew out —, dropped —, explained
about —, fell on —, found —, gestured
with —, glanced at —, glanced between
—, got —, grabbed —, gripped —, hated
—, held —, held up —, kept —, knew of
—, laid —, laid aside —, leaned on —,
leaned with —, left —, lifted —, lifted
up —, liked —, looked at —, lost —,
lowered —, moved —, nodded at —,
passed back —, picked up —, placed —,
pointed with —, pressed —, pulled —,
pulled out —, pushed —, pushed against
—, put —, put down —, raised —, ran
with —, reached —, reached for —,
reached with —, recognized —,
remembered —, saw —, set —, set down
—, slammed —, slammed down —,
slipped out —, stared at —, struck with
—, studied —, swung —, thought about
—, thought of —, threw —, threw down
—, took —, took out —, took up —,
tried —, used —, waved —, went under
—, wiped —, wished for —, worked
with —, wrapped —; — appeared, —
appeared at, — appeared in, — appeared
with, — began to, — called, — came, —
came at, — came down, — came
forward, — came out, — came up, —
caught, — caught in, — cut, — cut
across, — cut down, — cut into, — died,
— disappeared, — dropped, — dropped
from, — dropped to, — drove into, —
fell, — fell from, — fell into, — fell to,
— felt, — felt like, — flew away, — flew
from, — fought in, — found, — glanced

off, — gripped in, — handed, — handed
down, — held, — held back, — held
out, — held to, — hesitated, — hung in,
— laid on, — lay between, — lay on, —
left, — left to, — lifted, — looked, —
looked like, — made, — made of, —
meant for, — moved, — moved down,
— moved on, — moved with, — passed,
— passed by, — paused, — pointed at,
— pressed against, — pressed down, —
pressed into, — pushed down, — raised,
— rang in, — rode beneath, — rode on,
— rose, — sank, — sank in, — sank
into, — sat on, — seemed, — seemed to,
— shook, — shot, — showed in, —
slammed against, — slid beneath, — slid
between, — slid from, — slid in, — slid
onto, — slid past, — slipped, — slipped
away, — slipped between, — slipped
from, — slipped into, — slipped
through, — stayed out, — stopped, —
swung down, — swung from, — took,
— took down, — touched, — turned,
— turned in, — went, — went between,
— went in, — went into

knuckle

verbs

— began to, — came away, — covered
with, — dropped against, — glanced off,
— grew, — gripped, — hit, — kept, —
left in, — looked, — pressed against, —
remained, — said, — screamed, —
shifted, — shook, — showed, — started
to, — stood out, — struck, — touched,
— turned, — went, — went in

lab

verbs

called —, called from —, came into —,
came to —, crossed —, disappeared into
—, entered —, flew across —, glanced

around —, left —, lived in —, looked
across —, looked around —, loved —,
reached —, returned to —, spent in —,
stepped inside —, stepped into —,
swung by —, walked across —, walked
into —, went into —, went to —,
worked in —

ladder

verbs

arrived at —, came down —, came up —
, cleared —, climbed —, climbed down
—, climbed off —, climbed up —,
dropped down —, fell off —, found —,
got to —, grabbed —, grabbed for —,
hesitated before —, hung from —, hung
on —, left —, needed —, nodded at —,
opened up —, pointed to —, pulled up
—, raised —, ran down —, ran to —,
reached —, returned to —, saw —,
shifted on —, slid down —, started up
—, stepped from —, stepped off —,
stepped to —, stood at —, stood by —,
turned to —, turned toward —, walked
to —, waved toward —, went down —,
went over —, went to —

lake

verbs

became —, bought —, came off —,
came to —, continued around —,
crossed —, glanced across —, got to —,
hit —, left —, looked across —, looked
at —, looked into —, looked over —,
made —, passed —, pointed across —,
pointed to —, reached —, said from —,
saw —, stared across —, stared at —,
stared toward —, stood to —, stopped
beside —, studied —, turned from —,
turned toward —; — began to, —
brought, — came in, — came into, —
caught, — closed, — covered with, —

cried out, — cut into, — died away, — filled with, — happened to, — heard, — jumped forward, — kept, — lay, — lay between, — looked like, — looked out, — looked to, — met, — opened out, — poured in, — ran up, — rode, — rode together, — rose, — seemed, — seemed at, — seemed to, — slammed into, — sounded, — started, — stood, — took, — tried to, — turned, — went from, — went to

lamp
verbs
blew out —, drew —, dropped —, filled —, found —, glanced at —, got —, grabbed —, held up —, lifted —, lit —, lowered —, picked up —, pointed to —, raised —, reached for —, set down —, slid —, snapped off —, stood beneath —, swung —, took —, turned off —, turned on —, turned out —, watched —, went to —; — began to, — blinked off, — came on, — came up, — did, — dropped from, — fell on, — fell through, — filled, — held forth, — held in, — hit, — hung, — hung from, — hung over, — hung upon, — lay on, — lit, — lit by, — made, — made of, — sat, — seemed to, — set about, — set on, — shot, — showed up, — stood on, — swung above, — swung from, — threw, — took to, — turned, — turned on, — turned up, — went, — went on, — went out, — worked

land
verbs
— became, — began, — began in, — began to, — broke, — brought, — came down, — caught, — caught in, — changed to, — cleared by, — covered

with, — disappeared, — dropped away, — dropped down, — dropped off, — fell, — fell away, — fell into, — filled with, — grew, — held, — joined together, — laid, — lay, — lay about, — lay under, — left, — lit, — looked, — looked like, — lost, — lost to, — made, — moved, — moved on, — opened, — opened into, — opened up, — paused, — put on, — ran down, — remained, — returned to, — rolled, — rolled past, — rose, — rose from, — rose in, — rose into, — rose to, — rose up, — sank beneath, — seemed, — seemed to, — settled onto, — shook under, — took, — took on, — turned, — went, — worked in

lantern
verbs
— appeared, — appeared on, — came into, — disappeared, — fell, — fell on, — fell over, — held, — helped, — hung, — hung above, — hung between, — hung from, — hung in, — hung inside, — hung over, — joined to, — lit, — lit at, — lit by, — made, — made of, — played on, — raised, — rose in, — sat on, — seemed to, — set into, — set on, — set upon, — slammed against, — swung, — swung from, — swung on, — swung over, — went, — went out

laptop
verbs
bent over —, bent to —, brought —, brought up —, carried —, checked —, closed —, demanded —, dropped —, gestured at —, gestured to —, glanced at —, glanced between —, glanced to —, got —, grabbed —, held out —, kept —, leaned to —, leaned toward —, looked

at —, nodded at —, opened —, opened up —, picked up —, pointed to —, pulled out —, put —, put down —, reached for —, remembered —, returned to —, set —, set aside —, set up —, settled with —, shifted to —, shut —, shut down —, slid open —, stared at —, took —, took out —, turned —, turned off —, turned on —, turned to —, used —, waved at —, waved to —, went to —

lash
verbs

— came up, — caught, — did, — dropped over, — fell across, — frowned, — handed, — laughed, — lay against, — leaned, — leaned back, — left, — looked around, — looked at, — looked down, — looked out, — looked through, — looked up, — lowered, — moved, — picked up, — sat in, — shoved, — slipped, — smiled, — stared at, — started to, — stood in, — stood up, — stopped, — tossed, — touched, — tried to, — turned to, — walked into, — walked out, — walked through, — went across, — went around, — went over

laugh
verbs

added with —, admitted with —, agreed with —, answered with —, asked between —, asked with —, blew out —, breathed out —, broke into —, continued with —, did —, did with —, felt —, forced —, forced out —, gasped —, gave —, heard —, held back —, laughed —, let out —, liked —, looked for —, loved —, made —, managed —, needed —, offered —, repeated with —,

replied with —, said around —, said through —, said with —, saw —, shouted with —, swallowed —, tried for —, watched —; — became, — began in, — blew out, — broke, — broke into, — broke out, — came, — came from, — came in, — came out, — came up, — carried down, — cut off, — died, — died away, — ended in, — fell out, — filled with, — followed, — grew, — held, — hung in, — made, — rang off, — rang out, — rang with, — rolled around, — rolled out, — rose in, — rose up, — said, — seemed to, — slid, — slid over, — sounded, — sounded behind, — sounded like, — sounded through, — stopped, — told, — turned, — turned into, — went out

laughter
verbs

— added to, — began, — breathed, — broke, — broke against, — broke from, — broke in, — broke off, — broke out, — brought, — brought on, — called back, — came, — came between, — came from, — came in, — came out, — carried back, — carried on, — carried over, — caught, — changed to, — continued, — continued on, — cut off, — died, — died at, — died away, — died down, — died on, — died out, — disappeared, — ended, — filled, — filled out, — filled with, — followed, — got, — grew, — joined, — knocked out, — left inside, — let loose, — made, — met, — passed, — poured out, — put, — ran through, — rang, — rang in, — rang out, — rang through, — rang with, — reached, — rolled down, — rolled in, — rolled like, — rolled up, — rose, — rose from, — rose in, — rose to, — rose up,

— seemed to, — shook, — shot up, — slipped between, — sounded, — sounded from, — started, — started to, — stopped, — turned into, — turned to, — turned up, — went, — went around, — went on, — went up

leaf
verbs

— appeared to, — became, — began to, — blew across, — blew around, — blew over, — broke from, — brought, — came, — came with, — caught, — caught in, — covered, — disappeared, — disappeared into, — fell, — fell from, — fell in, — fell off, — fell to, — filled, — fought, — grew, — lay across, — lay on, — made, — made up, — passed over, — pressed into, — remained, — rode, — rose on, — sank into, — seemed to, — settled, — shifted in, — showed, — sighed, — sighed in, — started to, — turned in, — whispered

leg
verbs

bent —, broke —, brought back —, brought up —, caught —, checked —, closed —, crossed —, cut —, did —, drew up —, dropped —, felt —, felt between —, finished —, found —, gestured to —, glanced at —, glanced toward —, got in —, grabbed —, gripped —, kicked —, kicked out —, kicked with —, knew about —, knocked on —, leaned against —, lifted —, liked —, looked at —, lost —, lowered —, moved —, moved between —, needed for —, opened —, pointed at —, pointed out —, pointed to —, pulled —, pulled up —, pushed —, pushed open —, pushed with —, raised —, reached

between —, reached to —, rubbed —, saw —, shifted —, shook —, shot for —, slipped on —, stared at —, stared between —, stepped between —, stepped into —, stood between —, stopped —, studied —, swung —, thought —, threw —, took —, took from —, touched —, turned —, used —, walked up —, waved —, wiped —, worked —, wrapped around —; — appeared, — appeared to, — ate up, — became, — began, — began to, — bent, — bent at, — bent in, — bent on, — blew up, — bowed, — bowed out, — broke, — broke above, — brought, — came, — came around, — came back, — came down, — came into, — came out, — came up, — caught, — caught in, — closed, — continued, — continued to, — crossed, — crossed at, — crossed beneath, — crossed in, — crossed over, — crossed under, — cut, — cut off, — cut out, — did, — died, — disappeared from, — drew up, — drove in, — ended, — ended in, — ended with, — fell away, — fell from, — fell into, — fell out, — fell over, — felt, — felt like, — filled with, — flew across, — flew into, — flew over, — flew up, — followed, — forced, — found, — gave, — gave away, — gave in, — gave out, — gave under, — got, — got in, — grew, — held, — helped, — hit, — hung, — hung down, — hung from, — hung off, — hung over, — joined, — jumped, — kept up, — kicked, — kicked against, — kicked at, — kicked in, — kicked into, — kicked out, — laid out, — landed, — landed like, — lay, — lay at, — lay on, — lay over, — left, — let, — lifted off, — lifted over, — looked, — looked in, — looked like, — made, — made up, —

missed below, — missed beneath, — moved, — moved beneath, — moved forward, — moved in, — moved into, — moved through, — moved under, — needed, — opened, — opened in, — picked up, — pointed up, — pressed against, — pressed together, — pulled, — pulled into, — pulled up, — pushed off, — put, — raised, — ran to, — reached for, — remained, — returned to, — rolled up, — sank, — sank into, — screamed, — screamed inside, — screamed with, — seemed, — seemed to, — sent out, — set, — shifted, — shook, — shook beneath, — shook like, — shook on, — shook under, — shook with, — shot, — shot out, — shot up, — shut to, — slid, — slid away, — slid off, — slid over, — slipped, — slipped from, — slipped into, — snapped, — snapped from, — snapped like, — started to, — stayed, — stood, — stopped, — struck, — swung down, — swung from, — swung in, — swung off, — swung out, — swung to, — took, — took up, — touched, — touched on, — tried to, — turned, — turned out, — turned to, — wanted to, — waved in, — went down, — went from, — went on, — went out, — went over, — went through, — went to, — went up, — wore, — worked at, — wrapped, — wrapped around, — wrapped in

letter
verbs
answered —, called out —, came across —, carried —, closed —, dropped —, entered —, explained about —, filled in —, finished —, found —, frowned at —, glanced at —, glanced over —, got —, grabbed —, handed over —, held —,

held out —, held up —, kept —, kissed —, knew —, laid —, left —, lifted —, lifted up —, looked at —, looked over —, looked through —, lowered —, made —, missed —, needed —, nodded at —, opened —, picked up —, placed —, pointed at —, pointed to —, pointed toward —, pulled out —, put —, put down —, reached for —, read —, read off —, read over —, recognized —, said in —, saw —, sent —, sent along —, showed —, slid out —, smelled —, sounded out —, stared at —, studied —, swallowed —, thought about —, thought of —, took —, took out —, turned over —, waved —, wrote —, wrote down —; — appeared, — appeared in, — appeared on, — arrived, — asked for, — became, — began, — began to, — broke up, — came, — came from, — came out, — caught, — crossed, — cut from, — cut into, — dropped into, — dropped through, — ended with, — fell into, — filled with, — finished up, — gave, — got in, — got through, — grew, — lay in, — lay on, — lit, — lit with, — made, — meant, — meant to, — passed, — ran in, — ran on, — rang, — read, — remained, — said, — sat, — sat at, — sat in, — seemed to, — sent, — sent in, — shot out, — slid on, — slid out, — slipped to, — sounded, — stood for, — stopped, — talked about, — told, — took, — took off, — turned out, — waited for, — went, — went back, — went on, — went onto, — worked into

library
verbs
came from —, came into —, came to —, checked —, crossed to —, drove to —,

entered —, found —, gestured around —, glanced around —, glanced down —, headed for —, left —, looked across —, loved —, moved to —, passed —, pointed down —, pointed out —, reached —, returned to —, slept in —, slipped into —, started in —, stayed in —, stepped into —, turned to —, waited in —, walked into —, walked through —, walked toward —, went into —, went to —

lid
verbs
— began to, — came off, — came up, — closed, — closed like, — closed on, — closed over, — dropped, — fell back, — felt like, — flew, — flew open, — got, — kept in, — lay on, — lay open, — lifted, — lifted on, — lowered for, — made, — opened, — opened to, — rose, — seemed to, — shifted, — shut, — slid, — slid off, — slid open, — snapped back, — stayed on, — stood open, — swung, — swung up

lie
verbs
— became, — came, — came between, — came to, — crossed, — died in, — died on, — fell away, — felt, — held, — made in, — meant, — meant to, — passed from, — said, — seemed, — slipped off, — sounded, — spoke, — stood, — told, — told to, — turned, — turned to, — used by, — went, — went down, — worked for

life
verbs
appeared in —, approached —, became —, brought into —, came into —, came to —, changed —, chose —, decided —, did in —, entered —, felt —, felt in —, fought for —, found —, gave —, gave up —, got —, hated —, kept —, knew about —, left —, liked —, lived —, lost —, loved —, managed in —, needed —, ran for —, ran from —, saw —, settled into —, shifted —, snapped into —, stepped into —, stopped —, talked about —, thought about —, thought of —, took —, wanted —, wanted from —, wanted in —, went about —; — appeared, — appeared on, — appeared to, — became, — began, — began at, — began by, — began to, — began with, — came, — came at, — came back, — came down, — came from, — came in, — came to, — came with, — carried on, — caught up, — changed, — continued, — cut down, — cut off, — did, — died in, — disappeared in, — ended, — ended in, — fell away, — fell into, — fell to, — felt, — felt like, — figured out, — filled with, — fought to, — found, — glanced over, — got in, — grew, — happened in, — hated, — held, — hung, — hung around, — hung by, — hung in, — knew, — laid, — lay, — left, — left in, — left to, — lived, — lived at, — lived from, — lived in, — looked for, — looked over, — lost, — lost in, — lost to, — made, — made for, — meant, — meant for, — met, — moved on, — needed to, — offered, — passed before, — placed in, — played out, — poured, — poured out, — promised, — ran, — ran down, — ran from, — ran to, — remained, — returned, — returned to, — rolled over, — said, — sat on, — seemed, — seemed like, — seemed to, — shifted toward, — slid away, — slipped from, — sounded, — spent in, — spent

inside, — spent to, — spoke to, —
started at, — started to, — stepped
down, — stood, — stopped for, —
threw at, — took, — took out, —
turned into, — turned on, —
understood, — waited for, — walked
on, — went back, — went by, — went
in, — went off, — went on, — went out,
— wiped out, — worked

light
verbs
added —, bent —, blinked at —,
blinked in —, blinked into —, bought
—, broke —, brought —, called —,
called for —, came in —, came into —,
carried —, caught —, checked —,
continued toward —, covered —,
crossed against —, crossed at —, cut —,
dropped —, felt —, felt toward —,
followed —, followed with —, found —,
gave —, got out —, grabbed —, heard —
, held —, hit —, jumped —, jumped
into —, kicked into —, killed —, kissed
—, landed —, leaned into —, lifted —,
liked —, looked at —, loved —, lowered
—, missed —, moved into —, moved
through —, moved toward —, needed
—, noticed —, paused at —, picked up
—, pointed —, pointed with —, pulled
off —, pulled out —, put on —, put out
—, raised —, ran —, ran into —, ran on
—, reached —, rolled through —, rolled
toward —, said —, sat at —, sat in —,
saw —, set down —, set up —, shifted
—, shook —, shut down —, shut off —,
shut out —, smiled at —, snapped —,
snapped off —, snapped on —, spoke
with —, stared at —, stared into —,
stared toward —, stepped into —,
stepped toward —, stood before —,
stood in —, stood under —, stopped at

—, stopped for —, stopped under —,
struck —, swung —, threw on —, took
—, touched —, tried —, turned —,
turned at —, turned off —, turned on
—, turned out —, turned to —, turned
up —, used —, waited at —, waited for
—, walked through —, wanted —,
watched —; — added, — answered, —
appeared, — appeared above, —
appeared around, — appeared at, —
appeared behind, — appeared between,
— appeared down, — appeared in, —
appeared inside, — appeared on, —
appeared over, — approached, —
approached from, — became, — began
to, — blew out, — blinked, — blinked
at, — blinked from, — blinked in, —
blinked off, — blinked on, — blinked
out, — blinked to, — broke, — broke
out, — broke over, — broke through, —
brought, — came, — came around, —
came back, — came down, — came
from, — came in, — came into, — came
off, — came on, — came out, — came
over, — came through, — came to, —
came up, — carried, — caught, —
caught in, — caught on, — changed, —
changed at, — changed in, — changed
to, — cleared, — climbed, — continued,
— continued to, — cut across, — cut
off, — cut through, — did, — died, —
died away, — died down, — died in, —
died out, — disappeared, — disappeared
behind, — disappeared into, — drew, —
dropped, — dropped from, — dropped
off, — ended, — entered, — entered
through, — fell, — fell across, — fell
down, — fell from, — fell in, — fell
into, — fell on, — fell through, — fell
upon, — felt like, — filled, — finished,
— flew from, — flew into, — followed,
— followed by, — found, — gave, —

glanced off, — got, — grew, — grew
against, — grew beneath, — grew from,
— grew in, — grew to, — grew within,
— headed, — held, — held up, — hit,
— hung, — hung above, — hung
around, — hung at, — hung down, —
hung in, — hung over, — joined, —
landed in, — lay, — lay across, — lay
like, — lay on, — led, — left, — left
behind, — left in, — left on, — lit, — lit
up, — lived, — looked, — looked like,
— lowered, — made, — meant, — met,
— moved, — moved across, — moved
around, — moved away, — moved in,
— moved on, — moved over, — moved
through, — moved toward, — opened,
— opened in, — passed into, — passed
over, — passed through, — picked up,
— played across, — played along, —
played on, — played over, — pointed
out, — poured down, — poured from,
— poured in, — poured into, — poured
out, — poured over, — poured through,
— pushed, — pushed back, — put, —
put up, — ran, — ran away, — ran from,
— reached, — remained, — remained
in, — remained on, — remained to, —
returned, — returned to, — rode, —
rose, — rose from, — rose in, — rose
into, — rose like, — rose up, — sank
into, — sat in, — screamed toward, —
seemed, — seemed like, — seemed to, —
set into, — set on, — settled on, —
shifted, — shot, — shot away, — shot
down, — shot from, — shot out, —
showed, — showed around, — showed
beneath, — showed from, — showed in,
— showed on, — showed through, —
shut off, — slammed through, — slid
across, — slipped beneath, — slipped
through, — snapped, — snapped off, —
snapped on, — started from, — started

to, — stayed, — stayed behind, —
stayed off, — stayed on, — stayed out,
— stood in, — stopped, — struck, —
swung, — swung around, — swung
through, — took, — touched, —
touched open, — turned, — turned
around, — turned down, — turned off,
— turned on, — turned out, — turned
to, — turned up, — went after, — went
away, — went back, — went down, —
went from, — went off, — went on, —
went out, — went up, — went with

lightning
verbs
— added to, — appeared, — appeared
in, — ate at, — began to, — blinked in,
— came, — came to, — caught, — cut
at, — cut off, — died, — drove, —
entered, — filled, — followed, —
followed by, — got, — grew from, —
held in, — hit, — jumped, — lit, — lit
up, — moved to, — passed, — played
across, — played around, — played at,
— screamed for, — seemed to, — shot,
— shot from, — slammed into, —
started in, — struck, — struck from, —
threw, — turned, — went off, — went
to

limb
verbs
— bent down, — blew, — blew into, —
caught in, — closed out, — ended in, —
fell to, — felt, — felt like, — filled, —
filled with, — flew in, — gave, — grew,
— landed beside, — lay across, — left,
— lost, — made for, — made of, — met,
— moved, — reached, — reached out,
— rubbed, — seemed to, — started to,
— stood in, — went to

line

verbs

added —, answered —, approached —, asked over —, broke through —, called from —, came on —, continued down —, continued in —, crossed —, crossed out —, cut —, cut off —, drew —, dropped —, entered —, fell in —, fell into —, followed —, found —, glanced along —, glanced to —, got in —, got into —, got on —, grabbed —, held —, hung on —, joined —, jumped over —, killed —, knew —, laughed at —, led up —, left —, looked along —, looked at —, looked down —, moved along —, moved through —, needed —, opened —, picked up —, pointed down —, pulled —, pulled on —, pushed toward —, put on —, ran —, ran down —, read between —, returned to —, said —, said over —, saw —, shoved through —, shut off —, slammed into —, smiled at —, snapped —, spoke —, stayed in —, stayed on —, stepped into —, stood astride —, stood in —, stopped at —, studied —, swung —, threw in —, took —, tossed —, turned in —, waited for —, waited in —, waited on —, walked along —, walked down —, walked to —, wanted on —, went down —, went off —, whispered into —, worked —, worked down —; — added at, — added to, — answered on, — appeared, — appeared at, — appeared behind, — appeared between, — appeared in, — appeared on, — appeared to, — became, — began to, — blinked off, — broke, — brought, — brought down, — called, — came, — came down, — came from, — came into, — came out, — came to, — came together, — checked, — cleared, — closed about, — closed to, — continued around, — continued forward, — continued to, — crossed, — crossed out, — crossed over, — cut, — cut into, — cut off, — cut out, — cut through, — died, — died out, — disappeared, — disappeared around, — disappeared into, — drove, — fell, — fell into, — filled with, — flew out, — got, — grew, — grew at, — grew under, — held, — held on, — hung, — hung in, — joined in, — jumped, — jumped forward, — knocked over, — landed, — landed across, — laughed, — lay across, — led to, — left, — lit, — lit off, — lit up, — looked, — looked for, — looked in, — looked to, — lost under, — made, — met, — missed, — moved, — moved across, — moved forward, — moved on, — moved over, — moved up, — opened, — opened along, — opened up, — picked up, — played out, — pointed toward, — pulled, — pulled in, — put in, — ran, — ran across, — ran around, — ran down, — ran from, — ran into, — ran through, — ran to, — ran under, — rang, — rang on, — rang with, — reached, — remained, — rolled out, — rose, — said, — seemed, — seemed to, — set out, — settled within, — shifted, — slipped, — snapped, — sounded in, — spoke, — spoke in, — started, — started at, — started for, — started forward, — started to, — stayed, — stayed open, — stopped, — struck through, — swung, — threw, — took, — took up, — turned, — waited around, — waited at, — waited for, — walked over, — went down, — went forward, — went from, — went into, — went through, — went to, — whispered, — wrapped around

lip
verbs
asked —, bent —, blew out —, blew
through —, broke —, caught —, closed
—, drew from —, felt —, felt like —,
forced —, gasped against —, kept —,
kissed —, laughed against —, left —,
lifted —, looked at —, lost —, made —,
moved —, murmured against —,
murmured through —, offered —,
opened —, picked at —, pointed to —,
pressed —, pulled —, pulled at —,
pulled on —, pushed out —, raised —,
read —, recognized —, remembered —,
rolled —, rubbed —, said through —,
set —, slid over —, smiled with —,
stood at —, studied —, swallowed —,
touched —, turned —, used —, watched
—, wiped —, worked —; — appeared
to, — began to, — broke open, — broke
with, — came, — came down, — came
to, — came together, — caught, —
caught between, — caught in, — caught
on, — closed, — closed around, —
closed over, — continued to, — covered,
— did, — died, — disappeared, —
disappeared from, — disappeared into,
— drew, — drew away, — drew back, —
drew into, — drew out, — drew up, —
dropped, — fell open, — felt like, —
followed, — fought, — found, — gave
away, — grew, — held, — held with, —
hung open, — kissed, — kissed away, —
knew, — landed on, — led to, — left, —
left on, — lifted, — lifted at, — lifted in,
— lifted into, — looked, — made, —
made for, — managed, — met, —
moved, — moved across, — moved
against, — moved around, — moved
behind, — moved beneath, — moved
down, — moved for, — moved in, —
moved near, — moved on, — moved

over, — moved to, — moved up, —
moved without, — opened, — opened
over, — pressed, — pressed against, —
pressed down, — pressed in, — pressed
into, — pressed to, — pressed together,
— pulled, — pulled back, — pulled
down, — pulled in, — pulled into, —
pulled up, — pushed, — pushed out, —
raised, — reached, — remained, —
remembered, — repeated, — replied in,
— rose above, — said, — seemed, —
seemed to, — sent, — set, — set in, —
set into, — settled on, — shook, —
showed, — shut, — shut on, — shut to,
— slid along, — slid into, — slid over,
— slid up, — slipped open, — smelled,
— smiled, — spoke, — started to, —
stayed, — stood out, — suggested, —
took, — touched, — touched down, —
tried to, — turned, — turned down, —
turned up, — wanted to, — went, —
went from, — went in, — went
together, — whispered, — whispered
over, — worked, — wrapped around

liquid
verbs
— appeared on, — became, — began to,
— caught in, — cleared, — fell on, —
filled, — flew across, — held between,
— held in, — hung in, — left, — poured
from, — poured into, — poured out, —
ran down, — ran in, — ran through, —
rose around, — rose into, — rose up, —
sat in, — seemed to, — slid down, —
slid into, — slipped down, — touched,
— turned, — went down, — went in

list
verbs
asked for —, bent over —, blinked at —,
brought up —, checked —, checked off

—, considered —, continued down —,
dropped —, gave —, glanced at —,
grabbed —, handed over —, held up —,
hit —, killed —, left —, liked —, lived
by —, looked at —, looked down —,
looked over —, made —, passed over —,
picked up —, pointed at —, pointed to
—, pulled out —, pulled up —, put —,
ran through —, remained at —,
repeated —, saw —, slid back —, stared
at —, started down —, studied —,
talked through —, thought of —, took
—, took out —, tossed —, went down
—, went over —, went through —, went
to —, worked down —; — added up, —
asked for, — became, — began to, —
called, — came, — checked out, —
cleared, — continued, — continued to,
— disappeared, — followed, — forced,
— got, — grew, — kept, — meant, —
seemed, — started, — stopped, —
stopped at, — took, — turned up, —
used, — went in, — went on

lobby
verbs
ate in —, called from —, cleared —,
crossed —, entered —, gestured across
—, glanced across —, glanced around —
, headed through —, hit —, left —,
looked around —, looked toward —,
moved through —, moved toward —,
ordered —, paused in —, pointed
toward —, ran across —, ran into —,
ran to —, reached —, returned from —,
returned to —, rode to —, said in —, sat
in —, shot through —, started across —,
started for —, stepped inside —, stepped
into —, stood in —, stood outside —,
stopped in —, turned toward —, waited
in —, walked across —, walked between

—, walked into —, walked through —,
went in —, went into —, went to —

lock
verbs
broke —, changed —, checked —, cut
—, cut through —, felt for —, found —,
frowned at —, got —, heard —, kicked
at —, lifted —, looked at —, lost —,
nodded at —, opened —, picked —, put
—, reached for —, shot —, shot off —,
snapped open —, stepped into —,
studied —, took off —, touched —,
tried —, turned —, turned to —,
wanted —, worked —, worked at —; —
appeared, — appeared above, — began
to, — broke, — broke off, — broke
with, — called to, — came, — caught
up, — changed, — closed, — closed
with, — dropped across, — dropped
away, — fell off, — fell open, — fell
over, — fell to, — gave, — gave beneath,
— held, — hung, — looked, — opened,
— opened at, — opened with, — set, —
shut, — slid into, — slid open, —
snapped, — snapped into, — snapped
off, — snapped open, — snapped shut,
— sounded on, — started to, — stood
at, — swung open, — turned, — went
up

look
verbs
answered with —, caught —, did —,
followed —, gave —, got —, hated —,
held —, knew —, laughed at —, liked —
, loved —, met —, nodded with —,
noticed —, put on —, read —,
recognized —, replied with —, returned
—, said with —, saw —, shot —, smiled
at —, took —, turned with —,
understood —, wanted —, went for —;

— added to, — appeared on, — became, — brought back, — came across, — came back, — came from, — came in, — came into, — came onto, — came over, — came with, — changed, — continued for, — crossed, — cut off, — did, — disappeared from, — entered, — fell from, — filled, — filled with, — found in, — got, — grew, — grew in, — held for, — left, — lost, — made, — meant, — meant for, — meant to, — passed, — passed across, — passed over, — played on, — remained, — remained on, — returned, — said, — said without, — seemed to, — set, — settled, — settled on, — slept in, — started, — stayed in, — turned, — turned on, — turned to, — went, — went in, — wore off

lot
verbs
approached across —, ate —, ate in —, changed —, cried —, crossed —, did —, drank —, drove into —, explained —, frowned —, glanced around —, got to —, headed for —, helped —, knew —, laughed —, learned —, left —, liked —, looked around —, looked at —, moved —, nodded —, played with —, pulled into —, ran for —, reached —, realized —, saw —, screamed —, slept —, smiled —, spent —, stared at —, started toward —, stopped in —, talked —, turned into —, turned toward —, walked across —, walked through —, watched —, went from —, worked —, wrote —, yelled —

love
verbs
called —, chose —, demanded —, did for —, fell in —, felt —, got —, heard —, killed for —, knew of —, lost —, loved

—, made —, missed —, promised —, recognized —, remained in —, saw —, sent —, spoke of —, spoke with —, thought —, thought of —, understood —, waited in —, wanted —; — came, — changed into, — crossed, — did, — felt, — felt like, — filled, — got, — got for, — grew, — grew up, — happened, — left to, — looked like, — lost, — lost between, — made, — passed, — rode, — rose up, — slid through, — stared at, — told, — took, — turned into, — turned to, — went

lunch
verbs
asked over —, ate —, ate at —, bought —, brought —, finished —, got —, grabbed —, landed for —, left for —, made —, met for —, missed —, opened —, ordered —, returned after —, returned to —, said after —, said at —, sat for —, set down —, set out —, slept through —, stared at —, stayed through —, stopped for —, took —, took out —, walked to —, went for —, went to —, worked through —

lung
verbs
— began, — began to, — cried out, — felt, — felt about, — felt like, — filled up, — filled with, — forced, — forced out, — gave out, — got, — grew, — hit, — screamed, — screamed for, — screamed with, — seemed, — seemed to, — shook, — slipped past, — sounded, — started to, — stopped, — turned to, — went into, — worked

machine
verbs

bent over —, breathed without —,
brought —, checked —, closed —,
crossed to —, felt like —, found —,
frowned at —, gestured toward —,
glanced at —, got —, got off —, looked
at —, met at —, moved like —,
muttered to —, nodded at —, pointed
to —, reached —, said to —, sat at —,
shut down —, shut off —, sounded like
—, stared at —, started —, started up —
, stepped from —, stood beside —,
stopped —, stopped at —, studied —,
turned off —, turned on —, waited for
—, went to —; — answered, — ate, —
began, — began to, — called, — came at,
— came back, — came on, — came to,
— climbed, — continued on, — cut in,
— cut through, — did, — disappeared,
— drew, — filled, — found in, — found
out, — gave, — held, — lay, — left, —
made, — made of, — offered, — picked
up, — played, — put, — rang, —
returned, — said, — sat back, — sat on,
— seemed, — seemed to, — set up, —
shut down, — shut off, — sounded
above, — started up, — stood around,
— stood in, — stopped, — took, —
took off, — turned, — turned on, —
waited, — went, — worked, — worked
on

magazine
verbs
bought —, changed —, changed out —,
checked —, closed —, dropped —,
dropped out —, finished —, finished
with —, found —, glanced at —,
grabbed —, handed over —, looked at
—, lowered —, moved aside —, opened
—, picked up —, pointed to —, pulled
—, pulled out —, put down —, reached
for —, read —, rolled up —, shut —,

slammed in —, slid out —, snapped in
—, snapped off —, stared at —, studied
—, threw —, took out —, tossed aside
—, turned to —, waved away —

magic
verbs
— added to, — appeared, — became, —
began to, — brought out, — called, —
called forth, — came, — came from, —
came to, — came toward, — climbed, —
closed, — continued to, — cut through,
— decided, — did, — died away, —
disappeared, — drew, — felt, — felt like,
— filled, — flew through, — found, —
got, — happened, — happened in, —
held, — helped, — kept, — lay, — left,
— left to, — looked, — lost, — made,
— made by, — met, — moved down, —
needed, — needed to, — offered, —
passed by, — played, — remained, —
remained to, — returned, — rose in, —
rose to, — screamed into, — seemed, —
seemed to, — sent out, — settled
around, — shot forward, — showed, —
slammed into, — slid, — slid down, —
smelled, — spent, — started, — struck,
— swung, — took, — touched, — used,
— used for, — whispered, — worked,
— worked against, — worked by, —
worked on, — worked with

map
verbs
added —, asked for —, bought —,
brought —, brought up —, checked —,
did —, drew —, drew back —, explained
to —, fell off —, followed —, found —,
frowned at —, gestured at —, gestured
toward —, glanced at —, got out —,
grabbed —, held out —, held up —, laid
—, laid out —, leaned over —, lifted up

—, looked at —, looked over —, lost —, loved —, lowered —, made —, needed —, nodded to —, nodded toward —, opened —, picked up —, pointed at —, pointed to —, pulled open —, pulled out —, pulled up —, put —, reached for —, reached to —, read off —, remembered —, returned to —, rolled up —, saw —, shifted to —, shook open —, shoved —, stared at —, studied —, took —, took out —, touched —, turned from —, turned to —, walked to —, waved at —, went to —, worked —; — appeared, — appeared inside, — arrived, — became, — began to, — brought back, — brought in, — called, — came up, — changed, — covered, — disappeared, — drew back, — filled, — flew through, — laid out, — lay, — led to, — left behind, — looked like, — meant, — opened out, — pointed, — read, — remained, — seemed to, — showed, — slid in, — took up, — went, — went on

mare
verbs
— began to, — blew, — blew like, — broke, — came, — came to, — got, — joined in, — lifted, — looked, — lost, — made, — moved, — moved out, — picked up, — put, — put in, — reached, — rolled, — sat down, — seemed, — seemed to, — set, — set off, — shook, — started, — stood, — threw, — tossed, — tried to, — understood, — went, — went up

mask
verbs
caught inside —, dropped —, frowned behind —, grabbed —, gripped —, held

up —, kept on —, lifted —, looked at —, lowered —, picked up —, pointed at —, pulled away —, pulled down —, pulled off —, pulled on —, pulled out —, pulled up —, put on —, reached to —, said of —, saw —, shouted at —, sighed behind —, slipped off —, slipped on —, smiled behind —, smiled beneath —, smiled inside —, smiled under —, spoke through —, stared at —, studied —, suggested —, thought about —, thought of —, took —, took off —, touched —, turned —, turned over —, wore —; — appeared, — began, — came, — came back, — covered, — drew in, — dropped, — ended, — fell at, — fell away, — held, — held for, — held on, — hung, — lay inside, — moved out, — nodded on, — pointed, — pulled, — pulled below, — pulled down, — pulled over, — pushed up, — reached, — remained in, — rolled, — said, — said in, — sat in, — seemed, — seemed to, — shoved atop, — shut, — slammed, — slid into, — slipped, — slipped for, — slipped into, — smelled, — went into

mattress
verbs
carried —, checked under —, dropped —, dropped to —, fell into —, fell onto —, felt —, felt beneath —, grabbed —, hit —, kicked —, lay on —, lifted —, looked under —, passed —, pulled back —, put in —, reached under —, returned to —, sank against —, sat on —, settled onto —, shifted on —, slid off —, spoke into —, stood on —, turned —, turned from —, wanted —

meal
verbs

— arrived, — became, — began, — began to, — broke up, — brought to, — came around, — came from, — came through, — came to, — came up, — continued, — continued in, — drew to, — ended, — ended with, — finished, — got under, — hung in, — lay on, — made, — passed, — placed in, — seemed, — seemed to, — sent to, — sent up, — set, — set up, — smelled, — studied, — talked about, — went, — went back

meat
verbs
— approached, — began to, — cut into, — fell from, — fell to, — filled, — followed, — found, — grew, — hung, — hung off, — joined, — left, — left for, — made, — meant for, — rose up, — sat in, — seemed like, — set against, — slid down, — stopped, — swung from, — woke, — wrapped in

meeting
verbs
— began, — began to, — broke off, — broke up, — came to, — continued, — ended, — ended on, — ended with, — got under, — grew, — let, — moved into, — ran, — returned, — said, — seemed, — set up, — started, — started to, — took, — took on, — wanted to, — went, — went on, — went with

memory
verbs
asked —, became —, blinked away —, came by —, carried —, followed from —, found —, frowned at —, got into —, grinned at —, laughed at —, looked inside —, lost —, loved —, needed from

—, paused at —, picked through —, pressed —, pulled from —, pushed aside —, pushed away —, reached into —, shook at —, shook away —, shook off —, shrugged off —, shut down —, sighed at —, sighed with —, smiled at —, smiled with —, wiped —, worked from —, worked on —; — answered, — became, — began to, — began with, — broke down, — brought, — brought on, — brought to, — called to, — called up, — came, — came at, — came back, — came into, — came to, — came with, — carried on, — continued, — continued to, — disappeared, — disappeared into, — fell across, — felt like, — filled, — got, — grew, — grew like, — held, — held in, — held on, — held up, — kept, — kicked into, — knew, — left to, — lit up, — looked, — lost in, — made, — opened in, — opened up, — passed, — passed like, — picked out, — played, — pressed into, — ran, — ran between, — ran through, — remained, — remained of, — returned, — returned to, — rolled, — rose, — rose from, — rose in, — rose like, — rose to, — sat on, — seemed, — seemed to, — sent, — settled, — shifted, — shot, — slipped back, — stayed, — stopped, — took, — took over, — tried to, — went at, — worked, — wrapped up

menu
verbs
called for —, called up —, closed —, dropped —, glanced at —, grabbed —, handed over —, held up —, laid —, lifted —, looked at —, looked over —, lowered —, opened —, ordered from —, picked up —, pointed to —, put down —, raised —, reached for —, set aside —

, set down —, stared at —, studied —, took —, tossed aside —

message
verbs

brought —, brought up —, called up —, carried —, caught —, checked —, closed —, cried —, cut off —, found —, glanced at —, got —, held up —, left —, liked —, listened to —, looked at —, opened —, passed on —, played —, pulled up —, ran —, read —, repeated —, said in —, sat through —, saw —, sent —, stared at —, studied —, took —, understood —, waited for —, wrote in —, wrote out —; — appeared, — appeared in, — appeared on, — arrived at, — arrived on, — became, — began, — began in, — began to, — came, — came back, — came from, — came in, — came on, — came through, — came up, — carried on, — cleared, — continued, — cut off, — cut out, — ended, — fell into, — finished, — finished with, — got out, — got through, — hit, — kicked in, — lay in, — left in, — lifted, — made, — meant, — meant for, — offered, — passed, — passed through, — paused for, — played, — played in, — played on, — pressed into, — pulled up, — put on, — ran, — reached, — read, — said, — sent, — sent by, — sent to, — set, — slid into, — spoke of, — started, — stood against, — struck, — took, — went, — went on, — went out

metal
verbs

— appeared between, — ate into, — became, — began to, — called, — came from, — came under, — came up, — caught, — did, — dropped in, — fell

into, — fell on, — fell to, — felt, — felt like, — filled, — flew, — flew from, — gave, — gave away, — held, — hit, — hung, — hung from, — hung on, — lay across, — lay against, — lay in, — lay on, — looked, — lost, — made, — made of, — meant, — moved around, — moved in, — needed, — ran down, — ran through, — rang, — sank into, — screamed, — screamed against, — seemed, — seemed to, — set to, — shot up, — showed, — slid against, — slid through, — snapped, — snapped from, — stopped, — suggested, — threw, — took on, — touched, — went, — woke to

microphone
verbs

bent —, blew into —, called into —, covered —, dropped —, grabbed —, grinned into —, held —, hung up —, kept —, leaned into —, leaned near —, leaned to —, leaned toward —, lowered —, moved to —, murmured into —, needed —, ordered into —, picked up —, pressed —, pulled —, put down —, reached for —, returned to —, said into —, saw —, shouted into —, snapped on —, spoke into —, stepped to —, took —, took off —, touched —, turned —, turned off —, turned to —, whispered into —

mike
verbs

approached —, blew into —, called into —, covered —, cut —, dropped —, grabbed —, handed over —, hit —, leaned into —, leaned to —, left —, looked at —, picked up —, pressed —, pulled —, pulled on —, put down —,

reached for —, repeated into —,
returned to —, said into —, said on —,
said to —, shifted —, spoke into —,
stepped to —, threw down —, touched
—, tried —, went to —, whispered into
—, yelled into —

mind
verbs
changed —, cleared —, closed —,
crossed —, did —, entered —, fell into
—, felt —, filled —, forced —, found —,
found in —, held in —, kept —, knew
—, let —, looked inside —, lost —,
made up —, opened —, pushed with —,
put —, rang in —, read —, said in —,
screamed into —, shouted with —, shut
off —, spoke —, spoke in —, stood in —
, took —, touched —, went into —,
whispered in —; — added, — agreed, —
answered, — asked, — became, —
began, — began to, — broke, — broke
beneath, — came, — came at, — came
back, — caught, — caught up, —
checked in, — cleared, — cleared to, —
closed around, — closed down, —
continued to, — cried, — cried out, —
demanded, — did, — disappeared, —
drew, — drew at, — felt, — felt like, —
filled, — filled in, — filled with, — flew
back, — flew by, — flew to, — followed,
— fought, — fought for, — found, —
gave, — gave in, — got, — got on, — got
to, — grew, — heard, — held, — hit, —
joined, — jumped around, — jumped
to, — kept, — kicked up, — knew, —
lay, — lay open, — left, — left to, —
lifted off, — lost, — lost to, — made, —
made up, — moved near, — moved to,
— opened, — picked up, — played, —
pulled, — ran, — ran into, — ran like,
— ran over, — ran through, — reached

out, — recognized, — remained, —
repeated, — returned, — returned from,
— returned to, — rolled, — rose, —
said, — sat at, — saw, — screamed, —
screamed against, — screamed for, —
screamed in, — seemed, — seemed to,
— sent, — set at, — set on, — settled,
— settled on, — shifted to, — shouted,
— showed, — shut down, — shut off,
— slammed from, — slammed on, —
slept, — slipped into, — snapped back,
— snapped into, — snapped out, —
spent, — spoke up, — started to, —
stayed, — stopped, — suggested, —
thought, — told, — took, — took in, —
took over, — touched, — touched on,
— touched upon, — tried over, — tried
to, — turned, — turned down, —
turned in, — turned into, — turned on,
— turned over, — turned to, — turned
with, — understood, — waited for, —
waited in, — wanted to, — watched, —
went, — went at, — went back, — went
into, — went on, — went through, —
went to, — whispered, — wore, —
worked, — worked at, — worked in, —
worked like, — worked through, —
worked until, — wrote, — yelled

minute
verbs
appeared —, arrived —, arrived in —,
asked after —, called —, called within
—, considered —, considered for —,
continued for —, did for —, followed —
, fought for —, frowned —, frowned for
—, got —, held for —, held on —,
hesitated —, hesitated for —, hung for
—, laughed after —, laughed for —, lay
for —, left after —, left for —, listened
—, listened for —, looked away —,
looked for —, managed after —, needed

—, nodded after —, paused —, paused
for —, reached —, returned —, returned
after —, returned in —, said —, said
after —, sat for —, slept for —, spoke
for —, stared for —, stayed for —, stood
for —, stopped —, stopped after —,
stopped for —, thought —, thought for
—, took —, tried for —, waited —,
waited about —, waited for —, waited
over —, walked for —, watched for —;
— appeared in, — approached, —
arrived, — became, — came, — came
back, — caught up, — did, — felt like,
— flew, — grew into, — lay on, — left,
— left of, — left out, — left to, — left
until, — looked at, — looked for, —
looked through, — met, — passed, —
passed between, — passed by, — passed
in, — passed without, — played out, —
remained before, — remained for, —
said, — saw, — seemed like, — seemed
to, — shifted under, — slid by, —
slipped, — slipped away, — slipped by,
— slipped past, — stared at, — stood in,
— tried to, — turned into, — wanted
to, — went, — went around, — went
by, — went past, — went through, —
worked off

mirror
verbs
blinked into —, breathed on —,
checked —, checked in —, closed —,
dropped —, finished with —, found —,
frowned at —, frowned into —,
gestured at —, gestured toward —,
glanced at —, glanced in —, glanced
into —, glanced toward —, grinned in
—, held out —, leaned toward —, left
—, lifted —, looked at —, looked in —,
looked into —, lowered —, moved —,
moved to —, needed —, nodded into —

, nodded toward —, opened —, passed
—, passed by —, picked up —, pointed
to —, pulled out —, pushed away —,
put down —, remembered —, returned
to —, sat before —, saw —, screamed at
—, set down —, slammed at —, smiled
for —, smiled in —, stared at —, stared
in —, stared into —, stared toward —,
stood at —, stood before —, stood by —
, stopped at —, stopped before —, took
—, turned from —, turned in —, turned
to —, turned toward —, walked to —,
watched —, watched in —, waved
toward —, went to —; — broke, —
came out, — caught, — disappeared, —
fell on, — fell onto, — filled, — grew, —
held, — held up, — hung, — hung
above, — hung from, — hung on, —
leaned against, — looked, — made, —
made of, — remained, — rose up, — sat
on, — set up, — shook in, — showed,
— shut, — slid between, — slid into, —
stopped, — touched up, — turned away,
— went, — wore, — worked

mist
verbs
— appeared, — appeared around, —
appeared in, — became, — began, —
began to, — blew off, — broke, — broke
around, — came, — came across, —
came from, — came out, — came up, —
cleared, — cleared from, — cleared on,
— closed about, — closed behind, —
closed in, — continued, — continued
to, — covered, — drew back, — fell, —
fell across, — fell through, — fell upon,
— felt, — filled, — filled with, —
followed, — gave, — grew, — held, —
held on, — hung, — hung among, —
hung at, — hung in, — hung like, —
hung over, — lay, — lay on, — left by,

— lifted, — lifted from, — lost, — made, — moved, — poured from, — poured through, — pressed down, — pulled back, — ran from, — returned, — rolled away, — rolled over, — rolled up, — rose, — rose from, — rose in, — rose into, — rose off, — rose on, — rose over, — rose to, — seemed to, — settled in, — settled on, — settled through, — shifted, — shot out, — started to, — swallowed up, — took, — took on, — turned, — turned into, — turned to, — worked, — worked to, — wrapped

moan
verbs

— began, — began to, — broke, — broke from, — broke like, — broke out, — came, — came from, — came out, — caught in, — drew, — fell from, — followed, — grew, — left, — poured out, — rose from, — rose up, — seemed to, — sent, — shook, — slid from, — slid through, — slipped past, — slipped through, — sounded behind, — sounded out, — took on

moment
verbs

answered after —, appeared in —, asked after —, blinked for —, broke —, called at —, came at —, chose —, considered —, considered for —, continued after —, died within —, disappeared for —, drew after —, felt —, felt at —, felt in —, felt until —, forced —, found —, frowned —, frowned after —, frowned for —, glanced for —, held for —, hesitated —, hesitated for —, hung for —, knew —, knew at —, lay for —, leaned for —, listened —, listened for —, lived for —, looked around —, looked

down —, lost —, loved —, made in —, needed —, needed at —, nodded after —, paused —, paused for —, picked —, pressed for —, realized at —, remembered —, replied after —, said after —, said at —, sat —, sat for —, saw —, smiled for —, spoke for —, stared —, stared for —, stood —, stood for —, stopped —, stopped for —, studied —, thought —, thought about —, thought after —, thought at —, thought for —, took —, waited —, waited for —, watched for —, went for —, wrote after —; — agreed with, — appeared to, — arrived, — became, — began to, — broke, — called for, — came, — came back, — came through, — came to, — came up, — carried through, — caught, — checked over, — closed, — considered, — decided to, — did, — died away, — drank in, — ended, — expected, — fell into, — felt, — felt like, — filled with, — followed, — gave, — got, — grew, — happened, — happened in, — happened to, — held, — hung, — hung against, — hung in, — laid, — lay, — left open, — listened with, — looked, — looked around, — looked at, — made, — passed, — passed for, — passed in, — passed without, — placed, — played, — raised, — remembered, — said, — sat in, — saw, — seemed to, — slammed into, — slid by, — slipped, — slipped past, — spent, — spent together, — stood, — stood out, — thought, — thought about, — thought of, — turned, — turned into, — turned to, — walked out, — went, — went by, — went to, — wiped at, — wondered

money
verbs

came from —, checked —, considered
—, demanded —, drew out —, finished
with —, fought over —, found —,
frowned at —, gave —, gave away —, got
—, grabbed —, handed over —, held out
—, held up —, kept —, killed —, knew
—, left —, liked —, looked at —, looked
like —, made —, managed —, meant —,
needed —, offered —, passed over —,
picked up —, pulled —, raised —, sent
—, set down —, slipped —, smelled —,
snapped up —, spent —, spoke of —,
stared at —, started toward —, talked
about —, thought about —, thought of
—, took —, took out —, took up —,
touched —, turned over —, used —,
wanted —, waved —, worked for —; —
added, — arrived, — arrived by, —
began to, — bought, — brought in, —
brought out, — came, — came from, —
came in, — came through, — came to,
— came up, — changed, — covered, —
cut off, — disappeared, — drove, —
flew off, — gave, — gave out, — got, —
grew on, — held, — hit, — hit like, —
laid out, — landed, — lay on, — left, —
left over, — left to, — lifted, — lived, —
looked, — made, — meant, — moved
by, — passed, — passed from, — passed
through, — poured in, — put away, —
ran, — ran out, — rolled across, — sat
in, — sat on, — seemed like, — sent, —
set off, — smelled, — spent, — talked,
— turned into, — turned out, —
walked away, — went, — went down, —
went in, — went into, — went to, —
went up, — went with, — worked

monitor
verbs
bent over —, checked —, glanced at —,
grinned into —, leaned toward —,

looked at —, looked into —, looked
over —, moved to —, muttered at —,
picked up —, pointed at —, pointed to
—, pointed toward —, said to —, sat
behind —, saw —, shut off —, spoke to
—, stared at —, stepped from —,
studied —, turned on —, turned to —,
turned toward —, turned up —, walked
to —, watched —, watched on —,
waved to —

mood
verbs
— appeared to, — became, — began to,
— changed, — changed in, — changed
with, — continued to, — died, — fell,
— grew, — hung over, — lifted, —
lifted for, — looked, — made, — picked
up, — ran, — remained, — returned, —
said, — sank, — seemed, — seemed to,
— shifted to, — turned

moon
verbs
— appeared, — appeared above, —
appeared between, — appeared in, —
appeared through, — asked, — began,
— began to, — broke, — broke through,
— called, — came, — came down, —
came out, — came up, — continued to,
— cut through, — disappeared, —
disappeared behind, — disappeared
below, — drew, — filled, — filled up, —
followed, — gave, — got, — hung, —
hung above, — hung in, — hung like, —
lay over, — listened, — lit, — lit up, —
looked, — looked in, — made, — made
of, — meant, — passed, — reached, —
remained, — returned to, — rode, —
rode between, — rode on, — rolled
behind, — rose above, — rose around,
— rose behind, — rose in, — rose on, —

rose over, — rose up, — sank below, — sank into, — sat, — seemed to, — set, — shifted in, — showed, — showed up, — slid behind, — slid over, — slipped behind, — slipped beneath, — slipped into, — stared down, — stood above, — swung, — thought to, — threw, — took up, — turned, — turned out, — waited, — went, — went around, — went behind, — went by, — went down, — wore

moonlight
verbs
— brought out, — came from, — came in, — caught, — caught in, — chose, — continued to, — covered, — disappeared, — entered through, — fell, — fell across, — fell in, — gave, — hit, — lit, — made, — poured down, — poured in, — poured into, — poured through, — ran, — ran down, — ran like, — saw, — seemed to, — showed, — touched

morning
verbs
arrived —, arrived in —, asked —, called in —, came in —, checked —, continued about —, did —, did on —, died —, disappeared —, drank —, entered —, felt —, flew out —, found out —, got —, got up —, heard —, left —, left in —, nodded —, pulled out —, rode in —, said —, said in —, saw —, seemed off —, set off —, showed up —, sounded —, spent —, used —, waited until —, went inside —, whispered —, woke —, woke in —, woke up —, worked through —; — arrived, — arrived at, — became, — began, — began to, — broke, — brought, — called for, — came, — came

off, — came to, — came with, — drew on, — dropped, — felt, — felt like, — filled up, — flew, — followed, — found, — got on, — grew, — knew, — left, — left for, — let, — looked over, — meant, — moved, — moved past, — passed, — passed into, — passed with, — ran out, — rang around, — replied, — returned, — rolled around, — rolled over, — said, — sat on, — seemed, — seemed like, — seemed to, — slid toward, — slipped away, — slipped toward, — started, — struck with, — talked to, — thought about, — turned into, — turned to, — walked in, — went, — went at, — went by, — went on, — went through, — wore into, — wore on, — worked on

motion
verbs
— asked, — became, — came from, — caught, — changed from, — crossed, — drew, — felt, — joined by, — kicked up, — lifted, — looked like, — made, — meant, — passed, — pulled, — reached, — rose in, — seemed, — seemed to, — set, — set off, — started, — stopped, — used

motor
verbs
— began to, — came, — came to, — caught, — continued on, — continued to, — cut off, — cut to, — did, — died, — gasped, — grew, — lost, — made, — ran through, — reached, — screamed, — screamed in, — shut down, — shut off, — slipped in, — started, — started on, — started with, — took up, — turned, — turned over, — went on

mountain

verbs
came from —, came to —, cleared —, climbed —, continued into —, crossed —, felt like —, gestured at —, glanced up —, headed down —, headed for —, hit —, left —, looked at —, looked toward —, loved —, picked —, pointed at —, reached —, rolled into —, saw —, slipped down —, stared at —, wanted —, watched —; — appeared, — appeared in, — began to, — blew away, — blew up, — broke, — broke in, — broke off, — brought, — came into, — carried, — caught, — changed, — continued, — continued along, — drew, — fell, — fell down, — fell into, — fell on, — filled with, — gave, — grew, — grew up, — hung in, — left behind, — looked, — looked out, — looked up, — made of, — met, — moved with, — opened up, — picked up, — rang beneath, — remained, — rose, — rose above, — rose in, — rose into, — rose on, — sank away, — sat, — seemed to, — shifted, — shook, — showed, — slid past, — stood, — stood out, — struck, — struck down, — threw, — tossed, — touched, — turned to, — waited, — waited for, — went down, — went on, — wiped

mouth
verbs
ate at —, breathed into —, breathed through —, caught —, checked —, cleared —, closed —, covered —, covered up —, drew from —, felt —, felt in —, filled —, found —, gasped against —, gasped into —, got —, held —, kept —, kissed —, left —, lifted —, liked —, looked at —, lowered —, moved —, murmured against —, muttered through —, needed —, offered —, opened —,

opened up —, placed —, put —, raised —, reached —, reached for —, reached into —, rubbed —, said against —, said through —, set —, shoved into —, shut —, smelled —, smiled against —, smiled under —, smiled with —, spoke from —, spoke near —, spoke through —, stared at —, stood by —, thought of —, threw open —, took —, touched —, turned —, used —, wanted —, watched —, whispered against —, whispered into —, wiped —, wiped around —, wiped at —; — appeared, — became, — began, — began to, — broke, — broke into, — came down, — came open, — came together, — caught, — caught in, — changed, — changed from, — closed, — closed around, — closed down, — closed on, — closed over, — closed to, — continued, — continued to, — covered, — covered with, — cried out, — demanded, — did, — disappeared from, — disappeared into, — drank, — drew away, — drew back, — drew down, — drew from, — drew into, — dropped, — dropped at, — dropped in, — dropped open, — fell, — fell away, — fell into, — fell on, — fell open, — felt, — felt against, — felt like, — filled, — filled with, — flew, — flew open, — followed, — followed after, — forced, — forced open, — found, — gave, — glanced off, — got, — grew, — grinned, — hung, — hung open, — joined, — joined in, — kissed, — led to, — left, — lifted, — lifted at, — lifted in, — lifted into, — lifted up, — looked, — looked like, — lost, — lowered, — made, — made for, — meant for, — met, — met for, — met in, — missed, — moved, — moved against, — moved along, — moved down, — moved for, — moved in, — moved like, — moved over, — moved to, — moved under, — moved with, — opened, — opened by, — opened for, — opened in, — opened into, — opened like, — opened of, — opened to, — opened under, — opened with, — played over, — pointed at, — pressed, — pressed against, — pressed down, — pressed in, — pressed into, — pressed to, — pulled, — pulled back, — pulled down, — pulled into, — pulled up, — pushed aside, — ran, — remained, — remained open, — returned to, — rose, — said, — said to, — sat beneath, — screamed, — seemed, — seemed to, — set, — set in, — set into, — settled over, — shifted, — shook, — shouted, — showed, — shut, — shut at, — shut for, — shut in, — shut on, — shut out, — shut to, — slammed against, — slid across, — slid from, — slid over, — slid up, — slipped, — slipped open, — smiled, — snapped open, — spoke, — spoke at, — started to, — stayed open, — swallowed, — swung, — swung open, — talked of, — thought, — took, — took on, — touched, — tried, — tried to, — turned, — turned down, — turned to, — turned up, — wanted to, — went to, — went up, — wiped, — wore, — worked, — worked against, — worked at, — worked for, — worked in, — worked inside, — worked into, — worked like, — worked to, — worked with, — worked within, — wrapped, — wrapped around

movement
verbs

— became, — began, — began to, — broke, — brought, — came, — came from, — came on, — came to, — caught, — drew, — fell upon, — felt, — filled with, — forced, — helped, — made, — played, — pulled, — pulled up, — returned to, — seemed, — seemed to, — sent, — settled on, — shifted, — sounded, — started to, — stood out, — stopped, — swung around, — used

mug
verbs

blinked at —, brought —, drank from —, filled —, found —, frowned into —, gestured with —, got out —, grabbed —, gripped —, held out —, held up —, lifted —, looked at —, looked into —, lowered —, murmured into —, picked up —, played with —, pointed to —, pulled out —, pushed —, put —, put down —, raised —, reached for —, set —, set down —, took —, took up —

muscle
verbs

— added to, — appeared on, — became, — began, — began to, — came from, — did, — drew, — fell away, — fell into, — felt, — felt like, — gave, — grew, — grew to, — jumped, — jumped at, — jumped in, — lay against, — looked like, — lost, — made, — meant, — moved, — moved beneath, — moved in, — moved to, — moved under, — played against, — pulled, — ran in, — ran up, — remembered, — rolled beneath, — rose from, — screamed, — screamed beneath, — screamed in, — screamed with, — seemed to, — set off, — shifted in, — shifted under, — shifted underneath, — shook beneath, — snapped, — snapped in, — started to, — stood out, — threw, — took on, —

turned, — turned to, — went, — went into, — worked, — worked in

music
verbs
asked for —, asked over —, chose —, drove without —, flew toward —, followed —, gestured to —, hated —, headed toward —, heard —, killed —, liked —, listened to —, looked at —, loved —, made —, missed —, needed —, put down —, put on —, recognized —, rolled up —, said over —, shouted over —, studied —, thought of —, tried —, turned —, turned down —, turned off —, turned on —, turned up —, wanted —, wrote —, yelled above —; — became, — began, — began like, — began to, — brought, — called to, — came from, — came on, — came out, — came through, — came to, — came up, — caught, — changed, — closed, — continued, — continued to, — continued without, — cut off, — cut out, — died, — died away, — died down, — disappeared, — drew to, — dropped away, — ended, — fell, — filled, — filled with, — got, — grew, — heard in, — held for, — kept, — listened to, — made, — moved, — picked up, — played, — played at, — played from, — played in, — played inside, — played on, — played over, — played through, — played until, — poured out, — ran through, — rang in, — rang out, — reached, — remained, — rode, — rose in, — rose up, — screamed, — screamed in, — seemed to, — shook, — shut off, — snapped off, — sounded, — started, — started before, — started down, — started up, — stopped, — stopped for, — struck up, — took on, —

turned down, — turned off, — turned up, — went, — went from, — went on, — went out

name
verbs
added —, answered with —, asked —, blinked at —, breathed —, called —, called out —, caught —, changed —, checked —, considered —, cried —, cried out —, drew out —, entered —, filled in —, filled out —, found —, frowned at —, gasped —, gave —, gave out —, gave up —, got —, hated —, heard —, knew —, knew by —, laughed at —, learned —, left —, liked —, listened to —, looked at —, looked over —, lost —, loved —, made in —, made out —, made up —, missed —, murmured —, muttered —, needed —, nodded at —, noticed —, placed —, pointed to —, put —, ran —, read —, recognized —, remembered —, repeated —, returned with —, said —, saw —, screamed —, shot out —, shouted —, sighed —, sighed out —, smiled at —, sounded out —, spoke —, stared at —, studied —, thought about —, thought of —, thought up —, took —, took down —, tried —, used —, waited for —, wanted —, whispered —, wrote —, wrote down —, wrote out —, yelled —; — added to, — appeared at, — appeared in, — appeared on, — appeared to, — appeared under, — became, — became by, — began to, — began with, — brought, — called, — called by, — called in, — called out, — called up, — came, — came back, — came from, — came into, — came like, — came off, — came out, — came through, — came to, — came up, — caught, — caught in, —

caught on, — changed, — checked out,
— cleared, — continued to, — crossed,
— did, — disappeared from, —
dropped, — dropped into, — ended in,
— entered, — felt, — felt like, — filled
out, — followed by, — fought to, — got,
— got around, — grew at, — headed, —
helped, — hung for, — hung from, —
hung in, — jumped at, — kept to, —
left on, — left to, — lost in, — made, —
made for, — made up, — meant, —
meant in, — missed, — passed, —
passed down, — picked out, — played
through, — poured up, — pressed into,
— put, — put on, — put to, — raised,
— ran, — ran out, — rang, — reached
out, — read like, — remained, — rolled
off, — rolled through, — rose, — said,
— sank into, — seemed, — seemed to,
— sent, — set in, — settled in, — shot
out, — shouted, — shouted out, — slid
through, — slipped, — slipped from, —
slipped out, — slipped past, — sounded,
— sounded in, — sounded like, —
sounded on, — spoke, — started with,
— stood out, — stopped, — struck, —
took, — tried to, — turned, — turned
on, — turned out, — turned up, —
understood, — went, — went into, —
went off, — whispered, — whispered
through, — worked for, — wrapped

nausea
verbs
— began in, — brought, — brought on,
— came, — came across, — came back,
— crossed, — filled, — followed, —
fought in, — gripped at, — hit, — hit
below, — made, — passed, — passed
over, — returned, — rolled, — rolled in,
— rolled over, — rose, — rose at, —
rose from, — rose in, — tried to, —
went away

neck
verbs
bent —, blew on —, breathed down —,
broke —, checked —, covered —, felt —
, felt around —, grabbed —, grabbed at
—, gripped —, kissed —, looked at —,
moved —, murmured into —, nodded
against —, pointed at —, pointed to —,
reached around —, reached behind —,
reached to —, remembered —, rolled —
, rubbed —, rubbed at —, saw —,
smelled —, snapped —, studied —,
swung for —, touched —, tried —,
watched —, wiped —, wore about —,
wore around —; — became, — began
to, — bowed, — broke, — broke with,
— covered in, — did, — disappeared
down, — drew at, — ended in, — fell,
— felt, — felt like, — forced, — grew,
— held in, — hung, — hung down, —
joined, — lay across, — lay at, — left, —
lifted, — looked, — looked like, — lost,
— met, — opened, — opened like, —
opened up, — pressed against, — pulled,
— pulled up, — read, — remained, —
rose, — rose up, — sat down, — sat in,
— seemed to, — sent, — showed
through, — snapped, — snapped back,
— snapped to, — started, — started to,
— stood on, — stood out, — stood up,
— stopped, — told, — took, — turned,
— went, — wore

needle
verbs
— became, — began to, — caught in, —
cut into, — dropped from, — drove
into, — fell, — fell from, — fell to, —
fell with, — filled with, — flew past, —

hit, — lay on, — looked, — lowered, — moved, — paused, — remained, — rose, — sank into, — settled on, — settled to, — shook, — slid into, — slipped, — slipped between, — stood out, — stopped at, — turned, — went, — went in, — went into, — went through

news
verbs
— broke about, — brought, — came, — came from, — came in, — came on, — came out, — came to, — came up, — came with, — caught, — continued, — dropped into, — filled, — made, — moved on, — moved onto, — passed through, — picked up, — played on, — put out, — reached, — sank in, — seemed to, — sent, — took, — turned out, — went to

newspaper
verbs
asked for —, bent over —, bought —, called —, checked —, closed —, dropped —, found —, gestured to —, glanced at —, got —, grabbed —, held —, held out —, held up —, left —, lit —, looked at —, lowered —, nodded at —, nodded toward —, opened —, picked up —, pointed at —, pulled away —, put down —, ran for —, reached for —, read —, rolled up —, set aside —, shoved —, snapped open —, stopped for —, studied —, threw down —, took —, took out —, tossed down —, turned —, watched —, went to —, worked for —

night
verbs
arrived —, arrived during —, asked —, ate —, began —, called —, came —,

came at —, came over —, changed after —, did —, died —, died during —, disappeared —, disappeared during —, disappeared into —, drove through —, entered —, flew —, flew into —, flew through —, followed —, followed throughout —, got —, heard —, killed —, lay —, left —, left at —, liked —, listened to —, lit —, looked —, looked into —, loved —, needed —, ran —, ran through —, read into —, remembered of —, returned at —, rode —, rode by —, rode into —, rode through —, rose in —, said —, said to —, sat —, sat in —, saw —, shouted at —, shouted into —, slept —, slept at —, slept through —, slipped into —, smelled —, smelled like —, smiled into —, spent —, stared into —, started on —, stayed —, stayed over —, stayed up —, stepped into —, stood in —, stopped for —, thought —, thought about —, thought of —, thought to —, took —, tried —, tried at —, turned —, turned from —, used —, walked —, walked at —, watched —, waved —, went —, went at —, went to —, whispered to —, wished —, woke in —, wore —, worked —, worked at —, worked into —, worked through —, wrote —, wrote into —; — approached, — arrived, — became, — began, — began like, — began to, — brought, — came, — came back, — came down, — came inside, — came into, — came on, — came over, — came to, — came under, — came upon, — came with, — caught up, — changed, — closed about, — closed in, — closed over, — continued to, — covered, — covered with, — cut, — did, — drew down, — drew in, — drew on, — drew to, — dropped, — dropped like, — ended with, — fell, — fell by, — fell in, — fell into, — fell like, — fell over, — felt, — filled, — filled with, — followed, — forced, — found, — gave, — grew to, — held, — hung, — hung in, — hung like, — hung out, — killed, — lay, — lay across, — lay on, — left in, — lifted from, — lifted outside, — listened to, — lit up, — lit with, — looked for, — lost, — lost in, — made, — meant, — passed, — passed in, — passed to, — passed with, — played out, — poured down, — poured into, — pressed, — promised, — pulled back, — ran on, — ran through, — rang to, — rang with, — reached, — remained, — returned, — rose, — sat at, — screamed, — seemed, — seemed like, — seemed to, — sent, — settled down, — settled in, — settled into, — settled on, — settled onto, — settled over, — shook with, — slept, — slipped away, — smelled, — smelled like, — smelled of, — spent, — spent in, — spent on, — spoke into, — started with, — stayed, — studied in, — swallowed, — took, — took on, — took over, — tossed in, — tried to, — turned, — turned into, — turned out, — turned to, — went by, — went from, — went into, — went on, — went past, — went to, — wiped at, — wore on, — wrote about

nightmare
verbs
— appeared, — became, — began, — began to, — broke into, — came, — came after, — came on, — came to, — continued, — did, — drove, — ended, — filled with, — flew, — gave, — got, — made, — passed to, — realized, — returned in, — started, — stepped into,

— stood, — stood across, — stopped, — touched

noise
verbs
— added to, — asked, — became, — began, — began in, — began to, — broke, — brought, — came, — came from, — came out, — came through, — came up, — caught, — changed, — cleared, — continued, — continued until, — cut off, — cut out, — cut through, — died, — died away, — died down, — died for, — died off, — disappeared, — fell on, — filled, — filled with, — followed, — got, — grew, — left, — left behind, — made, — made up, — poured out, — rang through, — repeated, — returned, — rose, — rose with, — seemed to, — slammed into, — snapped through, — sounded, — sounded above, — sounded like, — sounded on, — sounded through, — started, — started to, — started up, — stopped, — struck, — turned into, — went away, — went off

nose
verbs
blew —, blew in —, breathed out —, breathed through —, broke —, covered —, drew up —, dropped —, felt —, followed —, gestured to —, got —, grabbed —, heard with —, held —, kept —, kissed —, knew —, landed on —, laughed through —, lifted —, looked down —, lost —, noticed —, picked —, picked at —, pulled at —, pulled on —, raised —, reached for —, rubbed —, rubbed at —, sighed through —, spoke through —, took —, touched —, wiped —, wiped at —, worked on —; —

appeared to, — began to, — bent, — bent to, — broke, — broke with, — came down, — came into, — closed, — closed with, — covered against, — covered with, — cut off, — dropped, — ended in, — felt, — filled with, — got, — held, — hit, — led, — lifted, — lifted to, — looked, — looked like, — lowered, — made, — met, — met with, — pointed, — pointed at, — pointed down, — pointed over, — poured with, — pressed against, — pressed into, — pressed to, — pushed against, — ran, — rang, — remembered, — rose, — rose like, — rubbed against, — said, — sat in, — seemed, — seemed to, — set, — set after, — shot, — shut, — shut down, — slammed down, — slammed into, — slid onto, — smiled, — sounded, — started to, — stepped out, — touched, — turned, — turned away, — went about, — went down, — went up, — wiped

note
verbs
added —, added to —, came with —, checked —, checked over —, continued with —, did —, drew out —, finished —, found —, glanced at —, glanced over —, got —, got out —, grabbed —, grinned at —, handed over —, held out —, jumped at —, kept —, knew —, left —, looked at —, looked over —, looked through —, looked up —, lowered —, made —, nodded at —, nodded to —, nodded toward —, opened —, passed back —, passed over —, picked up —, placed —, played —, pointed at —, pointed to —, pulled out —, pushed away —, pushed through —, put down —, read —, read from —, read through —, remembered —, returned to —,

rolled up —, saw —, sent —, set down —, smiled at —, spoke without —, stared at —, studied —, thought about —, threw away —, took —, took down —, took out —, turned over —, used —, waved —, went to —, wrote —; — admitted into, — asked, — began with, — blew, — came, — came out, — climbed, — continued on, — covered in, — cut, — died away, — dropped from, — ended, — fell from, — fell into, — filled, — followed on, — found, — happened for, — held in, — held up, — lay on, — left on, — made, — promised, — put, — ran over, — rang out, — read, — read in, — said, — seemed to, — sent up, — sounded in, — stayed in, — stood out, — took

notebook
verbs
bought —, checked —, closed —, closed down —, closed up —, found —, found in —, glanced at —, got —, got out —, grabbed —, held —, held up —, kept —, lifted —, looked at —, looked in —, looked through —, lowered —, nodded at —, opened —, opened up —, picked up —, placed —, pointed at —, pointed to —, pulled —, pulled out —, pulled over —, put —, put away —, put down —, reached for —, read from —, returned —, returned to —, set down —, shut —, slid over —, stared at —, stepped on —, studied —, threw down —, took —, took out —, took up —, went to —

notepad
verbs
closed —, found —, glanced at —, grabbed —, held up —, kept —, looked

at —, opened —, opened up —, picked
up —, pulled —, pulled out —, pulled
over —, put away —, raised —, reached
for —, returned to —, set aside —, set
down —, slid —, slid over —, stared at
—, took —, took out —, turned over —,
went to —, wished for —, wrote in —

number
verbs
called —, called from —, called in —,
called up —, checked —, chose —,
entered —, entered in —, finished —,
found —, gave —, glanced at —, got —,
handed over —, hated —, heard —, hit
—, knew —, left —, liked —, looked at
—, looked up —, loved —, made up —,
passed on —, pointed to —, pressed —,
pressed in —, read —, read off —, read
out —, recognized —, said —, saw —,
sighed at —, stared at —, studied —,
talked about —, took —, took down —,
tried —, understood —, watched —,
wrote —, wrote down —; — added, —
added to, — appeared, — appeared in,
— appeared on, — appeared under, —
began, — began to, — blinked on, —
called, — came across, — came back, —
came into, — came to, — came together,
— came up, — changed, — continued
to, — cut off, — dropped, — dropped
by, — filled, — filled up, — followed, —
found on, — grew, — handed out, —
killed, — lay, — lay open, — lit up, —
looked, — looked at, — made, —
meant, — needed for, — played for, —
poured forth, — rang, — rang out, —
remained, — seemed, — seemed to, —
set down, — showed, — showed up, —
stood, — stopped, — turned out, —
went, — went down, — went to, —
went up, — worked at

office
verbs
answered in —, approached —, arrived
at —, arrived in —, ate at —, called —,
called from —, called into —, came from
—, came into —, came to —, checked
with —, cleared —, climbed inside —,
considered —, continued into —,
continued toward —, crossed —,
crossed to —, disappeared from —,
disappeared into —, dropped by —,
drove into —, drove past —, drove to —
, entered —, fell into —, filled —, found
—, gave —, gave at —, gestured to —,
gestured toward —, glanced about —,
glanced around —, glanced into —,
glanced outside —, glanced toward —,
got to —, hated —, headed for —,
headed into —, headed to —, headed
toward —, hit —, kept —, knocked at
—, landed in —, leaned outside —, left
—, left for —, lived at —, looked across
—, looked around —, looked at —,
looked inside —, looked over —, missed
—, moved into —, moved to —, needed
—, nodded at —, nodded toward —,
opened —, passed —, picked —,
pointed at —, pointed to —, pushed
into —, ran from —, ran into —, ran to
—, reached —, remembered —,
returned to —, said —, said around —,
said in —, sat in —, saw —, shouted
from —, slammed into —, slept at —,
slept in —, slipped inside —, started for
—, started toward —, stayed in —,
stepped from —, stepped inside —,
stepped into —, stepped outside —,
stood in —, stopped at —, stopped by
—, stopped outside —, swung by —,
swung into —, thought of —, took —,
took in —, tried —, turned to —, waited

at —, walked across —, walked by —,
walked into —, walked through —,
walked to —, walked toward —, wanted
—, watched —, went in —, went inside
—, went into —, went to —, worked in
—, yelled from —; — agreed to, —
answered, — asked for, — became, —
began to, — called, — called to, —
came, — came in, — came over, —
checked for, — cleared, — closed, —
closed after, — covered in, — cried into,
— did, — drank, — dropped into, —
felt, — filled with, — flew, — flew open,
— followed by, — got, — grew, — held,
— held in, — hit, — lit with, — looked,
— looked at, — looked like, — made, —
nodded, — opened, — opened at, —
passed on, — picked, — played, — read,
— said, — sat, — sat behind, — sat on,
— seemed, — seemed to, — sent down,
— set, — smelled, — smelled like, —
smelled of, — stood, — suggested, —
swung, — swung open, — took, — tried
to, — turned into, — used, — wanted,
— waved, — went, — went to, — wore,
— worked during, — worked on

opening
verbs

arrived at —, began —, came through —
, climbed to —, closed —, crossed past
—, drew from —, dropped through —,
felt for —, flew into —, found —,
glanced toward —, heard —, kept —,
kissed —, leaned near —, leaned over —,
left —, looked at —, looked for —,
looked into —, moved through —,
moved toward —, needed —, passed
through —, pointed at —, pointed to —
, pushed against —, reached —, reached
through —, saw —, slid into —, slid
through —, slipped into —, slipped

through —, stared at —, stared through
—, stared toward —, started —, stepped
into —, stepped through —, stepped to
—, stepped toward —, stepped under —
, stood in —, stood over —, stopped by
—, took —, used —, waited for —,
walked through —, walked toward —

order
verbs

believed in —, called for —, called out
—, carried out —, changed —,
considered —, did like —, entered —,
explained —, filled —, finished —,
followed —, gave —, got —, held out —,
joined —, kept —, left —, left with —,
liked —, made —, placed —, put in —,
put through —, remembered —,
repeated —, shouted —, snapped —,
snapped out —, started —, took —,
took over —, turned in —, understood
—, waited for —, watched with —,
wrote out —; — appeared, — appeared
on, — arrived, — began to, — blew out,
— broke down, — brought to, — called,
— came, — came down, — came from,
— came in, — came into, — came on,
— came out, — came to, — came under,
— carried out, — closed in, — covered,
— demanded, — did, — dropped in, —
followed, — found, — got, — held out,
— hit, — killed, — knew, — knew by,
— left, — lived in, — looked, — lost, —
made, — meant to, — moved into, —
needed, — needed to, — nodded, —
offered, — opened, — picked, — placed,
— pulled, — pushed back, — put, —
rang in, — rang out, — remained, —
returned to, — said, — sat with, —
seemed to, — sent, — sent to, — set
upon, — spoke, — stared at, — stepped
in, — stood, — stood behind, — stood

in, — thought of, — took, — took out,
— took over, — took up, —
understood, — used to, — waited for,
— wanted, — went back, — went out,
— went through, — went to

owl
verbs

— appeared, — appeared with, — began
to, — blinked in, — called, — called
from, — called out, — called to, —
caught, — did, — dropped down, —
dropped from, — felt, — flew, — flew
away, — flew on, — glanced at, —
glanced over, — glanced up, — got to,
— grew, — heard, — hesitated, —
joined, — kept to, — landed, — landed
on, — laughed, — leaned, — leaned
back, — led, — let, — listened from, —
looked at, — looked for, — looked in,
— made, — nodded, — passed over, —
pulled up, — put, — raised, — reached
out, — reached over, — rode inside, —
said, — sat in, — set, — settled, —
settled on, — shifted, — shook, — shot
out, — shut, — slipped over, — smiled
at, — stared at, — stared down, —
stared into, — stood on, — swung, —
took, — tried to, — turned, — turned
to, — waited, — watched, — went

pack
verbs

caught —, closed —, crossed to —,
dropped —, dropped in —, found —,
glanced at —, glanced to —, got —,
grabbed —, handed over —, headed —,
held onto —, held out —, joined —,
kept —, kicked —, left —, lifted —,
moved to —, offered —, opened —,
passed —, picked up —, pulled off —,
pulled out —, put —, put down —,

raised —, ran in —, ran to —, reached
for —, reached inside —, reached into
—, reached to —, reached toward —, set
—, settled —, shifted —, shook —,
shrugged off —, shrugged on —, slipped
off —, swung to —, threw off —, took
—, took of —, took off —, went to —;
— appeared to, — became, — began to,
— broke forward, — called, — came, —
came on, — came to, — crossed, — did,
— died, — disappeared into, —
dropped to, — fell over, — felt, — filled
with, — gasped, — held, — kept, —
knew, — left, — lifted, — listened, —
looked, — looked like, — made for, —
moved in, — needed to, — ran in, —
ran up, — rubbed against, — sat, —
seemed to, — sent to, — slammed into,
— stopped, — turned, — wanted to, —
went, — went to

page
verbs

answered —, bent over —, came to —,
closed —, disappeared from —, dropped
—, finished —, found —, frowned at —,
glanced at —, glanced down —, glanced
through —, glanced to —, got to —,
grabbed —, gripped —, held out —,
held up —, kept —, leaned over —,
looked at —, looked down —, looked
inside —, looked through —, missed —,
nodded at —, opened —, opened to —,
picked up —, pulled out —, put down
—, read —, read down —, read from —,
read through —, repeated —, set out —,
shifted —, stared at —, stopped —,
stopped at —, stopped on —, studied —
, took —, took out —, touched —,
turned —, turned over —, turned
through —, turned to —, watched —,
went through —, went to —; —

appeared on, — appeared to, — asked, — became, — began to, — brought back, — brought up, — came into, — came up, — caught, — fell onto, — fell open, — filled with, — followed, — gave, — glanced at, — laid, — lay on, — leaned forward, — left in, — let out, — looked like, — moved to, — nodded, — offered by, — opened like, — pointed to, — pulled away, — ran, — ran off, — remained, — replied, — said, — screamed in, — seemed to, — settled, — settled together, — showed, — showed up, — shut, — stopped, — turned, — waved, — whispered, — wiped

pain
verbs
asked in —, ate —, blinked away —, blinked from —, blinked in —, cried in —, expected —, felt —, forced back —, fought —, fought back —, fought off —, fought through —, gasped at —, gasped from —, gasped in —, gasped out —, gasped through —, gasped with —, heard —, knew —, laughed in —, lay in —, learned about —, liked —, lived with —, looked at —, looked in —, loved —, meant —, moved with —, moved without —, muttered in —, needed —, nodded in —, played in —, pushed away —, pushed back —, recognized —, remembered —, saw —, screamed at —, screamed from —, screamed in —, screamed with —, seemed in —, shook with —, shouted in —, showed —, sighed in —, smiled through —, spoke with —, took —, understood —, used —, walked without —, wanted —, worked out —, worked through —, yelled in —, yelled with —; — added to, — arrived, — became, — began, —

began in, — began to, — broke through, — brought, — brought on, — came, — came after, — came back, — came behind, — came from, — came through, — came to, — came with, — cleared, — climbed up, — closed in, — continued, — continued to, — crossed, — cut in, — cut through, — disappeared, — drew, — drove, — drove through, — entered, — felt, — felt by, — felt like, — filled, — gave, — got, — grew, — grew in, — helped, — hit, — hit below, — jumped to, — left, — lit off, — made, — meant, — passed, — passed over, — pressed against, — pulled on, — ran down, — ran through, — ran up, — rang out, — remained, — returned, — returned to, — rolled through, — rolled up, — rose into, — sank into, — screamed through, — screamed up, — seemed, — seemed to, — settled into, — settled over, — shook, — shot, — shot across, — shot behind, — shot down, — shot from, — shot into, — shot through, — shot up, — slammed, — slammed into, — slammed through, — slipped away, — started, — started to, — stayed, — stopped, — struck, — took, — took over, — turned to, — waited for, — went, — went away, — went off, — went on, — went through, — went up, — whispered past

pair
verbs
— appeared around, — appeared at, — approached, — arrived, — began to, — came, — came forward, — came into, — continued, — continued to, — crossed, — died, — disappeared over, — flew to, — followed, — got in, — held, — held up, — landed, — landed like, —

laughed, — leaned, — left, — lit, — made, — moved through, — moved toward, — realized, — replied, — replied together, — returned to, — said in, — sat, — sat across, — seemed to, — stepped inside, — stepped into, — stood, — stood in, — stopped, — took off, — tried to, — walked, — walked into, — watched, — went down, — wrapped in

palm
verbs
caught —, checked —, closed —, fell into —, gestured to —, held open —, held out —, held up —, kissed —, leaned into —, leaned on —, lifted —, looked at —, lowered —, opened —, placed —, pointed behind —, pressed into —, put —, put out —, put up —, raised —, reached out —, rubbed —, shifted —, shook —, showed —, smiled into —, stared at —, stepped onto —, studied —, took —, touched —, turned —, turned up —, waved —, wiped —; — became, — began, — began to, — broke, — broke out, — came at, — came away, — came down, — came to, — came up, — covered, — fell away, — fell into, — fell open, — fell to, — felt, — felt like, — found, — grew, — gripped, — held, — held out, — held together, — hit, — landed on, — lay, — made, — meant, — met, — moved over, — moved up, — pressed, — pressed against, — pressed into, — pressed on, — pressed to, — pressed together, — pushed into, — raised, — returned to, — rose, — rubbed against, — sent, — set on, — settled, — shot out, — shoved against, — slid onto, — slid over, — slid through, — slipped, — slipped against,

— slipped up, — started to, — stood out, — took up, — touched, — turned, — turned out, — turned up, — went, — went in, — went to

panel
verbs
— appeared to, — began to, — came away, — came to, — closed, — covered, — cut from, — drew back, — kicked in, — lifted, — lit up, — made up, — nodded, — opened, — opened in, — raised from, — seemed to, — set into, — shot open, — shut, — slid, — slid into, — slid open, — swung, — swung open, — turned, — turned to, — went

panic
verbs
asked in —, cried in —, felt —, fought —, fought against —, fought back —, fought down —, fought off —, got —, heard —, remembered —, said in —, saw —, screamed —, screamed in —, shook off —, shouted in —, sounded near —, swallowed —, thought in —, turned in —, went into —, whispered in —, woke in —, yelled in —; — began to, — blew across, — blew over, — broke out, — came, — came on, — came out, — came upon, — caught in, — cleared, — climbed, — climbed in, — climbed into, — closed, — closed in, — closed up, — crossed, — ended, — entered, — fell, — filled, — forced, — got, — gripped, — held, — hit, — hit through, — kicked in, — lit, — made, — pulled, — ran, — ran like, — rang within, — reached out, — returned, — rolled, — rolled over, — rose, — rose in, — rose up, — rose with, — sat, — seemed to, — set, — set in, — shook, — shot through,

— showed in, — slammed into, — slid down, — slid through, — started, — started in, — stopped, — struck, — struck like, — thought, — took, — took over, — touched, — tried to, — went with

pants
verbs
changed into —, checked —, climbed into —, found —, grabbed —, kicked off —, left —, needed —, picked up —, pointed at —, pulled —, pulled down —, pulled off —, pulled on —, pulled up —, pushed —, put on —, reached for —, reached into —, rolled up —, said between —, saw —, shoved down —, slipped off —, slipped on —, stared at —, stepped from —, threw on —, took —, wore —; — began to, — came off, — came to, — changed, — dropped to, — fell, — filled with, — gave, — grabbed, — held up, — hit, — hung off, — hung over, — lay, — looked, — made, — opened, — pulled down, — pulled up, — pushed down, — raised, — rolled up, — sat on, — set, — settled into, — showed off, — spoke of, — started to, — went, — went down

paper
verbs
bent over —, bent to —, bent toward —, bought —, brought —, called —, checked —, cleared —, cleared away —, dropped —, finished —, found —, gestured at —, glanced at —, glanced toward —, grabbed —, grabbed for —, handed —, handed over —, held —, held out —, held up —, kept —, laid down —, leaned over —, lifted —, lit —, looked at —, looked in —, looked over —, looked through —, lowered —, moved around —, moved for —, nodded at —, nodded to —, offered —, opened —, passed —, passed over —, picked up —, pointed at —, pointed to —, pulled —, pulled at —, pulled off —, pulled out —, pushed aside —, put down —, ran —, reached for —, reached over —, read —, read from —, remembered —, returned to —, rolled up —, saw —, set aside —, set down —, shook —, slid —, slid away —, slipped —, slipped open —, stared at —, studied —, thought of —, threw down —, told —, took —, took back —, took down —, tossed —, tossed aside —, tossed down —, touched —, turned —, turned over —, turned through —, used —, waved —, waved at —, went for —, went through —, went to —; — added, — arrived at, — arrived in, — began to, — blew across, — blew off, — blew over, — came around, — came out, — came through, — came to, — carried, — caught, — caught in, — closed, — covered in, — covered with, — cut of, — did, — disappeared into, — ended, — fell onto, — fell out, — felt, — felt like, — filled, — filled out, — flew about, — flew through, — flew up, — followed, — found, — found on, — got, — grew, — grew in, — hung along, — hung from, — knew, — laid out, — lay around, — lay beside, — lay in, — lay on, — lay underneath, — led to, — led with, — looked, — looked for, — lowered, — made, — made out, — played up, — pressed into, — ran, — read, — rolled out, — rose into, — said, — sat on, — shifted, — shook, — shook between, — shook in, — showed, — slipped from, — slipped into, — stood

by, — stood out, — tried to, — used, —
waved, — wrapped, — wrapped around

part
verbs
— became, — broke open, — called, —
came after, — came from, — came
through, — cut through, — did, — felt,
— figured out, — finished, — flew
away, — hit, — laid out, — landed in,
— left to, — lit, — looked like, — made,
— meant, — pulled, — remained, —
returned to, — sat in, — seemed, —
took up, — used by, — walked toward,
— wanted to, — went on, — went
through

party
verbs
— agreed, — appeared, — approached,
— became, — began, — began to, —
broke up, — came, — came at, — came
into, — came out, — came to, — came
up, — came upon, — caught up, —
checked, — climbed, — continued, —
continued on, — continued to, —
crossed, — drew, — ended, — fell upon,
— filled, — followed, — fought to, —
found, — gave, — got, — grew, — held,
— held in, — kept, — kicked in, —
knew of, — left, — listened, — looked
at, — looked down, — looked for, —
looked to, — lost, — made, — meant,
— met, — moved, — moved forward,
— moved inside, — moved off, —
moved over, — moved up, — needed, —
passed by, — poured, — pushed
forward, — ran down, — reached, —
returned from, — rolled around, —
rolled on, — sat against, — sat outside,
— seemed, — seemed to, — sent, —
settled in, — showed, — showed up, —

stared at, — stared down, — started, —
started forward, — stepped in, —
stopped, — stopped at, — studied, —
took, — took off, — understood, —
waited by, — walked forward, — walked
into, — walked through, — wanted to,
— watched from, — went across, —
went along, — went on, — went to

path
verbs
approached along —, came along —,
came up —, chose —, climbed —,
continued —, continued along —,
continued down —, continued on —,
continued up —, crossed —,
disappeared down —, entered —, fell
onto —, flew along —, followed —,
found —, glanced at —, glanced toward
—, headed off —, hit —, knew —, left
—, looked at —, looked up —, lost —,
made for —, moved off —, nodded
along —, paused on —, placed in —,
pointed down —, ran up —, reached —,
recognized —, rode down —, saw —,
slipped into —, stared down —, started
along —, started down —, started for —
, started toward —, started up —, stayed
in —, stayed on —, stepped in —,
stepped into —, stepped off —, stood in
—, stood on —, stopped on —, turned
from —, turned in —, turned into —,
turned off —, turned onto —, turned up
—, walked —, walked along —, walked
down —, walked up —, watched —,
went off —; — appeared on, —
appeared to, — became, — began, —
began to, — came, — came out, —
cleared, — climbed, — closed in, —
continued beyond, — continued in, —
continued on, — continued through, —
continued to, — crossed, — crossed in,

— cut, — cut back, — cut into, — cut
through, — demanded, — disappeared,
— disappeared beneath, — ended, —
entered, — finished, — followed, —
happened to, — joined, — laid out, —
lay, — lay in, — lay open, — led, — led
away, — led down, — led from, — led
into, — led through, — led to, — led
up, — left by, — lit by, — looked, —
looked like, — made, — made of, —
meant, — met, — opened out, —
passed, — ran, — ran along, — ran out,
— ran through, — ran to, — reached,
— rose, — seemed, — seemed to, — set
with, — slid around, — took, — took
to, — turned, — turned into, — turned
to, — went, — went on

pause
verbs
added after —, agreed after —, answered
after —, answered without —, asked
after —, continued after —, continued
without —, drew out —, expected —,
gave —, heard —, hit —, left —, moved
without —, nodded after —, pressed —,
replied after —, replied without —,
returned without —, rode without —,
said after —, said without —, took —,
understood —, waited through —

pen
verbs
asked for —, brought out —, crossed —,
dropped —, felt —, found —, got —,
got out —, grabbed —, gripped —,
handed —, held —, held out —, held up
—, jumped into —, kept —, laid down
—, lay down —, lifted —, looked to —,
lowered —, needed —, picked up —,
pointed with —, pulled —, pulled from
—, pulled out —, pushed —, put —, put

away —, put down —, raised —, reached
for —, returned with —, rolled inside —
, set —, set aside —, set down —, slid —,
slipped out —, stepped into —, threw
down —, took —, took out —, took up
—, tossed aside —, walked around —,
waved —

pencil
verbs
broke —, drew —, dropped —, found
—, gestured with —, got out —, grabbed
—, grabbed up —, gripped —, held —,
held up —, laid —, lifted —, picked up
—, played with —, pulled off —, pulled
out —, put —, put away —, put down
—, reached for —, set aside —, set down
—, took —, took out —, took up —,
tossed aside —, tossed down —, used —,
wanted —

phone
verbs
answered —, asked about —, asked at —
, asked into —, asked on —, asked over
—, blinked at —, bought —, breathed
into —, brought —, brought out —,
called —, called into —, called on —,
came off —, came on —, came onto —,
came to —, carried —, caught —,
checked —, chose —, closed —, closed
down —, closed up —, continued into
—, continued on —, covered —, cried
into —, crossed to —, cut off —,
demanded into —, drew —, drew out —
, dropped —, felt —, felt for —, found
—, frowned at —, gestured at —,
gestured for —, gestured to —, gestured
toward —, gestured with —, glanced at
—, glanced toward —, got —, got off —,
got on —, got out —, grabbed —,
grabbed at —, grabbed for —, grabbed

up —, grinned at —, gripped —, handed back —, handed over —, headed for —, headed to —, heard —, held —, held out —, held up —, hit —, hoped —, hung up —, jumped on —, kept —, kicked —, laid down —, laughed into —, laughed over —, leaned to —, left —, lifted —, listened into —, listened to —, lived by —, looked at —, looked for —, lost —, lowered —, moved to —, moved toward —, murmured into —, muttered into —, muttered over —, needed —, nodded at —, nodded into —, nodded to —, nodded toward —, noticed —, opened —, passed —, passed back —, passed over —, picked up —, placed —, played with —, pointed —, pointed at —, pointed to —, pulled —, pulled back —, pulled out —, put —, put away —, put back —, put down —, raised —, ran for —, ran to —, reached for —, reached through —, reached under —, remembered —, repeated into —, repeated over —, returned —, returned to —, said —, said into —, said on —, said over —, sat by —, saw —, screamed down —, screamed into —, screamed over —, set aside —, set down —, shifted —, shook —, shouted down —, shouted into —, showed —, shut —, shut down —, shut off —, sighed into —, sighed through —, slammed —, slammed down —, slid —, slid out —, slipped out —, smiled at —, smiled into —, snapped into —, snapped off —, snapped open —, spoke by —, spoke from —, spoke into —, spoke on —, spoke through —, stared at —, stared between —, stared into —, started for —, started toward —, stayed at —, stayed off —, stayed on —, stepped to —, stopped at —, talked into —, took

—, took back —, took out —, took up —, tossed —, touched —, tried —, turned from —, turned off —, turned on —, turned over —, turned to —, turned up —, used —, waited on —, walked to —, walked toward —, wanted —, waved —, waved for —, went for —, went to —, whispered into —, woke —, worked —, worked on —, yelled at —, yelled into —; — answered, — appeared, — appeared from, — appeared in, — began to, — blinked, — broke, — brought, — came, — came to, — came with, — caught, — changed, — chose, — closed, — continued to, — cut, — cut in, — cut into, — cut off, — cut out, — cut through, — did, — died, — died in, — disappeared into, — dropped, — dropped from, — dropped to, — expected, — fell, — fell out, — fell to, — gave, — got, — gripped in, — held, — held to, — hit, — hung around, — hung on, — landed in, — landed on, — lay, — lay beside, — lay on, — let out, — lit up, — looked, — looked for, — made, — needed, — opened up, — ordered, — picked up, — played, — pressed, — pressed against, — pressed into, — pressed to, — put in, — ran out, — rang, — rang after, — rang at, — rang before, — rang during, — rang for, — rang from, — rang in, — rang inside, — rang off, — rang on, — rang out, — rang through, — rang with, — remained, — remained on, — said, — sat, — sat in, — sat on, — seemed, — seemed to, — sent, — set, — set in, — shifted in, — showed, — shut, — shut off, — slammed down, — slipped from, — slipped in, — sounded, — sounded in, — started to, — started up, — stayed, — stayed in, — stood on, —

stopped, — took, — turned off, —
turned up, — waited for, — went, —
went down, — went into, — went off,
— went to, — worked

photo
verbs
arrived with —, asked for —, called up
—, changed —, checked —, did for —,
dropped —, found —, frowned at —,
gestured to —, glanced at —, got —,
held —, held out —, held up —, kept
—, kissed —, laid —, laid down —, leaned
toward —, lifted —, liked —, looked at
—, looked through —, moved to —,
nodded at —, opened —, passed —,
picked up —, pointed at —, pointed to
—, pulled —, pulled out —, pulled up
—, put away —, put back —, put down
—, reached behind —, reached for —,
recognized —, remembered —, returned
—, saw —, saw in —, set down —,
showed —, slid out —, slipped —,
snapped —, stared at —, studied —,
took —, took down —, took out —,
touched —, turned over —, turned to
—, waved —, waved away —, went
through —; — appeared, — appeared
in, — appeared on, — began to, — came
along, — came from, — came through,
— came up, — carried, — changed, —
covered, — disappeared, — dropped
from, — dropped into, — dropped
onto, — filled, — finished, — followed,
— gave, — hit, — kept, — laid out, —
lay on, — looked, — looked like, —
made, — made for, — moved in, —
placed, — put together, — ran with, —
sat by, — seemed, — seemed to, — sent,
— showed, — showed off, — stood in,
— stopped at, — went on

photograph
verbs
closed —, considered —, drew out —,
explained about —, finished —, found
—, gestured at —, gestured to —,
glanced at —, grinned in —, handed
back —, handed over —, held —, held
up —, laid out —, lifted —, looked at —
, looked over —, lowered —, nodded at
—, nodded toward —, passed over —,
picked out —, picked up —, pointed at
—, pointed to —, pulled out —, pushed
—, put down —, reached for —,
remembered —, returned —, said to —,
saw —, set down —, shook —, slid back
—, snapped off —, spoke to —, stared at
—, studied —, thought about —,
thought of —, took —, took out —,
turned over —, turned to —, waved to
—, went through —

picture
verbs
asked —, asked about —, bought —,
came into —, carried —, continued
through —, drew —, dropped —,
entered —, found —, frowned at —,
glanced at —, got —, grabbed —,
gripped —, handed over —, hated —,
held out —, held up —, hung up —,
killed —, left —, lifted —, looked at —,
looked through —, loved —, lowered —
, needed —, nodded at —, nodded
toward —, opened —, passed on —,
picked up —, pointed at —, pointed to
—, pointed toward —, put down —,
recognized —, remembered —, returned
—, rolled up —, saw —, sent —, showed
—, smiled at —, snapped —, stared at —
, stepped into —, stepped toward —,
stopped with —, studied —, swung
from —, thought about —, threw —,

told —, took —, took back —, took
down —, took in —, took out —, took
up —, touched —, turned from —,
turned to —, used —, walked to —,
wanted —, waved at —, went to —,
worked from —; — appeared, —
appeared on, — arrived, — became, —
began, — began to, — blinked off, —
blinked to, — called, — called to, —
came, — came from, — came in, —
came into, — came on, — came onto, —
came out, — came to, — came up, —
changed, — changed to, — cut out, —
died, — disappeared, — fell down, —
fell from, — fell out, — fell over, — fell
to, — filled, — finished, — gave, —
grew, — held, — held in, — hit, —
hung by, — hung in, — hung on, —
hung over, — leaned against, — liked to,
— looked, — made, — made of, —
made on, — missed from, — reached, —
remained, — returned to, — rolled, —
rose in, — seemed, — shot through, —
showed, — snapped, — stared, — stared
at, — told, — took, — turned, —
turned out, — went, — went by, —
went to, — wore on

piece
verbs
ate —, broke off —, covered over —, cut
—, drew —, entered —, fell in —, fell to
—, glanced at —, knew —, loved —,
lowered —, opened —, picked up —,
played —, ran over —, reached for —,
read —, returned —, said —, screamed
at —, snapped off —, spoke —, stood by
—, thought about —, took —, touched
—, waved —, went to —, wrote —; —
began, — began to, — broke away, —
brought to, — came back, — came from,
— came off, — came together, —

disappeared beneath, — dropped past,
— ended, — ended with, — fell, — fell
away, — fell from, — fell in, — fell into,
— fell off, — fell to, — flew in, — hung
from, — landed on, — lay in, — left to,
— looked like, — made, — made in, —
missed from, — remained, — said, —
sat in, — seemed, — showed above, —
snapped, — snapped into, — struck, —
took, — took on, — touched, — turned,
— went in, — worked through

pillow
verbs
asked into —, brought —, cried against
—, dropped —, dropped into —,
dropped onto —, fell against —, fell into
—, fell on —, fell onto —, fought —,
found —, gasped into —, got —,
grabbed —, hit —, kicked —, lay against
—, lay on —, leaned into —, leaned on
—, lifted —, looked at —, looked under
—, needed —, picked up —, pulled off
—, pushed away —, put —, reached
behind —, reached for —, reached
under —, returned with —, rose on —,
said into —, sank in —, sank into —,
sank on —, sat against —, sat between
—, saw —, settled against —, shifted on
—, shouted into —, smiled into —,
threw —, took —, tossed —, tossed
away —, touched —, wanted —, waved
—, whispered into —

pistol
verbs
broke open —, brought out —, carried
—, checked —, drew —, dropped —,
felt —, felt for —, found —, gestured
with —, glanced at —, got —, grabbed
—, grabbed for —, gripped —, handed
—, handed over —, held —, held out —,

held up —, kept —, lifted —, liked —,
looked at —, looked over —, lowered —
, needed —, picked up —, placed —,
pointed —, pointed with —, pulled —,
pulled down —, pulled out —, put —,
put away —, put down —, raised —,
reached for —, recognized —,
remembered —, saw —, set —, shifted
—, slipped out —, stared at —, studied
—, swung —, thought of —, took —,
took out —, took up —, tossed —,
turned —, watched —, waved —, went
to —, wore —; — appeared, — came
back, — came out, — came up, — cut,
— disappeared into, — dropped from,
— fell, — fell away, — fell from, — fell
out, — fell to, — felt, — felt like, —
flew, — flew from, — gripped in, —
held, — held at, — held back, — hit, —
hung at, — hung by, — hung from, —
lay, — lay in, — lay on, — left, —
lowered, — missed from, — pointed at,
— pointed down, — pressed, — pressed
between, — pressed to, — raised, —
raised at, — raised in, — remained
within, — rose into, — sat, — shook in,
— shot to, — slipped from, — snapped
up, — spoke, — swung, — swung in, —
talked about, — touched, — went into,
— went off

place
verbs

approached —, bought —, came in —,
checked —, chose —, cleared —,
considered —, dropped into —, drove
by —, entered —, fell from —, fell into
—, felt to —, found —, found in —,
glanced around —, got —, hated —,
headed to —, held —, kept —, knew —,
knew about —, knew of —, left —, liked
—, lived in —, looked about —, looked

around —, looked at —, looked over —,
looked toward —, lost —, loved —,
made —, moved into —, needed —,
nodded in —, opened —, passed —,
passed by —, picked —, pointed to —,
pushed at —, ran in —, reached —,
recognized —, remained in —,
remembered —, returned to —, rose
from —, sat at —, sat in —, saw —, set
—, settled into —, slept above —,
slipped into —, stared at —, stayed at —
, stayed in —, stepped into —, stood in
—, stopped in —, studied —, swung in
—, took —, took of —, touched —,
turned in —, understood —, walked
around —, walked from —, walked in
—, walked into —, walked to —, went
to —, worked at —; — added to, —
appeared, — appeared to, — became, —
began at, — blew out, — brought, —
brought back, — called, — called for, —
came after, — came to, — carried, —
caught, — changed, — closed down, —
closed to, — did, — disappeared in, —
ended, — fell, — felt, — felt like, —
filled up, — filled with, — got, —
happened, — held, — held back, — held
in, — helped, — hung around, — kept,
— lay, — left, — left for, — left in, —
left to, — lit up, — looked for, —
looked in, — looked like, — made, —
made for, — meant, — meant for, —
nodded, — opened for, — opened in, —
opened out, — opened up, — pulled, —
put, — ran, — ran together, — reached,
— reached through, — sat, — saw, —
screamed, — seemed, — seemed to, —
set for, — set on, — set up, — shut
down, — slept in, — smelled, — smelled
like, — smelled of, — sounded, —
started to, — swung, — swung open, —

told, — took up, — turned, — turned
to, — wanted, — went, — went up

plan
verbs
began —, changed —, considered —,
continued —, continued with —,
explained —, glanced at —, got —,
hated —, heard —, knew —, laid —, laid
out —, leaned over —, liked —, listened
to —, looked at —, made —, needed —,
pointed at —, put —, remembered —,
set out —, studied —, talked through —
, thought about —, thought of —,
understood —, wanted —, whispered —
; — agreed, — appeared to, — became,
— began, — began to, — began with, —
called for, — came, — came into, —
came to, — came together, — changed,
— changed by, — continued to, — fell,
— made, — met with, — passed
through, — rolled through, — seemed
to, — settled, — showed, — snapped
into, — started to, — took, — went, —
worked, — worked for, — worked like

plane
verbs
approached —, ate on —, brought —,
came by —, climbed —, climbed aboard
—, climbed into —, climbed on —,
climbed onto —, entered —, felt like —,
gestured to —, got off —, got onto —,
left —, looked around —, looked at —,
met —, pointed at —, returned to —,
sat on —, saw —, slept on —, started for
—, stepped aboard —, stepped from —,
stepped inside —, stepped off —,
stepped onto —, took —, walked from
—, walked off —, walked onto —, yelled
into —; — appeared, — appeared above,
— arrived at, — became, — began, —

began to, — blew up, — broke through,
— came to, — came together, —
carried, — climbed through, — closed
in, — continued, — did, — disappeared,
— dropped through, — ended, — fell
from, — fell through, — filled, — flew,
— flew on, — flew over, — flew
through, — fought for, — got, — got
about, — got in, — headed for, — hit,
— landed, — landed at, — landed
before, — landed in, — landed on, —
landed with, — lay on, — left, — left on,
— lifted off, — looked, — looked in, —
made, — meant, — moved, — moved
down, — moved forward, — moved on,
— passed, — passed through, — picked
up, — pulled, — pulled up, — put on,
— ran along, — ran down, — reached,
— remained, — remained in, —
returned, — rolled on, — rolled over, —
rolled to, — rose, — rose into, — sat in,
— sat on, — seemed, — set off, —
settled in, — shook, — shot down, —
shot forward, — slammed into, — slid
down, — started, — started to, —
stopped, — stopped at, — took, — took
off, — took on, — took to, — touched
down, — turned, — turned out, —
waited, — waited to, — went, — went
beyond, — went down, — went into, —
went over

plate
verbs
blinked at —, brought —, brought over
—, carried —, checked —, cleared —,
dropped —, filled —, finished —,
finished with —, found —, glanced at —
, got —, grabbed —, grabbed up —,
heard about —, held out —, held up —,
lifted —, looked at —, made —, moved
—, nodded toward —, picked at —,

picked up —, pointed at —, pointed to
—, pulled on —, pushed —, pushed
aside —, pushed away —, put —, put
down —, ran —, reached for —, read —,
said about —, set —, set down —, set
out —, snapped to —, stared at —,
stood over —, stood with —, studied —,
took —, took off —, touched —, turned
—, turned to —, walked to —; — began
to, — broke into, — came, — covered
by, — covered with, — dropped, — fell
away, — filled with, — held, — held in,
— held on, — hit, — hung out, — lay
on, — led, — left at, — made, — moved
forward, — pointed to, — pulled into,
— pulled up, — ran, — read, — said, —
sank to, — sat atop, — sat on, — seemed
to, — sent, — set in, — set into, —
shifted, — shook, — slid, — stopped, —
turned, — waited on

pocket
verbs
carried in —, checked —, felt —, felt in
—, felt of —, grabbed —, looked in —,
looked to —, nodded toward —, picked
—, picked up —, pointed to —, pulled
from —, put in —, reached for —,
reached in —, reached inside —, reached
into —, reached to —, slipped into —,
touched —, turned —, wanted —, went
into —, went through —

point
verbs
approached —, came around —,
considered —, continued to —, drove
—, felt —, found —, got —, got to —,
looked past —, made —, missed —,
nodded —, passed to —, placed —,
pressed —, pushed —, raised —, reached
—, saw —, stayed on —, stood on —,

took —, took in —, turned at —,
understood —, went on —; — added to,
— appeared, — appeared in, — broke,
— called, — came, — came from, —
came out, — came to, — came up, —
caught between, — caught in, —
decided to, — did, — dropped, — drove
through, — entered, — fell away, — fell
from, — fell on, — felt like, — filled, —
flew past, — found, — held, — hit, —
jumped, — lay, — lay under, — left, —
lived in, — made, — made up, —
remained, — said, — sank, — sank in,
— seemed, — seemed like, — seemed to,
— sent, — showed, — slammed into, —
slid inside, — stopped at, — struck, —
talked about, — touched, — turned, —
went, — went in, — went into

pool
verbs
arrived at —, bent over —, crossed —,
dropped into —, gestured to —, headed
for —, hit —, jumped into —, left —,
looked across —, looked at —, nodded
across —, passed —, pointed at —,
pointed beyond —, reached —,
recognized in —, remained in —,
returned to —, sat by —, stared at —,
stared into —, stopped by —, turned
from —, turned to —, walked around —
, walked past —, went to —, yelled from
—; — became, — began to, — blinked
on, — caught, — covered with, — did,
— dropped, — dropped by, — filled
with, — grew in, — helped, — knew of,
— lay, — looked around, — looked like,
— put on, — remained, — sat, — sat in,
— sat within, — sent, — took, — took
back, — took on, — waited for, —
watched, — went, — worked

porch
verbs

appeared on —, approached —, called from —, came on —, came onto —, checked —, climbed —, climbed onto —, crossed —, entered —, fell to —, flew off —, headed for —, hit —, jumped off —, left —, liked —, looked at —, looked toward —, moved off —, moved toward —, nodded toward —, paused at —, paused inside —, paused on —, pointed to —, reached —, remained on —, returned to —, said from —, sat on —, screamed from —, stared at —, started for —, started on —, stepped from —, stepped inside —, stepped into —, stepped off —, stepped on —, stepped onto —, stood on —, turned from —, turned on —, waited on —, walked across —, walked off —, walked onto —, walked to —, walked toward —, went to —

power
verbs

added —, believed in —, came into —, came to —, carried —, climbed under —, cut —, explained —, felt —, found —, gave —, got —, held —, hit —, killed —, knew —, let —, liked —, lost —, loved —, missed —, needed —, recognized —, remembered —, saw —, showed —, stood under —, stopped —, thought about —, took —, turned off —, turned on —, understood —, used —, wanted —; — appeared at, — appeared in, — began to, — came back, — came from, — came in, — came of, — came through, — came to, — came up, — came with, — checked, — continued to, — died, — dropped, — entered, — fell, — fell over, — felt, — felt like, — filled,

— gave, — grew, — grew in, — grew to, — held, — hung about, — joined with, — knocked out, — lay, — lay behind, — lay in, — lay on, — lay over, — left, — liked to, — lost, — made, — made for, — met, — moved, — moved in, — moved through, — needed, — offered by, — passed down, — passed into, — put, — raised, — ran out, — remained, — remained in, — returned, — rode, — rode like, — rose against, — rose off, — rose up, — saw, — seemed, — seemed to, — shifted in, — shifted to, — shut off, — slammed into, — slid, — slipped away, — spent, — struck, — struck around, — took, — tried to, — turned, — turned into, — wanted to, — went, — went against, — went off, — went out, — went through, — worked in, — wrapped around

pressure
verbs

— became, — began to, — broke, — came, — came from, — came with, — climbed, — continued, — disappeared, — dropped, — dropped into, — dropped through, — entered, — fell, — filled, — forced, — got to, — grew, — gripped, — lifted, — lifted with, — made, — pushed, — returned to, — rose, — rose to, — said, — shook, — shot up, — snapped, — took

prompt
verbs

— appeared, — appeared after, — appeared in, — appeared on, — appeared to, — appeared with, — began to, — blinked in, — blinked on, — brought, — came from, — came up, — caught, — changed, — changed to, —

continued to, — disappeared, — filled, — held, — made, — meant, — raised, — remained in, — returned, — said, — seemed to, — waited at, — waited for

pulse
verbs

— began, — began to, — dropped down, — followed, — gave, — hit, — jumped, — jumped in, — jumped into, — jumped like, — kicked, — kicked against, — kicked at, — kicked in, — kicked into, — kicked up, — kicked with, — missed, — picked up, — rang in, — reached, — remained, — seemed to, — sent out, — shot down, — shot up, — slammed against, — slammed into, — slipped away, — sounded, — started to, — stopped, — struck, — took off, — went

purse
verbs

brought out —, came across —, carried —, checked —, closed —, dropped —, felt —, felt in —, filled —, found —, glanced into —, glanced toward —, got —, grabbed —, grabbed up —, gripped —, held up —, kept in —, left —, lifted —, looked at —, nodded at —, nodded to —, opened —, picked up —, pointed to —, pulled open —, put —, put away —, put down —, ran to —, reached for —, reached in —, reached inside —, reached into —, reached toward —, returned —, saw —, set —, set down —, shut —, snapped open —, started for —, stood with —, swung —, threw —, took —, took out —, took up —, tossed —, went for —, went into —, went to —

question

verbs

answered —, answered with —, asked —, began —, blinked at —, called for —, called with —, changed —, considered —, decided on —, felt about —, finished —, followed without —, frowned at —, frowned away —, frowned in —, got —, got in —, heard —, held —, hesitated at —, jumped at —, knew —, knew without —, laughed at —, laughed off —, liked —, listened to —, looked —, moved onto —, nodded at —, nodded to —, passed along —, raised —, ran through —, read —, repeated —, replied to —, replied with —, sent —, shouted —, shrugged off —, slid past —, slipped in —, smiled —, smiled at —, snapped —, snapped out —, stared at —, started at —, started with —, studied —, swallowed at —, thought —, thought about —, thought of —, thought over —, took up —, tossed in —, turned at —, turned without —, understood —, waited for —, wanted —, waved away —, waved off —, went without —, whispered —, wondered about —, worked —; — answered, — answered through, — asked, — asked by, — asked for, — became, — began, — brought, — brought back, — brought on, — called, — called for, — came, — came back, — came down, — came from, — came in, — came on, — came out, — came to, — caught, — continued, — continued to, — crossed, — cut, — cut into, — cut off, — died, — died away, — died in, — drew, — fell from, — felt, — filled, — flew into, — flew over, — flew through, — gave, — got, — happened to, — held back, — hung, — hung between, — hung in, — hung on, — joined, — lay, — lay beyond, — left, — left for, — lit,

— made, — meant, — met with, — moved in, — needed, — passed, — poured forth, — poured out, — pushed, — put, — ran through, — rang, — remained, — repeated, — repeated in, — rolled in, — rolled off, — rolled out, — rose, — rose in, — rose to, — said, — seemed, — seemed to, — sent, — showed, — slipped, — slipped into, — slipped past, — sounded, — started, — stepped forward, — stopped for, — struck, — struck from, — took, — took on, — took over, — turned, — turned into, — went, — went on, — went through, — wrote

radio
verbs
answered —, answered over —, asked —, asked into —, asked over —, asked through —, called from —, called into —, called over —, came on —, checked —, cut off —, demanded into —, dropped —, finished with —, found —, gasped over —, gestured toward —, glanced at —, got —, got on —, grabbed —, grabbed up —, heard —, heard on —, held —, held out —, hit —, killed —, lifted —, listened for —, listened to —, looked at —, loved —, lowered —, murmured into —, nodded at —, picked up —, pointed at —, pointed to —, pressed —, pulled —, pulled out —, put —, put on —, raised —, reached for —, replied over —, returned to —, said into —, said on —, said over —, said to —, screamed on —, screamed over —, set —, set up —, shouted at —, shouted into —, shouted over —, shoved aside —, shut off —, snapped into —, snapped off —, snapped up —, spoke into —, spoke over —, stared at —, talked into —,

took —, took off —, took out —, tried —, turned down —, turned off —, turned on —, turned to —, turned up —, waved away —, waved for —, went to —, whispered on —, whispered over —, yelled into —; — became, — broke in, — came, — came from, — came into, — came on, — came to, — died, — fell, — gave, — heard from, — knew, — left inside, — looked, — looked like, — moved to, — picked up, — played, — played in, — remained, — said, — sounded, — spoke, — stayed, — turned up, — went, — went on

rage
verbs
— ate, — ate at, — began to, — blew, — blew through, — broke, — brought out, — came from, — continued in, — disappeared, — fell from, — felt, — filled, — gave, — grew with, — lay beyond, — lifted on, — made, — poured off, — poured through, — put, — rolled, — rolled through, — rose in, — rose into, — screamed, — seemed to, — shook, — shook through, — snapped back, — started, — started to, — turned, — went, — went from, — went through, — went up

rail
verbs
approached —, bent over —, climbed onto —, climbed over —, crossed to —, glanced at —, glanced over —, grabbed —, gripped —, hung over —, jumped on —, leaned against —, leaned on —, leaned over —, moved along —, moved to —, pointed over —, pushed off —, ran to —, reached for —, slipped under —, stared over —, stared past —,

stepped from —, stepped to —, stood at —, stood by —, walked along —, walked to —, went to —

railing
verbs
approached —, bent over —, caught onto —, climbed —, climbed off —, climbed onto —, climbed over —, fell against —, fell through —, glanced over —, grabbed —, grabbed onto —, gripped —, held onto —, held to —, hung to —, jumped over —, leaned against —, leaned on —, leaned over —, looked over —, moved to —, pushed off —, ran to —, reached —, sat on —, shouted over —, slid from —, stepped to —, stood at —, stood by —, turned from —, turned to —, walked to —, went over —, went to —

rain
verbs
blinked —, blinked away —, cried like —, disappeared into —, fought in —, hated —, laughed in —, liked —, listened to —, looked at —, looked through —, loved —, ran into —, ran through —, remembered —, rode through —, shouted into —, shouted over —, smelled of —, smiled despite —, stared into —, stared through —, stepped into —, stood in —, walked through —, watched —, worked in —, yelled in —; — arrived, — became, — began, — began at, — began in, — began over, — began to, — blew into, — blew through, — broke, — came, — came down, — came in, — came like, — caught in, — continued, — continued for, — continued to, — decided to, — did, — disappeared behind, — ended, — ended on, — fell, — fell across, — fell against, — fell around, — fell beneath, — fell by, — fell down, — fell from, — fell in, — fell into, — fell like, — fell off, — fell on, — fell outside, — fell through, — fell with, — felt, — flew against, — flew from, — flew into, — followed, — followed by, — held back, — hit, — hit with, — kept, — knocked down, — knocked on, — left, — lost behind, — lowered, — made, — meant, — moved in, — moved up, — passed, — passed through, — picked up, — poured down, — poured from, — poured out, — poured outside, — pressed, — put, — put out, — ran down, — ran in, — ran into, — ran off, — remained, — returned, — returned to, — rolled across, — rolled down, — rolled off, — rolled through, — seemed to, — settled on, — showed up, — slammed, — slammed down, — slammed into, — slid down, — sounded in, — started, — started on, — started to, — started up, — stopped, — stopped for, — struck, — took on, — turned, — turned into, — turned to, — used to, — went on, — whispered on, — whispered over, — worked

rat
verbs
— appeared, — began to, — called, — came on, — came with, — caught in, — climbed onto, — did, — dropped to, — got in, — held, — knew, — lifted, — lost, — made, — managed to, — nodded, — pointed to, — poured out, — ran, — ran across, — ran for, — ran in, — ran on, — ran through, — returned, — rose from, — shook, —

threw, — took off, — turned in, — turned into, — used, — wrapped

realization
verbs
— began to, — broke over, — broke through, — brought, — came, — came to, — came upon, — carried, — crossed, — cut, — did, — drove, — fell over, — fell upon, — filled, — grew in, — made, — raised, — rose in, — sank in, — sank into, — sent, — settled on, — settled over, — shot around, — shot down, — slammed into, — struck, — turned

receiver
verbs
breathed into —, continued into —, covered —, dropped —, glanced at —, grabbed —, grabbed for —, grabbed up —, grinned into —, gripped —, handed over —, held —, held onto —, held out —, held up —, hung up —, laid down —, laughed into —, lay down —, lifted —, listened to —, looked at —, lowered —, nodded into —, picked up —, pulled —, put down —, raised —, reached for —, said into —, screamed into —, set down —, shouted into —, slammed down —, spoke into —, stared at —, threw —, threw down —, took —, turned off —, yelled into —

recorder
verbs
felt —, glanced at —, got —, got to —, held out —, held up —, leaned toward —, looked at —, nodded toward —, picked up —, played —, pointed at —, pressed —, pulled —, pulled out —, raised —, reached for —, set up —, shut off —, snapped off —, spoke into —,

started —, stopped —, took —, took out —, touched —, turned off —, turned on —

red
verbs
— appeared, — appeared in, — appeared on, — began to, — blinked in, — came to, — felt, — laughed, — looked at, — looked down, — made, — passed over, — ran down, — remained, — rose, — rose from, — rose in, — rose of, — sank through, — spoke, — stood at, — stood with, — threw out, — turned, — turned to

refrigerator
verbs
began with —, checked —, checked in —, checked out —, closed —, crossed to —, found in —, headed for —, headed to —, leaned against —, looked at —, looked in —, moved to —, opened —, opened up —, pointed out —, pulled open —, ran to —, reached into —, returned to —, shut —, started toward —, stepped to —, turned to —, walked to —, went into —, went to —

relief
verbs
breathed —, breathed in —, breathed with —, came into —, felt —, gasped in —, gasped with —, grinned in —, grinned with —, heard —, laughed in —, laughed with —, murmured in —, needed —, nodded in —, realized with —, said in —, said with —, saw with —, screamed in —, sighed —, sighed at —, sighed in —, sighed with —, smiled —, smiled in —, smiled with —, swallowed with —, thought with —, wanted —,

yelled with —; — arrived, — began to,
— blew, — brought, — came, — came
in, — came to, — came with, —
changed to, — crossed, — disappeared,
— fell over, — felt like, — filled, —
followed, — followed by, — hit, — lit,
— made, — moved, — passed, —
played, — poured over, — poured
through, — ran through, — saw, —
seemed, — settled over, — settled
through, — showed in, — showed on,
— slid, — turned to, — went through,
— whispered past

reply
verbs
asked in —, ate without —, breathed —,
called in —, considered —, cried in —,
cut off —, gasped in —, gave —, got —,
grinned in —, heard —, hesitated in —,
hit —, laughed in —, listened for —,
listened to —, made —, managed in —,
murmured —, muttered in —, needed
—, nodded in —, nodded without —,
said in —, shouted in —, shrugged in —,
shrugged off —, snapped in —, waited
for —, waved in —, whispered —,
whispered in —, yelled —, yelled in —

report
verbs
began —, brought up —, called in —,
came to —, came with —, checked —,
closed —, continued —, did for —,
dropped —, expected —, finished —,
finished off —, frowned at —, gave —,
gestured at —, glanced at —, glanced
down —, got —, grabbed —, handed —,
handed over —, heard —, held —, held
up —, listened to —, looked at —,
looked over —, looked through —,
made —, needed —, nodded at —,

opened —, passed —, passed over —,
picked up —, pulled —, pulled out —,
put down —, read —, read through —,
returned to —, saw —, set aside —, set
down —, shouted for —, stared at —,
thought about —, took —, wrote —,
wrote up —; — arrived at, — began to,
— blinked into, — brought back, —
called for, — came across, — came back,
— came down, — came from, — came
in, — came out, — came over, —
continued, — cut, — cut back, —
demanded, — ended, — ended with, —
kicked in, — lay on, — made, — meant,
— ran, — rang out, — reached, — read,
— rolled inside, — said, — sat in, —
seemed, — showed, — turned in, —
waited on, — walked in, — went to

response
verbs
asked as —, asked in —, considered —,
frowned at —, gave —, got —, grinned
in —, heard —, heard in —, held back
—, laughed in —, liked —, listened for
—, listened to —, loved —, made —,
murmured in —, muttered in —,
nodded in —, paused for —, read —,
said in —, screamed in —, shouted —,
shouted in —, shrugged —, shrugged in
—, shrugged off —, sighed in —, smiled
in —, stared at —, thought of —, waited
for —, waved in —, whispered in —

rest
verbs
— agreed with, — became, — came, —
came after, — came from, — came off,
— came on, — came out, — came with,
— continued, — covered in, — drew
away, — drew back, — drew off, —
dropped to, — fell from, — fell in, —

fell upon, — felt like, — followed, — grew, — happened, — happened on, — held, — held in, — joined in, — laughed, — lay, — lay in, — lay upon, — left, — left for, — lit, — looked, — looked like, — lost in, — made, — moved in, — moved off, — needed, — nodded, — passed, — passed in, — put into, — ran, — reached, — remained, — remained in, — rode on, — sat on, — screamed in, — seemed, — seemed to, — slipped away, — smiled, — spoke, — stayed inside, — stood, — stood in, — stopped, — waited, — walked along, — wanted to, — went, — went down, — went into, — went to, — wore, — worked over

restaurant

verbs

arrived at —, called —, came to —, chose —, drove past —, entered —, glanced around —, glanced at —, headed for —, left —, left for —, looked across —, looked around —, nodded at —, nodded toward —, passed —, reached —, stepped into —, suggested —, turned into —, turned toward —, walked into —, walked past —, walked through —, watched —, went into —, went to —, worked at —, worked in —

revolver

verbs

broke open —, carried —, checked —, drew —, drew out —, dropped —, got out —, gripped —, held —, held up —, kept —, left —, lifted —, looked at —, lowered —, opened —, picked up —, pointed to —, pulled —, pulled out —, put down —, raised —, reached for —,

stared at —, studied —, took —, took out —

rifle

verbs

carried —, checked —, dropped —, found —, gestured to —, glanced at —, grabbed —, gripped —, handed over —, held —, held up —, kicked under —, let —, lifted —, lifted out —, liked —, looked at —, lost —, lowered —, needed —, nodded at —, opened —, picked up —, pointed —, pointed at —, pulled out —, put —, raised —, reached —, reached for —, set aside —, set down —, shifted —, shot —, shoved —, shrugged off —, stared at —, stared down —, swung —, swung up —, thought about —, took —, took out —, touched —, used —, wanted —, waved —, went for —; — added, — brought back, — came, — came after, — came around, — caught, — disappeared, — dropped from, — fell, — filled, — held, — held across, — held against, — held in, — hit, — hung at, — jumped against, — kicked, — kicked against, — lay on, — leaned, — left to, — looked under, — made, — moved in, — opened, — opened together, — opened up, — pointed, — pointed at, — pointed out, — pressed to, — raised, — ran down, — rang out, — returned, — rose, — sank, — seemed like, — set, — slid from, — slid to, — slipped from, — started, — stepped, — stood up, — struck, — swung in, — threw, — took, — took out, — took up, — tried to, — went, — went off

right

verbs

broke to —, continued to —, cut to —,
did —, felt —, flew to —, followed in —
, gestured to —, glanced to —, got —,
headed to —, heard —, hung —,
jumped to —, kept to —, leaned to —,
looked —, looked to —, made —,
moved to —, nodded to —, pointed to
—, pointed toward —, pulled to —,
raised —, ran to —, rolled to —, sat at
—, sat on —, sat to —, seemed —,
shifted to —, slid toward —, slipped —,
slipped off —, slipped to —, stared to —
, started to —, started toward —,
stepped to —, stood at —, stood to —,
swung —, swung to —, took —, tried —
, turned to —, understood —, walked in
—, walked to —, wanted —, went to —

ring
verbs
answered after —, answered at —,
answered on —, bent over —, bought —
, broke through —, brought out —, felt
across —, fought in —, found —,
frowned at —, got —, got out —,
grabbed —, gripped —, handed over —,
heard —, held —, held out —, held up
—, jumped for —, kept on —, kissed —,
lifted —, lifted out —, listened to —,
looked around —, looked at —, noticed
—, paused at —, picked up —, pulled on
—, put on —, reached —, remembered
—, returned —, saw —, sent —, shook
—, slipped —, slipped off —, stared at
—, stared into —, stepped into —,
stepped toward —, stood in —, stopped
inside —, studied —, took —, took off
—, took out —, turned on —, wanted
—, wore —; — appeared in, — appeared
on, — appeared to, — began to, —
broke loose, — caught, — caught in, —
cut into, — cut out, — did, —

disappeared into, — ended, — fell off,
— felt, — filled, — got, — held, —
hung from, — hung on, — lay, — lay
on, — left, — let, — looked like, —
made, — made for, — made from, —
made of, — pushed up, — put through,
— remained, — repeated, — sat on, —
set in, — set into, — showed, — slid
into, — slipped off, — sounded, —
stopped, — took on, — turned, —
turned on, — went, — went in, — went
into, — went to

river
verbs
approached —, called across —, came to
—, cleared —, crossed —, drove across
—, drove to —, entered —, fell in —,
fell into —, flew across —, followed —,
gestured at —, gestured toward —,
glanced across —, glanced at —, got to
—, headed toward —, hit —, kept —,
knew —, left —, looked across —,
looked at —, looked up —, loved —,
moved to —, nodded to —, pointed
across —, pointed to —, ran into —,
reached —, remembered —, saw —,
shoved into —, slid into —, smelled —,
stared across —, stared at —, turned at
—, turned from —, turned toward —,
walked along —, walked to —, walked
toward —, wanted —, watched —, went
along —; — appeared, — became, —
began to, — bent, — broke, — brought
in, — called, — came, — came to, —
came together, — caught, — changed,
— closed over, — continued, —
continued to, — cried out, — cut
through, — did, — disappeared into, —
drew, — drew near, — entered, — fell
with, — followed, — got, — grew, —
held, — laid, — lay, — lay like, — led to,

— left, — looked, — looked for, — looked like, — lost, — made, — met, — moved, — moved beneath, — murmured, — offered, — opened, — opened up, — passed through, — poured in, — poured into, — ran, — ran at, — ran behind, — ran down, — ran from, — ran in, — ran into, — ran out, — ran through, — ran with, — reached, — remained, — rolled, — rose, — rose in, — said, — seemed, — seemed to, — settled, — slid beneath, — spoke with, — stood, — stopped, — took, — turned, — went, — whispered in

road
verbs
ate on —, broke from —, called from —, came across —, came to —, came up —, checked —, closed —, continued down —, continued up —, crossed —, crossed over —, cut across —, cut off —, drove across —, drove through —, drove up —, fell onto —, fell to —, fell toward —, followed —, found —, gestured down —, gestured toward —, glanced across —, glanced at —, glanced down —, glanced to —, glanced toward —, glanced up —, got off —, got on —, headed down —, headed for —, headed toward —, headed up —, hit —, knew —, left —, looked across —, looked at —, looked down —, looked toward —, looked up —, missed —, moved up —, nodded over —, nodded toward —, nodded up —, pointed across —, pointed along —, pointed at —, pointed down —, pointed toward —, pointed up —, pulled across —, pulled off —, pulled onto —, ran —, ran across —, ran along —, ran down —, ran into —, ran to —, reached —, rode down —, saw —, saw

across —, shouted across —, smiled at —, stared at —, stared down —, stared up —, started across —, started down —, started toward —, started up —, stayed in —, stayed on —, stepped into —, stepped off —, stepped onto —, stood beside —, stood in —, stood on —, stopped by —, stopped in —, studied —, swung off —, took —, took to —, turned down —, turned in —, turned into —, turned off —, turned onto —, turned toward —, walked —, walked across —, walked along —, walked down —, walked into —, walked to —, watched —, watched down —, went down —, went on —; — appeared, — appeared to, — became, — began on, — began to, — brought, — came out, — carried on, — cleared away, — climbed, — climbed into, — continued on, — continued through, — crossed, — cut, — cut through, — did, — disappeared in, — disappeared into, — ended, — ended against, — ended at, — ended in, — fell away, — followed, — gave, — grew, — headed into, — joined to, — lay, — lay like, — led, — led down, — led from, — led into, — led off, — led on, — led past, — led through, — led to, — led up, — left, — left in, — lifted to, — lit up, — looked, — looked down, — looked into, — made, — made by, — met, — opened out, — opened up, — passed, — passed down, — passed on, — put, — ran, — ran across, — ran along, — ran away, — ran beside, — ran between, — ran from, — ran on, — ran through, — remained, — rose, — rose up, — seemed, — seemed to, — shook, — shook to, — shot in, — shut down, — slid, — slid past, — started, — started to, — stayed, — stood, —

stopped, — took, — turned, — turned away, — turned to, — went, — went down, — went on, — went over, — went under, — went up, — worked

roar
verbs
— approached from, — became, — began in, — began to, — broke, — broke from, — brought, — brought around, — came from, — came out, — came up, — continued to, — died away, — filled, — followed by, — got, — grew, — reached, — returned to, — rose from, — shook, — sounded, — sounded behind, — started in, — turned into, — went up

robe
verbs
changed —, climbed into —, closed —, drew —, drew on —, dropped —, entered with —, felt beneath —, found —, got —, grabbed —, gripped —, held —, liked —, looked at —, opened —, picked up —, pulled at —, pulled on —, put on —, reached for —, reached into —, reached to —, rolled up —, shook out —, shrugged into —, slid into —, slipped into —, slipped off —, slipped on —, stepped into —, studied —, threw off —, threw on —, took —, took off —, went to —, wore —; — appeared, — appeared in, — blew up, — came forward, — came into, — came off, — caught, — closed, — closed across, — closed against, — closed over, — closed to, — cut, — did, — dropped on, — fell back, — fell open, — fell to, — flew, — flew open, — gave, — hung, — hung about, — hung from, — hung like, — hung on, — lay across, — lifted, —

looked, — made of, — moved, — pulled up, — remained, — said, — sat, — sat on, — seemed to, — settled against, — shifted, — shut, — slipped down, — stepped into, — stood behind, — stood out, — stood over, — tossed on, — turned to, — waved in, — whispered against, — whispered in

rock
verbs
came around —, climbed —, climbed off —, crossed —, disappeared among —, dropped —, dropped like —, fell like —, felt —, found —, grabbed —, heard —, hit —, kicked —, kicked at —, leaned against —, left —, let loose —, lifted —, looked at —, moved —, moved against —, moved aside —, moved onto —, moved to —, passed beyond —, picked up —, played —, pressed against —, pressed on —, pushed off —, put —, raised —, reached —, rolled —, rolled behind —, rolled off —, rose from —, sat behind —, sat on —, saw —, sent —, settled onto —, slept like —, slid across —, slid off —, slid over —, stood like —, stood on —, studied —, swung —, threw —, took —, turned over —, walked around —, walked on —, watched —; — became, — began, — began to, — blew, — broke, — broke into, — broke off, — broke through, — broke under, — came, — caught, — changed, — closed about, — closed behind, — continued, — covered with, — cut, — cut into, — did, — disappeared, — disappeared into, — drew together, — dropped away, — dropped from, — dropped in, — dropped into, — drove, — fell, — fell away, — fell from, — fell like, — flew,

— flew from, — flew into, — flew like, — flew out, — flew past, — forced, — gave, — gave under, — grew, — held, — helped, — hit, — jumped up, — landed, — landed on, — lay, — lay at, — lay in, — lay near, — lay on, — lay upon, — led to, — looked to, — made, — met, — moved, — poured down, — pushed down, — pushed out, — rang with, — recognized, — rolled, — rolled under, — rose, — rose around, — rose behind, — rose in, — rose toward, — said, — seemed to, — settled in, — shifted, — showed, — slammed down, — slid from, — slipped from, — snapped in, — sounded, — stood out, — suggested, — took down, — took over, — turned, — turned under, — used, — went atop, — went off

roof
verbs
— appeared to, — began to, — blew off, — bought with, — called, — came, — came down, — came to, — came together, — caught, — covered, — covered with, — ended in, — fell in, — fell on, — fell through, — gave, — held, — landed inside, — let in, — looked, — looked like, — made, — made for, — met, — opened down, — passed, — promised, — put, — ran beneath, — remained, — sat atop, — seemed to, — set on, — showed, — stood at, — turned, — turned into, — went up

room
verbs
appeared from —, approached —, arrived at —, arrived in —, asked —, asked around —, asked from —, asked in —, ate in —, called —, called across

—, called from —, came across —, came in —, came into —, came to —, changed —, changed in —, checked —, checked into —, checked out —, chose —, cleared —, climbed into —, climbed to —, continued across —, continued to —, cried at —, crossed —, crossed into —, crossed through —, disappeared from —, disappeared inside —, disappeared into —, drove past —, entered —, fell into —, felt —, felt in —, filled —, finished in —, flew about —, flew across —, flew into —, found —, frowned across —, gave —, gestured across —, gestured around —, gestured at —, gestured inside —, gestured to —, gestured toward —, glanced about —, glanced across —, glanced around —, glanced at —, glanced inside —, glanced into —, glanced toward —, got —, got inside —, got to —, grinned across —, hated —, headed across —, headed for —, headed into —, headed to —, headed toward —, heard from —, kept —, kept in —, kept to —, knew —, lay in —, left —, left for —, left through —, liked —, lit up —, looked about —, looked across —, looked around —, looked at —, looked in —, looked inside —, looked into —, looked over —, looked toward —, lost —, made —, made for —, met in —, moved about —, moved across —, moved around —, moved into —, moved through —, moved to —, murmured into —, needed —, nodded around —, nodded toward —, passed —, passed by —, passed through —, paused at —, paused in —, paused outside —, picked —, pointed across —, pointed around —, pointed into —, pointed to —, poured into —, pushed into —, put —, ran across —, ran around —, ran for —, ran from —, ran into —, ran through —, ran to —, ran toward —, reached —, reached into —, recognized —, remained across —, remained in —, remembered —, returned to —, rolled around —, said from —, said to —, sat across —, sat in —, sat outside —, saw —, screamed at —, shot through —, shouted across —, shouted from —, slipped across —, slipped from —, slipped inside —, slipped into —, spoke into —, spoke to —, stared across —, stared around —, stared at —, stared into —, started across —, started from —, stayed in —, stepped across —, stepped from —, stepped in —, stepped inside —, stepped into —, stepped outside —, stepped through —, stood across —, stood in —, stood inside —, stood outside —, stopped by —, stopped in —, studied —, swung into —, thought of —, told —, took in —, tried out —, turned around —, turned into —, turned to —, turned toward —, used —, waited in —, waited inside —, walked —, walked about —, walked across —, walked around —, walked down —, walked from —, walked in —, walked inside —, walked into —, walked through —, walked to —, walked toward —, wanted —, watched —, watched from —, watched over —, waved around —, waved to —, went across —, went around —, went in —, went inside —, went into —, went through —, went to —, wiped down —, woke in —, worked —, worked from —, worked in —, yelled across —, yelled from —, yelled to —; — appeared, — appeared to, — became, — began, — began to, — blew off, — breathed out, — broke into, — brought, — called, —

called back, — came, — came from, — came into, — came through, — came to, — carried, — caught, — changed, — cleared, — closed, — closed in, — continued, — continued to, — covered with, — crossed, — cut off, — did, — drank up, — drew back, — drew up, — dropped, — dropped into, — expected, — fell, — fell away, — fell into, — fell to, — felt, — felt like, — filled up, — filled with, — flew open, — followed, — fought for, — gasped, — gave, — glanced over, — glanced through, — got, — grew, — happened to, — heard, — held, — helped, — joined, — jumped, — kept, — knew, — knocked against, — laughed, — lay, — lay beyond, — leaned across, — leaned in, — leaned over, — leaned toward, — led to, — left, — left for, — listened, — lit, — lit behind, — lit by, — lit up, — lit with, — lived in, — looked, — looked at, — looked away, — looked for, — looked like, — looked over, — looked to, — looked up, — lost, — made, — made of, — made out, — made to, — made up, — met, — missed, — moved, — moved in, — murmured, — needed, — needed to, — nodded, — nodded in, — offered, — opened, — opened off, — opened on, — opened onto, — opened up, — passed in, — paused, — picked up, — played, — pulled, — pulled down, — pushed open, — raised, — ran, — rang in, — rang with, — read, — remained, — remained under, — repeated, — returned, — returned to, — rose, — rose from, — rose in, — rose to, — rubbed, — said, — said in, — sank to, — sat, — sat at, — screamed, — seemed, — seemed to, — sent, — set aside, — set up, — settled down, —

shifted, — shifted in, — shook, — shook in, — shot, — shouted, — showed, — slammed to, — slid off, — slid open, — smelled, — smelled like, — smelled of, — smiled, — snapped, — snapped into, — sounded, — spoke, — stared at, — started to, — stayed, — stepped, — stepped on, — stood, — stood out, — stopped, — studied, — swung in, — swung open, — took, — took off, — took to, — tried to, — turned, — turned out, — turned to, — turned up, — used, — waited, — waited around, — waited in, — watched, — went in, — went out, — went up, — went with, — wore, — worked, — wrapped in

rope
verbs

caught —, climbed —, climbed down —, climbed through —, climbed up —, cut —, dropped —, fell against —, felt —, felt like —, fought —, found —, got out —, got to —, grabbed —, grabbed onto —, gripped —, headed for —, headed up —, held onto —, held out —, held up —, hung on —, knew —, left —, let —, liked —, lit —, looked at —, picked up —, played out —, pointed to —, pulled —, pulled at —, pulled on —, reached —, reached for —, rolled up —, shook —, slid down —, slipped past —, stared at —, stepped over —, stepped through —, studied —, threw —, took —, took out —, tossed —, turned to —, used —, walked to —, went up —, worked on —, wrapped —; — became, — broke, — came, — came down, — came off, — came up, — cut, — cut into, — cut through, — cut with, — did, — dropped down, — fell away, — fell down, — fell into, — gave, — grew, — held, — hit, — hung down, — hung from, — hung in, — hung off, — hung up, — lay at, — lay in, — led, — led to, — let, — lowered from, — made, — made of, — moved in, — pulled, — pulled on, — ran from, — remained in, — sank into, — seemed to, — shook, — slid against, — slid through, — slipped, — snapped, — snapped off, — swung, — took, — turned to, — used, — went, — went under, — wrapped around, — wrapped in

round
verbs

— appeared to, — began to, — blew, — blew into, — blew off, — blew through, — called out, — came from, — came out, — came through, — carried on, — caught, — continued to, — cut across, — cut out, — dropped into, — fell with, — felt, — filled, — flew through, — found, — held up, — hit, — hit with, — landed, — left, — left in, — made, — missed, — noticed, — passed through, — put, — saw, — shot, — slammed into, — snapped through, — stayed in, — struck, — struck around, — took, — went, — went through, — went to

rumor
verbs

— became, — began to, — came to, — caught, — crossed, — died down, — dropped to, — fell, — flew, — grew of, — led, — lifted, — meant, — passed, — ran, — reached, — remained behind, — said, — spoke of, — stared, — started, — stayed at, — went, — went about, — went on, — went with, — worked in

saddle

verbs

came to —, climbed into —, dropped from —, fell from —, glanced at —, grabbed —, lay in —, leaned against —, leaned from —, leaned in —, moved in —, noticed —, rode in —, rose in —, sat in —, settled in —, shifted in —, shook in —, shrugged in —, slid from —, slid off —, slipped from —, stayed in —, stood in —, stood on —, swung from —, swung into —, threw —, took —, turned in —

sand

verbs

became —, covered with —, crossed —, dropped to —, fell in —, fell into —, fell to —, felt —, found —, hated —, hit —, kicked at —, landed on —, lay in —, lay on —, pointed to —, ran across —, reached —, sat on —, settled to —, shifted on —, slipped along —, stared toward —, stood on —, took —, touched —, walked onto —, walked through —; — appeared, — began to, — blew against, — blew on, — blew up, — bowed, — brought, — came, — came down, — caught in, — did, — fell over, — fell through, — felt, — filled, — flew over, — gave, — got between, — grew, — led away, — made, — made for, — poured down, — poured out, — poured over, — ran, — ran on, — rode, — rose up, — rubbed, — said in, — sank under, — settled, — showed, — slid through, — slipped in, — turned to, — went over

sandwich

verbs

ate —, bought —, brought —, carried —, chose —, considered —, dropped —,

finished —, finished off —, got —, grabbed —, lifted —, looked at —, lowered —, made —, met for —, opened —, ordered —, picked among —, picked at —, picked up —, pulled out —, put away —, put down —, reached for —, stared at —, started on —, studied —, thought of —, took —, walked to —, worked on —, wrapped —

scar

verbs

— appeared, — appeared on, — became, — began to, — came from, — covered, — crossed, — cut through, — disappeared from, — felt, — frowned, — lay, — left behind, — looked, — looked like, — lost, — made, — paused, — pulled, — ran across, — ran along, — ran down, — ran from, — ran out, — ran through, — remembered, — seemed like, — showed on, — stood out, — struck, — went

scene

verbs

arrived at —, began with —, came onto —, checked —, considered —, continued toward —, died at —, drove to —, glanced around —, glanced at —, hit —, knew —, laid out —, left —, looked at —, looked over —, looked upon —, made —, moved to —, nodded toward —, reached —, read —, recognized —, saw —, shot —, smiled at —, stared at —, stayed with —, studied —, took in —, turned to —, walked around —, walked into —, walked onto —, watched —, waved at —, went through —; — appeared, — appeared on, — appeared to, — arrived to, — asked, — became, — began to, — came,

— came back, — came together, — changed, — continued, — disappeared, — felt, — hung from, — left to, — lit to, — looked, — looked like, — made, — played in, — played out, — put, — put on, — raised, — remained, — reminded, — repeated over, — repeated through, — rose from, — said, — seemed, — set, — shifted, — showed, — stayed, — went, — went from, — worked, — worked on

school

verbs

arrived at —, began —, called —, came to —, checked with —, cut —, drove around —, entered —, finished —, gestured toward —, got to —, happened at —, hated —, headed for —, left —, left for —, liked —, liked at —, lived near —, looked at —, looked toward —, loved —, met after —, missed —, nodded toward —, passed —, played in —, pointed to —, remembered —, returned to —, said about —, started —, stopped at —, thought about —, turned toward —, walked into —, walked past —, wanted in —, went to —, worked at —, worked through —; — agreed to, — became, — began, — bought, — broke for, — brought in, — called, — called back, — came, — came back, — came to, — caught on, — did, — did to, — disappeared atop, — ended, — fell, — felt like, — found out, — gave, — gave out, — got, — got out, — grew, — kept for, — knew, — let in, — let loose, — let out, — looked on, — made, — met, — needed, — opened, — played, — raised, — said, — saw, — sent, — showed up, — slammed, — started, — stood, — stood in, — took, — took up,

— used, — waited in, — wanted, — went, — went in, — went to

scream

verbs

— became, — began, — began from, — began to, — broke, — broke into, — broke off, — broke through, — brought, — came, — came from, — came out, — came to, — carried into, — carried on, — carried to, — caught in, — changed, — continued, — continued from, — cut, — cut off, — cut through, — died, — died away, — died in, — died into, — died out, — died with, — drew, — ended, — filled, — followed, — grabbed, — grew, — left, — lifted into, — lost in, — made, — made up, — poured down, — rang, — rang out, — rang through, — reached, — reached through, — rose, — rose above, — rose from, — rose in, — rose on, — rose over, — rose to, — rose with, — seemed to, — sent, — shot up, — snapped off, — sounded, — sounded about, — sounded behind, — sounded from, — sounded like, — started, — started to, — stopped, — told of, — turned into, — turned to, — went on, — went up

screen

verbs

appeared on —, asked —, blinked at —, called up —, changed —, checked —, cleared —, closed —, closed down —, filled —, frowned at —, frowned on —, gestured at —, gestured to —, gestured toward —, glanced at —, got —, grabbed —, held open —, held up —, kicked —, killed —, leaned into —, leaned to —, leaned toward —, looked across —, looked at —, looked over —,

looked through —, looked to —,
lowered —, murmured at —, nodded at
—, nodded to —, nodded toward —,
opened —, paused —, paused behind —,
pointed at —, pointed to —, pulled —,
pulled open —, pulled up —, pushed
open —, reached for —, reached to —,
read —, read from —, read off —,
returned to —, said on —, said to —, sat
at —, sat through —, saw —, saw on —,
set aside —, shouted at —, shrugged on
—, sighed at —, slid —, smiled at —,
stared at —, stepped behind —, stepped
from —, stepped toward —, stood
beyond —, studied —, told —, took —,
took in —, touched —, turned —,
turned from —, turned off —, turned
on —, turned to —, turned toward —,
used —, walked to —, watched —,
waved at —, waved to —, went to —,
worked —, yelled at —; — appeared, —
appeared in, — appeared to, — appeared
with, — became, — began to, —
blinked, — blinked out, — came, —
came back, — came into, — came on, —
came to, — came up, — carried, —
caught, — changed, — changed to, —
cleared, — closed off, — covered in, —
cut, — cut back, — cut off, — cut out,
— cut to, — drew back, — dropped
from, — fell, — filled in, — filled up, —
filled with, — grew, — grew in, — held,
— held in, — jumped, — jumped to, —
lit, — lit up, — made, — played, —
pressed, — pulled up, — ran for, —
read, — remained, — returned, —
rolled down, — rolled into, — rose
above, — said, — set into, — shifted, —
showed, — slammed behind, — slid
into, — slid open, — slid out, —
snapped into, — spoke, — started to, —
stayed, — stood in, — stood on, —

swung open, — tried to, — turned, —
turned on, — turned up, — walked out,
— went back, — went down, — went
from, — went off, — went to, — woke
underneath

sea
verbs
— appeared, — appeared amid, —
became, — began to, — broke, —
brought, — changed, — continued, —
did, — drew, — dropped away, — fell
upon, — felt, — felt like, — filled with,
— found in, — got, — grew, — held, —
lay, — lay in, — lay on, — looked, —
looked like, — meant, — met, —
moved, — moved in, — opened, —
poured, — pushed, — pushed over, —
ran from, — ran in, — reached out, —
remained, — rose, — rose in, — rose on,
— rose over, — seemed, — seemed to,
— shoved, — spoke, — started to, —
threw, — took up, — turned, — turned
up, — went, — went from

seat
verbs
arrived at —, asked for —, asked from
—, bent over —, called from —, came in
—, checked —, checked under —, chose
—, climbed from —, climbed into —,
climbed off —, climbed over —,
dropped from —, dropped in —,
dropped into —, fell against —, fell into
—, felt under —, filled up —, found —,
glanced across —, glanced at —, got in
—, got into —, got off —, grabbed —,
gripped —, held onto —, held to —, hit
—, jumped from —, jumped in —,
jumped into —, jumped off —, jumped
over —, kept —, kept beneath —, lay
across —, lay against —, lay between —,

lay in —, leaned across —, leaned against
—, leaned between —, leaned from —,
leaned in —, leaned on —, leaned over
—, left —, lifted —, lifted from —,
lifted in —, looked across —, looked
over —, looked toward —, lowered —,
moved in —, moved on —, moved to —,
nodded toward —, pointed at —,
pointed to —, pulled out —, pulled up
—, raised —, reached —, reached across
—, reached behind —, reached beneath
—, reached into —, reached over —,
reached through —, reached under —,
remained in —, returned to —, rolled to
—, rose from —, said from —, sank
against —, sank in —, sank into —, sank
to —, sat against —, sat at —, sat in —,
sat on —, settled in —, settled into —,
settled to —, shifted —, shifted in —,
shifted on —, shot from —, shot past —
, shouted from —, slid across —, slid
along —, slid from —, slid in —, slid
into —, slid off —, slid on —, slid onto
—, slipped between —, slipped into —,
slipped off —, slipped onto —, spoke
from —, stared under —, started to —,
started toward —, stayed in —, stood at
—, stood from —, stood near —, swung
on —, took —, tossed —, turned in —,
turned on —, turned to —, walked to —
, waved at —, waved from —, waved to
—, went to —; — asked, — blinked, —
closed, — disappeared from, — drew, —
fell, — felt, — filled with, — got out, —
got up, — hit, — landed, — lay on, —
leaned out, — left, — looked, — looked
out, — made, — put, — said, — sat, —
screamed in, — seemed, — set at, —
shot out, — stood, — threw up, — took,
— turned

second

verbs
called —, chose —, filled —, followed in
—, found —, grabbed for —, hesitated
—, hesitated for —, listened at —,
listened for —, needed —, opened —,
paused for —, played —, pulled —, saw
—, stared for —, started on —, stepped
into —, stood —, stood for —, thought
—, thought for —, took —, took on —,
turned to —, went with —, whispered
off —; — appeared in, — began to, —
came, — closed to, — continued to, —
died of, — drew into, — drew on, —
drew out, — fell, — fell off, — fell out,
— felt like, — followed, — found, —
gave, — held, — led, — led to, — left,
— left in, — left until, — let, — looked
across, — made, — opened, — passed,
— ran down, — ran into, — ran out, —
remained before, — screamed in, —
seemed, — seemed like, — seemed to, —
showed on, — slammed into, — slipped
by, — sounded like, — thought about,
— took, — tried to, — turned into, —
went, — went by, — went into, — went
onto, — worked up

sensation

verbs
— became, — began to, — came, —
came back, — came from, — continued
to, — covered, — disappeared, —
entered, — felt like, — kicked off, —
lifted by, — meant, — passed, —
returned, — returned in, — returned to,
— seemed, — seemed to, — sent, —
settled in, — started to, — took, —
turned into, — went, — went out

sense

verbs

— began to, — came, — came back, — came to, — caught, — decided to, — drank in, — felt like, — filled with, — fought in, — gripped in, — jumped up, — kept, — kicked in, — knew, — knocked out, — left, — left to, — lit up, — lost in, — picked out, — pressed, — pulled, — reached out, — remained, — returned, — returned to, — said, — screamed for, — seemed, — seemed at, — seemed to, — showed off, — started, — told, — took over, — went, — went on, — went out

shade
verbs
came into —, closed —, drew —, dropped —, found —, gripped —, kept in —, lifted —, looked through —, lowered —, moved into —, promised —, pulled —, pulled down —, pulled off —, raised —, reached —, sat in —, slipped into —, slipped off —, slipped on —, stood in —, threw away —, took off —, wore —; — approached, — asked, — began to, — came forward, — came to, — closed, — covered, — fell across, — felt, — gave, — hung, — looked, — made, — moved, — opened, — picked, — pointed, — pointed at, — pulled, — pulled against, — pulled down, — remained, — said, — seemed to, — spoke, — stared down, — stood atop, — stopped, — stopped in, — suggested, — threw, — told, — turned to, — went down, — whispered

shadow
verbs
appeared from —, became —, broke into —, disappeared into —, entered —, followed in —, glanced into —, hit —,

kept in —, kept to —, knew —, lay in —, leaned into —, listened from —, lived in —, looked into —, moved between —, moved in —, moved into —, moved through —, needed —, nodded toward —, noticed —, picked up —, played —, pointed at —, pointed to —, ran through —, reached for —, remained in —, rode in —, sat in —, saw —, slid into —, slipped from —, slipped into —, stared into —, stayed in —, stepped from —, stepped into —, stood in —, stopped in —, studied —, waited in —, walked in —, walked through —, watched —, watched from —, whispered to —, worked from —; — added, — agreed, — answered, — appeared, — appeared at, — appeared in, — appeared on, — approached, — asked, — ate, — became, — began, — began to, — bent down, — blew, — bought, — breathed out, — broke off, — brought, — came, — came back, — came between, — came from, — came in, — came out, — came to, — came up, — carried, — caught in, — caught up, — changed, — checked, — climbed into, — climbed to, — closed, — closed about, — continued to, — covered, — crossed, — crossed over, — cut, — cut across, — decided, — decided to, — demanded, — did, — disappeared, — disappeared from, — disappeared in, — disappeared through, — drew, — drew back, — dropped, — drove, — drove back, — fell, — fell across, — fell along, — fell away, — fell down, — fell from, — fell like, — fell on, — fell onto, — fell out, — fell over, — fell upon, — felt, — felt like, — filled, — filled with, — finished, — flew across, — flew among, — flew at, — flew through, — followed,

— fought, — fought in, — fought through, — found, — gave, — gave up, — glanced about, — glanced at, — glanced down, — glanced into, — got, — got out, — got to, — got up, — grabbed, — grew, — grew across, — grew around, — grinned, — heard, — held, — hesitated, — hung, — hung about, — hung from, — joined, — jumped out, — kept back, — knew, — knocked, — laughed, — lay, — lay across, — lay before, — lay by, — lay in, — lay like, — lay on, — lay over, — left, — let, — let out, — lifted, — lifted at, — listened with, — looked, — looked around, — looked at, — looked away, — looked down, — looked out, — looked over, — looked to, — looked up, — made, — made of, — met, — moved, — moved across, — moved against, — moved along, — moved around, — moved at, — moved away, — moved behind, — moved in, — moved inside, — moved into, — moved like, — moved on, — moved through, — moved toward, — moved up, — murmured, — nodded, — nodded to, — noticed, — offered, — opened, — ordered, — passed, — passed above, — passed across, — passed behind, — passed by, — passed over, — passed through, — picked at, — picked up, — placed, — played, — played across, — played over, — pulled, — pulled away, — pulled down, — pulled on, — pulled open, — pulled up, — pushed, — pushed against, — pushed open, — put, — put down, — put on, — put out, — raised, — ran, — ran through, — reached, — reached for, — reached into, — reached out, — reached over, — read, — recognized, — remained behind, — remained on, — remembered, — returned to, — rode, — rolled, — rolled across, — rolled over, — rose, — rose behind, — rose from, — rose in, — rose on, — said, — sat, — sat down, — sat in, — sat on, — sat up, — saw, — seemed, — seemed to, — set, — shifted, — shifted across, — shifted against, — shifted in, — shifted on, — shifted with, — shifted within, — shook, — showed, — shrugged, — shut, — sighed, — slid, — slid through, — slipped, — slipped across, — slipped in, — slipped into, — slipped over, — slipped through, — smiled, — smiled at, — spent, — spoke, — stared, — stared at, — stared into, — started, — started to, — started toward, — stayed, — stayed in, — stepped, — stepped into, — stepped out, — stepped over, — stood, — stood against, — stood behind, — stood for, — stood in, — stood out, — stood over, — stood to, — stood up, — stopped, — stopped in, — stopped on, — swallowed, — swung, — swung away, — thought, — thought about, — thought for, — thought of, — threw, — threw across, — took, — took off, — took on, — touched, — tried, — tried to, — turned, — turned around, — turned off, — turned onto, — turned to, — waited, — waited for, — walked, — walked across, — walked along, — walked alongside, — walked down, — walked in, — walked inside, — walked into, — walked out, — walked over, — walked through, — wanted, — wanted to, — watched, — waved, — went before, — went on, — went out, — went through, — whispered into, — woke up, — woke with, — wondered, — wondered about

shape
verbs
— appeared, — appeared above, — appeared at, — appeared between, — appeared in, — appeared like, — became, — began to, — broke, — broke from, — came at, — came into, — came to, — changed, — closed on, — cut out, — disappeared, — drew, — dropped from, — dropped through, — filled, — followed, — got, — grew, — hesitated, — hung, — hung before, — hung from, — laid on, — lay on, — leaned forward, — left, — looked like, — looked to, — lost in, — made, — made of, — met, — moved, — moved against, — moved amid, — moved around, — moved beneath, — moved forward, — moved in, — moved through, — moved within, — nodded, — passed across, — passed over, — pressed into, — ran, — ran across, — rose, — rose in, — rose up, — seemed, — seemed like, — seemed to, — settled, — shifted, — shifted in, — shot, — slipped around, — started to, — stood around, — stood behind, — stood outside, — stood within, — took, — walked across, — watched from, — went, — went in, — went into, — went through, — wrapped in

sheet
verbs
changed —, checked —, cut —, drew back —, dropped —, found —, frowned at —, glanced at —, got —, got to —, grabbed —, grabbed for —, gripped —, handed —, held up —, hit —, kicked off —, laid out —, lay under —, lifted —, lifted up —, looked around —, looked at —, looked beneath —, looked down —, looked over —, looked under —,

lowered —, missed —, picked up —, pointed to —, pulled —, pulled at —, pulled away —, pulled back —, pulled down —, pulled out —, pulled up —, pushed aside —, pushed off —, put down —, ran to —, reached for —, read from —, read off —, rolled back —, saw —, shook out —, slid between —, slid through —, slipped out —, stared at —, threw —, threw aside —, threw back —, threw off —, took —, took back —, took down —, tossed aside —, touched —, turned over —, turned to —, waved —, went down —; — arrived, — changed, — covered, — dropped, — ended, — fell, — filled with, — hung from, — hung off, — kicked, — listened to, — looked, — looked for, — made, — made of, — meant, — moved with, — pulled, — pulled across, — pulled back, — pulled down, — pulled to, — pulled up, — rolled across, — sat, — showed, — slid off, — slid out, — went into, — went off, — whispered against, — wrapped around

shield
verbs
carried —, dropped —, grabbed —, held —, held up —, jumped off —, kept —, laid —, lifted —, looked at —, looked over —, looked past —, lowered —, made —, noticed —, pointed to —, pulled at —, pulled out —, pushed back —, raised —, showed —, slammed —, swung —, took —, took down —, took out —, tossed —, tossed aside —, touched —; — appeared around, — appeared in, — became, — came up, — continued for, — continued to, — covered, — did, — dropped, — fell, — felt, — got in, — grew, — grew into, —

held, — held in, — held up, — hung, — hung before, — hung from, — kept, — lit with, — made for, — moved to, — pushed against, — raised, — rolled out, — rose from, — seemed to, — settled to, — shifted into, — showed, — slammed against, — slid down, — took, — turned to, — went, — went down, — went up

ship
verbs

approached —, asked —, asked about —, ate on —, closed with —, demanded of —, found —, gestured to —, glanced at —, got —, got to —, hated —, headed toward —, held —, knew —, left —, looked around —, looked at —, looked between —, lost —, loved —, met —, nodded at —, nodded to —, passed over —, pulled —, ran —, ran to —, reached —, rolled with —, saw —, spoke to —, took —, walked along —, walked to —, watched —, waved to —, yelled toward —; — agreed, — appeared, — appeared in, — appeared on, — approached, — arrived, — arrived at, — became, — began, — began to, — bent to, — broke, — broke off, — broke out, — called, — called at, — came, — came about, — came around, — came in, — came into, — came over, — came to, — came together, — came up, — carried, — caught, — changed, — cleared, — closed on, — continued on, — continued to, — cut across, — cut through, — did, — disappeared from, — drew, — drove through, — drove toward, — entered, — fell, — felt, — filled, — filled with, — flew, — flew in, — flew on, — flew over, — fought, — gave, — got, — got away, — grew, — grew in, — headed, —

headed up, — heard, — held together, — hit, — joined with, — knew, — landed without, — lay, — lay at, — lay in, — lay on, — left, — left on, — left out, — lifted, — lifted from, — looked, — looked for, — looked like, — lost, — lost at, — made, — missed, — moved, — moved against, — moved along, — moved forward, — moved through, — moved to, — needed, — offered, — opened, — passed in, — passed over, — picked up, — pointed, — pulled into, — raised, — ran before, — ran into, — ran on, — ran to, — reached, — reached open, — remained on, — returned, — rode, — rode at, — rolled, — rolled in, — rolled over, — rolled to, — rose, — rose from, — rose into, — rose on, — said, — sank, — sank in, — sat, — sat on, — sat with, — screamed toward, — seemed, — seemed to, — set, — set forth, — set on, — set out, — settled, — settled beneath, — shook, — shouted, — showed, — showed up, — sighed around, — slammed into, — slid down, — slid through, — slipped into, — snapped in, — started to, — stayed in, — stood out, — stopped, — struck, — suggested, — swung around, — swung toward, — took, — took off, — took on, — tried, — tried to, — turned, — waited for, — waited over, — waited to, — wanted, — went, — went about, — went back, — went down, — went out, — went through, — went up, — went with

shirt
verbs

bought —, called —, carried —, changed —, checked out —, climbed up —, closed —, drew on —, dropped —,

dropped off —, found —, glanced at —, got —, grabbed —, grabbed at —, grabbed for —, gripped —, handed over —, held —, held out —, held up —, laid out —, left —, lifted —, lifted up —, looked at —, lost —, lowered —, moved —, nodded into —, opened —, passed —, picked at —, picked up —, pulled —, pulled at —, pulled off —, pulled on —, pulled open —, pulled out —, pulled up —, put on —, raised —, reached for —, reached in —, reached inside —, reached into —, reached under —, rolled —, shoved —, shrugged into —, shrugged off —, shrugged on —, slid into —, slipped off —, slipped on —, stared at —, stood in —, threw —, threw off —, threw on —, took —, took off —, tossed —, tossed down —, touched —, wore —; — asked, — called to, — came off, — came out, — changed, — closed, — closed at, — continued, — covered, — covered in, — covered with, — cut, — fell away, — fell out, — fell to, — felt, — got, — got back, — got out, — held in, — hung, — hung from, — hung in, — hung inside, — hung on, — hung open, — joined, — jumped out, — laid, — lay on, — looked like, — made, — opened at, — opened in, — pulled, — pulled over, — pushed up, — rolled up, — rubbed, — said, — sent, — showed off, — slid along, — slid to, — smelled of, — snapped, — spoke of, — stepped up, — stood behind, — stood in, — stood up, — stopped at, — struck, — swallowed, — took, — tossed over, — turned, — watched, — went, — wrapped around, — yelled

shock
verbs

asked in —, blinked in —, blinked with —, covered —, cried in —, expected —, felt —, fought through —, gasped in —, gasped with —, got —, got over —, heard —, jumped in —, lay in —, listened in —, muttered in —, nodded in —, nodded through —, noticed with —, read —, realized in —, remembered —, repeated in —, said in —, said with —, sat in —, saw —, screamed in —, seemed in —, shook off —, snapped in —, stared in —, started in —, stood in —, stopped in —, swallowed in —, waited for —, watched in —, went for —, went into —, whispered in —, yelled in —; — appeared on, — began to, — called for, — came, — came over, — covered, — crossed, — died away, — disappeared in, — drew up, — filled, — gave, — killed, — looked like, — made, — passed, — passed like, — passed through, — ran over, — ran through, — seemed to, — settled on, — shot up, — showed in, — showed on, — slammed into, — struck, — took, — turned into, — turned to, — went through, — wore off

shoe
verbs

bent for —, bought —, brought —, brought out —, carried —, changed —, checked —, dropped —, explained about —, followed —, found —, got —, grabbed —, handed back —, held out —, kicked off —, laid down —, left —, lifted —, liked —, looked at —, looked through —, lost —, loved —, needed —, picked at —, picked up —, played with —, pulled off —, pulled on —, put —, put down —, put on —, raised —, recognized —, said about —, said to —, saw —, shook —, slipped —, slipped off —, slipped on —, stared at —, stepped into —, stopped by —, studied —, threw away —, took —, took off —, took out —, tossed —, wanted —, wore —, worked —, worked off —; — appeared to, — broke through, — came down, — came from, — came off, — came to, — caught, — covered, — dropped, — felt, — flew into, — found at, — got, — got to, — held in, — hit, — hung around, — kept in, — kicked, — kicked at, — kicked off, — lay among, — looked, — looked like, — made, — made of, — moved across, — moved along, — moved on, — moved out, — needed, — placed, — pointed down, — pointed up, — sank, — sank into, — sat, — sat on, — sent, — showed, — slid on, — slipped on, — touched, — turned around, — walked into, — walked out, — whispered on, — wore

shop
verbs

arrived at —, bought —, bought at —, broke into —, called —, called from —, called into —, came in —, came into —, closed —, closed up —, continued into —, entered —, gestured to —, gestured toward —, glanced around —, glanced at —, glanced inside —, glanced toward —, handed over —, knew —, left —, looked around —, loved —, moved through —, opened —, passed —, ran through —, saw —, set up —, started —, stepped inside —, stepped into —, stopped at —, stopped by —, stopped outside —, talked —, waited outside —, walked around —, walked into —,

walked through —, went into —, went to —, worked in —

shore
verbs

approached —, crossed to —, fought toward —, frowned at —, glanced toward —, kicked for —, lay on —, left —, looked at —, looked to —, looked upon —, pointed toward —, pulled into —, pulled onto —, ran from —, reached —, remained on —, sat on —, started along —, started toward —, stepped onto —, stood by —, stood on —, took to —, turned at —, turned toward —, walked —, walked along —, walked up —, went along —

shot
verbs

appeared in —, called —, checked —, drank —, finished —, finished off —, found —, glanced at —, got —, heard —, held —, hit —, leaned into —, let fly —, listened for —, looked —, made —, meant —, missed —, ordered —, poured —, returned —, said —, said about —, saw —, snapped —, snapped off —, studied —, took —, tried —, tried for —, waited for —, wanted —, went for —; — added, — answered, — appeared to, — approached, — began to, — blew off, — blew past, — broke, — broke out, — brought down, — came, — came from, — came in, — came near, — carried over, — caught, — continued, — continued to, — cut, — cut to, — drew, — dropped, — ended, — fell, — fell on, — felt, — flew, — flew forward, — followed, — followed behind, — found, — got, — hit, — landed, — landed without, — lay, — lay against, — left, —

lifted, — lit, — made, — meant for, — missed, — passed through, — poured through, — promised, — put, — rang in, — rang out, — rang past, — rang through, — rose, — screamed, — seemed, — set, — showed, — slammed, — slammed into, — sounded, — sounded in, — stopped, — struck, — told, — took, — waited on, — went, — went off, — went over, — went through, — wore, — wore off, — worked for

shotgun
verbs
ate —, broke open —, carried —, caught —, dropped —, gestured with —, glanced at —, got —, grabbed —, grabbed up —, gripped —, held —, held up —, kept —, leaned into —, lifted —, lowered —, moved with —, picked up —, pulled down —, put away —, raised —, reached for —, rode —, set down —, shifted —, took —, took up —, turned with —, waved —, waved with —

shoulder
verbs
added over —, answered over —, appeared at —, appeared over —, asked over —, called over —, caught —, caught at —, checked —, checked behind —, checked over —, cleared —, covered —, cried over —, crossed —, drew in —, dropped —, drove onto —, explained over —, felt —, followed at —, frowned over —, gestured over —, gestured toward —, gestured with —, glanced at —, glanced over —, got —, grabbed —, grinned over —, gripped —, heard over —, held —, hit —, kissed —, landed on —, laughed over —, leaned against —, leaned over —, left —, lifted —, looked at —, looked over —, loved —, lowered —, moved —, murmured at —, murmured into —, murmured over —, muttered against —, needed —, nodded over —, placed on —, pointed over —, pointed past —, pointed to —, pressed —, pulled —, pulled at —, pulled in —, pulled onto —, pulled to —, pushed —, raised —, ran on —, reached for —, reached over —, reached past —, reached to —, replied over —, rolled —, rubbed —, rubbed at —, said into —, said over —, saw —, sent over —, set —, settled —, settled onto —, shifted —, shifted on —, shook —, shot over —, shouted over —, shoved —, shoved at —, shrugged —, smiled over —, snapped over —, spoke at —, spoke over —, stared over —, stayed at —, stepped off —, stepped onto —, stood at —, stood behind —, stood by —, stood over —, swung onto —, threw over —, took —, took in —, tossed over —, touched —, turned —, turned onto —, used —, walked to —, watched —, watched over —, waved over —, whispered over —, yelled over —; — appeared, — became, — began to, — bowed, — bowed by, — broke, — broke through, — brought back, — came back, — came down, — came in, — came into, — came up, — caught, — caught against, — caught in, — climbed, — continued to, — covered by, — covered in, — covered with, — disappeared in, — drew, — drew back, — drew in, — dropped, — dropped from, — dropped in, — dropped like, — drove, — fell, — felt, — felt like, — filled, — flew, — followed, — gave, — grew, — held in, — hit, — hit on, — hung, — joined, —

jumped, — lay, — leaned against, — led to, — let down, — let out, — lifted, — lifted in, — looked, — looked around, — looked for, — lowered, — made, — met, — moved, — moved beneath, — moved in, — pressed against, — pressed to, — pulled, — pulled in, — pushed down, — pushed into, — raised in, — ran at, — ran with, — rode, — rolled, — rolled forward, — rolled in, — rolled with, — rose, — rose in, — rose off, — rubbed, — said to, — sank, — sank in, — sank into, — sank with, — sat, — sat behind, — screamed, — screamed in, — seemed, — seemed to, — set, — set like, — set out, — shifted, — shifted under, — shifted with, — shook, — shook beneath, — shook from, — shook like, — shook through, — shook with, — shot, — shot up, — shoved against, — showed, — showed above, — shrugged, — slammed against, — slammed into, — slid along, — slipped, — slipped into, — started, — started to, — stayed, — stepped out, — stood, — stood in, — took, — touched, — turned, — turned to, — waited for, — went, — went back, — went down, — went from, — went up, — worked for

shout
verbs

— became, — began to, — broke out, — came, — came back, — came from, — came over, — carried across, — carried on, — continued, — continued to, — cut, — cut through, — did, — drew, — drew around, — filled, — followed, — gave, — grew, — joined, — led, — lost in, — rang, — rang across, — rang out, — rang up, — repeated, — rose, — rose around, — rose from, —

rose to, — rose up, — sent, — snapped, — sounded behind, — sounded from, — turned to, — went up

shower
verbs

called —, climbed into —, entered —, finished —, finished in —, got —, got from —, got in —, got into —, grabbed —, headed for —, heard —, hit —, jumped into —, leaned into —, left —, liked —, listened to —, moved into —, needed —, paused before —, reached into —, saw —, shut off —, slipped into —, snapped off —, started —, stepped from —, stepped inside —, stepped into —, stood in —, stood under —, took —, turned in —, turned off —, turned on —, used —, walked into —, wanted —, went for —, went into —, went to —; — began, — came, — came on, — cut off, — felt, — filled, — helped, — hit, — looked, — made, — played over, — ran in, — shut off, — slipped off, — sounded, — started to, — started up, — stood in, — stopped, — turned, — turned into, — turned off, — turned on, — went on, — worked

side
verbs

appeared at —, appeared on —, approached —, began down —, broke to —, brought from —, called from —, came from —, came out —, came to —, changed —, checked —, climbed —, climbed into —, crossed to —, dropped over —, entered at —, fell on —, fell onto —, fell to —, felt —, felt up —, flew to —, followed on —, gestured to —, glanced at —, glanced to —, got in —, got on —, got to —, grabbed —,

grabbed onto —, grinned on —, gripped at —, held —, hit on —, jumped in —, jumped off —, jumped over —, jumped to —, kept at —, kept to —, landed on —, lay on —, lay to —, leaned into —, leaned onto —, leaned over —, leaned to —, left —, liked —, looked at —, looked over —, looked to —, moved —, moved along —, moved to —, moved toward —, murmured at —, nodded at —, nodded to —, opened —, passed to —, paused by —, pointed around —, pressed —, pressed on —, pulled into —, pulled to —, raised —, ran around —, ran to —, reached —, reached over —, reached to —, reached toward —, remained at —, remained by —, returned to —, rode at —, rode to —, rolled from —, rolled on —, rolled onto —, rolled over —, rolled to —, rubbed —, said at —, said from —, sank to —, sat at —, sat by —, sat on —, settled on —, shifted onto —, shifted to —, shoved to —, slept on —, slid out —, slid over —, slid to —, slipped over —, slipped to —, spoke at —, stayed at —, stayed by —, stayed on —, stepped to —, stood at —, stood by —, stood on —, stood to —, stopped on —, studied —, swung to —, took —, touched —, tried —, turned on —, turned onto —, turned to —, waited on —, walked around —, walked at —, walked to —, wanted on —, went around —, went down —, went over —, went to —, whispered at —, whispered from —, worked —; — added to, — agreed to, — appeared, — asked, — became, — began, — began to, — blew off, — came, — cleared, — closed, — closed in, — covered with, — did, — dropped, — fell, — fell to, — felt like, — finished in, — fought for, — gave, —

held, — hung, — kept, — kicked in, — knew, — lay, — lived in, — looked at, — looked like, — lost, — made, — met, — needed, — opened, — opened to, — opened up, — pulled up, — put, — raised, — ran, — ran off, — remained, — rose, — rose at, — rose up, — said, — sat, — screamed out, — seemed to, — sent, — settled into, — shook, — shook with, — showed, — showed through, — slammed into, — slid off, — slid open, — snapped, — spoke, — stepped, — stepped away, — stood, — stopped, — struck, — took, — touched, — tried, — turned, — turned in, — used, — wanted, — wanted to, — wore

sidewalk

verbs

came down —, came up —, checked —, continued along —, continued down —, crossed —, dropped to —, flew off —, followed —, glanced at —, glanced to —, got across —, got to —, headed down —, hesitated on —, hit —, lay across —, left —, looked at —, moved along —, paused on —, pointed at —, pulled onto —, ran across —, ran to —, reached —, stared at —, stared up —, started along —, started down —, started onto —, started up —, stayed on —, stepped off —, stepped onto —, stepped to —, stood on —, stopped on —, turned on —, walked along —, walked down —, walked to —, walked up —, went down —

sigh

verbs

added with —, admitted on —, admitted with —, agreed with —, answered on —, answered with —, asked on —, asked with —, blew out —, breathed —, breathed out —, did —, drew in —, expected —, felt —, fought back —, fought down —, gave —, gave up —, got —, heard —, held back —, held in —, leaned with —, let loose —, let out —, managed —, murmured with —, nodded with —, promised with —, pushed out —, repeated with —, replied with —, returned —, returned with —, rose with —, said on —, said through —, said with —, sank with —, spoke on —, stood with —, suggested with —, swallowed —, thought with —, threw —, waited for —, watched —

sight
verbs
blinked at —, came in —, came within —, disappeared from —, drank in —, dropped —, dropped from —, found —, frowned at —, gasped at —, got —, grinned at —, knew by —, looked —, looked along —, looked down —, lost —, loved —, lowered —, nodded at —, paused at —, sank from —, shifted —, sighed at —, smiled at —, stared at —, stared down —, started at —, swung into —, took in —, turned from —

sign
verbs
carried —, caught —, checked —, dropped —, followed —, found —, gave —, gestured to —, glanced at —, grabbed —, held —, held up —, knew —, let out —, looked at —, looked for —, made —, nodded toward —, passed —, picked up —, pointed at —, pointed out —, pointed to —, raised —, read —, read from —, recognized —, repeated —, said in —, saw —, showed —, stared at

—, studied —, threw up —, took —, took down —, waited for —, wanted —, watched —, watched for —, waved —; — added to, — appeared in, — arrived, — began to, — blinked in, — blinked on, — called, — came in, — came out, — covered, — flew, — gave, — held in, — held up, — hung by, — hung from, — hung in, — hung inside, — hung on, — hung out, — made, — made of, — meant, — pointed, — pointed in, — pointed to, — read, — remained, — remained in, — said, — said to, — showed, — stood, — swung over, — told, — took out, — waved in, — went up

silence
verbs
answered with —, asked —, asked after —, asked for —, asked in —, asked into —, ate in —, broke —, continued —, continued in —, demanded —, dropped —, dropped into —, drove in —, entered in —, expected —, fell into —, filled —, filled in —, followed in —, found —, gave —, gestured for —, got —, hated —, heard —, held —, jumped into —, kept —, lay in —, leaned into —, left in —, liked —, listened in —, listened to —, managed after —, missed —, moved in —, nodded in —, noticed —, offered after —, played —, played in —, replied with —, rode in —, said after —, said into —, sat in —, shrugged into —, spoke into —, stared in —, stepped into —, stood in —, thought about —, thought in —, took —, tried —, understood —, waited for —, waited in —, waited out —, waited through —, walked in —, wanted —, watched in —, went with —, wished for —, wondered

at —, wondered in —, worked in —; — answered, — became, — began to, — bowed, — broke, — brought, — came, — came over, — came upon, — closed in, — continued, — continued for, — continued to, — cut, — demanded, — did, — drew on, — drew out, — dropped, — dropped over, — ended, — fell, — fell about, — fell across, — fell around, — fell between, — fell beyond, — fell for, — fell in, — fell like, — fell on, — fell over, — fell upon, — fell with, — felt, — felt like, — filled, — filled up, — filled with, — followed, — followed by, — forced, — found, — gave, — got, — grew, — grew between, — grew in, — gripped, — held, — held for, — hung, — hung around, — hung between, — hung for, — hung in, — hung on, — hung over, — lay, — lay over, — left, — lifted, — looked, — looked at, — made, — met, — nodded, — opened up, — passed, — poured in, — promised, — pushed on, — put, — rang in, — rang out, — rang through, — remained, — replied, — returned, — rolled in, — rose, — said, — sank in, — sat for, — seemed, — seemed like, — seemed to, — settled, — settled down, — settled for, — settled into, — settled on, — settled over, — shook, — slipped toward, — smiled, — spoke for, — swallowed, — took, — took on, — turned, — understood, — waited, — went, — went by, — went on, — wore on, — worked on, — wrapped

silhouette
verbs
— appeared, — appeared in, — approached, — began to, — caught on, — demanded, — entered, — flew into,

— got, — kept to, — laughed, — moved against, — moved among, — moved around, — moved past, — passed, — ran to, — remained, — rose, — said, — sat on, — screamed into, — sighed, — slid to, — stepped into, — stood in

sink
verbs
approached —, bent over —, came around —, checked under —, crossed to —, filled —, glanced toward —, leaned against —, leaned into —, leaned on —, leaned over —, left —, left in —, looked toward —, looked under —, moved toward —, passed —, paused at —, ran to —, reached into —, reached toward —, slid down —, stepped from —, stepped to —, stood at —, stood between —, stood by —, stood near —, stood over —, turned from —, turned off —, turned to —, turned toward —, waited by —, walked to —, went to —, wiped —

siren
verbs
— approached, — approached in, — arrived, — began, — began to, — came, — came from, — came into, — came on, — came to, — came up, — cleared, — closed on, — continued to, — cried in, — cut, — cut out, — cut through, — died, — drew, — filled, — gave, — grew, — headed toward, — joined in, — reached, — rose, — rose behind, — screamed, — screamed by, — screamed into, — screamed through, — screamed up, — shut off, — sounded, — sounded along, — sounded at, — sounded in, — started, — started to, — started up, —

stopped, — swallowed, — went, —
went off, — went on

situation
verbs
— became, — began to, — called for, —
changed, — changed in, — demanded,
— drew, — ended in, — felt, — filled
with, — kept, — looked, — made, —
offered, — placed upon, — pressed
down, — seemed, — seemed on, —
seemed to, — settled in, — settled into,
— sounded, — turned, — went, —
went from

skill
verbs
— added, — brought in, — brought up,
— came from, — came in, — came into,
— came to, — gave, — kept, — lay in,
— learned in, — let, — made, — meant,
— passed down, — picked up, —
remained at, — seemed, — seemed like,
— seemed to, — set about, — showed,
— started, — stayed at, — took, —
turned on, — used to, — went up

skin
verbs
— appeared, — appeared to, — became,
— began to, — broke, — broke into, —
broke open, — broke out, — brought
up, — called to, — came, — came up, —
caught between, — covered, — covered
in, — covered with, — cut, — cut to, —
did, — drew, — felt, — felt against, —
felt like, — filled, — filled with, —
found under, — got, — grew, — held,
— helped, — hung, — hung from, —
hung in, — hung on, — joined with, —
jumped, — kissed, — left to, — lit by,
— looked, — looked like, — lost, —

made, — met, — missed from, —
moved, — pressed against, — pulled, —
pulled over, — pulled up, — ran from,
— sat, — sat in, — seemed, — seemed
to, — sent, — set off, — showed, —
showed above, — showed in, — slid
across, — slid over, — slipped off, —
smelled, — smelled of, — started to, —
stayed, — took on, — touched, —
turned, — went, — went away, — went
with, — wiped, — wiped off

skirt
verbs
bought —, called —, caught up —,
changed from —, dropped —, found —,
gripped —, lifted —, lifted up —, liked
—, picked up —, pulled down —, pulled
on —, pulled out —, pulled up —,
pushed down —, put on —, raised —,
remembered —, rolled up —, settled —,
shoved up —, stepped into —, studied
—, took —, took off —, wore —; —
appeared, — began, — came, — came
out, — caught, — covered up, — fell
back, — fell to, — finished up, — flew
up, — gave, — got, — held, — held up,
— lay, — looked out, — pulled, —
pulled up, — rode up, — rose up, —
settled at, — showed off, — stood
beneath, — stopped at, — swung with,
— walked under

skull
verbs
— appeared, — appeared on, — became,
— began to, — broke, — broke like, —
brought back, — felt, — felt like, —
filled, — filled with, — flew, — gave, —
hung in, — joined, — knocked, —
landed with, — made, — made of, —
nodded, — opened in, — picked out, —

pushed through, — remained, —
replied, — rolled from, — rolled to, —
said, — sat atop, — sat on, — screamed,
— seemed to, — settled on, — shot out,
— stared down, — struck, — swung
around, — turned

sky
verbs
asked —, checked —, disappeared into
—, gestured toward —, glanced around
—, glanced at —, glanced to —, glanced
toward —, glanced up —, liked —,
looked at —, looked into —, looked to
—, looked toward —, nodded at —,
pointed at —, pointed into —, pointed
to —, pointed toward —, reached —,
said to —, saw —, screamed at —,
shouted into —, smiled at —, stared at
—, stared toward —, studied —,
thought to —, watched —, waved at —,
yelled into —; — appeared, — appeared
in, — appeared to, — became, — began,
— began to, — broke, — broke open, —
called, — changed, — changed from, —
cleared, — cleared in, — cleared into, —
continued to, — cried, — did, —
disappeared, — disappeared to, —
dropped, — dropped upon, — fell, —
fell down, — fell in, — fell on, — fell to,
— felt, — filled, — filled with, —
found, — got, — grew, — headed
toward, — held, — hung, — knew, —
lit, — lit with, — looked, — looked for,
— looked like, — lost, — made, — met,
— moved, — opened, — opened above,
— opened like, — opened up, —
promised, — put on, — remained, —
rolled, — said, — saw, — seemed, —
seemed like, — seemed to, — shifted, —
shook, — shook with, — showed, —
stayed, — swallowed up, — took on, —

touched, — touched with, — turned, —
turned from, — turned into, — turned
to, — wanted to

sleep
verbs
blinked away —, caught —, did —, died
in —, fell into —, fell to —, felt —,
fought —, gasped in —, got —, let —,
liked —, lost —, moved in —,
murmured in —, needed —, passed in
—, passed into —, said in —, sank into
—, shifted in —, shook in —, sighed in
—, sighed into —, slid into —, slipped
into —, smelled of —, smiled in —,
started in —, talked in —, turned in —,
wanted —, wanted to —, watched —,
whispered in —, woke from —

sleeve
verbs
caught —, caught at —, checked —,
dropped —, grabbed —, gripped —,
held out —, held up —, lifted —, lifted
up —, looked at —, picked up —, pulled
off —, pulled on —, pulled up —,
pushed up —, reached into —, rolled —,
rolled down —, rolled up —, shook out
—, shoved up —, slid up —, touched —,
wiped off —, wore —; — appeared to,
— caught, — cut off, — fell back, — fell
to, — hung down, — left, — made, —
needed, — opened up, — pressed
against, — pulled back, — pulled up, —
pushed down, — pushed up, — ran to,
— reached to, — rode up, — rolled, —
rolled above, — rolled to, — rolled up,
— said, — shot out, — shoved above, —
showed, — slipped down, — snapped in,
— stood up, — stopped, — stopped on,
— turned

slope

verbs

climbed —, climbed up —, fell against
—, flew down —, gestured down —,
gestured up —, headed down —, headed
up —, lay on —, looked down —,
looked to —, looked up —, nodded to
—, pointed along —, pointed down —,
reached —, rolled down —, sank to —,
slid down —, slid on —, started up —,
stopped on —, turned to —, walked up
—, went down —

smell

verbs

— began to, — brought, — brought
back, — brought on, — came, — came
from, — came in, — came off, — came
to, — came with, — caught, — changed,
— cleared out, — did, — disappeared,
— filled, — got, — grew, — hit, —
hung in, — hung on, — left, — left
behind, — made, — meant to, — ran
from, — reached, — remained in, —
remained of, — returned, — rolled
across, — rose from, — rose into, —
rose up, — seemed, — seemed to, —
told, — went up

smile

verbs

added —, added with —, agreed with —
, answered with —, approached with —,
arrived with —, asked with —, ate —,
began with —, bowed with —, broke —,
broke into —, caught —, continued
with —, covered —, cut —, did —,
dropped —, expected —, explained with
—, felt —, finished with —, forced —,
forced out —, forced up —, fought —,
found —, gasped —, gave —, hated —,
held —, held back —, kept —, kept up

—, killed —, left amid —, let —, liked
—, listened with —, lived for —, lost —,
loved —, loved with —, made —,
managed —, missed —, murmured with
—, muttered with —, nodded with —,
nodded without —, offered —, offered
up —, offered with —, ordered up —,
pointed at —, promised with —, put on
—, raised —, recognized —,
remembered —, repeated with —,
replied on —, replied with —, returned
—, returned with —, rose with —, said
on —, said through —, said with —, said
without —, saw —, showed —,
shrugged with —, slipped into —,
smiled —, spoke with —, started —,
started with —, swallowed —, thought
with —, tossed —, tried —, tried for —,
tried on —, tried out —, turned on —,
turned with —, waited for —, wanted
—, watched —, whispered behind —,
whispered with —, wondered with —,
wore —, worked at —, worked up —;
— appeared, — appeared on, —
appeared under, — appeared upon, —
ate up, — became, — began, — began
to, — broke, — broke across, — broke
into, — broke out, — broke over, —
broke through, — brought, — brought
back, — came, — came across, — came
at, — came back, — came on, — came
out, — came over, — came through, —
came to, — came up, — came with, —
caught, — changed, — climbed over, —
continued to, — crossed, — cut across,
— did, — died, — died in, — died on,
— disappeared, — disappeared from, —
disappeared under, — dropped, —
dropped away, — dropped from, —
dropped off, — expected, — fell, — fell
away, — fell from, — fell off, — fell
over, — felt, — felt like, — filled, —

filled with, — found, — gave, — got, — grew, — grew on, — grew to, — held, — helped to, — hit, — hung on, — lay on, — left, — left on, — lifted, — lit, — lit up, — looked, — looked like, — looked over, — lost, — made, — made up, — meant for, — meant to, — opened, — passed across, — passed over, — passed through, — played about, — played across, — played along, — played around, — played at, — played on, — played over, — played upon, — pulled at, — put, — put away, — reached, — reached out, — remained, — remained in, — remained on, — returned, — returned for, — returned to, — said, — said to, — seemed, — seemed to, — sent, — shifted, — shook on, — showed, — showed on, — slid, — slid across, — slid away, — slid from, — slid off, — slipped, — slipped away, — slipped from, — slipped off, — spoke for, — started, — started on, — started to, — stayed, — stayed in, — stayed on, — suggested, — took, — took on, — tossed, — touched, — tried to, — turned, — turned down, — turned into, — turned on, — turned to, — turned up, — walked over, — went, — went away, — went from, — whispered across, — wiped from, — worked

smoke

verbs

blew —, blew in —, blew out —, breathed in —, drew in —, finished —, fought through —, hated —, held in —, left —, let out —, lit —, lit up —, needed —, pointed to —, pulled in —, ran through —, remembered —, saw —, slid into —, smelled —, smelled like —, smelled of —, stared at —, took —,

turned toward —, wanted —, watched —, waved away —; — appeared, — became, — began to, — blew, — blew around, — blew from, — blew on, — blew out, — came, — came from, — came out, — came through, — carried on, — caught, — caught in, — cleared, — cleared away, — climbed into, — closed in, — continued to, — covered, — drew, — drove, — felt, — felt like, — filled, — flew, — flew from, — got, — got in, — grew, — grew into, — hung, — hung in, — hung like, — hung over, — jumped, — lay, — left, — lifted, — made, — meant, — moved, — poured from, — poured into, — poured off, — poured out, — poured over, — poured through, — pushed through, — reached into, — remained, — rolled, — rolled forward, — rolled in, — rolled out, — rolled through, — rose, — rose about, — rose above, — rose at, — rose before, — rose behind, — rose from, — rose in, — rose inside, — rose into, — rose over, — rose through, — rose to, — rose toward, — rose up, — seemed to, — settled across, — settled in, — shifted, — shot, — shot up, — smelled, — smelled like, — started to, — stood, — went on, — went up, — worked

snake

verbs

— arrived, — began, — began to, — called, — came out, — continued to, — drew back, — dropped into, — hung from, — joined in, — killed, — left, — lifted, — liked to, — lowered, — made, — moved, — moved across, — offered to, — paused, — raised, — ran, — reached, — remained, — said, — slid, — slid past, — slid through, — snapped, —

started to, — tried to, — turned, —
turned to, — watched from, — went, —
wrapped around

snow
verbs
climbed through —, drove through —,
flew like —, hit —, kicked against —,
kicked at —, kicked away —, lay in —,
loved —, moved into —, picked up —,
ran through —, rolled in —, rolled
through —, sat in —, shot across —,
smelled —, smelled like —, stared across
—, stared at —, stepped through —,
stood amid —, stood in —, struck —,
talked about —, touched —, understood
—, used —, walked across —, walked
through —, watched —, went to —; —
added, — became, — began, — began
to, — blew, — blew across, — blew
around, — blew in, — blew over, —
broke, — came, — came down, — came
from, — came in, — came up, — carried
on, — cleared, — continued to, —
covered, — disappeared, — dropped, —
dropped from, — fell, — fell against, —
fell down, — fell from, — fell in, — fell
on, — fell through, — fell to, — felt, —
filled, — flew in, — flew under, —
followed in, — got, — grew, — headed
in, — held, — held off, — hit, — kept,
— landed on, — lay, — lay in, — lay on,
— lay under, — lifted, — lifted on, —
made, — meant, — pushed aside, —
put, — put on, — rose around, —
seemed, — seemed to, — settled, —
settled across, — settled on, — settled
over, — slid down, — slid from, — slid
off, — started, — started to, — stopped,
— struck, — took, — took on, —
turned into, — turned to

sob
verbs
— became, — began to, — broke, —
broke from, — broke in, — came, —
came from, — came in, — came out, —
came through, — caught, — caught at,
— caught in, — cut off, — cut through,
— died away, — filled, — jumped from,
— poured from, — poured out, —
rolled out, — rolled toward, — rose, —
rose from, — rose in, — rose up, —
shook, — sounded, — sounded over, —
started, — started to, — took, — turned
into, — turned to, — worked

sofa
verbs
chose —, crossed around —, dropped
onto —, fell on —, fell onto —, flew off
—, gestured at —, gestured to —,
gestured toward —, glanced at —, got
off —, headed for —, kicked —, lay on
—, leaned against —, leaned into —,
leaned on —, left —, looked at —,
lowered onto —, moved from —, moved
off —, moved to —, nodded toward —,
ordered —, paused on —, pointed at —,
pointed to —, reached across —,
remained on —, returned —, returned
to —, rolled off —, rose from —, sank
into —, sank onto —, sat on —, settled
on —, settled onto —, shifted on —,
shot off —, shoved off —, slept on —,
slid off —, stared at —, stayed on —,
stepped behind —, stood behind —,
stood by —, stood from —, stood on —,
took —, turned to —, walked to —,
watched from —, waved at —, waved to
—, went to —, woke on —

song
verbs

— appeared to, — became, — began, — began to, — broke off, — brought, — called, — came, — came from, — came on, — came out, — came to, — carried, — changed, — continued, — continued to, — cut off, — ended, — fell, — filled, — finished, — finished to, — followed, — grew, — grinned, — lifted, — lost to, — made, — passed into, — played, — played for, — played in, — played on, — rang out, — reached out, — rolled over, — rose, — rose into, — said, — said in, — screamed, — seemed to, — shook, — smiled, — sounded, — spoke of, — started, — started in, — started up, — stood on, — stopped, — told, — turned to, — went, — went on, — went onto, — went through, — wrote for

soul
verbs

— agreed, — agreed to, — began to, — breathed, — brought, — came at, — came from, — cut into, — died, — entered, — fell into, — felt, — felt like, — filled, — flew over, — found, — gave, — grew from, — hung from, — killed, — knew, — knew of, — left to, — lit up, — lost in, — made, — made of, — moved, — needed, — remained, — seemed to, — set, — slipped into, — spoke, — stayed, — stood, — struck, — swung about, — took, — tossed, — tried to, — turned up, — waited for, — wanted to

sound
verbs

blinked at —, brought up —, caught —, died without —, fell without —, followed —, gasped at —, glanced at —, glanced toward —, got —, hated —,

headed toward —, heard —, jumped at —, knew —, let out —, liked —, listened for —, listened to —, looked toward —, loved —, made —, moved toward —, moved without —, noticed —, paused at —, pushed out —, ran toward —, recognized —, smiled at —, started at —, swallowed —, swung toward —, turned at —, turned down —, turned off —, turned on —, turned toward —, turned up —, used —; — appeared in, — approached, — approached from, — became, — began, — began to, — broke, — broke out, — brought, — brought back, — brought to, — came, — came back, — came forth, — came from, — came on, — came out, — came over, — came through, — came to, — came up, — carried, — carried across, — carried back, — carried in, — carried on, — carried over, — carried through, — caught, — caught at, — caught in, — changed, — checked, — closed around, — continued, — continued for, — crossed, — cut, — cut off, — cut out, — cut through, — did, — died, — died away, — died into, — died out, — disappeared, — disappeared at, — drew, — ended, — entered, — fell, — fell in, — fell out, — filled, — filled with, — finished, — followed, — followed after, — followed by, — gave, — got, — grew, — grew in, — happened at, — heard in, — held, — left, — lifted, — lit off, — lost in, — lost to, — made, — made up, — moved, — played in, — pressed on, — pulled at, — rang in, — rang out, — reached, — rode, — rose, — rose above, — rose behind, — rose in, — rose over, — rose up, — seemed, — seemed to, — sent, — set up, — shifted, — shot, —

shot through, — shut off, — slipped past, — started, — started out, — stopped, — stopped at, — stopped for, — stopped with, — struck, — told, — took, — took over, — turned, — turned into, — turned off, — went, — went away, — went in, — went into, — went off, — went on, — went up, — woke

space
verbs
called into —, chose —, cleared —, crossed —, dropped through —, entered —, fell through —, filled —, found —, frowned into —, gave —, glanced around —, looked around —, made —, moved into —, needed —, pointed at —, pulled into —, shot into —, slid into —, smiled into —, stared at —, stared into —, stepped into —, studied —, took in —, walked into —, walked through —, wanted —, went into —; — appeared, — appeared in, — became, — came from, — cleared, — covered with, — cut down, — cut up, — fell, — felt, — filled with, — hit, — hung, — hung between, — left by, — left for, — left over, — left to, — looked, — looked out, — made, — meant for, — opened behind, — ran, — remained before, — seemed, — seemed to, — set up, — settled in, — smelled, — spoke of, — stared, — went, — went through

spark
verbs
— appeared, — appeared at, — blew out, — broke off, — called out, — came, — came off, — caught, — caught in, — continued, — died after, — fell, — fell like, — flew, — flew from, — flew into, — flew like, — flew off, — flew onto, —

flew up, — flew with, — followed, — followed by, — got in, — grew into, — grinned, — hesitated, — jumped between, — landed, — landed on, — leaned over, — left in, — lit, — lit in, — lit on, — lit up, — looked, — made, — moved to, — needed to, — nodded, — pulled up, — rolled, — rose, — rose into, — sat back, — seemed to, — set off, — shot out, — shot through, — showed, — slipped through, — smelled, — smelled like, — snapped through, — stopped, — struck, — struck off, — threw down, — took, — turned, — turned away, — went off, — went on, — went out

speaker
verbs
— added, — answered, — appeared, — asked, — asked for, — began to, — called, — came, — came back, — caught, — climbed on, — continued, — cut off, — explained, — fell, — finished, — glanced at, — hung on, — laughed, — made, — nodded, — ordered, — placed in, — played, — pointed, — pointed to, — rose, — said, — sent, — shook, — shrugged, — smiled, — snapped, — stepped forward, — stood, — went on, — whispered

spear
verbs
— appeared, — arrived at, — became, — came, — came for, — crossed in, — cut, — did, — drew, — dropped to, — dropped with, — drove into, — drove past, — flew, — flew past, — flew through, — gripped in, — held, — held in, — hit, — laid over, — lay, — lay in, — lowered, — made for, — passed

through, — pointed at, — pointed to,
— pointed toward, — promised, —
raised, — remained, — rode, — seemed
to, — slammed into, — struck, — struck
at, — tried to, — turned to, — went
into, — wrapped around

spell
verbs
— appeared, — began, — began at, —
began to, — began with, — broke, —
called for, — came to, — continued, —
covered, — cut off, — did, — drew, —
dropped away, — fell over, — finished,
— found, — grew in, — held in, —
helped, — hit, — kept, — knew, — laid
on, — left behind, — lifted, — looked,
— made, — pressed on, — ran, —
reached, — seemed, — seemed to, —
sent to, — set into, — set on, — shot, —
shot out, — sounded, — sounded like,
— stopped, — struck, — studied, —
took, — took to, — touched, — went
off, — went up, — wore off, — worked,
— worked in

spider
verbs
— began to, — came through, —
climbed, — climbed into, — continued
to, — drew, — dropped, — fell off, —
gave up, — got, — joined, — jumped
back, — jumped off, — jumped to, —
kept to, — landed, — landed on, — lay,
— lived in, — made, — moved at, —
ran along, — remained under, — saw,
— screamed, — seemed to, — settled
down, — slipped under, — struck, —
took, — tried to, — turned, — turned
into, — used, — waited on, — walked
across, — watched, — went

spine
verbs
— bowed, — broke, — broke in, —
broke off, — came from, — came up, —
felt like, — held, — hit, — leaned
against, — lifted, — made, — needed,
— pressed against, — pressed to, —
rose, — seemed, — seemed to, —
shifted, — showed, — snapped, —
snapped open, — sounded, — sounded
like, — turned to, — went, — went into

spirit
verbs
— appeared, — appeared in, — became,
— began to, — broke, — brought down,
— called to, — came on, — came to, —
chose to, — closed in, — cried out, —
demanded, — did, — entered, — fell, —
felt, — flew, — followed, — got, — got
within, — grabbed, — happened to, —
held, — hit, — jumped, — knew, —
left, — left for, — left to, — lifted, —
looked, — looked up, — made, —
moved through, — remained, —
repeated, — returned to, — rose, — rose
at, — rose from, — said, — said
through, — sank, — sank at, — seemed
to, — set, — set upon, — settled down,
— shook, — showed in, — slipped
under, — smiled, — stepped out, —
stood, — stood beside, — swung, —
took, — walked, — went, — woke

spot
verbs
approached —, called from —, came to
—, chose —, cleared —, died on —,
found —, gave up —, got to —, held —,
jumped from —, kicked at —, kissed —,
knew —, left —, lit up —, looked at —,
loved —, missed —, passed —, picked

—, pointed at —, pointed to —, pulled into —, ran to —, reached —, remembered —, returned to —, rose from —, rubbed —, saw —, shot into —, slipped into —, spoke about —, stared at —, stopped on —, took —, touched —, tried at —, turned on —, turned to —, walked to —, went to —

staff
verbs

— began to, — closed, — entered, — gripped in, — headed for, — heard, — held in, — held of, — lay on, — leaned against, — looked at, — met, — opened, — raised to, — sat at, — slid into, — stood at, — stood to, — struck, — took, — used in, — waited for, — waited with, — walked with, — watched, — watched with, — went, — went to

stage
verbs

asked from —, called from —, cleared —, climbed —, climbed onto —, crossed —, gestured toward —, glanced at —, jumped off —, lay under —, left —, looked at —, moved around —, passed behind —, pointed at —, pointed to —, remained on —, shouted to —, stared at —, stared toward —, stepped off —, stepped onto —, stood on —, took —, walked to —, waved toward —, went through —

stair
verbs

appeared on —, appeared up —, approached —, bent over —, called down —, called from —, called up —, came down —, came off —, came up —, climbed —, climbed down —, climbed

up —, continued down —, continued up —, disappeared down —, disappeared up —, dropped down —, fell down —, fell on —, flew down —, followed up —, found —, gestured at —, gestured to —, glanced at —, glanced down —, glanced toward —, glanced up —, got off —, got up —, hated —, headed down —, headed for —, headed to —, headed toward —, headed up —, hit —, jumped down —, knew —, looked at —, looked down —, looked from —, looked to —, looked toward —, looked up —, made for —, managed —, moved down —, moved to —, moved toward —, nodded toward —, paused at —, paused on —, paused up —, pointed at —, pointed to —, pointed toward —, pointed up —, pushed off —, ran down —, ran for —, ran to —, ran up —, reached —, remained by —, sank to —, sat on —, saw —, shot down —, shouted down —, shouted up —, slid onto —, started down —, started for —, started toward —, started up —, stayed on —, stepped down —, stepped off —, stepped onto —, stepped toward —, stood by —, stood on —, stopped on —, stopped up —, took —, took to —, turned from —, turned on —, turned to —, turned toward —, used —, walked down —, walked to —, walked toward —, walked up —, watched —, waved toward —, went down —, went for —, went to —, went up —, yelled from —, yelled up —; — appeared to, — became, — began, — bent, — broke off, — came down, — came out, — came to, — caught, — climbed to, — continued, — continued below, — crossed, — cut, — cut into, — did, — died in, — drew, — ended, — gave, — got, — landed in, —

led, — led down, — led to, — led up, — listened to, — made, — opened, — passed, — passed up, — raised, — ran, — rose into, — said, — screamed, — set in, — stood, — stopped, — took, — tried to, — turned on, — went up, — wore, — wrapped

staircase
verbs

approached —, cleared —, climbed —, climbed down —, continued toward —, found —, gestured to —, gestured toward —, gestured up —, glanced toward —, glanced up —, headed toward —, headed up —, looked down —, looked toward —, moved to —, moved toward —, nodded to —, pointed to —, pointed toward —, ran for —, ran to —, reached —, stared down —, stared up —, started down —, started for —, started up —, stepped around —, used —, walked toward —, went down —, went to —, went up —

stairwell
verbs

arrived at —, cleared —, entered —, fell into —, found —, gestured to —, glanced at —, glanced to —, glanced toward —, glanced up —, looked up —, made for —, paused at —, paused in —, paused on —, pointed to —, reached —, shouted up —, stared down —, stared toward —, started for —, stepped into —, stood in —, stopped on —, swung into —, turned into —, turned to —, yelled toward —

star
verbs

flew —, frowned at —, heard —, heard about —, hit —, knew —, lifted —, looked at —, looked like —, looked to —, loved —, made —, picked —, placed —, pointed to —, remembered —, sat under —, saw —, smiled at —, stared at —, studied —, took —, turned to —, waited for —, watched —; — appeared, — appeared by, — appeared in, — began to, — blinked, — came away, — came back, — came down, — came from, — came out, — came to, — caught, — continued to, — cut, — died, — dropped into, — fell from, — fell like, — fell out, — felt, — flew into, — grew, — hung, — hung in, — hung over, — lay, — lit, — looked like, — made, — meant, — met, — missed, — moved along, — moved in, — needed, — ran across, — remained in, — returned, — rode down, — rose, — rose in, — sat, — seemed, — seemed to, — set, — set in, — showed, — showed in, — shut, — shut away, — slid forward, — stared, — stared down, — stayed in, — struck out, — turned, — turned into, — waited in, — went, — went in, — worked upon

stare
verbs

— became, — continued, — continued to, — fell over, — fell upon, — felt, — felt like, — found, — frowned, — gave, — grew, — held, — lifted to, — made, — met, — moved from, — put, — remained, — returned to, — seemed, — seemed to, — shot to, — swung, — turned, — went back, — went from

step
verbs

began —, called from —, came —, came down —, came off —, came up —, changed —, climbed —, climbed down —, climbed on —, climbed up —, continued down —, disappeared down —, drew back —, dropped back —, explained —, fell back —, fell into —, fell up —, flew down —, flew up —, followed in —, gave —, glanced at —, got —, headed down —, headed for —, headed toward —, headed up —, heard —, hesitated at —, hesitated for —, hesitated on —, hit —, jumped back —, jumped up —, knew —, landed on —, leaned across —, left —, left in —, left out —, lowered to —, made —, missed —, moved —, moved back —, moved down —, moved forward —, moved on —, moved onto —, moved toward —, moved up —, nodded at —, nodded toward —, nodded up —, paused by —, paused on —, paused to —, paused up —, picked up —, pointed to —, ran down —, ran toward —, ran up —, reached —, remained on —, returned to —, rose from —, sank onto —, sat on —, sat upon —, saw —, set —, settled on —, shifted back —, shifted on —, shot down —, shot up —, slid from —, slid into —, slipped down —, slipped on —, started back —, started down —, started toward —, started up —, stood —, stood on —, stopped —, stopped by —, stopped in —, stopped on —, threw down —, took —, turned —, turned on —, turned to —, turned toward —, waited on —, walked down —, walked for —, walked to —, walked toward —, walked up —, watched —, went by —, went down —, went up —; — approached, — became, — began to, — brought, — came, — came down, —

came toward, — came up, — came with, — crossed, — cut in, — cut into, — died out, — drew, — ended, — ended behind, — ended on, — explained, — fell, — felt, — felt like, — finished, — followed, — grew, — held, — hesitated at, — lay, — led down, — led from, — led into, — led to, — lifted, — listened for, — lived upon, — lost along, — made, — opened onto, — put, — ran, — ran out, — rose into, — rose to, — sat, — seemed, — seemed to, — sent, — sent off, — shook, — shook to, — sounded along, — sounded down, — started to, — stood, — stopped, — took, — turned away, — turned into, — waited for, — watched by, — waved, — went down, — worked

stick
verbs
brought —, drew on —, dropped —, found —, gestured with —, grabbed —, gripped —, held —, hit —, kept —, left —, lifted —, moved —, picked up —, pointed to —, pointed with —, pressed —, pulled on —, pulled out —, put down —, raised —, reached for —, studied —, threw —, took —, touched —; — appeared in, — ate, — became, — called, — came to, — caught, — caught between, — caught in, — chose to, — cut from, — fell from, — fell to, — flew from, — landed, — landed like, — lay across, — lay beneath, — lay on, — leaned against, — moved, — moved on, — pulled, — ran through, — reached, — rose, — sat against, — set, — shoved through, — shoved up, — slid into, — slipped out, — snapped, — went, — went up

stomach

verbs

checked —, dropped on —, dropped onto —, dropped to —, fell on —, fell onto —, felt —, frowned at —, gestured at —, got onto —, grabbed —, grabbed at —, gripped —, held —, hit —, kept on —, kissed —, landed on —, lay on —, lost —, pointed to —, pressed on —, rolled on —, rolled onto —, rolled to —, rubbed —, rubbed at —, shifted from —, shouted at —, slept on —, stared at —, told —, touched —, tried —, turned —; — answered, — became, — began to, — came into, — came to, — came up, — caught, — chose, — continued to, — covered with, — cried out, — demanded, — did, — dropped, — dropped at, — dropped in, — dropped like, — fell, — fell through, — felt, — felt like, — filled with, — forced, — gave, — got, — got in, — grew, — grew with, — gripped by, — hung over, — jumped, — kicked, — let out, — lifted, — looked, — made, — murmured in, — opened, — pressed over, — remained, — rolled, — rolled from, — rolled over, — rolled up, — rubbed, — said, — sank, — seemed, — seemed to, — sent, — set, — settled, — settled along, — shook, — slammed into, — started to, — took, — turned, — turned at, — turned in, — turned into, — turned over, — turned to, — went, — wore, — worked

stone

verbs

brought —, brought out —, carried —, climbed over —, climbed up —, crossed —, dropped —, dropped like —, fell like —, felt —, found —, frowned at —, gestured at —, gestured toward —,

grabbed —, gripped —, held —, held up —, kicked —, kicked at —, kissed —, landed on —, lay on —, leaned against —, let loose —, looked at —, lost —, lowered —, meant —, passed —, picked up —, placed —, pressed —, pulled —, pulled out —, sank like —, saw —, shoved on —, slammed —, slept like —, slipped on —, smelled —, stared at —, stepped to —, stood before —, stood like —, studied —, swallowed —, told —, took —, touched —, tried —, turned —, turned to —, walked between —, walked over —, whispered to —, worked with —; — appeared in, — appeared to, — arrived beneath, — became, — began to, — blew into, — blew throughout, — broke, — called, — called to, — came, — came out, — came to, — caught, — caught in, — climbed, — closed in, — covered with, — cut, — cut into, — dropped, — dropped in, — dropped into, — dropped out, — fell, — fell about, — fell among, — fell from, — fell in, — fell into, — fell on, — fell out, — fell over, — fell to, — felt, — filled, — flew, — flew past, — flew through, — flew to, — followed, — found, — gave, — gave off, — grew, — gripped in, — held, — held up, — hit, — hung, — hung about, — hung from, — kept, — knocked, — laid, — laid across, — landed in, — landed on, — lay behind, — lay beneath, — lay in, — lay on, — led to, — left, — lifted from, — looked, — looked like, — made, — met, — missed, — missed by, — moved, — moved across, — opened at, — picked up, — poured, — poured down, — pressed against, — pressed on, — promised, — pulled, — pulled out, — put, — put in, — raised against, — ran,

— ran down, — ran in, — reached, — remained, — rolled, — rolled in, — rolled under, — rose, — rose amid, — rose from, — rose like, — rose to, — rose up, — rubbed, — said, — sank through, — sat, — sat in, — sat on, — seemed to, — sent, — sent back, — set into, — set on, — set upon, — shifted, — shifted against, — shifted in, — shook beneath, — shook under, — shot up, — slammed, — slid, — slid open, — slid over, — slipped beneath, — spoke for, — stared, — stared from, — stared out, — stood to, — struck, — took, — tossed in, — turned, — turned beneath, — turned in, — turned over, — turned under, — turned up, — used, — went, — went into

stool

verbs

asked for —, brought —, carried —, climbed off —, climbed onto —, drew up —, dropped from —, dropped on —, dropped onto —, fell off —, fell over —, found —, gestured at —, gestured to —, got —, got off —, got on —, grabbed —, jumped off —, leaned on —, left —, lifted —, missed —, moved —, moved off —, moved on —, moved to —, picked up —, pointed at —, pointed to —, pulled —, pulled across —, pulled out —, pulled up —, pushed back —, pushed off —, raised —, reached for —, remained on —, returned to —, rose from —, sank onto —, sank to —, sat at —, sat on —, settled onto —, shifted on —, slid from —, slid off —, slid onto —, slipped from —, slipped off —, slipped onto —, stayed on —, stepped off —, took —, turned on —, walked to —, waved at —, waved to —

store

verbs

approached —, called —, checked —, disappeared behind —, disappeared into —, drove by —, drove to —, entered —, found —, glanced around —, glanced toward —, got inside —, got to —, knew —, left —, looked across —, looked around —, looked over —, looked to —, loved —, nodded at —, passed —, pushed into —, ran behind —, ran to —, returned to —, shut down —, spoke to —, stopped at —, stopped outside —, talked of —, walked into —, walked through —, walked to —, watched —, went in —, went into —, went to —; — agreed to, — appeared to, — became, — brought, — called, — came up, — caught, — closed, — did, — filled with, — gave, — held in, — kept, — knew, — lay in, — left, — lost, — opened, — opened up, — put in, — ran, — remained, — said, — sat, — seemed, — slid off, — turned on, — waited on, — went, — went along, — went out, — went to

storm

verbs

— appeared to, — approached, — arrived, — arrived before, — began, — began to, — blew from, — blew in, — blew over, — blew up, — breathed, — broke, — broke in, — broke out, — broke over, — brought, — came, — came around, — came from, — came in, — came into, — came on, — came to, — came up, — caught, — caught up, — cleared up, — closed, — continued, — continued to, — did, — died, — drew, — dropped, — drove to, — ended, —

fell, — fell on, — followed, — got, — grew, — held, — hit, — knocked, — knocked out, — lifted, — made for, — moved, — moved in, — moved on, — moved under, — passed, — passed in, — picked up, — remained in, — rode up, — rolled over, — rolled past, — screamed, — screamed in, — seemed to, — set, — set loose, — started, — struck, — waited for, — waited in, — walked, — went down, — wore

story
verbs
began —, believed —, believed in —, bought —, broke —, came on —, climbed —, considered —, continued — , continued with —, did —, finished —, finished with —, found —, frowned on —, glanced at —, got —, hated —, heard —, knew —, liked —, listened to —, looked at —, loved —, made up —, needed —, needed for —, opened —, picked up —, pointed to —, ran down —, read —, remembered —, repeated — , said —, shot —, smiled at —, stared at —, started —, stopped —, thought about —, thought of —, told —, took over —, took up —, wanted —, went into —, went over —, went through —, worked on —, wrote —; — agreed on, — appeared, — appeared in, — appeared on, — arrived, — began, — began in, — began to, — began with, — broke, — broke about, — brought, — called, — came from, — came in, — came out, — came to, — came up, — carried, — caught, — changed, — closed with, — continued, — continued on, — continued to, — ended, — felt, — felt like, — figured out, — filled with, — finished, — followed, — found, — gave,

— got out, — got to, — grew, — grew from, — held, — hit, — hit in, — jumped inside, — led to, — left, — lost, — made, — made around, — moved, — played, — played out, — poured forth, — ran, — ran in, — ran on, — rang, — read, — remained, — repeated, — rolled, — said, — seemed, — seemed like, — seemed to, — sent, — set, — set in, — showed, — showed up, — told, — told about, — told by, — told in, — told of, — told to, — took, — took on, — went, — went against, — went around, — went on, — went onto, — went out, — worked, — worked out

stove
verbs
asked from —, closed —, crossed to —, glanced at —, glanced toward —, leaned against —, left —, lit —, looked at —, looked in —, moved to —, nodded at — , opened —, remained at —, saw —, stood against —, stood at —, stood by —, threw —, touched —, turned from —, turned off —, turned on —, turned to —, turned toward —, walked to —, went to —

stream
verbs
— became, — began to, — cut, — did, — disappeared beneath, — fell into, — filled with, — got from, — grew, — grew to, — hit, — led to, — lit up, — made, — met, — picked up, — ran, — ran by, — ran down, — ran from, — ran into, — ran out, — ran over, — ran through, — rolled, — rose in, — said, — sat, — seemed, — seemed to, — sent down, — turned, — went over, — went toward

street

verbs

called from —, called toward —, came up —, changed —, checked —, continued along —, continued down —, continued up —, crossed —, crossed down —, crossed over —, drove around —, drove down —, drove up —, fell in —, fell onto —, fell to —, flew down —, found —, gestured to —, gestured toward —, glanced across —, glanced along —, glanced at —, glanced down —, glanced up —, got off —, headed across —, headed down —, headed for —, headed up —, hesitated in —, hit —, kept to —, knew —, lay in —, learned —, lived on —, looked across —, looked around —, looked at —, looked down —, looked into —, looked over —, looked up —, loved —, moved across —, moved along —, moved down —, moved into —, moved toward —, nodded across —, nodded toward —, passed on —, played on —, pointed across —, pointed along —, pointed down —, pointed toward —, pointed up —, pulled down —, pulled into —, pulled off —, pulled onto —, ran —, ran across —, ran down —, ran into —, ran to —, reached —, rolled into —, sat in —, saw —, shot into —, shouted toward —, slipped into —, slipped onto —, stared across —, stared around —, stared down —, started across —, started down —, started for —, started up —, stayed in —, stayed off —, stayed on —, stepped into —, stood across —, stood by —, stood in —, stood on —, stopped in —, studied —, took to —, turned down —, turned from —, turned in —, turned into —, turned off —, turned on —, turned onto —, turned to —, turned toward —, waited in —, walked —, walked across —, walked along —, walked down —, walked into —, walked through —, walked up —, wanted —, watched —, watched for —, went across —, went along —, went down —, went into —, went to —, went up —, wondered at —, yelled at —; — appeared to, — became, — began, — began to, — blew by, — brought back, — called, — came, — came into, — came through, — came to, — carried on, — caught, — climbed, — closed up, — continued to, — covered by, — covered in, — disappeared into, — disappeared under, — drew, — dropped, — ended, — ended at, — fell, — filled, — filled with, — gave, — got, — grew, — heard, — jumped back, — lay, — led, — led from, — led off, — looked, — looked for, — made, — managed to, — moved with, — offered to, — opened out, — opened up, — pushed, — ran, — ran like, — ran up, — ran with, — remained, — returned to, — rolled by, — seemed, — seemed to, — showed, — snapped to, — stayed, — stood at, — stood between, — took, — turned to, — went, — went to, — went up, — wore

strength

verbs

— began to, — came back, — came from, — came into, — continued to, — cut through, — gave out, — grew, — grew with, — held up, — lay in, — left, — left in, — left to, — lifted, — made, — meant, — needed to, — ran beneath, — ran out, — remained, — remained to, — returned, — returned to, — seemed, — seemed to, — started to, —

turned, — went from, — went out, —
wore out

stuff
verbs
— began to, — brought up, — came
down, — came in, — came into, —
came off, — carried out, — covered, —
fell down, — fell to, — flew from, — got
to, — grew, — handed down, —
happened, — happened to, — lay
around, — looked, — made, — moved,
— poured out, — ran down, — ran into,
— seemed to, — shot out, — started to,
— turned, — went, — went down, —
went in, — went up

suit
verbs
bought —, carried —, changed from —,
changed into —, climbed into —,
decided against —, followed —, got —,
got to —, grabbed —, hated —, heard —
, left —, nodded inside —, ordered —,
picked out —, pulled out —, put down
—, put in —, put on —, reached for —,
recognized —, slept in —, slipped into
—, slipped on —, stepped into —, stood
in —, threw off —, took —, took in —,
tossed —, tried —, went with —, wore
—; — appeared, — appeared at, —
appeared from, — approached, —
approached to, — asked, — blinked, —
breathed, — came, — came around, —
came into, — came to, — carried, —
caught, — continued, — cut for, — cut
in, — dropped in, — entered, — fell
away, — fell open, — felt, — felt like, —
got out, — held, — hung off, — landed
on, — left, — looked, — looked at, —
looked like, — made, — made of, —
made up, — missed, — nodded, —

opened, — pulled, — pushed, — put, —
ran, — rose, — said, — sat, — sat at, —
sat with, — saw, — seemed, — shook,
— showed up, — spoke in, — stared, —
stepped on, — stepped out, — stood
around, — stood at, — stood on, —
stood out, — talked at, — thought
about, — took, — turned to, — waited,
— walked, — walked alongside, —
walked in, — went on, — went to

suitcase
verbs
brought —, brought down —, carried
—, carried out —, closed —, dropped —
, followed with —, found —, gestured at
—, gestured to —, glanced at —,
grabbed —, held —, held up —, kicked
—, left —, left with —, lifted —, lifted
out —, looked at —, moved —, nodded
at —, nodded to —, nodded toward —,
noticed —, opened —, picked up —,
pointed at —, pulled out —, put —, put
down —, reached for —, reached in —,
set down —, shoved into —, stared at —
, stopped —, threw —, threw open —,
took —, took out —, tossed —, walked
to —, went to —

summer
verbs
— arrived, — arrived in, — began to, —
came, — came around, — came in, —
came on, — drew to, — gave, — got to,
— lay down, — left, — meant, —
moved from, — passed in, — passed on,
— promised, — raised, — sat back, —
saw, — seemed to, — showed, — slid
away, — slid toward, — stood over, —
took, — took on, — tried to, — turned
to, — waved in, — went, — wore on, —
worked on

sun
verbs
blinked —, blinked in —, came into —,
changed —, checked —, glanced at —,
lay in —, liked —, looked at —, looked
into —, looked to —, loved —, missed
—, needed —, pointed to —, rose with
—, sat in —, saw —, smelled of —,
stepped into —, stood in —, wanted —,
watched —, woke before —, woke with
—, worked in —; — appeared, —
appeared at, — appeared like, —
approached, — became, — began, —
began to, — broke, — broke across, —
broke over, — broke through, —
brought, — came, — came back, —
came down, — came out, — came
through, — came up, — caught, —
cleared, — climbed, — climbed in, —
climbed into, — climbed over, —
climbed to, — climbed up, —
continued, — continued to, — covered,
— cut, — did, — disappeared, —
disappeared behind, — disappeared
below, — disappeared beneath, —
disappeared from, — disappeared into,
— disappeared over, — dropped, —
dropped behind, — dropped below, —
dropped toward, — fell, — fell across,
— fell away, — fell behind, — fell
below, — fell beneath, — fell beyond, —
fell from, — fell in, — fell upon, — felt,
— filled, — flew into, — flew over, —
followed, — gave, — gave off, —
glanced over, — got, — got around, —
got up, — grew, — hit, — hung, —
hung above, — hung in, — hung on, —
kept at, — kissed, — laid, — lay, — left,
— left to, — lifted in, — lifted over, —
lifted to, — lit, — lit up, — looked, —
looked up, — lost, — lowered, —
lowered in, — made, — moved, —
moved across, — moved behind, —
offered, — passed, — passed behind, —
passed over, — played, — played over,
— poured, — poured down, — poured
through, — pushed up, — raised, —
reached, — remained, — returned, —
returned to, — rode down, — rose, —
rose above, — rose at, — rose behind, —
rose from, — rose in, — rose on, — rose
over, — rose through, — rose up, —
sank, — sank away, — sank behind, —
sank below, — sank beneath, — sank
beyond, — sank down, — sank in, —
sank into, — sank over, — sank toward,
— sat, — sat below, — sat on, —
seemed to, — sent, — sent forth, — sent
out, — set, — set by, — set in, — set off,
— set on, — set over, — settled, —
settled down, — settled into, — settled
over, — shifted, — showed, — showed
through, — sighed, — slid toward, —
slipped across, — slipped behind, —
slipped below, — slipped beneath, —
slipped in, — slipped past, — stared
down, — started to, — stayed, —
stepped behind, — stood at, — stood in,
— struck, — struck across, — struck
into, — threw, — touched, — turned,
— went, — went back, — went behind,
— went down, — went out, — went
over, — worked

sunglasses
verbs
changed —, dropped —, frowned
behind —, got —, got out —, grabbed
—, lifted —, lost —, lowered —, picked
up —, pulled off —, pulled on —,
pushed at —, pushed up —, put on —,
reached for —, slid off —, slid on —,
slipped off —, slipped on —, slipped up

—, started toward —, took off —, took out —, wore —

sunlight
verbs

— appeared through, — began to, — broke, — broke through, — came, — came in, — came off, — came through, — caught, — crossed like, — fell, — fell from, — fell in, — fell like, — fell through, — fell upon, — felt, — filled, — filled with, — got to, — hit, — left in, — lit up, — looked, — looked like, — made, — meant, — poured over, — poured through, — returned, — seemed to, — shifted across, — shot down, — showed through, — slipped across, — slipped below, — stood, — struck, — threw, — touched, — turned

surprise
verbs

asked in —, asked with —, blinked —, blinked back —, blinked in —, blinked with —, caught —, checked —, covered —, demanded in —, demanded with —, expected —, felt —, found to —, frowned in —, gasped in —, gasped with —, glanced in —, got —, grinned in —, heard —, held —, hesitated in —, jumped in —, laughed at —, laughed in —, laughed with —, leaned in —, meant by —, murmured in —, nodded in —, recognized in —, remembered —, replied in —, replied with —, said in —, said with —, saw —, screamed in —, shook off —, shouted in —, shouted with —, showed —, smiled in —, stared in —, started in —, started with —, stopped in —, swallowed —, thought in —, turned in —, turned with —, understood —, watched in —,

whispered in —, wondered in —, yelled in —; — appeared, — became, — broke into, — came, — came from, — came in, — crossed, — followed by, — gave, — got on, — left, — left behind, — left for, — lit, — lit up, — looked up, — lost, — made, — passed across, — passed over, — played across, — ran through, — rolled through, — rose from, — seemed, — set up, — settled on, — settled over, — showed, — showed in, — showed on, — sounded in, — turned into, — turned to, — waited for, — went through, — went up, — wore off

suspicion
verbs

— ate away, — became, — began to, — came, — came from, — came into, — carried, — continued to, — covered, — crossed, — entered, — filled, — followed, — grew, — hung over, — lay in, — left, — passed over, — pointed to, — raised, — ran, — ran down, — rang in, — rose, — rose off, — seemed, — seemed to, — settled in, — settled on, — showed in, — started to, — turned to, — worked

sweat
verbs

— appeared, — appeared on, — began to, — broke across, — broke from, — broke on, — broke out, — broke over, — came from, — continued to, — covered, — fell from, — fell into, — flew from, — flew in, — got, — lay, — lay against, — left, — made, — poured, — poured down, — poured from, — poured off, — poured through, — ran, — ran down, — ran from, — ran in, — ran into, — ran like, — ran off, —

returned to, — rolled, — rolled down, — rolled over, — rose on, — seemed, — seemed to, — showed on, — slid between, — slid down, — slid in, — slid into, — slipped across, — stood on, — stood out, — struck, — turned, — went down, — worked up

sword
verbs
brought —, called —, carried —, caught —, checked out —, crossed —, drew —, dropped —, felt —, felt for —, finished —, found —, gestured with —, got —, grabbed —, grabbed at —, grabbed for —, gripped —, handed —, hated —, held —, held out —, held up —, hung —, kept —, laid —, laid aside —, laid down —, lay down —, leaned on —, learned —, let —, let loose —, lifted —, looked at —, looked for —, lost —, lowered —, moved —, needed —, nodded to —, picked up —, placed —, pointed at —, pointed with —, pulled —, pulled out —, pushed —, put —, put down —, raised —, reached for —, remembered —, rode with —, said —, sank around —, saw —, shoved —, stared at —, studied —, swung —, threw —, took —, took off —, took out —, took up —, touched —, tried —, turned —, turned over —, used —, waved —, went for —, wiped —, wore —; — answered, — appeared, — appeared from, — appeared in, — became, — began to, — broke, — broke in, — came, — came across, — came at, — came down, — came from, — came in, — came out, — came to, — came together, — came up, — caught, — covered with, — crossed, — cut, — cut above, — cut at, — cut from, — cut in, — cut through, — did, — disappeared, — disappeared before, — dropped by, — dropped from, — dropped to, — entered, — entered beneath, — fell, — fell back, — fell from, — fell in, — fell to, — felt, — filled, — finished, — flew, — flew at, — flew down, — flew from, — flew like, — flew through, — found, — gave off, — glanced across, — glanced off, — got, — gripped by, — gripped in, — held, — held across, — held at, — held down, — held in, — held out, — held to, — hit, — hung, — hung at, — hung down, — hung from, — hung in, — hung on, — jumped at, — kissed, — laid, — laid down, — laid upon, — landed on, — lay, — lay beneath, — lay in, — lay within, — led, — left, — left in, — left to, — lifted, — looked, — lowered, — made, — made at, — made by, — made for, — made from, — made in, — made of, — met, — met in, — missed, — missed by, — moved in, — moved like, — moved to, — moved with, — offered to, — passed, — passed over, — passed through, — played, — pointed at, — pressed against, — pressed into, — pushed, — raised, — raised above, — raised in, — raised like, — raised over, — rang, — rang in, — rang on, — rang together, — remained, — rose, — said, — sank, — sat inside, — saw, — seemed to, — settled onto, — shifted from, — shot, — shot through, — slid, — slid down, — slid from, — slid into, — slipped from, — snapped in, — started down, — started to, — stood up, — struck, — swung beneath, — swung down, — swung on, — swung through, — swung to, — took, — touched, — waved in, — went, — went back, — went into, — went out, —

went through, — whispered from, — whispered through, — woke, — wore, — worked on

system
verbs

— appeared to, — became, — began to, — blew, — broke down, — called, — came on, — cut off, — did, — fell, — gave, — got, — kicked in, — knocked out, — lit up, — made, — needed, — ordered, — passed by, — put, — ran through, — remained, — saw, — sent out, — settled, — showed, — shut down, — told, — went into, — went on, — worked

table
verbs

appeared at —, approached —, arrived at —, ate at —, bent over —, bought —, came around —, came by —, came to —, checked —, cleared —, continued to —, covered —, crossed to —, crossed under —, dropped to —, fell across —, felt —, flew past —, found —, frowned across —, frowned at —, gestured across —, gestured at —, gestured to —, gestured toward —, glanced across —, glanced along —, glanced around —, glanced at —, glanced down —, glanced over —, glanced to —, got —, got off —, got on —, got to —, grabbed —, gripped —, hit —, hung from —, jumped off —, jumped on —, jumped onto —, jumped over —, kept on —, kicked at —, kicked over —, knocked into —, knocked on —, knocked over —, laid —, lay on —, leaned across —, leaned against —, leaned around —, leaned into —, leaned on —, leaned onto —, leaned over —, leaned under —, left —, looked across —, looked along —, looked around —, looked at —, looked down —, looked over —, looked toward —, moved among —, moved around —, moved down —, moved past —, moved to —, moved toward —, needed —, nodded at —, nodded to —, nodded toward —, opened —, ordered for —, passed —, paused at —, paused beside —, paused by —, paused near —, picked out —, pointed across —, pointed down —, pointed to —, pointed under —, pressed against —, pressed onto —, pushed —, pushed from —, pushed off —, ran from —, ran into —, ran through —, ran to —, ran under —, reached —, reached across —, reached behind —, reached beneath —, reached for —, reached onto —, reached over —, reached to —, reached under —, remained at —, remained by —, returned to —, rose from —, said around —, said from —, said to —, sat across —, sat around —, sat at —, sat before —, sat behind —, sat beside —, sat by —, sat from —, sat on —, saw —, set —, set on —, set up —, settled at —, settled on —, shifted on —, shot around —, shouted across —, shoved from —, shoved off —, slammed —, slammed into —, slid across —, slid between —, slid off —, slid on —, slipped off —, smiled across —, stared across —, stared around —, stared at —, stared down —, started toward —, stayed at —, stepped around —, stepped behind —, stepped from —, stepped to —, stepped toward —, stood at —, stood behind —, stood beside —, stood by —, stood from —, stood near —, stood on —, stood over —, stopped at —, stopped by —, studied —, took —, turned from —, turned to —, turned toward —, waited —, waited at —, waited on —, walked along —, walked around —, walked past —, walked to —, walked toward —, waved to —, went around —, went to —, whispered across —, wiped —, wiped down —, woke on —; — added to, — appeared, — appeared in, — appeared to, — ate, — became, — brought up, — called for, — came from, — caught, — changed, — cleared, — climbed to, — covered, — covered in, — covered with, — demanded, — did, — died, — drank, — dropped, — fell, — fell into, — felt, — felt like, — filled, — filled with, — flew into, — flew open, — followed, — gave, — glanced over, — got, — got to, — got up, — grinned, — held, — hit, — hung, — joined in, — jumped, — knocked over, — laid, — laid out, — laid with, — laughed, — lay, — lay in, — lifted, — looked, — looked at, — looked like, — looked over, — looked to, — looked up, — made, — made for, — made of, — made out, — meant for, — moved, — nodded, — opened, — paused from, — played, — pressed against, — pressed into, — pulled together, — pushed, — pushed off, — pushed to, — pushed underneath, — ran, — ran down, — ran in, — rang, — remained in, — replied, — said, — sat, — sat in, — sat near, — sat on, — sat under, — saw, — screamed, — set, — set aside, — set beneath, — set for, — set out, — set up, — set with, — shifted, — shifted in, — shook, — shouted, — shoved, — spoke, — stared, — stared at, — stood, — stood along, — stood at, — stood beside, — stood between, — stood by, — stood in, — stood to, — stood up, — stood with, — stopped, — struck, —

studied, — talked to, — threw, — took, — tried to, — turned, — turned for, — turned in, — turned to, — waited in, — waited on, — went, — worked at, — worked on

tail
verbs

— became, — began to, — came, — came off, — came up, — covered, — covered with, — cut across, — disappeared into, — fell down, — fell over, — fought to, — gave, — got, — held, — hesitated, — hit, — hung, — hung down, — hung from, — hung past, — lay across, — made of, — pointed at, — raised, — rose, — rose into, — sank, — seemed to, — sent, — shook, — shot forward, — struck, — struck at, — suggested, — swung, — swung through, — turned out, — waved like, — went into, — went up, — wrapped around, — wrapped in

tale
verbs

— became, — began, — began to, — came back, — changed, — ended, — filled with, — got out, — grew, — grew around, — grew in, — grew up, — held in, — led to, — made, — made in, — rang at, — seemed to, — spoke of, — told, — told in, — told of, — told on, — told to, — went

talk
verbs

— began in, — broke down, — broke out, — came, — continued in, — did, — died, — died down, — died for, — died with, — ended, — got, — got about, — grew, — happened on, —

picked up, — remained, — said, — seemed to, — shifted to, — started, — stopped, — turned, — turned from, — turned to, — went on

tank
verbs
— blew, — blew up, — came down, — caught, — continued to, — drew, — filled, — hit, — left in, — looked like, — made, — nodded, — poured through, — put together, — ran, — ran out, — reached, — remained, — returned, — rolled, — rolled across, — rolled in, — rolled through, — sat in, — screamed through, — screamed toward, — seemed like, — seemed to, — shook, — stopped, — waited on, — went around, — went with

tape
verbs
asked for —, bought —, broke —, brought —, changed —, checked —, cut —, dropped —, explained —, filled —, finished with —, found —, glanced at —, got —, handed over —, heard —, held —, held up —, left with —, listened to —, looked at —, moved down —, muttered under —, paused —, picked up —, played —, pulled —, pulled at —, pulled on —, put —, ran —, remained at —, remembered —, said on —, screamed beneath —, screamed into —, screamed through —, set —, shoved in —, shut off —, snapped off —, started —, stopped —, took —, took out —, touched —, tried —, turned off —, turned to —, waited out —, watched —; — began, — began at, — began to, — came off, — came on, — came to, — closed off, — continued, — covered, —

held, — lay across, — lay on, — left in, — let, — looked, — played, — played on, — pulled off, — ran, — ran on, — rolled, — rolled on, — said, — sat in, — shut, — shut off, — snapped, — started, — started to, — stopped, — touched off, — turned, — went, — went on, — wrapped around

taxi
verbs
— appeared, — appeared in, — approached, — approached in, — arrived, — came at, — came to, — disappeared, — disappeared around, — drove away, — drove off, — drove up, — got, — hit, — left, — made, — passed, — pulled away, — pulled in, — pulled into, — pulled over, — pulled to, — pulled up, — raised, — reached, — rolled down, — sat in, — sat with, — smelled of, — started up, — stopped, — stopped at, — stopped in, — swung, — took, — took off, — turned, — turned away, — waited by, — waited in

tea
verbs
asked for —, blew on —, bought —, brought —, brought out —, carried —, drank —, drank down —, finished —, got —, got out —, hated —, left —, lifted —, looked into —, made —, nodded into —, nodded over —, offered —, ordered —, picked up —, poured —, poured out —, put down —, rang for —, reached for —, returned to —, returned with —, sat with —, set aside —, set down —, set out —, smelled —, stared into —, studied —, thought —, told —, took —, tried —, wanted —, went to —

tear

verbs

asked through —, blinked —, blinked against —, blinked away —, blinked back —, blinked through —, broke into —, brought —, expected —, felt —, fought —, fought against —, fought down —, got —, hated —, heard —, kissed —, laughed through —, looked —, nodded through —, remembered —, rubbed at —, said through —, saw —, shouted through —, smiled against —, smiled through —, spoke through —, stared through —, swallowed —, swallowed down —, tried —, waited for —, wanted —, whispered through —, wiped —, wiped at —, wiped away —, wished for —, wore —; — appeared, — appeared across, — appeared in, — appeared on, — appeared to, — became, — began, — began behind, — began to, — broke, — broke loose, — broke through, — called up, — came, — came at, — came back, — came down, — came for, — came in, — came into, — came on, — came out, — came through, — came to, — came up, — closed, — continued, — continued to, — cut, — cut through, — did, — dropped for, — dropped from, — dropped onto, — fell, — fell down, — fell from, — fell in, — fell into, — fell on, — fell onto, — fell to, — fell upon, — filled, — flew from, — followed, — fought against, — gave, — gave off, — got into, — grew, — grew in, — held, — left, — left to, — looked, — looked like, — lost in, — made, — meant, — offered to, — opened in, — poured down, — poured out, — poured over, — pressed at, — ran, — ran down, — ran from, — ran into, — ran out, —

returned, — returned to, — rolled, — rolled across, — rolled down, — rolled from, — rolled out, — rolled over, — rose, — rose in, — rose inside, — rose up, — seemed, — seemed to, — showed in, — slid, — slid down, — slid from, — slid into, — slid onto, — slid over, — slipped, — slipped down, — slipped from, — slipped out, — slipped over, — slipped past, — started, — started from, — started in, — started to, — started up, — stood in, — stood out, — stopped, — tried to, — turned into, — turned to, — understood, — wanted to, — wished to

telephone

verbs

answered —, approached —, dropped —, gave —, glanced at —, grabbed —, grabbed up —, gripped —, heard —, hung up —, leaned into —, lifted —, lifted up —, looked at —, picked up —, pointed to —, pointed toward —, pulled over —, put down —, reached —, reached for —, said into —, said on —, screamed into —, smiled at —, smiled into —, stared at —, started toward —, stepped toward —, talked on —, threw out —, used —, went to —

television

verbs

gestured at —, glanced at —, glanced toward —, grabbed —, leaned toward —, learned from —, looked at —, made for —, moved to —, moved toward —, murmured to —, muttered at —, nodded toward —, pointed to —, put down —, put on —, said to —, sat near —, saw on —, shut —, shut off —, slammed into —, snapped off —, stared

at —, tried —, turned off —, turned on
—, turned to —, wanted —, watched —
, went to —; — began to, — came, —
came on, — caught, — cut, — cut back,
— cut out, — fell, — hung, — hung
from, — hung on, — looked, —
murmured in, — played in, — played
inside, — played on, — played over, —
rolled over, — sat in, — sat on, — set,
— set across, — set for, — set from, —
set in, — set off, — set on, — set to, —
stood in, — took up, — turned off, —
turned up, — went, — went off, —
went on

temperature
verbs
— became, — began to, — came down,
— changed, — climbed, — continued
to, — dropped, — dropped down, —
dropped in, — dropped to, — dropped
with, — fell, — fell away, — fell by, —
hit, — kept, — let out, — liked to, —
lowered, — made, — passed, — passed
through, — promised, — pushed, —
rose, — rose above, — rose around, —
rose to, — rose with, — seemed to, —
stood at, — took, — turned on, — went
from

tension
verbs
— began to, — broke, — climbed, —
disappeared from, — disappeared with,
— fell away, — felt like, — filled, — got,
— grew, — grew in, — grew with, —
gripped, — hung in, — lay, — left, —
made, — moved through, — passed, —
pulled, — pulled at, — ran, — ran out,
— returned to, — rose in, — rose off, —
seemed to, — settled around, — shot
down, — slipped away, — snapped, —

started to, — touched, — went out, —
went through

tent
verbs
appeared at —, approached —, arrived
at —, brought —, called from —,
entered —, felt —, finished with —,
gestured to —, gestured toward —,
glanced around —, glanced at —,
grabbed —, headed to —, left —, lived
in —, looked at —, nodded at —,
nodded to —, nodded toward —,
pointed out —, put up —, ran into —,
sat in —, set —, set up —, slipped inside
—, slipped into —, started for —, stayed
in —, stepped inside —, stepped into —,
stood in —, walked into —, walked
through —, walked underneath —,
went into —, went to —; — began, —
began to, — came into, — caught, —
covered, — did, — disappeared, — fell,
— filled with, — got, — grew, — hung,
— lay, — looked, — made, — made of,
— made up, — moved, — opened, —
opened up, — rose along, — seemed, —
seemed to, — set up, — shifted, —
stood, — stood at, — stood on, — stood
toward, — stopped, — took, — went up

terror
verbs
— began, — began to, — called, —
came up, — came upon, — came with,
— crossed, — fell away, — fell upon, —
felt like, — filled, — gave, — gripped, —
lay, — left over, — made, — opened, —
opened like, — ran through, —
returned, — rose, — rose in, — rose
into, — rose up, — screamed up, —
seemed to, — settled in, — shifted to, —
shot back, — shot down, — shot

through, — slipped into, — snapped, — took, — took away, — turned, — went before, — wrapped around

text
verbs
— appeared, — appeared on, — appeared to, — arrived, — began to, — called, — came, — came back, — came in, — came through, — came to, — caught, — changed, — continued, — continued to, — filled in, — found on, — hung on, — jumped around, — landed in, — lay open, — moved across, — read, — said, — seemed, — seemed to, — spoke of, — went through, — went to

thought
verbs
added —, began —, blinked at —, broke from —, broke into —, carried out —, caught —, cleared —, continued —, continued with —, cut into —, cut off —, dropped —, explained —, fell into —, filled —, finished —, followed —, forced aside —, forced down —, fought off —, found —, frowned at —, frowned in —, gave —, grinned at —, hated —, heard —, held —, kept to —, knew —, laughed at —, lived with —, lost —, murmured with —, offered —, ordered —, paused for —, paused in —, picked up —, pushed away —, put —, read —, sank into —, sat in —, saw —, sent —, shook —, shook at —, shook away —, shook off —, shouted with —, shoved —, shrugged at —, shrugged away —, shrugged off —, shut down —, sighed at —, smiled at —, spoke —, spoke without —, stared into —, stopped —, swallowed at —, thought —, threw off

—, took over —, tossed in —, waved away —, waved off —, went at —, went to —, went without —, wore —, wrote down —; — appeared, — arrived in, — became, — began to, — broke off, — broke through, — broke up, — brought, — brought on, — brought to, — called out, — called up, — came, — came back, — came before, — came from, — came into, — came to, — came with, — carried on, — caught, — cleared, — cleared up, — closed, — closed off, — continued to, — continued without, — crossed, — did, — died away, — drew, — ended, — entered, — fell, — fell away, — fell like, — felt like, — filled, — filled with, — flew away, — flew back, — followed, — followed from, — forced out, — gave, — gave away, — got, — grew, — happened, — held, — held on, — hit from, — hung, — hung in, — joined, — jumped, — jumped to, — kept, — landed, — landed on, — led, — led to, — left, — lifted, — lost, — made, — moved in, — opened up, — passed, — passed in, — passed through, — paused for, — played over, — poured, — poured like, — pressed on, — pushed through, — put, — ran, — ran around, — ran away, — ran in, — ran on, — ran through, — rang in, — reached out, — remained, — remained inside, — returned, — returned along, — returned to, — rode, — rolled through, — rose up, — said, — sank into, — screamed, — screamed in, — seemed, — seemed to, — sent, — settled, — settled down, — settled in, — settled into, — settled on, — shifted, — shifted to, — shot through, — shoved into, — showed in, — shut, — slammed, — slammed into, — slid into, — slipped, — slipped away,

— slipped into, — snapped into, — spoke, — started to, — stopped, — struck, — told, — took, — touched, — tried to, — turned, — turned away, — turned in, — turned over, — turned to, — went around, — went away, — went back, — went into, — went on, — went out, — went through, — went to, — whispered, — whispered to, — woke, — wrapped up

throat
verbs
checked —, chose —, cleared —, cut —, felt —, found —, gasped against —, gestured to —, grabbed —, held —, kissed —, laughed in —, muttered against —, opened —, pointed to —, raised —, reached —, reached to —, rubbed —, rubbed at —, shook —, snapped at —, stared at —, swallowed on —, swallowed past —, swallowed with —, thought with —, took out —, touched —, wore at —; — answered, — became, — began to, — broke, — brought, — came, — came on, — caught, — caught in, — cleared, — cleared from, — closed, — closed in, — closed on, — closed up, — closed with, — cut, — cut across, — cut behind, — decided to, — did, — died, — drank, — fell to, — felt, — felt like, — filled, — filled with, — gave, — got, — grew, — laid open, — lay, — lay open, — let out, — looked, — looked like, — made, — moved, — moved up, — needed, — opened, — opened in, — opened to, — pulled in, — put, — said, — screamed with, — seemed to, — sent, — showed, — shut, — shut up, — sounded, — started to, — stood, — went, — worked,

— worked in, — worked on, — worked with

thumb
verbs
asked around —, brought —, closed —, dropped —, felt —, forced —, gestured with —, held —, held out —, held up —, kept —, lifted —, looked at —, made —, made with —, moved —, placed —, pointed with —, pressed —, pulled —, put —, raised —, ran —, rubbed —, said around —, shifted —, stared at —, took —, touched —, used —; — drove into, — found, — landed on, — moved across, — moved over, — passed, — pointed to, — pressed, — pressed against, — pressed into, — pressed to, — pulled, — pulled back, — rolled, — rolled in, — rose from, — rubbed, — rubbed along, — rubbed at, — rubbed over, — seemed to, — shoved at, — slid along, — slid beneath, — slid between, — slid into, — slid over, — slipped under, — stopped, — went back, — went in, — wiped, — worked along

thunder
verbs
— added to, — became, — began to, — broke, — broke over, — came, — cleared, — continued to, — filled, — followed, — gave, — grew, — made, — muttered, — passed, — ran, — rolled, — rolled across, — rolled down, — rolled in, — rolled on, — rolled out, — rolled over, — rolled past, — rolled through, — shook, — sounded, — sounded beneath, — sounded in, — took on, — turned to

tie

verbs

— appeared under, — arrived at, — asked, — came back, — came out, — came through, — came to, — crossed, — cut into, — flew back, — held together, — hung, — lay against, — lay around, — meant to, — played, — pulled, — pulled down, — ran, — remained, — set off, — shook, — stepped forward, — stood up, — suggested, — swung over, — yelled across

time

verbs

added —, answered —, appeared on —, arrived in —, arrived on —, asked —, asked after —, asked for —, blinked —, bought —, breathed for —, called —, called at —, called for —, called out —, came —, came to —, changed for —, checked —, chose —, considered —, continued after —, continued for —, cried at —, cried for —, cried out —, decided —, did —, dropped in —, explained —, explained at —, fell for —, felt —, figured —, finished —, finished in —, followed —, followed in —, fought —, fought for —, found —, gasped for —, gave —, gave up —, gestured —, glanced at —, got —, got away —, got on —, got out —, grinned for —, heard —, hesitated for —, knew about —, knocked —, laughed —, laughed at —, laughed for —, lay for —, left about —, liked —, listened for —, lived —, looked —, looked at —, looked for —, looked up —, lost —, made —, meant for —, missed —, murmured —, needed —, nodded —, noticed —, opened on —, passed —, paused for —, picked —, picked up —, played for —,

pointed out —, realized —, realized for —, realized in —, remembered —, remembered in —, repeated for —, returned —, said —, said after —, said at —, said for —, said on —, sat for —, set off —, shifted —, shouted at —, slept for —, smiled —, smiled for —, spent —, spoke —, spoke for —, spoke with —, stared for —, started —, stayed —, stayed for —, stood for —, stopped —, stopped in —, struck —, talked —, talked for —, thought about —, thought at —, thought for —, took —, tried —, turned —, turned in —, used —, waited —, waited for —, walked for —, wanted —, watched —, watched for —, woke —, woke at —, woke for —, woke up —, wondered for —, wrote down —; — added, — appeared to, — approached, — approached for, — arrived, — asked, — asked about, — became, — began, — began to, — believed, — brought up, — called for, — came, — came along, — came around, — came at, — came back, — came for, — came from, — came on, — came to, — carried, — caught, — caught for, — caught up, — changed, — checked, — climbed, — closed, — closed in, — covered in, — did, — drew, — drew near, — drew on, — drew onto, — drew to, — dropped, — dropped from, — drove, — explained to, — felt, — filled, — finished, — finished up, — flew, — flew by, — followed, — fought, — found, — found out, — gave, — gestured, — got, — got by, — got loose, — got on, — got onto, — got through, — grabbed, — grew, — gripped, — gripped by, — happened to, — hated, — headed in, — heard, — held, — held back, — helped, — hit, — hung up, — hung with, — knew, — knocked off, —

landed, — lay, — leaned over, — left, —
left for, — left in, — left on, — left to,
— let, — listened to, — lit, — lived on,
— lived to, — looked, — looked at, —
looked for, — looked in, — lost, —
made, — managed to, — meant, —
missed, — moved, — moved on, —
needed, — needed to, — noticed, —
opened, — passed, — passed by, —
passed in, — passed inside, — paused
for, — picked up, — poured, — pulled,
— pulled at, — pulled out, — pushed
into, — ran in, — ran out, — ran
through, — ran to, — read before, —
recognized, — remained, — remained
for, — remembered, — returned, —
rolled by, — rolled on, — rose on, —
said, — sat by, — sat in, — saw, —
screamed about, — seemed, — seemed
like, — seemed to, — set, — shot, —
showed, — slept, — slept until, — slid
down, — slipped, — slipped away, —
slipped by, — slipped forward, —
slipped through, — sounded, —
sounded like, — spent, — spent
between, — spent in, — spent on, —
spent with, — spoke, — stared at, —
stared out, — started up, — stayed on,
— stepped into, — stood for, — stood
on, — stopped, — stopped for, —
struck, — studied, — swung from, —
talked about, — thought about, — told,
— took, — took in, — took on, —
touched, — tried to, — turned, —
turned to, — used, — waited for, —
walked to, — walked up, — wanted to,
— watched, — went, — went against,
— went at, — went beyond, — went by,
— went down, — went on, — went out,
— went through, — went underneath,
— woke, — wore, — wore down, —
wore on, — worked, — worked after, —
worked against, — worked in, —
worked on

tip
verbs
— began to, — came back, — came
from, — came in, — came out, — came
to, — changed, — died, — disappeared
into, — drew back, — drove through, —
ended in, — found, — hit, — made, —
pointed at, — pointed into, — pointed
toward, — pressed against, — pressed
on, — pulled over, — pushed out, —
reached to, — rose from, — said, —
sank into, — seemed, — stepped into,
— stopped, — touched, — turned, —
turned out

tire
verbs
— ate up, — began to, — blew, — blew
out, — came off, — hit, — kissed, —
laid out, — left, — looked, — made, —
pulled off, — rolled over, — sank into,
— screamed, — screamed against, —
screamed on, — shot out, — slammed
into, — slid on, — slipped, — slipped
against, — started to, — touched, —
touched down, — turned, — went

toe
verbs
felt —, frowned at —, glanced at —,
glanced to —, grabbed —, held —,
kissed —, lifted —, lifted on —, looked
to —, moved —, pointed —, pressed
with —, rose on —, rose onto —, rose to
—, stared at —, stared between —,
stood on —, studied —, took —,
touched —, tried —, walked on —,
wanted —, watched between —, went
off —

toilet

verbs

asked about —, came from —, checked out —, crossed to —, found —, gestured to —, left —, moved to —, needed —, pointed around —, ran to —, reached behind —, reached into —, rose from —, sat on —, slipped into —, started on —, stayed on —, stood from —, stood near —, stood on —, stood over —, used —, went into —, went to —

tone

verbs

added in —, admitted in —, answered —, asked in —, called in —, caught —, changed —, considered —, continued in —, explained in —, felt at —, frowned at —, got —, hated —, heard —, kept —, knew —, knew from —, loved —, ordered in —, picked up —, read —, recognized —, repeated in —, replied in —, replied with —, said in —, said with —, set —, spoke in —, thought from —, thought with —, took on —, understood —, whispered in —; — added, — asked, — became, — broke into, — brought, — came, — came from, — came out, — came through, — came with, — carried, — changed, — changed from, — covered, — cut in, — cut off, — drew, — dropped, — dropped away, — fell from, — filled with, — gave, — got, — got through, — grew, — held, — left, — lit, — lost, — lowered, — lowered to, — made, — meant, — rang to, — remained, — returned, — returned to, — rose with, — said, — seemed, — seemed to, — sent, — set, — shifted, — shook with, — sounded, — sounded in, — spoke, —

stayed, — suggested, — took on, — tried, — turned, — turned to, — went, — went from, — went up, — wondered

tongue

verbs

asked in —, brought out —, caught —, checked —, felt —, found —, got —, held —, kept —, learned —, left —, lifted —, lost —, met —, moved —, opened to —, pointed —, pulled back —, put out —, ran —, said in —, slid over —, spoke —, spoke in —, touched —, used —; — appeared, — began, — began to, — blew out, — broke down, — broke through, — came into, — came out, — closed around, — cut out, — did, — dropped to, — entered, — fell, — fell out, — felt, — felt like, — filled, — followed, — found, — gave, — glanced over, — got to, — grew, — hit, — hung between, — hung in, — hung out, — hung over, — joined, — knew, — lay, — lay like, — lay on, — led, — left, — made, — met, — met in, — moved, — moved behind, — moved in, — moved on, — moved over, — played along, — pressed, — pressed against, — pressed to, — pulled out, — pushed at, — pushed into, — pushed out, — pushed past, — ran across, — ran around, — ran over, — reached, — rolled out, — rubbed over, — said, — seemed, — seemed to, — sent, — set between, — shot out, — slammed into, — slid, — slid across, — slid along, — slid between, — slid from, — slid like, — slid out, — slid over, — slid past, — slid up, — slipped back, — slipped inside, — slipped into, — slipped out, — took over, — touched, — turned, — turned into, — turned to, — waved in,

— went, — went down, — went to, — worked for, — worked over, — wrapped

tooth
verbs
breathed through —, came to —, closed —, felt —, grinned —, grinned through —, kissed —, liked —, lost —, picked —, picked at —, pulled with —, said between —, said through —, sank —, saw —, set —, showed —, smiled through —, smiled with —, snapped —, spoke through —, touched —, used —, whispered through —; — appeared, — began to, — broke off, — came away, — came down, — came into, — came out, — caught, — closed around, — closed on, — cut across, — cut into, — disappeared, — fell out, — felt, — felt like, — filled, — filled with, — flew, — flew from, — flew like, — flew out, — followed, — found, — got, — grew, — hit, — hung around, — kicked in, — knocked, — knocked out, — knocked together, — left, — lifted from, — lit up, — looked, — looked like, — made, — missed, — passed, — pressed, — pressed against, — pressed into, — pulled, — pulled back, — raised, — ran like, — remained in, — sank, — sank in, — sank into, — screamed, — seemed to, — set, — set against, — showed, — showed in, — showed through, — showed under, — showed up, — shut, — slammed, — slammed together, — slid from, — snapped, — snapped at, — snapped near, — snapped together, — started to, — started up, — stepped up, — touched, — wanted to

top
verbs

— became, — began to, — bent, — came off, — covered with, — cut, — cut off, — fell, — filled with, — grew, — heard, — lay, — left, — left of, — left off, — lifted, — lifted off, — made of, — meant to, — opened, — pulled up, — put back, — rode up, — rose from, — rose into, — sat, — seemed to, — shoved, — slipped up, — stared at, — started, — took

torch
verbs
asked for —, carried —, dropped —, found —, got out —, grabbed —, handed —, held —, held out —, held up —, killed —, left —, lifted —, lit —, looked at —, looked for —, lowered —, moved —, picked up —, pulled out —, put down —, raised —, saw —, swung —, threw —, took —, took out —, took up —, turned off —, turned on —, used —; — appeared, — became, — began to, — breathed out, — came, — came in, — came into, — came near, — came to, — carried by, — caught, — climbed into, — continued to, — cut through, — disappeared, — fell, — fell through, — felt, — flew, — flew away, — flew from, — headed, — hung, — hung from, — kept, — lay, — led, — lifted to, — lit, — lit with, — lowered, — made, — moved across, — moved on, — played across, — poured, — pressed against, — pressed into, — pushed at, — raised, — remained to, — said, — set in, — set into, — shot out, — snapped down, — stopped, — stopped at, — took, — turned to, — went before, — went out

touch
verbs

— appeared, — became, — caught, — cut through, — felt, — followed, — gave, — kept, — lifted from, — made, — meant to, — moved, — moved on, — opened, — put, — said, — seemed, — seemed to, — sent, — slid away, — slipped to, — stayed, — turned into, — went through, — went to, — went up, — woke

towel
verbs
bought —, came with —, carried —, changed out —, checked —, dropped —, found —, got —, grabbed —, grabbed for —, lifted —, opened —, passed in —, paused with —, picked up —, pulled —, pulled on —, put down —, reached for —, returned with —, rolled on —, saw —, set down —, shook out —, stared at —, stepped over —, stood in —, threw —, threw in —, took —, took off —, tossed —, tossed down —, wanted —, waved —; — closed between, — covered, — fell, — fell away, — fell like, — fell onto, — fell to, — followed, — gripped, — held in, — helped, — hung before, — hung in, — hung on, — hung over, — laid along, — laid out, — lay on, — left, — raised to, — rode up, — slid open, — slipped, — slipped off, — smelled, — went away, — wrapped about, — wrapped around, — wrapped in

tower
verbs
— asked, — began to, — blinked, — called, — came down, — came on, — cleared, — did, — disappeared into, — fell, — fell on, — felt, — flew, — joined by, — lay, — looked like, — lost, —

made of, — moved, — moved behind, — placed in, — reached, — reached for, — rose, — rose about, — rose above, — rose from, — rose like, — seemed, — seemed to, — shook, — slid into, — stood, — stood in, — stood on, — stood upon, — struck, — swallowed in, — went, — went up, — wrapped in

town
verbs
arrived in —, came by —, came from —, came into —, chose —, drove across —, drove into —, drove through —, drove to —, entered —, got about —, got in —, got into —, got to —, knew in —, left —, lived in —, moved across —, ran through —, settled in —, settled into —, walked around —, went across —, went in —, went into —, went to —; — asked about, — became, — began to, — believed, — brought out, — came, — came in, — came into, — came out, — came to, — carried, — considered, — did, — disappeared from, — ended in, — figured, — filled with, — gave, — got, — got to, — grew, — heard, — held, — joined in, — kept, — knew about, — lay, — lived, — looked like, — lost, — met up, — needed, — needed to, — passed, — passed through, — paused, — put in, — put to, — reached, — said, — sat in, — saw, — seemed, — seemed on, — seemed to, — set in, — slept, — slid by, — smelled of, — stepped in, — stood, — stopped by, — talked of, — thought, — took, — turned out, — understood, — waited for, — walked, — wanted to, — went, — went to, — wondered

track

verbs
came across —, came upon —, changed
—, covered —, crossed —, drove down
—, felt —, followed —, found —,
gestured toward —, got off —, headed
for —, kept —, kept to —, lay on —,
leaned across —, left —, lost —, ran —,
ran across —, ran along —, saw —,
started along —, started down —,
started up —, stayed on —, stepped
onto —, stood on —, stopped in —,
studied —, turned toward —, walked
over —; — appeared, — appeared on, —
approached, — became, — began, —
began to, — brought, — came to, —
came up, — covered, — cut across, —
disappeared, — laid onto, — led, — led
into, — led off, — led to, — led toward,
— looked, — made for, — met, —
passed, — ran along, — ran alongside,
— ran between, — ran into, —
remained, — rose, — rose like, —
seemed to, — sounded, — sounded like,
— started, — started to, — stood, —
stood out, — stopped at, — turned to,
— walked up

traffic
verbs
— appeared to, — began to, — came, —
came at, — came down, — came in, —
came off, — came on, — came to, —
came toward, — cleared, — continued
to, — crossed, — died down, —
disappeared, — disappeared behind, —
got, — grew, — grew by, — headed
across, — headed for, — headed toward,
— kept, — lit, — moved, — moved in,
— moved past, — moved through, —
opened up, — passed in, — passed on,
— passed through, — picked up, —
returned to, — rolled forward, — rolled

on, — seemed, — started to, — stopped,
— took, — waited at, — went, — went
in, — went out

trail
verbs
broke —, broke from —, caught —,
crossed —, cut off —, followed —,
found —, gestured down —, hit —, lay
in —, left —, let —, lost —, moved off
—, nodded to —, noticed —, picked up
—, pointed to —, poured along —,
reached —, saw —, started down —,
stayed on —, stopped on —, turned off
—, went off —; — began, — began to,
— called, — came, — changed, —
cleared, — climbed, — climbed up, —
continued on, — crossed, — cut, — cut
through, — disappeared, — disappeared
at, — disappeared into, — disappeared
with, — ended, — ended at, — ended
in, — ended on, — felt like, — followed,
— got, — grew, — led, — led down, —
led into, — led on, — led to, — left, —
left by, — looked like, — passed to, —
pointed to, — promised, — ran, — ran
along, — ran behind, — ran down, —
ran out, — ran through, — remained, —
rose, — rose from, — seemed, —
seemed to, — set off, — slid down, —
snapped into, — stopped, — took, —
turned down, — turned into, — turned
off, — turned to, — went, — went into,
— went on, — went up, — wrapped

train
verbs
— approached, — approached with, —
arrived, — arrived at, — arrived in, —
began, — began to, — came, — came at,
— came on, — came to, — crossed, —
disappeared, — drew, — drew into, —

drew to, — entered, — headed toward,
— hit, — kept, — left, — left at, — left
for, — lifted up, — lit, — looked like, —
looked to, — made, — moved, —
moved away, — moved off, — moved
on, — passed, — passed on, — passed
through, — picked up, — pulled away,
— pulled forward, — pulled in, —
pulled out, — pulled to, — pushed
through, — ran, — ran at, — ran on, —
reached, — rolled, — rolled in, — rolled
on, — rolled out, — rolled past, — rose
into, — rose off, — screamed, —
screamed by, — seemed, — seemed like,
— set, — slammed on, — slammed past,
— slid away, — started to, — started up,
— started with, — stopped, — stopped
at, — stopped in, — took, — used, —
walked over, — went, — went into, —
went off

tray
verbs
arrived with —, ate —, bent to —,
brought —, brought in —, brought up
—, carried —, carried in —, carried on
—, checked —, dropped —, filled —,
finished —, gestured at —, got —, got
out —, grabbed —, gripped —, handed
over —, heard from —, held out —, laid
—, leaned over —, lifted —, looked at
—, picked up —, pointed at —, pointed
to —, pointed toward —, pulled out —,
pushed aside —, put down —, rang for
—, reached for —, reached to —,
reached toward —, returned with —,
rose with —, set —, set down —, set on
—, set up —, settled —, shifted —,
stared at —, took —, took in —,
touched —, turned to —, went to —

tree
verbs
approached —, blinked at —, called —,
came down —, cleared —, climbed —,
climbed down —, climbed into —,
climbed past —, disappeared among —,
disappeared into —, dropped from —,
drove between —, drove through —,
entered —, fell against —, fell into —,
felt with —, figured —, flew from —,
flew through —, found —, frowned at
—, gestured at —, gestured toward —,
glanced above —, glanced at —, glanced
into —, got into —, gripped —, hit —,
hung on —, kept to —, kicked —, knew
about —, lay against —, leaned against
—, leaned off —, left —, listened to —,
looked around —, looked at —, looked
behind —, looked down —, looked out
—, looked through —, looked toward
—, looked under —, loved —, made —,
moved into —, moved through —,
needed —, nodded to —, noticed —,
passed —, paused among —, pointed at
—, pointed into —, pointed to —,
pointed up —, promised —, pushed off
—, ran among —, ran through —, ran to
—, ran toward —, reached —, rode into
—, rose above —, sat beneath —, sat
under —, saw —, shifted in —, slid
down —, slipped behind —, slipped
through —, smiled at —, spent in —,
stared at —, started into —, stayed in —
, stayed inside —, stepped behind —,
stepped from —, stepped into —,
stepped to —, stood behind —, stood by
—, stood in —, stopped behind —,
stopped by —, stopped near —, studied
—, thought about —, told —, touched
—, turned from —, turned to —, turned
toward —, waited behind —, walked
beneath —, walked into —, walked
through —, walked to —, walked

toward —, walked under —, watched —
, watched from —, went to —; —
agreed, — appeared, — appeared in, —
appeared to, — ate, — became, —
began, — began to, — blew up, —
bowed away, — bowed beneath, —
broke, — broke in, — called to, — came,
— came back, — came into, — came to,
— caught, — caught in, — cleared, —
closed about, — closed in, — continued
to, — covered, — covered in, — covered
with, — crossed, — cut down, — did,
— died, — disappeared, — drew, —
drew back, — ended, — ended in, —
fell, — fell across, — fell away, — fell in,
— fell into, — fell on, — felt, — filled,
— filled with, — flew past, — gave, —
grew, — grew against, — grew around,
— grew from, — grew in, — grew
inside, — grew on, — grew over, —
grew through, — grew throughout, —
grew up, — headed, — heard, — held,
— helped to, — hit, — hung, — hung
between, — hung from, — hung over,
— joined in, — kept, — laid, — lay, —
lay across, — lay on, — lay over, —
leaned, — leaned out, — leaned over, —
leaned toward, — left, — let, — let fly,
— lifted, — lifted in, — lifted up, —
looked, — looked like, — lost, — made,
— managed to, — met, — moved, —
moved back, — moved in, — offered, —
opened into, — opened up, — placed to,
— pointed at, — pressed in, — pulled
back, — pushed down, — raised, — ran,
— reached, — reached from, — reached
out, — reached over, — remained, —
returned, — rolled up, — rose, — rose
from, — rose in, — rose like, — rose off,
— rose on, — rose to, — rubbed, —
said, — sank, — sat, — seemed, —
seemed like, — seemed to, — sent, —

shifted, — shook, — shut out, — sighed,
— slammed against, — slid past, —
slipped, — spoke, — stayed up, —
stood, — stood above, — stood beneath,
— stood in, — stood like, — stood off,
— stood to, — struck, — struck by, —
suggested, — swung, — threw, — took,
— took over, — tossed, — turned, —
turned into, — turned out, — turned to,
— used to, — watched over, — went
down, — went over, — went up, —
worked upon, — wrapped around

trepidation
verbs
— blew through, — caught in, — closed
around, — closed up, — crossed, — fell
across, — felt like, — filled, — grew in,
— gripped, — lifted from, — lit, —
made, — played across, — played over,
— poured through, — pressed against,
— ran down, — ran through, — ran up,
— rolled down, — rolled through, —
rose in, — settled in, — shot down, —
shot up, — showed in, — showed on, —
slammed into, — slid down, — turned,
— went through

trouble
verbs
— approached, — began, — began
inside, — called up, — came by, — came
from, — caught, — did in, — filled, —
followed, — found, — got, — got off, —
headed, — heard, — held, — lay, —
made, — made out, — meant, — met,
— passed, — picked up, — pulled, —
ran with, — reached, — reached behind,
— read, — rose up, — said, — seemed,
— started, — stayed on, — struck, —
took, — walked on

truck

verbs

approached —, arrived in —, bought —, called —, climbed from —, climbed in —, climbed into —, closed up —, drove —, fell off —, followed —, followed in —, found —, gestured at —, glanced at —, glanced inside —, glanced toward —, glanced under —, got —, got in —, got inside —, got into —, got to —, headed for —, headed to —, heard —, hit —, jumped from —, jumped in —, leaned against —, leaned into —, leaned on —, left —, looked around —, looked at —, looked past —, looked toward —, needed —, nodded toward —, passed — , passed near —, paused outside —, picked up —, pointed to —, pulled —, pushed off —, put —, ran around —, ran for —, ran to —, reached —, reached inside —, reached into —, recognized —, returned to —, rolled underneath —, said to —, sat in —, saw —, shouted from —, shut down —, slammed into —, slid into —, stared at —, started —, started for —, started to —, started up —, stayed in —, stepped from —, stood beside —, stood by —, stopped —, stopped at —, stopped beside —, took —, turned —, turned off —, turned to —, turned toward —, walked around —, walked to —, walked toward —, watched —, waved at —, went to —, yelled from —; — appeared, — appeared at, — approached, — arrived, — arrived at, — began to, — blew, — blew through, — blew up, — broke, — broke down, — came, — came after, — came around, — came at, — came back, — came down, — came over, — came to, — came up, — carried, — climbed up, — closed, — continued on,

— crossed, — cut into, — cut out, — cut through, — did, — died, — disappeared into, — drew, — dropped into, — dropped off, — drove, — drove away, — drove by, — drove off, — drove on, — drove through, — fell away, — filled, — filled with, — flew forward, — fought, — found, — glanced at, — got, — grew, — headed, — held together, — hit, — kept, — kept on, — kicked up, — lay across, — lay in, — lay on, — left, — let, — looked like, — lost, — made, — moved forward, — moved through, — needed, — passed, — passed by, — passed in, — passed over, — paused, — picked up, — pulled away, — pulled in, — pulled into, — pulled onto, — pulled out, — pulled over, — pulled through, — pulled up, — ran, — ran out, — ran over, — reached, — rolled, — rolled away, — rolled forward, — rolled inside, — rolled to, — rolled up, — sat, — sat for, — sat in, — sat on, — sat out, — screamed by, — screamed to, — seemed to, — sent, — shifted, — shook, — shot off, — showed, — slammed, — slammed into, — slammed to, — slid onto, — slipped, — started, — started along, — started down, — started to, — started up, — started with, — stayed, — stood, — stood at, — stood like, — stopped, — stopped at, — stopped in, — stopped to, — struck, — swung, — swung over, — took, — turned, — turned around, — turned in, — turned into, — turned off, — waited for, — went, — went back, — went by, — went into, — went past, — went up, — worked in

trunk

verbs

— arrived at, — began to, — brought to,
— called, — came, — came up, —
closed, — fell across, — filled with, —
grew around, — lay open, — led, —
lifted, — lifted into, — made, —
opened, — opened with, — reached out,
— rose up, — set at, — shut, — took on,
— turned, — used, — wrapped with

truth
verbs
— became, — began, — broke down, —
came, — came from, — came out, —
came together, — did, — explained, —
felt like, — hung, — jumped to, — lay,
— lay below, — lay within, — pushed
back, — rang in, — sank in, — sat, —
seemed, — stared from, — started to, —
struck, — told, — took, — went

tunnel
verbs
came through —, continued through —,
crossed —, drove down —, entered —,
followed —, found —, glanced to —,
headed toward —, left —, looked at —,
looked down —, moved along —,
moved down —, moved into —, moved
through —, nodded down —, nodded
to —, paused in —, picked —, pointed
to —, pointed up —, pushed into —,
ran down —, recognized —, returned to
—, shoved down —, stared into —,
started down —, started into —,
stepped into —, stopped in —, swung
into —, turned to —, used —, walked
down —, walked in —, walked through
—, walked to —, walked toward —,
watched —, went down —, went to —;
— began, — began to, — called, —
came, — carried, — climbed in, —
continued, — continued at, —

continued into, — continued on, —
continued through, — continued to, —
cut, — cut into, — cut through, —
ended, — ended at, — ended in, —
entered, — filled with, — followed, —
gave out, — grew, — led, — led beneath,
— led down, — led on, — led to, — led
under, — made, — met, — opened, —
opened into, — opened on, — opened
onto, — opened out, — played, — ran,
— ran in, — ran off, — ran out, — rang
out, — remained, — remained open, —
rose, — seemed to, — set into, — shook,
— shook like, — shot by, — shouted, —
shut, — slid, — smelled, — stayed, —
stood, — struck, — swung open, —
took, — turned, — turned to, — waited
for, — went, — went to, — went with

turn
verbs
admitted in —, approached —, asked in
—, began —, bowed in —, came around
—, came through —, continued —, did
—, entered —, fought —, gestured in —
, laughed in —, made —, missed —,
nodded in —, paused in —, reached —,
said in —, saw —, slid through —,
smiled in —, started into —, stood —,
stood in —, stopped —, studied in —,
swung in —, took —, waited —, waited
for —, wanted —, watched —, waved in
—, went in —, worked —; — admitted,
— began with, — brought, — came
around, — carried, — cut down, —
drew, — entered into, — filled up, —
forced, — gave, — gave to, — handed
over, — joined, — led to, — left, — left
at, — left out, — left past, — lifted, —
looked through, — lost, — made, —
opened, — passed on, — pulled, — put
out, — reached for, — read, — repeated,

— set out, — set up, — spoke to, — started to, — thought, — walked to, — waved

TV
verbs
crossed to —, gestured at —, gestured toward —, glanced at —, heard —, kept —, killed —, left —, looked at —, looked to —, lowered —, moved to —, needed —, nodded at —, pointed at —, pointed to —, put —, put on —, returned to —, said to —, saw —, saw on —, shouted at —, shut off —, snapped off —, snapped on —, spoke above —, stared at —, told —, turned off —, turned on —, turned up —, walked to —, watched —, went on —

uniform
verbs
— added, — arrived, — arrived on, — arrived to, — asked, — brought out, — came, — came into, — came off, — came out, — came through, — came to, — came with, — carried, — changed, — checked, — covered, — entered, — felt like, — got on, — got out, — grew, — hung off, — hung over, — kept, — knocked on, — laid out, — lifted, — made, — meant, — nodded, — opened, — poured into, — poured out, — pulled against, — pushed, — ran through, — reached into, — said, — said from, — said in, — sat, — sat behind, — sat on, — sat with, — seemed, — seemed to, — slid, — stared for, — stepped forward, — stepped into, — stepped out, — stood, — stood by, — stood in, — stood off, — stood out, — stood to, — stood up, — turned, — turned out, — waited by, — walked, — walked by, — went on

valley
verbs
— appeared, — began to, — bent, — came, — came out, — continued on, — disappeared behind, — fell away, — fell under, — felt, — filled with, — lost in, — made, — made for, — offered, — opened beneath, — opened off, — opened onto, — opened up, — rang with, — rose up, — seemed to, — shut at, — shut in, — stood, — went

van
verbs
arrived with —, bought —, checked —, checked out —, climbed in —, climbed into —, continued to —, disappeared around —, drove —, found —, gestured at —, glanced at —, got in —, got into —, got to —, headed toward —, jumped in —, jumped into —, jumped off —, kicked —, knew —, left —, looked across —, looked around —, looked at —, looked inside —, nodded to —, opened —, passed —, passed alongside —, pointed toward —, pulled —, pulled alongside —, put —, ran around —, ran to —, reached —, reached into —, returned to —, rode in —, sat in —, saw —, slipped —, stared at —, started —, started toward —, started up —, stayed with —, stepped behind —, stepped into —, stopped —, stopped near —, threw —, took —, walked around —, walked behind —, walked to —, wanted —, waved at —, went to —; — appeared, — appeared around, — began, — began to, — blew up, — came for, — came from, — came into, — came over, — came to, — caught, — crossed, — did, — did in, — disappeared, — disappeared down,

— disappeared from, — dropped off, — drove, — drove by, — drove into, — drove off, — drove past, — drove through, — drove with, — entered, — felt, — filled with, — followed at, — grew, — headed toward, — hit, — joined, — jumped forward, — kept, — kicked up, — led, — left, — let out, — looked, — looked to, — moved, — moved along, — moved around, — moved forward, — moved into, — moved on, — opened, — passed on, — paused at, — pointed, — pulled away, — pulled back, — pulled in, — pulled into, — pulled out, — pulled to, — pulled up, — pushed, — reached, — returned to, — rode, — rolled by, — rolled forward, — rolled on, — rolled to, — sank with, — sat, — sat for, — sat outside, — seemed to, — shifted with, — shook, — shook in, — shot out, — showed, — slammed into, — slid open, — slid toward, — smelled of, — started, — started up, — stopped, — stopped by, — swung up, — took, — took off, — turned, — turned on, — turned to, — waited, — watched, — went, — went away, — went by, — went in, — went through, — went to

vehicle
verbs
approached —, broke for —, came in —, checked for —, climbed from —, climbed in —, drove for —, found —, gestured to —, glanced at —, got in —, got into —, heard —, jumped off —, left —, looked at —, looked for —, looked into —, needed —, noticed —, paused outside —, put —, ran between —, ran toward —, reached —, remained beside —, returned to —, saw —, shouted at —

, slipped between —, started —, started toward —, started up —, stayed in —, stepped around —, stepped from —, stopped —, threw —, touched —, walked around —, went toward —; — added to, — appeared, — approached, — approached at, — became, — began, — began to, — broke down, — came, — came along, — came around, — came down, — came over, — came through, — came to, — continued, — continued to, — did, — drew, — drove, — drove along, — drove away, — drove up, — filled with, — grew, — headed for, — headed in, — hit, — jumped on, — jumped over, — knew, — lay on, — left, — lifted, — looked, — looked for, — made, — met, — moved, — moved away, — opened, — passed, — pulled into, — pulled to, — pulled up, — put into, — reached, — remained, — remained on, — rolled, — rolled on, — rolled onto, — rolled out, — rolled up, — rolled with, — sat, — sat in, — seemed, — shook, — shot forward, — stayed in, — stood, — stood in, — stood outside, — stopped, — struck, — swung around, — swung into, — took off, — took up, — turned, — turned around, — turned out, — went, — went in, — went into, — went off

vein
verbs
— became, — began to, — came, — came to, — came up, — carried, — felt like, — filled with, — grew, — jumped in, — jumped out, — left, — lit up, — lost, — made, — ran, — ran across, — ran up, — seemed to, — showed in, — started to, — stood, — stood out, — turned to, — went

vessel

verbs

— appeared in, — arrived, — began to, — broke, — came into, — came up, — closed in, — continued to, — drew alongside, — filled, — filled with, — kept, — lay at, — lay on, — led to, — looked at, — looked like, — lost, — made, — moved toward, — needed, — raised, — ran through, — reached, — rose up, — settled in, — shook, — took

video

verbs

— appeared, — appeared on, — appeared to, — began, — began to, — began with, — came from, — came on, — came through, — came to, — came up, — caught, — closed, — continued, — cut off, — ended, — finished, — happened, — jumped, — made at, — moved in, — moved on, — opened, — paused, — played, — played on, — played out, — pulled up, — ran on, — seemed to, — showed, — showed up, — started, — started up, — stopped, — swung, — went, — went off, — went up

view

verbs

came into —, changed —, checked —, climbed from —, climbed into —, crossed —, disappeared from —, flew into —, gestured to —, knew —, leaned into —, liked —, loved —, meant —, moved —, moved into —, pulled down —, rose into —, shifted —, shifted into —, slid from —, slipped into —, stared at —, stepped into —, studied —, took in —, turned from —, turned to —, walked into —, waved at —

village

verbs

— appeared in, — appeared on, — appeared to, — became, — began to, — believed in, — broke, — called, — came by, — came into, — came to, — caught, — cried out, — did, — ended, — fell, — filled with, — got, — heard, — held, — hoped for, — kept, — knew about, — looked like, — lost, — made, — needed, — needed to, — put to, — ran, — ran to, — remained, — rode, — sat beside, — sat in, — sat like, — sat on, — saw, — seemed, — seemed to, — settled in, — showed, — showed through, — smelled of, — started to, — stood on, — took, — turned into

vision

verbs

— appeared in, — became, — began, — began in, — began to, — brought, — brought to, — came, — came back, — came from, — came in, — came on, — came to, — carried, — carried to, — changed, — cleared, — cleared after, — cleared at, — cleared from, — cleared in, — cleared to, — continued, — continued to, — crossed, — disappeared, — drew, — ended, — entered, — felt, — filled with, — got, — grew, — headed off, — left off, — left to, — looked out, — made, — meant, — moved, — opened, — opened up, — played out, — pulled back, — ran through, — returned, — returned in, — returned to, — rose in, — seemed, — seemed to, — shifted, — shifted into, — shifted to, — shifted with, — shut off, — slammed into, — started to, — stood on, — swung around, — took, — took on, — turned, — went away, — went to, — worked

voice
verbs
added —, added in —, admitted in —, agreed in —, answered —, answered in —, asked —, asked in —, began in —, began with —, called in —, called with —, came by —, changed —, cleared —, continued in —, cried in —, demanded in —, demanded with —, drew toward —, dropped —, explained in —, felt —, filled —, followed —, fought for —, found —, found in —, got —, hated —, heard —, heard in —, jumped at —, kept —, knew —, lifted —, liked —, listened for —, listened to —, lost —, loved —, lowered —, made —, managed in —, murmured in —, muttered in —, needed —, raised —, ran toward —, rang in —, recognized —, remembered —, repeated in —, replied in —, said in —, said toward —, said with —, screamed in —, spoke in —, spoke with —, started at —, talked in —, thought about —, told —, tried —, tried for —, turned at —, turned to —, turned toward —, used —, waited for —, whispered in —, yelled in —; — added, — added to, — agreed, — answered, — answered on, — appeared, — appeared in, — approached inside, — arrived on, — asked, — asked for, — asked from, — asked off, — asked on, — asked over, — became, — became like, — began, — began in, — began to, — blew, — blew into, — breathed, — broke, — broke at, — broke in, — broke into, — broke like, — broke off, — broke on, — broke out, — broke through, — broke under, — broke with, — brought, — brought

back, — called, — called across, — called around, — called back, — called from, — called in, — called on, — called out, — called through, — called to, — came, — came across, — came at, — came back, — came behind, — came down, — came from, — came in, — came into, — came like, — came on, — came out, — came over, — came through, — came to, — came up, — came with, — carried, — carried across, — carried back, — carried from, — carried in, — carried on, — carried out, — carried over, — carried through, — carried throughout, — carried to, — caught, — caught around, — caught at, — caught for, — caught in, — changed, — changed at, — changed into, — changed to, — cleared, — climbed, — climbed in, — climbed to, — climbed toward, — climbed up, — climbed with, — continued, — continued from, — continued over, — continued to, — cried, — cried from, — cried in, — cried out, — cut, — cut across, — cut in, — cut into, — cut off, — cut out, — cut through, — demanded, — demanded from, — did, — died, — died away, — died in, — died off, — died out, — died to, — disappeared into, — drew, — dropped, — dropped at, — dropped away, — dropped from, — dropped in, — dropped into, — dropped off, — dropped on, — dropped to, — ended in, — entered, — explained, — fell, — fell away, — fell into, — fell off, — fell to, — felt, — felt like, — filled, — filled with, — finished, — followed, — forced, — gasped, — gasped into, — gave, — gave out, — got, — got into, — got to, — grabbed, — grabbed at, — grew, — grew in, — grew toward, —

happened to, — heard, — heard in, — held, — helped, — hesitated, — hit, — joined, — joined in, — kicked in, — killed, — laid, — laughed, — laughed at, — leaned on, — left, — left behind, — lifted, — lifted across, — lifted over, — lifted to, — lifted up, — lifted with, — lost, — lost to, — lowered, — lowered in, — lowered to, — lowered with, — made, — made of, — managed to, — meant, — meant for, — moved away, — moved off, — murmured, — murmured in, — muttered, — muttered from, — offered, — ordered, — paused, — paused for, — picked up, — played out, — played over, — pointed out, — poured into, — poured out, — promised from, — pulled at, — pulled back, — put, — put in, — raised, — raised in, — raised to, — ran down, — ran up, — rang, — rang across, — rang against, — rang behind, — rang down, — rang from, — rang in, — rang like, — rang off, — rang out, — rang through, — rang to, — rang with, — reached, — reached from, — reached out, — read, — remained, — repeated, — replied, — replied from, — replied in, — replied through, — replied to, — replied with, — returned, — returned at, — returned to, — returned with, — rolled across, — rolled into, — rolled like, — rolled over, — rolled through, — rolled with, — rose, — rose above, — rose along, — rose behind, — rose between, — rose for, — rose from, — rose in, — rose into, — rose like, — rose on, — rose over, — rose through, — rose to, — rose toward, — rose up, — rose with, — said, — said above, — said at, — said down, — said for, — said from, — said in, — said on, — said over, — said through, —

said to, — said with, — said without, — sank, — sank at, — sank down, — sank into, — sank to, — sank with, — sat back, — screamed, — screamed for, — screamed in, — screamed inside, — seemed, — seemed like, — seemed to, — sent, — set, — set off, — shifted, — shifted from, — shifted to, — shifted with, — shook, — shook in, — shook like, — shook on, — shook with, — shot, — shot like, — shot up, — shouted, — shouted at, — shouted behind, — shouted for, — shouted from, — shouted in, — shouted out, — shut up, — sighed, — sighed across, — slid, — slid across, — slid like, — slid through, — slipped down, — slipped to, — snapped, — snapped out, — snapped with, — sounded, — sounded behind, — sounded for, — sounded from, — sounded in, — sounded like, — sounded off, — sounded on, — sounded out, — sounded outside, — sounded over, — sounded to, — spoke, — spoke at, — spoke behind, — spoke by, — spoke for, — spoke from, — spoke in, — spoke inside, — spoke on, — spoke out, — spoke over, — spoke through, — spoke to, — spoke up, — spoke with, — started to, — stayed, — stopped, — struck, — suggested, — swallowed by, — talked, — talked in, — talked to, — told, — took, — took on, — took over, — took up, — touched, — touched with, — tried for, — tried to, — turned, — turned away, — turned loose, — turned to, — wanted to, — went, — went back, — went before, — went from, — went on, — went onto, — went through, — went up, — whispered, — whispered among, — whispered from, — whispered in, —

whispered into, — whispered through,
— whispered with, — wore, — yelled,
— yelled from, — yelled in, — yelled
into, — yelled out

wagon
verbs

— began to, — bought, — broke
through, — came, — came to, —
continued, — gave, — got, — hit, —
jumped, — kept up, — leaned against,
— lost, — moved forward, — pulled
into, — pulled out, — pulled over, —
pulled up, — rode, — rolled, — rolled
down, — rolled forward, — rolled into,
— rolled past, — rolled to, — seemed
to, — shifted, — shut, — stopped, —
struck, — swung, — turned over, —
turned to

walk
verbs

began —, came up —, carried on —,
continued —, continued on —, flew
along —, followed with —, headed up
—, landed at —, landed on —, liked —,
needed —, ran down —, reached —,
recognized —, started at —, started
down —, started up —, stood on —,
stopped in —, took —, walked down —,
walked up —, watched —, went down
—, went for —, went up —

wall
verbs

approached —, broke —, called beyond
—, called from —, came to —, checked
—, cleared —, climbed —, climbed onto
—, climbed through —, continued
along —, continued toward —, covered
over —, crossed to —, dropped off —,
fell against —, fell at —, felt —, felt

along —, finished —, flew into —, flew
over —, followed —, found —, frowned
at —, gave —, gestured at —, gestured
toward —, glanced at —, glanced to —,
glanced toward —, got off —, grabbed
—, grabbed at —, grabbed for —,
gripped —, hit —, hung against —,
hung over —, jumped over —, kept to
—, kicked —, kicked off —, knocked on
—, landed against —, lay against —,
leaned against —, leaned on —, leaned
over —, leaned to —, leaned toward —,
left —, liked —, listened at —, looked at
—, looked over —, looked upon —,
made for —, moved along —, moved
toward —, needed —, nodded at —,
nodded to —, nodded toward —,
noticed —, passed —, pointed at —,
pointed to —, pointed toward —,
pressed against —, pressed into —,
pushed against —, pushed at —, pushed
off —, raised —, ran along —, ran into
—, reached —, reached for —, reached
to —, reached toward —, sank against
—, sat against —, sat behind —, sat by
—, sat on —, saw —, screamed —,
shifted against —, shoved off —,
slammed against —, slammed into —,
slid along —, slid down —, slipped
against —, slipped down —, slipped
over —, spoke to —, stared —, stared
across —, stared at —, started along —,
started toward —, stayed against —,
stayed to —, stepped along —, stepped
from —, stepped to —, stepped toward
—, stood against —, stood at —, stood
by —, stood outside —, struck —,
studied —, swung behind —, thought of
—, told —, touched —, turned from —,
turned to —, turned toward —, walked
along —, walked through —, walked to
—, watched —, waved to —, went over

—, went to —, wiped down —, worked around —; — appeared, — became, — began to, — bent, — blew out, — bowed, — broke beneath, — called, — came at, — came down, — came into, — came to, — came together, — came up, — carried, — caught, — changed beneath, — cleared, — closed, — closed about, — closed behind, — closed off, — continued, — covered in, — covered with, — cut to, — did, — disappeared, — disappeared into, — drew, — ended, — fell, — fell away, — fell down, — fell on, — felt, — felt like, — filled with, — flew through, — fought to, — gave, — grew, — held, — hung, — hung with, — joined into, — kept, — kept out, — lay, — led to, — left, — lit, — lit by, — lit up, — looked, — looked like, — made, — made of, — made to, — meant for, — meant to, — met, — moved, — muttered, — needed, — opened, — opened from, — opened on, — opened onto, — opened up, — pressed, — pressed against, — promised, — pulled down, — ran, — ran along, — ran off, — rang, — rang with, — reached, — read, — remained, — rolled, — rose, — rose above, — rose against, — rose beside, — rose from, — rose in, — rose into, — rose up, — said, — sank, — sat, — sat back, — seemed, — seemed to, — shook, — shot, — shot out, — shot up, — showed, — shut out, — slammed, — slammed into, — slammed together, — slid, — slid open, — slid past, — slid to, — started to, — stood, — stood in, — stood open, — swung, — swung open, — threw, — told, — took up, — turned, — turned into, — went, — went up

wallet

verbs
added —, checked —, checked through —, closed —, dropped —, felt for —, found —, glanced in —, glanced into —, got —, got out —, grabbed —, held up —, kept —, kept in —, looked in —, looked inside —, looked over —, lost —, nodded to —, opened —, opened up —, picked up —, placed —, pulled —, pulled out —, put —, put down —, reached for —, reached in —, reached into —, remembered —, returned —, set —, shoved —, started for —, started with —, thought of —, took —, took out —, tossed —, wanted —, went into —

war
verbs
— began, — began between, — began in, — began to, — broke out, — brought out, — came, — came to, — changed, — continued, — continued to, — demanded, — did, — did to, — ended, — ended in, — ended with, — fought by, — fought over, — fought with, — grew, — happened, — happened to, — lay between, — opened, — remained, — seemed, — slid across, — started, — started in, — took, — used up, — went on

warmth
verbs
— answered, — began in, — began to, — came, — came from, — came in, — came through, — came with, — disappeared, — entered, — fell from, — felt, — filled, — grew in, — hit, — left, — missed from, — passed, — poured off, — poured out, — ran down, — reached, — realized, — remained, —

remained in, — returned to, — rolled
beneath, — rose from, — rose up, —
seemed to, — shot through, — slid
down, — took, — touched, — went
from

warning
verbs
called out —, cried —, cried out —,
drew —, felt —, frowned in —, gave —,
got —, heard —, left —, remembered —
, repeated —, said in —, said without —,
screamed —, shouted —, slid back —,
smiled at —, thought about —, thought
of —, took —, understood —,
whispered —, whispered in —, yelled —
, yelled in —

watch
verbs
checked —, checked at —, closed —,
died on —, felt —, found —, frowned at
—, glanced at —, glanced between —,
glanced on —, glanced to —, glanced
toward —, got —, grabbed for —, held
up —, kept —, looked —, looked at —,
loved —, nodded at —, picked up —,
pointed at —, pointed to —, pulled out
—, put —, put away —, reached for —,
set —, shook —, stared at —, stood —,
studied —, took —, took back —, took
off —, took out —, tossed —, touched
—, wanted —, wore —

water
verbs
asked for —, blinked back —, breathed
—, broke from —, brought —, brought
over —, came for —, carried —, climbed
from —, crossed to —, cut off —, cut
through —, died in —, disappeared
under —, drank —, drew in —, entered

—, fell into —, felt —, filled with —,
finished —, finished off —, flew from —
, fought —, found —, gasped for —,
gave —, gestured for —, gestured toward
—, glanced across —, glanced at —,
glanced toward —, got in —, hated —,
heard —, helped —, hit —, hung in —,
jumped into —, kicked against —, killed
—, landed in —, left —, lifted —,
looked across —, looked at —, looked in
—, looked into —, looked over —,
looked through —, loved —, meant —,
moved through —, moved toward —,
needed —, nodded across —, nodded at
—, nodded toward —, offered —,
opened —, ordered —, picked up —,
played in —, pointed across —, pointed
at —, pointed into —, pointed to —,
poured —, put —, put down —, ran —,
reached —, reached for —, reached into
—, reached through —, returned with
—, rolled in —, rose from —, sank into
—, sank through —, sank under —, sat
by —, saw —, set down —, set out —,
settled for —, shifted in —, shut off —,
slid into —, slid under —, slipped
beneath —, slipped into —, smelled —,
stared across —, stared at —, started
toward —, stayed above —, stayed under
—, stepped into —, stepped under —,
stood beside —, stood by —, stopped in
—, struck —, studied —, swallowed —,
took —, took out —, touched —, tried
—, turned in —, turned off —, turned
on —, turned to —, turned toward —,
turned up —, used —, walked into —,
walked on —, walked to —, wanted —,
watched —, went into —, went under
—, went with —, yelled for —; —
appeared, — appeared to, — arrived, —
asked, — became, — began, — began to,
— breathed, — broke, — brought, —

brought forward, — brought up, — came, — came down, — came from, — came in, — came into, — came on, — came out, — came over, — came through, — came to, — came up, — carried, — caught, — cleared, — closed over, — continued, — continued in, — continued to, — covered, — cut into, — cut off, — cut through, — demanded, — did, — disappeared in, — ended in, — entered, — fell, — fell back, — fell from, — fell in, — fell into, — fell on, — fell onto, — fell over, — fell to, — fell upon, — felt, — felt like, — filled, — filled with, — flew, — flew from, — flew like, — flew up, — followed in, — forced through, — forced up, — found, — gave, — got, — got in, — got into, — grew, — held, — helped, — hit, — hung, — hung beside, — hung from, — joined, — kicked up, — landed, — lay, — lay at, — lay beside, — left, — lifted, — lived, — looked, — looked over, — made, — meant to, — met, — moved, — moved under, — passed over, — passed through, — played, — played across, — poured, — poured down, — poured forth, — poured from, — poured in, — poured into, — poured onto, — poured out, — poured over, — poured through, — pressed against, — pressed at, — pushed against, — ran, — ran across, — ran along, — ran beneath, — ran between, — ran down, — ran from, — ran in, — ran into, — ran like, — ran off, — ran on, — ran onto, — ran out, — ran over, — ran through, — ran toward, — reached, — reached to, — remained, — remained in, — returned to, — rolled, — rolled beneath, — rolled onto, — rolled out, — rolled over, — rose, — rose around, — rose from, —

rose in, — rose over, — rose past, — rose to, — rose under, — rose up, — sank in, — sat, — sat on, — screamed with, — seemed, — seemed to, — sent, — settled, — settled in, — shot, — shot out, — shot to, — showed through, — shut off, — slid by, — slid down, — slid over, — slid up, — slipped down, — smelled, — smelled of, — sounded, — sounded like, — spoke, — spoke to, — started, — started to, — stayed down, — stood, — stood between, — stood in, — stood on, — stopped, — struck, — swallowed, — took, — took on, — tossed, — touched, — tried to, — turned, — turned into, — turned off, — turned on, — turned to, — waited for, — went away, — went in, — went on, — went under, — went up, — whispered, — whispered from, — whispered on, — whispered past, — worked, — worked on

wave
verbs

answered with —, arrived in —, came in —, cried in —, disappeared with —, entered on —, felt —, gave —, gestured with —, heard —, jumped —, listened to —, offered —, reached under —, remembered —, replied with —, returned —, said with —, sank into —, sent —, shot up —, shouted at —, turned to —, turned with —, watched —, went to —; — appeared to, — approached, — arrived, — began, — began to, — blew, — blew out, — broke, — broke against, — broke around, — broke from, — broke on, — broke over, — broke upon, — called, — came, — came down, — came in, — came out, — came to, — came up, — caught, —

climbed into, — continued to, — did, — drove, — fell, — fell down, — fell from, — fell like, — fell over, — filled, — gave, — grew, — hit, — hung over, — kicked, — looked like, — made, — passed, — pushed, — ran, — ran on, — ran under, — ran up, — reached, — rolled across, — rolled on, — rolled onto, — rolled over, — rolled to, — rolled up, — rose, — rose above, — rose from, — rose to, — rose up, — screamed in, — seemed to, — shifted around, — sighed for, — slammed up, — started to, — stood, — struck, — threw up, — took, — tossed, — went through, — whispered along

way
verbs
added in —, became —, came —, came from —, came out —, continued on —, died —, disappeared down —, fell —, felt —, followed in —, forced —, fought —, found —, gave —, glanced —, glanced out —, got —, got in —, got under —, grinned in —, headed —, held on —, kissed —, knew —, knew in —, laughed in —, led —, lit —, lived —, looked —, lost —, made —, moved into —, nodded in —, passed —, passed along —, picked —, pointed —, ran —, returned by —, said —, said in —, saw —, sent —, settled for —, shifted —, smiled in —, stayed —, stepped in —, stood in —, stopped in —, swung —, thought —, took —, took off —, tried —, turned —, walked in —, wanted —, went —, went on —, went out —, went up —, worked —; — became, — came into, — came to, — climbed, — closed, — closed behind, — closed in, — did, — drove against, — felt, — filled, —

gave, — knew, — lay, — led out, — led to, — led toward, — left, — left in, — left to, — lit by, — looked, — looked for, — made, — met, — offered, — opened for, — opened into, — put, — ran under, — sat, — saw, — seemed, — seemed to, — set out, — shut, — smiled at, — sounded, — stood, — stopped, — struck, — told, — took, — took on, — turned from, — wanted, — went down, — went on, — went up, — went with, — wore, — worked, — wrote

weapon
verbs
broke —, brought out —, brought up —, carried —, checked —, checked for —, closed —, drew —, dropped —, found —, gestured to —, got out —, grabbed —, gripped —, held —, knew —, laid down —, leaned on —, lifted —, looked at —, looked for —, lowered —, needed —, nodded to —, picked up —, pointed —, pressed —, pulled —, pulled away —, pulled out —, put down —, raised —, reached for —, recognized —, returned —, saw —, set up —, shifted —, snapped up —, stared at —, studied —, swung —, swung up —, thought about —, thought of —, threw down —, took —, took back —, took off —, took out —, used —, watched —, waved —, went for —; — added to, — appeared, — appeared to, — began to, — came forward, — came out, — changed, — cut, — cut through, — did, — dropped, — dropped into, — dropped to, — drove, — fell, — fell from, — fell to, — felt, — filled, — flew, — flew across, — flew from, — flew into, — flew past, — followed, — found, — gave, — glanced off, — grew, — gripped in, — held, —

hung, — hung off, — hung on, — laid out, — landed with, — lay in, — lay on, — leaned against, — lifted, — lit up, — looked, — looked like, — lost, — lowered, — made, — made for, — made of, — made to, — made up, — meant to, — met, — moved in, — moved toward, — opened up, — passed from, — passed through, — pointed, — pointed at, — pointed in, — pointed toward, — pulled back, — pushed aside, — raised, — raised to, — ran, — rang out, — rang under, — remained, — rose, — rose from, — sank into, — sank through, — seemed, — seemed of, — seemed to, — shifted in, — shook in, — shot out, — shut down, — slid, — slid off, — snapped up, — sounded, — sounded like, — spoke to, — stayed, — stayed in, — stood, — stood in, — struck, — took, — turned into, — went down, — went into, — went off, — went with, — wrapped in

weather
verbs
— appeared, — approached, — became, — broke, — came, — came from, — came on, — came out, — changed, — cleared, — continued, — felt, — followed, — got, — grew, — held, — helped, — kept, — looked, — remained, — shifted, — started, — stayed, — took, — turned, — turned to, — worked on

week
verbs
— added to, — added up, — answered, — began, — began in, — began to, — came, — came down, — carried, — closed, — continued to, — decided to, — did, — ended, — flew by, —

followed, — kept, — laughed, — left, — left of, — left to, — offered, — passed, — passed away, — passed with, — passed without, — raised, — remained, — rolled away, — rose from, — sat at, — sat behind, — seemed, — showed, — started, — turned, — turned into, — used, — went, — went by, — went on, — went past, — wore on

weight
verbs
— became, — began to, — broke, — brought, — came down, — came on, — changed, — cut off, — dropped, — dropped across, — dropped in, — dropped on, — dropped onto, — fell against, — fell back, — fell from, — fell through, — felt, — forced, — gave, — grew, — hung against, — hung from, — landed, — lifted, — lifted from, — lifted off, — looked, — lost in, — made, — moved back, — pressed, — pressed down, — pressed on, — pressed over, — pulled, — pushed against, — returned, — rolled off, — sank into, — seemed to, — set off, — settled, — settled in, — settled on, — settled onto, — shifted, — shifted from, — shifted on, — shifted to, — slammed, — slammed against, — slid forward, — slipped behind, — struck, — threw off

wheel
verbs
climbed behind —, cut —, dropped behind —, explained about —, fell behind —, fought —, fought with —, got behind —, grabbed —, grabbed at —, grabbed for —, gripped —, held —, hit —, hung onto —, hung over —, jumped behind —, leaned on —, leaned over —,

looked at —, moved to —, needed —,
nodded at —, paused on —, ran for —,
reached for —, rode —, sat behind —,
settled behind —, shouted into —,
shoved —, shrugged at —, slammed —,
slid behind —, slipped behind —,
slipped under —, stayed behind —,
stepped around —, stepped behind —,
stood at —, swung —, took —, tried —,
turned —, turned to —, waited behind
—, wiped —, worked —; — began to,
— broke, — came down, — came off, —
came to, — caught in, — cleared, —
covered with, — crossed, — cut
through, — dropped, — flew off, —
flew over, — got away, — hit, —
jumped, — jumped up, — landed on, —
left, — left to, — let out, — lifted from,
— lifted off, — looked after, — nodded,
— placed alongside, — raised, — ran
along, — rolled along, — rolled away, —
rose, — rose off, — said, — screamed, —
seemed in, — sent, — set in, — set into,
— snapped, — spoke up, — stared at, —
started to, — stood in, — stopped, —
took up, — touched, — touched down,
— tried to, — turned, — turned against,
— turned in, — waited, — walked in, —
went along, — went at, — wore, —
wore down

whisper
verbs
added in —, agreed in —, answered in
—, answered on —, answered with —,
asked in —, began in —, continued in
—, demanded in —, explained in —,
finished in —, heard —, listened for —,
listened to —, managed —, murmured
on —, promised in —, reminded in —,
repeated in —, replied in —, said in —,
said on —, screamed in —, spoke above

—, spoke in —, turned at —, yelled —;
— asked, — became, — began, — broke
through, — brought, — came, — came
back, — came into, — came through, —
came to, — carried in, — caught, —
continued, — cut, — died, — died away,
— fell into, — filled, — followed, —
held, — landed beside, — left, — made,
— meant for, — passed around, — ran
out, — ran through, — rose, — said, —
shook, — started, — started up, —
stopped, — turned, — turned to, —
went, — went around

wind
verbs
asked —, asked over —, bent in —, bent
into —, blinked against —, broke —,
caught —, checked —, drank —, drove
like —, felt —, fought —, fought against
—, found —, got —, grinned into —,
headed into —, heard —, kept —,
laughed into —, leaned into —, let —,
listened to —, muttered through —,
needed —, passed —, ran like —, said
into —, said to —, saw —, shouted
above —, shouted against —, shouted
into —, shouted over —, stood in —,
talked about —, thought —, turned to
—, walked into —, walked with —,
whispered to —, worked in —, yelled
over —; — appeared, — appeared to, —
asked, — ate, — became, — began, —
began to, — blew, — blew about, —
blew across, — blew against, — blew
around, — blew at, — blew beneath, —
blew by, — blew down, — blew from, —
blew in, — blew off, — blew on, — blew
open, — blew over, — blew through, —
blew up, — bowed, — breathed in, —
breathed through, — broke over, —
broke up, — brought, — brought about,

— brought in, — called, — came, — came back, — came down, — came from, — came in, — came off, — came on, — came out, — came through, — came to, — came up, — came upon, — came with, — carried, — carried away, — caught, — caught at, — caught in, — caught up, — changed, — continued to, — cut, — cut off, — cut through, — cut to, — did, — died, — died away, — died down, — died to, — dropped, — drove, — drove at, — drove away, — fell, — felt, — felt in, — felt like, — filled, — flew into, — followed, — fought to, — gave, — gave out, — got, — got in, — got up, — grew, — held, — hit, — kicked, — kicked at, — kicked up, — kissed, — knocked out, — left, — let up, — lifted, — made, — made in, — moved, — moved in, — moved through, — passed in, — passed on, — passed through, — picked up, — played with, — poured through, — pulled, — pulled at, — pushed, — pushed against, — pushed back, — raised, — ran, — ran through, — reached out, — remained, — returned, — rose, — rose in, — rose to, — rose with, — screamed, — screamed across, — screamed over, — seemed to, — sent, — sent down, — set, — shifted, — shifted from, — shifted to, — shook, — sighed, — sighed across, — sighed against, — sighed over, — sighed through, — slammed, — slammed against, — slammed into, — smelled, — smelled like, — smelled of, — snapped at, — spent, — spoke with, — started, — started to, — stood, — stopped, — struck, — swallowed, — threw, — took, — took down, — tossed, — touched, — turned, — turned toward, — walked, — went, — went like, — went on, — whispered, — whispered across, — whispered through, — worked

window
verbs

appeared at —, approached —, asked through —, asked to —, breathed on —, broke —, called out —, called through —, came to —, came toward —, checked —, climbed out —, climbed over —, climbed through —, closed —, considered —, covered —, crossed to —, crossed toward —, disappeared from —, drew near —, dropped —, drove past —, drove through —, fell from —, flew to —, found —, frowned out —, frowned toward —, gestured at —, gestured to —, gestured toward —, glanced at —, glanced out —, glanced through —, glanced to —, glanced toward —, got to —, grabbed —, grinned out —, headed toward —, hesitated outside —, jumped from —, jumped out —, kicked out —, kissed by —, knew —, knocked on —, lay against —, leaned against —, leaned in —, leaned into —, leaned out —, leaned through —, leaned toward —, left —, lifted —, listened at —, looked at —, looked in —, looked into —, looked out —, looked through —, looked to —, looked toward —, lowered —, moved at —, moved from —, moved on —, moved through —, moved to —, moved toward —, muttered to —, nodded at —, nodded out —, nodded to —, nodded toward —, opened —, passed —, paused at —, paused by —, pointed at —, pointed out —, pointed to —, pointed toward —, pressed against —, pressed open —, pulled through —, pushed open —, pushed up —, put —, put down —, raised —, ran at —, ran to —, ran toward —, reached —, reached for —, reached through —, remained at —, returned to —, rolled down —, rolled to —, rolled up —, said from —, said out —, said to —, sat at —, sat behind —, sat beside —, sat by —, sat in —, saw —, screamed at —, shifted to —, shook —, shouted into —, shouted out —, shouted through —, shut —, slid down —, slid open —, slid toward —, slipped to —, slipped under —, smiled to —, spoke by —, spoke to —, stared at —, stared from —, stared out —, stared outside —, stared through —, stared toward —, started by —, started toward —, stayed at —, stayed by —, stayed in —, stepped from —, stepped to —, stood against —, stood at —, stood before —, stood beside —, stood by —, stood in —, stood near —, stood outside —, stopped at —, stopped by —, studied —, swung from —, swung through —, threw open —, threw up —, took —, tried —, turned from —, turned to —, turned toward —, waited by —, walked —, walked to —, walked toward —, watched —, watched from —, watched out —, watched through —, waved at —, waved from —, waved out —, waved to —, waved toward —, went from —, went in —, went out —, went through —, went to —, whispered at —, wished for —, yelled at —, yelled out —, yelled through —, yelled toward —; — added, — admitted, — answered, — appeared, — appeared in, — appeared to, — ate, — became, — began, — began to, — blew in, — blew out, — broke, — broke like, — broke open, — brought in, — came, — came down, — came on, — came open, — carried, — caught, —

changed, — closed, — closed despite, — closed off, — covered with, — did, — died away, — disappeared, — dropped, — fell, — fell on, — felt like, — filled with, — flew open, — gave, — gave on, — gave onto, — got, — got up, — grew, — held, — hung, — kept, — knocked out, — left open, — let, — let in, — listened in, — lit, — lit up, — looked, — looked at, — looked down, — looked into, — looked like, — looked on, — looked onto, — looked out, — looked over, — lowered, — made, — made of, — made out, — meant, — met, — moved, — moved up, — needed, — offered, — opened, — opened behind, — opened in, — opened into, — opened like, — opened on, — opened onto, — opened to, — opened with, — picked up, — pointed at, — poured, — pulled up, — ran along, — ran down, — reached, — remained, — rolled down, — rolled shut, — rolled up, — rose, — said, — said to, — sat, — sat atop, — saw, — seemed, — seemed to, — set, — set at, — shook, — showed, — showed off, — shut, — shut behind, — shut to, — shut up, — slid, — slid down, — slid open, — slid past, — smelled, — stared, — stared down, — started to, — stayed up, — stood, — stood in, — stood open, — stopped, — swung open, — swung up, — threw, — turned, — watched, — waved, — went back, — went down, — went out, — whispered

wine

verbs

arrived with —, bought —, brought —, brought back —, called for —, came with —, checked out —, demanded —, drank —, drank from —, drank of —, dropped —, felt —, finished —, finished off —, frowned into —, got —, grabbed —, grabbed up —, knew —, knocked back —, laughed into —, lifted —, liked —, looked at —, looked into —, loved —, needed —, opened —, ordered —, passed on —, picked —, picked up —, poured —, poured out —, put down —, reached for —, shouted for —, smelled —, smelled of —, smiled into —, stared at —, stared into —, studied —, took —, took up —, tried —, wanted —; — appeared, — arrived, — brought, — came from, — came out, — caught, — continued to, — covered, — fell out, — gave out, — grew, — helped, — made, — made for, — opened, — poured, — poured over, — raised, — ran, — ran down, — rose, — sat in, — sat on, — seemed to, — slid down, — stepped into, — stood beside, — stood on, — stood open, — turned, — turned to, — waited to, — went to, — worked, — wrapped in

wing
verbs
— appeared, — arrived, — became, — began to, — blew off, — blinked, — broke, — came, — caught, — caught on, — closed, — did, — drew, — drove, — ended in, — fell off, — felt, — filled, — filled with, — flew, — flew off, — forced, — grew, — headed for, — held, — hesitated, — hung, — hung at, — hung from, — kept, — landed on, — lifted, — lifted from, — looked, — looked like, — made, — made of, — missed by, — moved forward, — moved in, — needed, — opened, — ran, — ran off, — reached for, — returned, — rose, — rose behind, — rose from, — rose up,

— seemed, — seemed to, — set up, — settled into, — shot up, — slammed, — snapped, — snapped forward, — snapped like, — snapped open, — sounded by, — stared at, — stood, — stood in, — took up, — touched with, — turned, — went between, — went with, — wrapped

winter
verbs
— arrived, — brought, — came, — came before, — came down, — came on, — came with, — covered, — drew on, — fell, — fell away, — kept, — lay, — lay on, — looked, — passed, — passed away, — passed by, — passed in, — put out, — returned to, — rolled down, — seemed, — seemed to, — settled down, — showed, — went on, — wore on

wire
verbs
— began at, — came in, — came out, — changed, — covered, — covered with, — crossed, — cut into, — cut off, — cut through, — fell into, — felt like, — found, — held in, — hit, — hung, — hung from, — lay on, — ran down, — ran from, — ran in, — ran into, — ran like, — ran up, — remained on, — seemed to, — went through, — wrapped

wolf
verbs
— became, — blew at, — blinked, — broke out, — brought to, — came, — came back, — came down, — came for, — came on, — came to, — carried back, — cried in, — did, — did to, — did with, — drew, — drew on, — dropped, — fell, — figured out, — filled, — flew

over, — fought for, — gave, — got, —
got back, — got in, — got to, —
gripped, — held, — jumped in, —
landed, — laughed at, — laughed
without, — lay at, — lay down, — led,
— left, — lifted, — liked, — looked at,
— looked out, — looked up, — lowered,
— made, — made for, — made off, —
made out, — opened, — poured out, —
poured through, — ran, — ran at, —
returned to, — said, — sat on, — saw,
— seemed to, — sent up, — set at, —
smiled with, — snapped at, — spoke to,
— started back, — started up, —
stepped forward, — stood in, — stood
on, — stood up, — took, — turned, —
walked to, — wanted to, — watched, —
went down, — went for, — went with,
— whispered in

woods
verbs
broke from —, came into —, came
through —, cut through —, disappeared
into —, found —, frowned into —, got
into —, got to —, headed into —, kept
to —, knew —, lay in —, left —, left for
—, lived in —, looked at —, looked into
—, moved into —, moved through —,
passed into —, pointed at —, pointed
toward —, pulled into —, ran from —,
ran into —, ran through —, reached —,
rode for —, shouted into —, slipped
into —, smelled in —, stared at —,
stepped from —, stepped into —,
turned toward —, walked around —,
walked in —, walked into —, walked
toward —, went into —, went through
—, went toward —

word
verbs

added —, believed —, blew out —,
blinked at —, breathed —, breathed out
—, broke —, caught —, checked —,
chose —, closed with —, considered —,
cut —, cut off —, drew out —, ended on
—, entered —, felt —, felt for —,
finished —, followed without —, forced
out —, fought for —, found —, frowned
at —, frowned over —, gasped —,
gasped out —, gave —, glanced at —, got
—, hated —, heard —, hung on —,
jumped at —, kept —, kept to —, knew
—, laughed at —, leaned on —, learned
—, left without —, let out —, liked —,
listened between —, listened to —,
listened without —, lived by —, looked
at —, looked for —, loved —, made out
—, meant —, murmured —, muttered
—, nodded at —, offered —, passed —,
passed without —, paused on —, picked
—, picked over —, played with —, read
—, recognized —, remembered —,
repeated —, rose without —, said —,
saw —, screamed —, sent —, shouted —
, shrugged off —, sighed out —, smiled
at —, snapped —, snapped off —,
snapped out —, spoke —, stared at —,
started at —, stepped without —, stood
without —, studied —, swallowed —,
swallowed at —, thought —, thought
about —, thought of —, thought over
—, took —, took in —, tried —, turned
on —, turned without —, understood
—, used —, waited for —, wanted —,
watched —, waved away —, went over
—, whispered —, wrote down —, yelled
—; — answered, — appeared, —
appeared from, — appeared in, —
appeared on, — arrived, — became, —
began to, — began with, — blew across,
— breathed out, — broke, — broke
from, — broke into, — broke off, —

broke up, — brought, — brought back, — brought on, — brought to, — came, — came at, — came back, — came down, — came for, — came forth, — came from, — came in, — came into, — came like, — came on, — came out, — came through, — came to, — came with, — came without, — carried, — carried away, — carried over, — carried through, — carried to, — caught, — caught in, — climbed into, — continued to, — cried out, — cut, — cut into, — cut like, — cut off, — cut through, — cut to, — decided, — did, — died away, — died in, — died off, — died on, — died out, — disappeared, — disappeared amid, — disappeared in, — drew, — drew out, — dropped, — dropped like, — dropped to, — drove into, — ended, — explained, — fell, — fell away, — fell behind, — fell between, — fell from, — fell in, — fell into, — fell like, — fell on, — fell out, — felt, — felt like, — filled, — filled with, — flew, — flew from, — flew in, — flew like, — flew out, — flew to, — followed, — fought, — found, — gave, — got around, — got back, — got out, — got past, — got to, — grew, — held, — hit, — hit like, — hung, — hung between, — hung in, — hung like, — jumped across, — jumped into, — jumped out, — landed, — landed like, — lay, — left, — left behind, — left for, — left to, — lifted, — lit up, — lost, — lost in, — made, — made for, — managed to, — meant, — meant for, — moved across, — needed, — passed, — passed on, — paused, — picked up, — played, — played in, — played on, — poured forth, — poured forward, — poured out, — put, — raised, — ran, — ran around, — ran away, — ran down, — ran on, — ran out, — ran over, — ran through, — rang, — rang against, — rang in, — rang like, — rang of, — rang off, — rang out, — rang through, — rang with, — reached, — read, — read out, — remained, — repeated in, — repeated over, — returned, — returned to, — rode, — rode over, — rolled on, — rolled out, — rolled over, — rolled past, — rose, — rose from, — rose in, — rose like, — rose to, — rose up, — rubbed over, — said, — said over, — said to, — sank in, — sank into, — sat, — sat like, — screamed from, — screamed in, — seemed, — seemed in, — seemed like, — seemed to, — sent, — sent back, — sent through, — set off, — set up, — settled, — settled in, — shook, — shot, — shot around, — shot out, — shot to, — shouted from, — showed, — slammed into, — slid through, — slipped, — slipped from, — slipped off, — slipped out, — slipped over, — slipped past, — slipped through, — snapped back, — snapped out, — sounded, — sounded in, — sounded like, — spoke, — spoke of, — spoke to, — started for, — started to, — stayed, — stayed with, — stood out, — stopped, — stopped at, — struck, — struck like, — struck with, — suggested, — swallowed up, — told, — took, — took on, — took over, — touched, — touched off, — turned, — turned into, — turned to, — used, — used for, — used in, — went, — went from, — went into, — went out, — went through, — whispered in, — whispered like, — whispered of, — whispered through, — woke, — worked, — wrapped

work

verbs
arrived at —, arrived for —, arrived from —, began —, believed in —, called —, chose —, continued with —, did —, drove into —, finished —, gave —, got —, headed into —, kept at —, knew —, knew through —, left —, left for —, liked —, loved —, missed —, paused —, paused at —, paused in —, put in —, reached with —, settled into —, started —, stopped —, took —, tried at —, watched —, went about —, went to —, wore for —; — appeared in, — began, — came back, — came before, — came through, — came to, — changed, — continued at, — continued on, — cut out, — cut through, — drew to, — filled, — filled with, — finished, — found, — got, — got in, — got under, — grew, — helped, — hung on, — kept, — lay, — lay in, — led to, — left behind, — made, — noticed, — placed in, — saw, — seemed to, — showed, — stopped, — took, — went, — went into, — went on, — went to

world

verbs
— appeared, — became, — began, — began to, — believed, — bent, — bowed, — broke, — broke in, — broke up, — came, — came down, — came from, — came in, — came to, — came together, — carried, — chose to, — cleared with, — closed, — closed together, — continued to, — demanded, — did, — died, — died from, — disappeared, — disappeared beneath, — disappeared beyond, — dropped away, — ended, — ended in, — fell, — fell away, — fell back, — fell by, — fell into, — fell out, — fell with, —
felt, — felt in, — felt like, — filled with, — followed, — followed into, — gasped, — gave, — got to, — happened to, — held, — held out, — hesitated, — hung, — jumped, — jumped back, — kept, — knew, — knew about, — lay, — lay beyond, — lay on, — left for, — lit up, — lit with, — lived, — lived by, — lived in, — looked, — looked away, — looked for, — looked like, — looked up, — made, — missed, — moved, — moved beneath, — moved in, — moved on, — moved onto, — moved out, — moved outside, — needed, — needed to, — opened, — opened up, — passed by, — paused, — paused to, — played, — ran on, — remembered, — returned, — returned to, — rolled, — rolled away, — rolled out, — rose around, — rose up, — sank in, — sank into, — saw, — seemed, — seemed to, — set, — shifted, — shook, — shut out, — slept at, — slipped, — slipped away, — slipped between, — snapped back, — started to, — stopped, — thought, — took, — took on, — tried to, — turned, — turned beneath, — turned on, — turned out, — turned over, — turned through, — turned to, — used, — waited, — waited for, — waited inside, — wanted, — watched, — watched in, — went, — went about, — went away, — went by, — went in, — went on, — went to, — worked, — wrapped around

worry

verbs
— ate, — began to, — came to, — crossed, — disappeared into, — drew, — filled, — followed, — grew in, — knew, — lifted from, — lit, — put, — returned, — rose from, — settled on, —

showed, — slid across, — slid away, — slid down, — slipped into, — started at, — started in, — turned to, — went from, — went out

wound
verbs
— appeared in, — appeared to, — became, — began to, — came from, — caught up, — closed, — closed beneath, — closed up, — closed with, — continued to, — covered, — cut, — cut across, — felt, — gave, — gave off, — held open, — hung in, — looked, — looked like, — made by, — meant to, — needed, — opened up, — ran down, — reached through, — remained, — rubbed, — seemed, — seemed to, — stayed open, — struck, — told, — took

wrist
verbs
broke —, caught —, caught at —, checked —, crossed —, cut —, cut across —, dropped —, explained about —, felt —, found —, glanced at —, glanced to —, grabbed —, grabbed for —, gripped —, held —, held out —, held to —, held up —, kissed —, lifted —, looked at —, moved —, offered —, offered up —, pointed to —, raised —, raised up —, reached for —, reached to —, rolled —, rubbed —, rubbed at —, saw —, shook —, shot out —, snapped —, stared at —, stepped on —, took —, touched —, turned —, turned over —, wore on —; — appeared in, — appeared to, — began to, — broke, — came, — came to, — came together, — continued, — continued to, — covered, — cut, — ended in, — felt, — felt like, — forced, — gave to, — held, — held in,

— held to, — hit, — left, — looked, — looked after, — needed, — passed by, — passed through, — pressed together, — rubbed at, — seemed, — shut, — slipped through, — snapped, — snapped in, — snapped under, — spoke in, — stood out, — struck, — threw, — told, — tossed, — turned, — wrapped with

yard
verbs
bought —, called from —, came across —, continued across —, crossed —, cut across —, cut through —, drove forward —, entered —, felt —, flew off —, glanced about —, glanced across —, glanced around —, landed in —, left —, looked across —, looked around —, looked at —, looked into —, missed by —, moved through —, paused inside —, pointed to —, ran —, ran across —, ran from —, ran into —, ran through —, reached —, rolled into —, said —, shouted into —, slid —, stared around —, started across —, stepped —, stepped forward —, stepped into —, stood in —, turned into —, walked —, walked about —, walked across —, walked around —, walked through —, walked to —, waved across —, waved toward —, went through —, worked in —; — came, — entered, — fell, — felt, — flew open, — grew, — held, — lay, — looked, — looked for, — opened, — put, — ran from, — rang to, — seemed to, — set, — shook, — shouted, — slammed open, — stood, — stood between, — stopped, — swung, — turned out, — went, — went by, — yelled down

year

verbs

— became, — began, — began to, — brought, — came back, — came down, — came in, — changed, — continued for, — covered, — did, — died, — disappeared from, — drew on, — drew onto, — drew over, — dropped away, — drove, — ended, — ended in, — ended with, — fell, — fell away, — fell out, — fell together, — flew by, — followed, — gave, — happened to, — helped, — kept, — laid on, — lay in, — lay on, — left, — left on, — left to, — looked for, — looked over, — lost to, — made, — missed, — moved across, — passed, — passed in, — passed with, — passed without, — picked, — played, — put together, — ran, — returned to, — rolled away, — rolled by, — saw, — seemed like, — seemed to, — sent, — showed, — slid by, — slipped by, — slipped from, — started to, — stepped onto, — stepped up, — stood at, — thought on, — turned, — turned out, — turned to, — turned up, — waited for, — wanted to, — went by, — went into, — went on, — wore on, — worked, — worked in, — worked with, — worked within reached out, — screamed, — seemed to, — started to, — stepped into, — stopped, — swung around, — took, — tried to, — turned, — turned around, — walked to, — went

zombie

verbs

— appeared, — appeared in, — began to, — came, — came toward, — caught, — continued to, — died, — dropped, — dropped to, — fell, — fell down, — fell into, — fell over, — fell to, — grabbed, — grabbed at, — held, — hit, — landed on, — looked at, — made, — managed to, — moved, — moved into, — paused, — paused for, — raised, —